NARRATORS AND FOCALIZERS

NARRATORS AND FOCALIZERS

THE PRESENTATION OF
THE STORY IN THE ILIAD

Irene J.F. de Jong

Second Edition

Bristol Classical Press

This impression 2011
First edition published in 1987
Second edition first published in 2004 by
Bristol Classical Press
An imprint of Bloomsbury Academic
Bloomsbury Publishing Plc
50 Bedford Square, London WC1B 3DP
and
175 Fifth Avenue, New York, NY 10010, USA

Text © 1987, 2004 by Irene J. F. de Jong

A catalogue record for this book is available
from the British Library and the Library of Congress.

ISBN 978 1 8539 9658 0

Typeset by Ray Davies

www.bloomsburyacademic.com

CONTENTS

ACKNOWLEDGEMENTS

This study was submitted as a doctoral thesis to the Faculty of Arts of the University of Amsterdam. It was written under the supervision of Professors J.M. Bremer and M. Bal. I have always considered it a great privilege and a great joy to work with these two supervisors, each a specialist in his (Greek literature) and her (narratology) field, both equally generous in giving their time, professional interest and personal attention. Not only as scholars, but also as supervisors, they complemented each other, Professor Bremer discussing the interpretation of the Homeric text with me, Professor Bal helping me to shape the overall presentation of my argument.

My friend and colleague S.R. van der Mije has spent almost as much energy on this book as I did myself. From the very beginning of writing the application for a scholarship until the final stage of proof-reading, but especially in between, he has been a constant support to me. Quick in detecting weak spots in the text, he has always been the first to offer an alternative formulation. This study has profited enormously from having had such an 'ideal reader', for, as Homer says:

μοῦνος δ᾽ εἴ πέρ τε νοήσῃ,
ἀλλά τέ οἱ βράσσων τε νόος᾽ λεπτὴ δέ τε μῆτις.

I am also very grateful to A Rijksbaron for turning what I considered to be my ultimate version into a penultimate one. Heated debates, but also numerous corrections and improvements of the text resulted of this confrontation between a linguist and a narratologist on the battlefield of the 'text'.

I further wish to thank Professor C.J. Ruijgh not only for reading the manuscript with his usual accuracy, but in general for his instructive seminars on Greek linguistics and Mycenaean Greek and for the many times he discussed problems of the Greek language with me; Professor D.M. Schenkeveld, M. Schmidt (Hamburg) and N. van der Ben for reading and commenting upon first drafts of my sections on Plutarch, the scholia, and the Muses, respectively.

H.A. Mulder expertly corrected my English. My husband W.H.M. Liesker developed in an amazingly short time a Greek laserprinter font, which is based on the original Greek type designed by J.L van Krimpen.

viii

Two scholarships provided by the Netherlands Institute for the Advancement of Pure Research (Z.W.O.) have enabled me to work on this thesis. The first one (1984) consisted of a stay as a 'Stipendiatin' at the *Thesaurus Linguae Graecae* at Hamburg. I have profited very much from the excellent Homer library there. I spent the second one (1985-7) at the University of Amsterdam. Z.W.O. has proved a generous employer, allowing me to revisit Hamburg on three occasions, to spend two periods (1985, 1987) of three weeks at the Fondation Hardt (Vandoeuvres, Switzerland), and to go to Oxford and Cambridge (1987) for one week.

Amsterdam, 1989

INTRODUCTION TO THE FIRST EDITION, 1987

> The novel began, we are told, with Cervantes,
> with Defoe, with Fielding, with Richardson,
> with Jane Austen, – or was it with Homer?
> (Wayne Booth, *The Rhetoric of Fiction*)

> All narrative poetry presents characters,
> recounts actions, describes a world, implies
> values and so on. At a certain level it makes no
> difference to a critical interpretation whether a
> poem is written or oral.
> (Anne Amory Parry, *Homer as Artist*)

If one were to take a bird's eye view of modern Homeric scholarship, i.e. scholarship since the publication of Wolf's *Prolegomena* in 1795, two issues would stand out most prominently. The first can be referred to briefly as the 'Homeric question', the debate between Analysts and Unitarians. The second is the oral-formulaic theory as initiated by Milman Parry in 1928. Both issues are concerned with the way in which the *Iliad* and *Odyssey* came about – in other words, they approach these texts from a *genetic* point of view. This is reflected in their interpretations. Thus, while Analysts mark certain passages as contradicting each other, Unitarians give an interpretation which accounts for these contradictions. Or, while hard-core Parryists make an ever growing inventory of formulas, repetitions or typical scenes, more liberal ones show how many of these formulas are subtly adapted to their context.

Some scholars have protested against the genetic approach, and, instead, advocated looking at the text as an object in itself, regardless of its origin. In this connection two names deserve to be mentioned. First, Samuel Bassett (1938), who is *de facto* a Unitarian, but does not let himself be provoked by Analysts to provide answers to *their* questions. Instead, he proclaims as the goal of his book the achievement of 'a clearer understanding of the principles of great poetry' (1938: 1). The other scholar is Jasper Griffin, who expresses his disappointment at the 'amount of light' that the oral-formulaic theory 'has shed on the poems themselves' (1980: xiii). He therefore decides to apply principles of literary criticism (again), 'approaching the epics in a manner not wholly different from the way in which the Greeks themselves approached them' (xiv).

This study, too, will try to account for the *Iliad* as it is rather than to reconstruct how it came about. More specifically, I intend to study the *Iliad* as a narrative text, analyzing it within the theoretical framework of narratology, i.e. the theory that deals with the general principles underlying narrative texts. Narratologists are concerned with such issues as characterization, chronology, suspense, space, plot-structure, point of view and the role of the narrator. A number of these issues have already been investigated in the Homeric epics. Some relevant monographs are: Hellwig (1964) on time and space, Duckworth (1933) on suspense, Van Erp Taalman Kip (1971) and Andersen (1978) on characterization.

I shall tackle a central aspect of narratology: the presentation of the story. In chapter 1 it will appear that there is a consensus among scholars to describe the presentation of the story in the *Iliad* as 'objective' and 'dramatic'. I shall argue, first, that these two terms are not very useful, because scholars apply them with different meanings, and, second, that a description involving these two terms *only* is incomplete and superficial. To give a more refined and comprehensive description requires an adequate terminology and a systematic approach. These two requirements are met by the narratological model developed by Gérard Genette and Mieke Bal, as will be shown in chapter 2. The most important concepts introduced there will be: the three layers (text, story, fabula); the two functions of narrator and focalizer, their activities (narration, focalization) and the addressees of their activities (narratee, focalizee); and embedding. Using these concepts it is possible to distinguish types of presentation or narrative situations. The three main narrative situations in the *Iliad* are:

1. simple narrator-text	
2. complex narrator-text	together 55% of the total text
3. character-text (speeches)	45% of the total text

To each of these narrative-situations a chapter will be devoted, chapters 3, 4 and 5, respectively. In each of these chapters I will start with a discussion of the general characteristics of the narrative situation under review and then turn to special subjects or problems. Chapter 6 deals with aspects of the relation between the three narrative situations.

In view of the vastness of my material I will in most cases choose one or a few examples for discussion in the main text and refer to other examples in the notes. The examples will be one to five verses in length and will be taken from all books of the *Iliad*. It may be a disadvantage of my method (division of the *Iliad* into narrative situations and discussion of different passages from all books) that in this manner the poem is fractured to a high degree. Indeed, not much will be learnt in this study about its *linear* structure, the way in which scenes follow upon one another, together forming a unified whole. On the other hand, what I hope will become clear is the poem's *narrative* structure, the way in which the reader gets to know its content, the events and the persons causing or experiencing those events, through the mediation of narrator(s) and focalizer(s). Once this structure has been systematically analyzed and illustrated with clear examples, it can be expected that future studies will profit from the insights gained here for the interpretation of complete scenes and books.

This study is written primarily with a view to further Homeric studies, but it may benefit narratology as well. To start with the second claim: Waldemar Görler, reviewing in the *Anzeiger für die Altertumswissenschaft* 36 (1983) two collections of papers on modern literary theory and the classics, raises two points of criticism, even scepsis, concerning narratology:

> Ist die Fülle konkurrierender Methoden nicht ein Idiz dafür, daß die 'Narratologie' zunehmend in eine Sackgasse gerät ... ? Auch folgendes gibt zu denken: Die Erzählanalyse, die nun schon auf eine nicht mehr ganz kurze Geschichte zurückblicken kann, widmet sich noch immer mit Vorliebe knappen und sehr einfachen Texten. (165-6)

The application of one model out of the 'abundance of rivalling methods' to a large-scale narrative text like the *Iliad* provides both that model in particular and narratology in general with an opportunity, indeed a challenge, to show what they are worth. This study does not contribute to the development or further refinement of the theoretical apparatus of narratology – I agree with Görler that too much energy is spent on the introduction of new terminology and classifications – but exploits an already existing theory to the full. Narratologists who are not Homeric specialists may be interested by the problems encountered and the roads of investigation opened in this process of the practical application of theory. As for the charge of choosing simple texts, I would propose to reverse it: narratology may prove capable of showing the complexity of texts reputed simple.

How about the Homerists, my 'primary addressees' in this book? In contrast to Görler, Joachim Latacz has expressed 'great expectations' with regard to the fruitfulness of narratology for Homeric research:

> Mit der allgemeinen Erzählforschung, deren Auswertung für die Homerphilologie (wie für die Klassische Philologie üiberhaupt) heute noch in den Kinderschuhen steckt, wird diese Erweiterung des Blickfeldes voraussichtlich ein weiteres Stück vorankommen: Die Gattungsgebundenheit der Oral poetry-Theorie und der mit ihr mitgegebenen vergleichenden Epenforschung wird aufgehoben werden durch eine zweite Erhöhung des Standpunktes: vom Subtyp 'Epos' hinauf zum Typ 'Erzählwerk'. (1981: 54)

The narratological approach to the *Iliad* as pursued in the present study aims at contributing to Homeric studies in the following three ways:

1. by offering a more systematic and refined analysis of the presentation of the story
2. by using the narratological model also as a heuristic device to tackle existing problems of interpretation or signal new ones
3. by trying to enrich genetic observations made by oralists with insights into the text on its own terms.

This last point calls for an explanation. All too often Homerists restrict their interpretation to observing a certain phenomenon in the text (e.g. repetition of phrases) and explaining it as due to the oral composition or, as I prefer to call it, oral background of the *Iliad*. A narratological approach invites the interpreter to ask whether the phenomenon can also be explained or given a significance in terms of the story. There is of course the risk of over-interpretation. I try to take a middle road between reading too much into a text which, after all, was created in a different way when compared with a novel, and *a priori* denying it those subtleties and meanings which the narrative genre allows.

I end with some remarks of a more practical nature.

Iliadic passages are quoted from the Monro-Allen text, Oxford [3]1920. Scholia are quoted from the recent Erbse edition. For Plato's *Republic* I have used Burnet's edition, Oxford 1902; for Aristotle's *Poetics* Kassel's edition, Oxford 1965; for Plutarch's *De audiendis poetis* the edition of W.R. Paton, I. Wegehaupt, M. Pohlenz, Leipzig 1974. All translations in the text are mine, except when stated otherwise. They do not aim at beauty, but at literalness.

Secondary literature is referred to by the name of the author and year of publication, in the case of commentaries, grammars or lexica by the name of author only. Full references are given in the Bibliography. For certain investigations I have made use of the computerized version of the *Iliad* produced by the *Thesaurus Linguae Graecae* (Irvine, USA). This text has been converted to meet the requirements of Query (a search program developed by the University of Amsterdam) and I have added the codes NAR (= narrator-text) and DR (= direct speech) in view of the special focus of my investigation.

A glossary of the most important terms introduced in chapter 2 is found on p. xxvii.

INTRODUCTION TO THE SECOND EDITION, 2004

In writing *Narrators and Focalizers* on the presentation of the story in the *Iliad*, I had three objectives in mind. In order of importance, these were: (i) to replace the nineteenth-century description of the Homeric narrative style as objective and impersonal by one more receptive to the subtle rhetoric of the invisible but powerful narrator; (ii) to contribute to the resurgence of *literary* interpretation of the Homeric epics, which, as a result of the success of Parry's oral-formulaic theory, had come to a standstill; and (iii) to show the fruitfulness of a new branch of literary theory, narratology, for the interpretation of ancient texts. Looking back after some fifteen years, I believe that the third objective has turned out to be the most important one. Not least as a result of the work of other pioneering narratological classicists, notably Fusillo on Apollonius Rhodius' *Argonautica* (1985), Richardson on Homer (1990), and Winkler on Apuleius' *The Golden Ass* (1985), narratology has become firmly established both within Homeric studies, as witness the overviews on Homeric narratology by Schein (1991), Schwinge (1991), de Jong (1997a), and Reichel (1998), and within classics in general, as witness the narratological section in Schmitz's overview of modern literary approaches to the classics (2002: 55-75), as well as the many narratological studies on individual authors.

For myself, however, the second objective has become the most enduring and most valuable. In dealing with a text whose oral background seemed to rule out literary sophistication and hence traditional literary criticism, it has been liberating to think in terms of a narrative rather than a poem, of a narrator and narratees rather than a singer and his public. For, as Anne Amory Parry once wrote:

> All narrative poetry presents characters, recounts actions, describes a world, implies values, and so on. At a certain level it makes no difference to a critical interpretation whether a poem is written or oral.[1]

---

[1] Amory Parry (1971: 14). For a more detailed discussion of my views on the relation between oral poetry and narratology, see De Jong (1991); to the defenders of the *literary* Hmsl t fR oral Homer should be added Rutherford (1985, esp. p. 133: '... it is not unreasonable to suppose that any story-teller, oral or literate ... should desire and be able to connect his ending with his beginning, to develop themes ...') and Holoka (1991; esp. 481: 'From the point of our own inescapably literate apprehension of them, the *Iliad* and *Odyssey* must be treated as independent entities, proper sources in themselves of verification for literary critical assertions. They may legitimately be viewed as poetic texts rather than exclusively as oral performances ...').

Indeed, approaching the Homeric epics as narratives and with the help of narratological concepts has led to the exploration of entirely new areas, the most exciting of which surely has been focalization (about which more below), and a renewed interest in old ones, such as verbal repetition, which gains significance when looked at in terms of its distribution across narrator and characters. My faith in narratology as a heuristic instrument led me to write a narratological commentary on the *Odyssey* (de Jong 2001a) which covers much more ground than this book. Though the latter has more than once been called by reviewers a 'handbook of narratology', it actually deals only with certain aspects, mainly the role of the narrator and his narratees, focalization, and the relationship between the narrative parts and the speeches. In my commentary many other aspects, such as plot, characterization, description, time, and structure (of scenes and speeches) are also discussed. Thus where my thesis offered a paradigmatic discussion of certain narratological aspects of Homer, this new study provides a syntagmatic and comprehensive pendant. The new *Iliad* commentary edited by J. Latacz, one volume of which (on Book I) has appeared so far, also pays considerable attention to narratological aspects of the text. Both commentaries contain an – almost identical – glossary or *Homerische Poetik in Stichwörtern*, which presents an overview of the most important narratological concepts and secondary literature.

Looking back again, but now at the presentation of my own 'story', there are no major things I would like to change, so that the main text of this second edition will be the same as the first (or rather the same as the 1989 reprint, which contained a number of corrections). There is only one minor point about which I now think differently: the designation of the narrator as NF_1 and the narratee as $NeFe_1$. These references, which earned my book the qualification of 'excellent if algebraically written',[2] were the result of an attempt to combine ideology (to bring home my central thesis that the story does not tell itself, but is told by a narrating and focalizing subject) with efficiency (writing 'primary narrator-focalizer' every time would have made the book at least ten pages longer).[3] An easy solution, which I have in fact adopted in my *Odyssey* commentary, is to state once and for all that when I use the word 'narrator', I mean the 'primary narrator-focalizer'.

[2]Hornblower (1994: 131).
[3]I also realize that I have been influenced in this respect by Genette (1980), who repeatedly uses 'algebraic' abbreviations, and himself writes on p. 114: '... or if we want to abbreviate with a pseudo-mathematical formula: $1N/1S$.'

What has changed, of course, is the scholarship: new studies have appeared on issues touched upon in *Narrators and Focalizers*, as well as studies on new issues. In the remainder of this introduction I will give an update of those studies, following roughly the order of my book (and abstaining from a critical discussion, as many of the monographs mentioned have been reviewed by me in *Mnemosyne*).

Chapter 1 contains among other things a discussion of the – rare – subjective elements in the Homeric epics which in the course of time had been put forward by scholars (pp. 15-26). In this overview the passage *Iliad* VI 61-2 ('The hero [Agamemnon] spoke like this and bent the heart of his brother, *since he urged justice*') is missing. Lattimore's translation, quoted here, represents the *communis opinio* and suggests that the narrator is passing a – positive – moral judgement on Agamemnon's speech, in which he urges Menelaus not to spare the life of the suppliant Adrestus. This interpretation is challenged by Yamagata (1990), who argues that 'the poet means that Agamemnon is skillfully measuring and balancing the issues in order to make up an excuse for his brother ...[and] only reports the eloquence of Agamemnon without expressing any moral approval or disapproval of his own'; by Goldhill (1990), who suggests that we take *aisima* as 'fateful' (for Adrestus); and by Taplin (1992: 51-2), who proposes to take *aisima* as representing Menelaus' implicit focalization. Another passage, which *is* mentioned (p. 26, and cf. n. 35 on p. 278), *Iliad* VI 234-6 ('but Zeus the son of Cronus *stole away the wits of* Glaucus, who exchanged with Diomedes the son of Tydeus armour of gold for bronze, for nine oxen's worth the worth of a hundred'), has since been further interpreted by Traill (1989), Scodel (1992), and Harries (1993), who all take this as a – negative – narratorial comment, but give various explanations as to why Zeus intervenes (to compensate Diomedes for being robbed of his victory as a result of the peaceful solution of the encounter with Glaucus; to illustrate the tragic warning which Glaucus has just given, namely that human life is changeable and luck unreliable; to demonstrate the fatal character flaw which Glaucus inherited from his ancestors, since his grandfather Bellerophon once exchanged a gold cup for a leather belt: 219-20).

One of the non-classical scholars discussed in my overview of descriptions of the Homeric narrative style is Auerbach, who claims that the subjectivistic-perspectivistic procedure, creating a foreground and a background, is not found in Homer (pp. 22-4). In de Jong (1985) I had already criticized this thesis, offering an alternative analysis of his star example, the digression on

Odysseus' scar in *Odyssey* 19.393-466. In de Jong (1999) I evaluate his views in greater detail, not only the lack of perspective, but also the absence of suspense, gaps and psychological complexity, and discuss other recent scholarship on Auerbach and Homer.

Chapter 3 is devoted to a search for the invisible but almighty narrator and his narratees. This same search is undertaken on an even grander scale by Richardson (1990), who partly covers the same ground (in his chapters on special abilities, commentary, and self-consciousness), partly includes more devices (mainly descriptions, summaries, and the handling of simultaneity; for all of these, see below). My list of the rare places which more or less explicitly reveal the presence of the narrator, Muse-invocations, apostrophe, questions, second-person optatives, *hoioi nun brotoi*-passages (pp. 44-5, 54-60) had been anticipated – without my being aware of this – by Frontisi-Ducroux (1986: 11-32). The Muses, of course, continue to capture the imagination of scholars. I will single out two contributions which strike me as particularly helpful. The most extensive discussion is that of Ford (1992: 13-56), who argues that it is primarily the presence of the Muses which defines the genre of epic poetry, and that they ensure not so much truth or beauty as vividness, the power of heroic poetry to evoke the past. If I may step briefly outside the boundaries of this introduction, his study forms part of a renewed surge of interest in aspects of the *performance* of the Homeric epics, which further explores the path opened by Parry; cf. especially Bakker (1997). My thesis that the narrator 'is not so much dependent on the Muses, but rather uses them to recommend his own activity as (primary) narrator and (primary) focalizer' (p. 46), is corroborated by Finkelberg (1990), who concludes: 'In the Greek tradition, the idea of the poet's inspiration by the Muse offers an excellent alibi for creative intervention. Thanks to this idea, each of the poet's innovations automatically gains the status of divine truth in virtue of its origin in divine inspiration' (1990: 296).

One of the places where we can see the narrator and his narratees interacting is what I have called the 'if not-situation': 'and now X would have happened, if someone had not done Y'. I argue that this device has both a narrative function, to create suspense or pathos, and an 'ideological' function, to stress that the version presented by the narrator is according to fate, thus underscoring his authority. Since then, this device has been discussed by no fewer than five other scholars: Lang (1989; 'unreal conditions'), Richardson (1990: 187-96; 'plot decisions'), Morrison (1992b; alternatives to the epic tradition), Nesselrath

(1992; 'Ungeschehenes Geschehen'), and Louden (1993; 'pivotal contrafactuals'). Richardson and Nesselrath favour the same narrative and ideological functions as I do; Lang suggests that the device serves to change the direction of the narrative; Louden points out that this device often (i) serves to mark a major turning point in the story, and (ii) functions as a narratorial comment. Morrison, finally, comes up with a function which is the complete opposite of my ideological one: rather than showing his adherence to the traditional – fated – course of events, the narrator, 'demonstrates his own freedom to move in accordance with or contrary to the tradition. In essence, Homer has defined an aesthetic position of independence not by violating the tradition, but by showing how easily he might have deviated from the story as it had been told for many generations' (1992: 69-70).

Perhaps the largest group of devices which reveal the hand of the narrator concerns his handling of time; of these, I discussed only the prolepses and analepses (pp. 81-90; cf. Richardson 1990: 132-9 and 100-8). Today we have discussions of many more aspects of time. In the first place, there is misdirection, the creation of false expectations among the narratees, which has been studied by Morrison (1992). These expectations may be based on familiarity with the epic tradition or on prolepses made in the text itself. The misdirection may take the form of (i) false anticipation, when the fulfilment of a prolepsis is delayed; (ii) epic suspense, when an unexpected episode is inserted which threatens to disturb the traditional course of events; and (iii) thematic misdirection, when prolepses are not fulfilled.

False anticipation, in fact, is a form of retardation, which has been studied by Reichel (1990). He defines it as the postponement of an announced event, either through the insertion of another episode or through a slowing down of the narrative rhythm. Retardation serves both a structural function, expanding the narrative, and a narrative function, creating suspense.

Suspense itself can take two forms: suspense in the strict sense, when the narratees know the outcome but not the way in which it will be reached (suspense of anticipation), and what is known in German as *Spannung* (tension), when the narratees are on tenterhooks as to how the story will develop or end (suspense of uncertainty). Of these, the first form has long been recognized for Homer and has recently been further explored by Schmitz (1994); he demonstrates how in the *Odyssey* suspense can arise from the contrast between what is said and what is left unsaid, between tradition and innovation, and between those who know the future and those who do not. Rengakos (1999) extends the discussion, pointing out forms of suspense such as retardation, gradual revelation, dramatic irony, and misdirection in both *Iliad* and *Odyssey*. As for the second, 'modern' type of suspense, which has long been deemed foreign to the Homeric style, I claim in my narratological commentary that it *is* found in Homer, at any rate in the *Odyssey*. The best example is Odysseus' revenge on the Suitors: although it is repeatedly announced, the narratees are long left in the dark about its form (violence or trick) and the final dénouement, Odysseus' use of the bow of the wedding contest for a first, forceful blow (see de Jong 2001a: 8-9).

A specific Homeric device for handling time, the so-called law of Zielinski, has been hotly debated of late. This law consists of two parts. (i) The Homeric narrator does not retrace his steps: when he moves from one storyline to another, time ticks on and storyline B continues where A left off. (ii) However, certain events which are narrated successively *should in fact be thought of as occurring simultaneously*. Thus Zielinski reconstructs a *real* action, as opposed to the *apparent* action which we find in the text. The second part of this law (successive = simultaneous) long went unchallenged (cf. e.g. Richardson 1990: 90-5), but recently Patzer (1990) and Rengakos (1995) have argued that successive really means successive, in that storyline B often reacts to storyline A, and that, when he so wishes, the narrator is perfectly able to present – small-scale – simultaneous actions. As for the first part, Rengakos (1998: 55-60) and Nünlist (1998) have brought forward a number of examples, in which we do go back in time: (Rengakos) I 365-92; VIII 53-9; X 299-301; XV 390-4; XVIII 429-61; 16 1-3; 17 492-3; 24 412-14; (Nünlist) V 319, 432; XIII 206-9, 660; XIV 440-1; XV 390-4, 484-5; XVI 508; 1 113, 325; 2 155. Danek (1999) takes issue with Rengakos and Nünlist, and suggests that in a case like XIV 1-8, the narrator is not so much going back in time as reactivating a storyline which has lain 'dormant' for two books, and synchronizing it with the main storyline. Among other things, he points out that this passage represents Nestor's focalization (first embedded focalization, then speech). Indeed, many of the examples mentioned by Rengakos and Nünlist concern passages of embedded focalization or speech which, in my view, should not be analyzed in terms of the *narrator* going back in time but rather one of the characters; such passages cannot therefore be seen as a breach of the law of succession. Zielinski himself acknowledges the possibility of going back in time via the speeches of a character. In de Jong (2001a: 590) I formulate my own views on what I call the 'continuity of time' principle as follows: in principle the Homeric narrator does not retrace his steps; the different storylines he handles are best thought of as parallel rather than simultaneous (reserving this term for actions which *are* simultaneous); while one storyline is in the foreground, the other remain stationary, i.e. time ticks on but nothing important happens. As always, this rule is proved by its exceptions: in 13 185-9; 16 1-3; and 17 492-3 the narrator does go back in time, and in 15 301-495 and 21 188-244 important developments do take place in the background. A final, quite radical approach to the problems of simultaneity in Homer which deserves mention here is that of Seeck (1998), who suggests that the Homeric narrator intentionally leaves open the question of whether storylines are simultaneous or successive; this is a compromise between the simultaneity of the events and the – inevitable – successiveness or linearity of narration: 'Homer, like any storyteller, simply wanted to avoid the word "meanwhile", which interrupts the smooth flow of the story' (1998: 143; my translation).

Chapter 4 is devoted to a phenomenon which was long regarded foreign to the Homeric narrative style, not only by Auerbach but also by others (for an overview, see de Jong 2001b): the presentation of events through the eyes of one of the characters, i.e. figural narration or embedded focalization. In Homer the passages of embedded focalization are usually very short, on average about two lines; they are marked, in principle, by a verb of seeing, etc. We are still far removed from the extended mind reading of our modern novels. Homeric focalization is less concerned with the psychology of the characters than with the moral or affective evaluation of events: as discussed in Chapter 1, the Homeric narrator rarely comments explicitly on the events he is recounting. Interestingly enough, many of the subjective words which we do exceptionally find in the narrator-text can, upon closer analysis, be ascribed to the focalization of characters rather than to that of the narrator (the discussion on pp. 136-45 is complemented by de Jong 1988). Since the narrator is the one who in the end verbally presents the embedded focalization of the character, there is always the methodological problem of *proving* that a certain word represents the focalization of the character rather than the narrator. For some, this is reason enough to reject the concept of embedded focalization altogether. In my view most cases are defensible and in all cases it is heuristically more interesting to allow for a broad range of perspectives than to ascribe everything to the one narrator. The three main methods of arguing that a word is focalized by a character are analyzing the syntax (often the moods used have traditionally been described by the grammars as representing the point of view of the agent rather than the speaker), considering statistics (when a word occurs once in narrator-text and many times in speech, the chances are high that we should ascribe it to the focalizing character), and adducing contextual evidence (when the view expressed in the passage of embedded focalization is also voiced by the same character in a speech).

In de Jong 1992 and 1997b I have expanded the discussion started in *Narrators and Focalizers*, looking not only at the exceptional use of evaluative language in the narrator-text, but arguing for the existence of character-language: words which are used exclusively or mainly by the characters, in speeches or in embedded focalization. Apart from obviously affective words, such as 'bad', 'sorrowful', 'miserable', etc., we may think here of periphrastic denomination, such as 'father' and 'mother', or relative terms, such as 'fatherland' and 'friend', as well as particles, subordinators, and pronouns. The notion of character-language can also be a useful instrument for the discussion of Homeric epithets (see de Jong 1998). All in all, there appears to be quite a large corpus of character-language which I am sure new studies will enlarge and refine. Acknowledging its existence will have interesting consequences for the interpretation of individual passages.

To my joy, the term focalization has become well accepted in Homeric studies, though occasionally it is employed incorrectly, that is to say in too broad a sense. Thus some scholars use it focalization as a synonym for evaluation, or they consider the focalizer the focal or central character; for a more detailed discussion, see Nünlist (2002). Rather than stretching the concept to the point where it loses its heuristic and descriptive value, I would like to see it used only in its original sense: to indicate the agent in the text through whose eyes the narratees perceive the events.

Chapter 5 discusses narrative aspects of character-text or speech. Of these, external analepses recounted by characters (discussed on pp. 160-8) have remained the main object of research. Alden (2000) discusses all of these analepses (which she calls para-narratives), and her analysis is intended to show the ways in which the poet uses them to influence the audience's interpretation of the main story. Edmunds (1997) discusses the same subject, but puts the case somewhat more strongly: 'Typically, a character's intentions for a myth that he or she narrates miscarry, while some further meaning, of which the character is unaware, becomes apparent in the context of the epic as a whole' (1997: 440). Both pay attention to that most famous, but notoriously complex analepsis about

Meleager (IX 524-99), which is also discussed by March (1987: 27-46), Swain (1988), and Grosshardt (2001: 9-24). For the Bellerophon-story in VI 156-202 we have a recent interpretation by Harries (1993). To do justice to the various interpretations of these passages requires more space than I have here, and I can do no more than note their existence.

Chapter 6 discusses the relations between narrator-text and character-text or speech. Three more recent studies have also explored this subject. Steinrück (1992) investigates the temporal relationship between narrator-text and speeches and concludes that speaking characters can never narrate something that has not been recounted or mentioned before by the narrator. Rabel (1997) looks at the confrontations between the perspectives of narrator and characters. Reichel (1994) is interested primarily in the compositional device of the cross-reference (*Fernverbindung*), but his discussion often involves the combination or confrontation of references to a person or event by the narrator and different characters.

In fact, Reichel's book discusses much more, viz. the structure of the *Iliad*. This brings me to the final part of my update, in which I would like to point out a number of important areas of narratological research not touched upon in *Narrators and Focalizers*. The first is structure and plot, which are not exactly the same thing. In point of fact, structure, by which I mean here the linear organization of the text, lies outside the domain of narratology. Nevertheless, I would like to signal here discussions of the structure of the *Iliad* by Taplin (1992), Stanley (1993), and Heiden (1996; strictly speaking he is analyzing the *performance* structure, which does, however, entail a discussion of narrative structure as well), and the examination of general structural principles by Schwinge (1991).

Plot (or *sjuzhet* or story) is a central narratological concept, by which I mean the events of a narrative looked at from the standpoint of causality and in the order of the text, as opposed to the fabula, which means the events abstracted from their order in the text and seen as a strictly chronological sequence (for an overview of the many definitions of plot, see Lowe 2000: 3-16). Two recent studies deal explicitly with the plot of the *Iliad*, the factors which make the narrative move. Lowe (2000: 103-28) discusses the plotting of time and space, the plot function of characters, and the heroic code as organizing principle of the narrative. Heiden (2002) proposes an analysis of the way in which the plot moves forward in the *Iliad* in terms of moves, each move consisting of a problem which leads, often via an auxiliary, to a solution. For example, Achilles' move which triggers the plot of the *Iliad* can be analyzed as: (problem) Briseis abducted – (auxiliary) call his mother Thetis – (solution) get help from Zeus. In my narratological commentary I revive an old distinction, which, I believe, is helpful when discussing plot, viz. narratorial motivation versus actorial motivation: the analysis of the 'why' of the way in which the story develops in terms of the aims and intentions of the narrator versus those of a character. Scodel (1999), finally, discusses the verisimilitude of plots: what mimetic flaws, inconsistencies, and implausibilities of character and plot do we find; what kind of authorial strategies attempt to mitigate these flaws; and which principles does an audience apply to deal with them.

In my overview of Homer and narratology dating from 1997 I noted that there exists no discussion of the methods of Homeric characterization. This lacuna has still not been filled. In my narratological commentary I suggest some basic distinctions (explicit versus implicit characterization, and narratorial versus actorial characterization), but the subject deserves a more detailed study, as has been done for tragic characterization, for example. Here the study on characterization by the narratologist Phelan (1989) could be helpful. He distinguishes between the mimetic, synthetic and thematic components of a character: the traits which make it real, those which reveal it as an artificial construct, and those which make it a representative of a certain class or type. One aspect of Homeric characterization which has been receiving a great deal of attention lately is the way in which their manner of speaking characterizes characters. Here much important work has been done by Martin (1989).

Finally, there is the description of objects or persons. This topic has been explored by Bernsdorff (1992), who looks at the way in which external description and internal qualification relate to each other, and Becker (1995), who offers a model to analyze *ekphraseis* (descriptions of works of visual art).

Looking back at the rich harvest of narratological studies on the *Iliad* produced in the past fifteen years, I can only conclude that this is a highly rewarding field of research, which will not quickly be exhausted and which will only increase our admiration for Homer's narrative genius.

Amsterdam   IdJ
November 2002

Bibliography

Alden, M. (2000). *Homer Beside Himself. Para-Narratives in the Iliad*, Oxford.

Amory Parry, A. (1971). 'Homer as Artist', *CQ* 21, 1-15.

Bakker, E.J. (1997). *Poetry in Speech. Orality and Homeric Discourse*, Ithaca, NY & London.

Becker, A.S. (1995). *The Shield of Achilles and the Poetics of Ekphrasis*, Lanham.

Bernsdorff, H. (1992). *Zur Rolle des Aussehens im homerischen Menschenbild*, Göttingen.

Danek, G. (1999). 'Synchronisation von Handlungssträngen in *Iliad* 14,1-40', in J.N. Kazazis and A. Rengakos (eds), *Euphrosyne. Studies in Ancient Epic and its Legacy in Honor of D.N. Maronitis*, Stuttgart, 76-88.

Edmunds, L. (1997). 'Myth in Homer', in I. Morris and B. Powell (eds), *A New Companion to Homer*, Leiden, 415-41.

Finkelberg, M. (1990). 'A Creative Oral Poet and the Muse', *AJPh* 111, 293-309.

Ford, A. (1992), *Homer. The Poetry of the Past*, Ithaca, NY & London.

Frontisi-Ducroux, F. (1986). *La cithare d'Achille*, Paris.

Fusillo, M. (1985). *Il tempo delle Argonautiche. Un'analisi del racconto in Apollonio Rodio*, Rome.

Goldhill, S. (1990). 'Supplication and Authorial Comment in the *Iliad*: *Iliad* Z 61-2', *Hermes* 119, 373-6.

Grossardt, P. (2001). *Die Erzählung von Meleagros. Zur literarischen Entwicklung der Kalydonischen Kultlegende*, Leiden.

Harries, B. (1993). 'Strange Meeting: Diomedes and Glaucus in *Iliad* 6', *G&R* 40, 133-46.

Heiden, B. (1996). 'The Three Movements of the *Iliad*', *GRBS* 37, 5-22.

―――― (2002). 'Structures of Progression in the Plot of the *Iliad*', *Arethusa* 35, 237-54.

Holoka, J.P. (1991). 'Homer, Oral Poetry Theory, and Comparative Literature: Major Trends and Controversies in Twentieth-Century Criticism', in J. Latacz (ed.), *Colloquium Rauricum II. Zweihundert Jahre Homer-Forschung*, Stuttgart & Leipzig, 456-81.

Hornblower, S. (1994). 'Narratology and Narrative Technique in Thucydides', in S. Hornblower (ed.) *Greek Historiography*, Oxford, 31-66.

Jong, I.J.F. de (1985). 'Eurykleia and Odysseus' Scar: *Odyssey* 19.393-466', *CQ* 35, 517-18.

―――― (1988). 'Homeric Words and Speakers: an Addendum', *JHS* 108, 188-9.

―――― (1991). 'Narratology and Oral Poetry: the Case of Homer', *Poetics Today* 12, 405-23.

―――― (1992). 'The Subjective Style in Odysseus' Wanderings', *CQ* 42, 1-11.

―――― (1997a). 'Homer and Narratology', in I. Morris and B. Powell (eds), *A New Companion to Homer*, Leiden, 305-25.

―――― (1997b). 'Narrator Language versus Character Language: Some Further

Explorations', in: F. Létoublon (ed.), *Hommage à Milman Parry. Le style formulaire de l'épopée homérique et la théorie de l'oralité poétique*, Amsterdam, 175-85.

—— (1999). 'Auerbach and Homer', in J.N. Kazazis and A. Rengakos (eds), *Euphrosyne. Studies in Ancient Epic and its Legacy in Honor of D.N. Maronitis*, Stuttgart, 154-64.

—— (2001a). *A Narratological Commentary on the Odyssey*, Cambridge.

—— 2001b. 'The Origins of Figural Narration in Antiquity', in W. van Peer and S. Chatman (eds), *New Perspectives on Narrative Perspective*, New York, 67-81.

Lang, M. (1989). 'Unreal Conditions in Homeric Narrative', *GRBS* 30, 5-26.

Latacz, J. (ed.) (2000). *Homers Ilias. Gesamtkommentar, Prolegomena, Band I.2, Kommentar 1.Gesang*, München-Leipzig.

Louden, B. (1993). 'Pivotal Contrafactuals in Homeric Epic', *CA* 12, 181-98.

Lowe, N. J. (2000). *The Classical Plot and the Invention of Western Narrative*, Cambridge.

March, J.R. (1987). *The Creative Poet. Studies on the Treatment of Myths in Greek Poetry*, London.

Martin, R. (1989). *The Language of Heroes: Speech and Performance in the 'Iliad'*, Ithaca, NY & London.

Morrison, J.V. (1992a). 'Alternatives to the Epic Tradition: Homer's Challenges in the *Iliad*', *TAPA* 122, 61-71.

—— (1992b). *Homeric Misdirection: False Predictions in the Iliad*, Ann Arbor.

Nesselrath, H.-G. (1992). *Ungeschehenes Geschehen. 'Beinahe-Episoden' im Griechischen und Römischen Epos*, Stuttgart.

Nünlist, R. (1998). 'Der Homerische Erzähler und das sogenannte Sukzessionsgesetz', *MH* 55, 2-8.

—— (2002). 'Some Clarifying Remarks on "Focalization" ', in F. Montanari, P. Ascheri (eds), *Omero tremila anni dopo*, Rome, 445-53.

Patzer, H. (1990). 'Gleichzeitige Ereignisse im homerischen Epos', in H. Eisenberger (ed.), *Hermeneumata, FS H. Hörner*, Heidelberg, 153-72.

Phelan, J. (1989). *Reading People, Reading Plots. Character, Progression, and the Interpretation of Narrative*, Chicago.

Rabel, R.J. (1997). *Plot and Point of View in the Iliad*, Ann Arbor.

Reichel, M. (1990). 'Retardationstechniken in der *Ilias*', in W. Kullmann, M. Reichel (eds), *Der Übergang von der Mündlichkeit zur Literatur bei den Griechen*, Tübingen, 125-51.

—— (1994). *Fernbeziehungen in der Ilias*, Tübingen.

—— (1998). 'Narratologische Methoden in der Homerforschung', in H.L.C. Tristram (ed.), *New Methods in the Research of Epic*, Tübingen, 45-61.

Rengakos, A. (1995). 'Zeit und Gleichzeitigkeit in den homerischen Epen', *AuA* 41, 1-33.

—— (1998). 'Zur Zeitstruktur der *Odyssee*', *WS* 111, 45-66.

—— (1999). 'Spannungsstrategien in den homerischen Epen', in J.N. Kazazis and A. Rengakos (eds), *Euphrosyne. Studies in Ancient Epic and its Legacy in Honor of D.N. Maronitis*, Stuttgart, 308-38.

Richardson, S. (1990). *The Homeric Narrator*, Nashville.

Rutherford, R.B. (1985). 'At Home and Abroad. Aspects of the Structure of the *Odyssey*', *PCPhS* 31, 133-50.

Schein, S.L. (1991). 'Narratology and Homeric Studies', *Poetics Today* 12, 577-90.

Schmitz, T.A. (1994). 'Ist die Odyssee "spannend"? Anmerkungen zur Erzähltechnik des homerischen Epos', *Philologus* 138, 3-23.

——— (2002). *Moderne Literaturtheorie und antike Texte*, Darmstadt.

Schwinge, E.-R. (1991). 'Homerische Epen und Erzählforschung', in J. Latacz (ed.), *Colloquium Rauricum II. Zweihundert Jahre Homer-Forschung*, Stuttgart & Leipzig, 482-512.

Scodel , R. (1992). 'The Wits of Glaucus', *TAPhA* 122, 73-84.

——— (1999). *Credible Impossibilities. Conventions and Strategies of Verisimilitude in Homer and Greek Tragedy*, Stuttgart & Leipzig.

Seeck, G.A. (1998). 'Homerisches Erzählen und das Problem der Gleichzeitigkeit', *Hermes* 126, 131-44.

Stanley, K. (1993). *The Shield of Homer. Narrative Structure in the Iliad*, Princeton.

Steinrück, M. (1992). *Rede und Kontext, zum Verhältnis von Person und Erzähler in frühgriechischen Texten*, Bonn.

Swain, S.C.R. (1988). 'A Note on *Iliad* 9.524-99: The Story of Meleager', *CQ* 38, 271-6.

Taplin, O. (1992). *Homeric Soundings. The Shaping of the Iliad*, Oxford.

Traill, D. (1989). 'Gold Armor for Bronze and Homer's use of Compensatory *timê*', *CPh* 84, 301-5.

Winkler, J.J. (1985). *Auctor & Actor. A Narratological Reading of Apuleius's Golden Ass*, Berkeley, Los Angeles & Oxford.

Yamagata, N. (1990). '*Aisima pareipon*: A Moral Judgement by the Poet?', *PP* 45, 420-30.

GLOSSARY

Fabula   a chronological series of events caused or experienced by characters in a fictional world.

Story   the elements of the fabula (events, characters, space, time) as perceived, ordered and interpreted by a focalizer.

Text   the focalized story (and by implication the fabula) put into words by a narrator.

Narrator (N)   function consisting of the verbal presentation of the story.

Focalizer (F)   function consisting of the perceptional, emotional and intellectual presentation of the fabula.

Narratee (Ne)   recipient of the narration by the narrator.

Focalizee (Fe)   recipient of the focalization by the focalizer.

Character (C)   imaginary person playing a role in a narrative.

Simple narrator-text: the external primary narrator-focalizer (NF_1) presents the events/persons. Recipient is an external primary narratee-focalizee ($NeFe_1$).

Complex narrator-text (embedded focalization): the external primary narrator-focalizer embeds in his narrator-text the focalization of one of the characters, who, thus, functions as an internal secondary focalizer (F_2). Recipients are a secondary focalizee (Fe_2), who is internal or external, and, ultimately, the external primary narratee-focalizee.

Character-text (speeches): the external primary narrator-focalizer embeds in his narrator-text a character-text, presented by a character, who, thus, functions as internal secondary narrator-focalizer (NF_2). Recipients are an internal secondary narratee-focalizee ($NeFe_2$) and, ultimately, the external primary narratee-focalizee.

1. THE PRESENTATION OF THE STORY IN THE ILIAD: THE STATE OF THE ART

> "The whole distinction between 'objective' and 'subjective' has in fact turned out to be less clear than is often suggested"
> (Jasper Griffin, *Homer on Life and Death*)

The aim of this first chapter is to survey ancient (1.1) and modern (1.2) opinions on the presentation of the story in the *Iliad*. Under the heading "the presentation of the story" I provisionally subsume - in chapter 2 I will give a more precise definition - three issues:

1. who is presenting the story
2. how explicitly is this presentator present in the text
3. what is the narrative style of this presentator.

In the concluding section (1.3) I will give a summary and indicate on which points existing scholarship needs correction, clarification and, above all, refinement.

1.1. Antiquity

Already in antiquity literature on Homer, the poet *par excellence*, was overwhelming and in this section only a selection of passages will be discussed. I shall start with two *theoretical* texts: Plato, *Republic* III 392c-394b and Aristotle, *Poetics* 1448a 19-28, 1460a 5-11. These passages have received ample attention, both from classical scholars, e.g. Koster (1970: 29-80) and Fuhrmann (1973: 1-98);

and from literary theorists, e.g. Friedman (1955: 1161-2), Genette (1969: 50-6, 1972: 184-91 = 1980: 162-71) and Lanser (1981: 19-21). Even so, it is worthwhile once more to take a close look at these texts, because their popularity, especially among literary theorists, has not always gone hand in hand with philological precision or regard for the context in which they occur and function.

The other passages in this section are taken from Plutarch, *De audiendis poetis* 19a 6-20c 25, and the Iliadic scholia. These texts have hardly played a role in the discussion so far. I have chosen Plutarch as representative of the moralistic-didactic interpretation of the Homeric epics, which has known a long tradition in antiquity. The scholia, together with Plutarch, give us a good insight into the *practice* of ancient literary criticism and as such form an interesting complement to the theoretical contributions of Plato and Aristotle.

Plato: Republic III 392c-394b

In the *Republic* Plato sketches the outlines of an Ideal State. Twice, he comes to speak of literature (II 376e-III 398b and X 595a-608b); the reason for the lavish attention paid to this subject becomes clear from his own words (esp. 606e 1-5): traditionally, the poets and especially Homer were considered the educators of the people and authorities in matters of government, politics and ethics.[1] As such they formed "Plato's main rivals" (White 1979: 247).

The passage 392c-394b belongs to the first discussion of literature, which itself forms part of an exposé on the education of the 'guardians', rulers of the Ideal State (376c-412a). Education starts with the stories children hear and which, because of the youth of the recipients, strongly influence them. Therefore, Plato maintains, it is absolutely necessary that the content of these stories be morally impeccable. This criterion induces him to blue-pencil many passages in traditional poetry. In 392c he turns from *subject-matter* (λόγος or ἃ λεκτέον) to *style of speech* (λέξις or ὡς λεκτέον), only to prescribe (394c-398b) that the mimetic style of speech (represented by drama and direct speech in the epic) should be avoided by the 'guardians' and in general all 'good citizens', since it involves the risk of contagion with vices. Thus, the short descriptive passage 392c-394b forms a tiny part of an elaborate structure erected by Plato to fight his formidable opponent, traditional poetry.

I will now give a systematical analysis of 392c-394b, thereby sometimes rearranging Plato's order of treatment. According to Plato all literature (both poetry and prose) consists of the *narration* (διήγησις) of things from the past, present or future (392d). There are three ways in which this narration can be accomplished:

1. ἁπλῇ διηγήσει: 'by single narration';
2. διὰ μιμήσεως γιγνομένῃ: '(by narration) that is effected through impersonation';
3. δι' ἀμφοτέρων: '(by narration that is effected) through both' (1 and 2).

These three manners of narration are connected by Plato to three genres of poetry (394c): dithyramb, drama and epic, respectively. To illustrate what he means by 'single narration' and 'narration that is effected through impersonation' Plato takes the epic genre (in casu, the beginning of the *Iliad*: Chryses' visit to the Greek camp). Epic texts can be divided into two elements (393b):

    a. the speeches (τὰς ῥήσεις) and
    b. the parts between the speeches (τὰ μεταξὺ τῶν ῥησέων).

Homer narrates both (a) and (b), yet in (b) 'the poet is speaking himself and does not even attempt to suggest to us that anyone but himself is speaking', whereas in (a) 'the poet speaks as though he himself were Chryses and tries as far as may be to make us think that not Homer is speaking, but the priest, an old man' (393a-b). This speaking 'as if being someone else' (ὥς τις ἄλλος ὤν) means that the poet assimilates his style of speech[2] to that of the character he is impersonating. In other words, in (b) the manner of narration is (1) ἁπλῇ διηγήσει, in (a) it is (2) διὰ μιμήσεως γιγνομένῃ, the *Iliad* as a whole belonging to (3) since it contains both (1) and (2).[3]

Of the two terms *diegesis haple* and *mimesis* used here by Plato, the second has attracted most scholarly attention. In the present context 'impersonation' is, I think, an adequate translation of this elusive term *mimesis*.[4] As for *diegesis haple*, a great number of scholars translate it with 'pure' or 'unmixed' narration[5] and contrast it to the third, mixed, manner of narration. In my opinion this is wrong. Plato had to add a specification to *diegesis*, since, as we saw earlier, he defines all literature as forms of diegesis and this term recurs in the definition of all three manners of narration. I submit that Plato has chosen the specification ἁπλοῦς ('single', 'one-layered') in contrast with mimesis: there the poet narrates and *at the same time* impersonates one of his characters, and one could speak of a double-layered narration, whereas in the *diegesis haple* he is speaking only as himself, a one-layered narration. Arguments in favour of my interpretation are:

- it is more in accordance with the Greek: ἁπλοῦς does not mean 'pure', but 'single-layered', the opposite being διπλοῦς ('double-layered');

- the first and second manner of narration stand on a par, whereas the third is a combination of 1 and 2. Hence, it is *a priori* more plausible that ἀπλῆ should contrast with 2 (διὰ μιμήσεως) than with 3 (δι' ἀμφοτέρων).[6]

In order to show what epic would look like without *mimesis* Plato rewrites *Iliad* A 12-42, replacing all direct speech by indirect speech (393d-394b). In a similar way, he says (394b), one could leave out all *diegesis haple* and make the epic completely mimetic, i.e. consisting of direct speech, dialogues (ἀμοιβαῖα) only. Genette, in his discussion of "distance" - the question of how much narrative information is provided to the reader and in what degree of directness - (1972: 184-91 = 1980: 162-71) has paid much attention to Plato's rewriting activity, but has at certain points, in my opinion, read too much into the Platonic text or even interpreted it incorrectly. According to Genette, Plato's transformation of *mimesis* into *diegesis haple* means that "the scene in direct dialogue" is turned into "a narrative mediated by the narrator". Accordingly, Genette claims "pure narrative" to be more distant than "imitation": "it says less, and in a more mediated way." Two simpler explanations for the condensation ("it says less") which Genette rightly points out seem to be that

- Plato is giving a prose (ἄνευ μέτρου: 393d) paraphrase and
- his chief didactic aim being to illustrate how *mimesis* (direct speech) can be turned into *diegesis haple*, he concentrates on the essentialia in order to cover as many speeches as possible in a relatively short space.

To speak of *diegesis haple* as "a narrative mediated by the narrator" is an incorrect rendering of Plato's ideas, since *mimesis* is also a narrative (better: manner of narration) and Plato would never think of *diegesis haple* as "mediated": on the contrary, in the *diegesis haple* the poet speaks as himself, *in propria persona* and if there is "mediation" at all, it is in the *mimesis*, where the poet impersonates a character. Genette also makes much of Plato's treatment of A 33-6, which is no direct speech, but all the same condensed by him. It becomes clear from Genette's own words here that he thinks that Plato considered these four verses *mimesis* and that he therefore suppressed e.g. 'along the shore of the loud-sounding sea' - according to Genette a "connotator of mimesis"- "as a feature incompatible with pure narrative". I think that Genette is mistaken: Plato did not consider A 33-6 *mimesis* (he had just defined *mimesis* very clearly as τὰς ῥήσεις: 'the speeches'). He simply had to include this passage of *diegesis haple* in his paraphrase, because it forms the transition to Chryses' prayer 37-42 and condenses it for the same two reasons (prose paraphrase, economy) as given above. In sum, Genette has given too much credit to Plato by ascribing to him certain ideas which are in fact his own.

Plato is also incorrectly credited with the distinction "showing" (the story seems to tell itself without the author becoming visible) and "telling", which is said to be the same as his distinction *mimesis* vs. *diegesis haple*.[7] This equation is incorrect, because "showing" encompasses far more than the use of direct speech (*mimesis*) alone. It might be the result of confusion between Plato's restricted concept of *mimesis* and Aristotle's much wider one (see below).

Having removed some growth which in the course of this century had accrued to Plato's text, I summarize what has remained, even in its trimmed form a valuable theoretical distinction:

	diegesis haple	*mimesis*
the poet speaks as:	himself	one of the characters
in the	parts between the speeches	speeches

Aristotle: Poetics 1448a 19-28 and 1460a 5-11

The *Poetics* is the first attempt to systematize the art of poetry, offering both descriptions and prescriptions. Its actual form has been characterized as "lecture notes", because of the many "interruptions, digressions and failures in connexion" (Lucas 1968: IX-X), which, together with textual problems, make this treatise so difficult to understand in detail. The two genres discussed in the first Book are tragedy and epic, which Aristotle considered as being closely connected.[8] This connection explains why he uses dramatic categories for the analysis of epic on the one hand - only in ch. 23-6 is the epic genre itself discussed, and even then in continual comparison to drama -, and amply illustrates features of drama with examples taken from Homer on the other: "there are more references to the Homeric epics in Aristotle's *Poetics* than to any of the tragedians" (Hogan 1973: 95).

At the outset of the *Poetics* (1447a 13-16) we are immediately confronted with an important difference between Aristotle and Plato's discussion of literature in *Republic* III 392c-394b.[9] Aristotle does not only call drama mimetic, but also epic (as a whole), dithyramb (which Plato, 394c, had mentioned as a representative of *diegesis haple*) and even music: "Mimesis umfaßt in der Poetik a l l e Aus-

drucksformen der Kunst, ..., wobei μιμεῖσθαι die spezifisch künstlerische Um-
setzung von Realität in die Sphäre des Kunstwerkes meint" (Söffing 1981: 46).
Within this group of mimetic arts, Aristotle distinguishes the forms of poetry
according to (1) the medium employed, (2) the object represented and (3) manner
of representation (1447a 16-18).

The passage 1448a 19-28 deals with the third of these criteria. Unfortunately,
the text confronts us with great difficulties of interpretation. There are two
possible ways of grouping the words

ἔστιν ὁτὲ μὲν ἀπαγγέλλοντα, ἢ ἕτερόν τι γιγνόμενον ὥσπερ
Ὅμηρος ποιεῖ ἢ ὡς τὸν αὐτὸν καὶ μὴ μεταβάλλοντα, ἢ πάντας
ὡς πράττοντας καὶ ἐνεργοῦντας τοὺς μιμουμένους.

resulting either in a tripartite division (like Plato's) or in a bipartite one. I
give a translation according to both interpretations:

'it is possible to represent
TRIPARTITE:
  1) by alternately narrating and becoming something else (a character)
  - as Homer does -;
or 2) by remaining the same, without changing;
or 3) by assuming the roles of all those who act and carry out (the action);

BIPARTITE:
either   1) by narrating,
          either   a) becoming (at times) something else (a character)
                    - as Homer does -;
          or   b) remaining the same, without changing;
or   2) by assuming the roles of all those who act and carry out (the action)'

Many pros and cons have been offered for both interpretations.[10] I refrain from
discussing these arguments here, because, whether we accept the tripartite or
the bipartite interpretation of the text, the description of Homeric presentation
as mixed remains the same. Both Aristotle and Plato divide the Homeric text
into the speeches and the rest, which I will henceforth - anticipating the introduction of narratological terminology in chapter 2 - call narrator-text. Plato
describes this division in terms of mimetic vs. non-mimetic, whereas Aristotle
considers both parts mimetic, the difference being one of manner of *mimesis*.

The passage 1460a 5-11 will be discussed in more detail, because here
Aristotle makes an interesting refinement in comparison to the passage just
discussed, which has as yet not been pointed out clearly. I first give my own
translation of the passage:

'Homer deserves to be praised in many other respects, but especially because he alone of the poets knows very well what he should do himself. For the poet must speak as little as possible in his own person, since he is not a *mimetes* in that respect. Now the other poets are asserting themselves throughout the poem and only occasionally represent a few things. But he (Homer), after a brief proem, at once brings a man or a woman or some other character on the stage.'

A number of commentators have taken αὐτὸν ... λέγειν in 1460a 7 as referring to the narrator-text and μιμοῦνται in 1460a 8-9 as referring to the speeches. Homer is unique in comparison to other epic poets, because he has so many speeches and so little narrator-text.[11] This interpretation raises a number of difficulties, which - as notes 12-16 make clear - have been noticed also by the commentators:

- the meaning of *mimesis* would here be restricted and differ from that in the rest of the *Poetics*.[12]
- the narrator-text would now be called non-mimetic, whereas in 1447a 13-16 it was stated that the epic genre as a whole is mimetic;[13]
- other epic texts are supposed to have no or very few speeches;[14]
- ἀγωνίζονται in 1460a 9 must be taken as a synonym of ἀγγέλλουσι;[15]
- the qualification ὀλίγα for the 55% narrator-text of e.g. the *Iliad* is strange.[16]

In view of these difficulties I propose a different interpretation, which may already have become apparent in my translation. The idea for this interpretation is not entirely new, but earlier advocates have remained unnoticed.[17] With αὐτὸν ... λέγειν Aristotle means the poet speaking personally, referring to himself in the first person, exactly as Homer does in his proems - the verb φροιμιασάμενος literally means 'make a proem'- to the *Iliad* (ἄειδε sc. μοι: A 1) and *Odyssey* (μοι: α 1). These passages are considered by Aristotle as non-mimetic, because here Homer is not representing others, but speaking as himself and about himself. According to Aristotle Homer only has little of this personal text (the proems: 7 and 10 verses, respectively), whereas other poets speak personally and assert themselves all through their poems (δι' ὅλου as opposed to φροιμιασάμενος, only in the opening lines of the poem).

If we briefly recall Plato's analysis:

diegesis haple:	poet speaks as poet
mimesis:	poet speaks as character

Aristotle's refinement of this description (and his own analysis in 1448a 19-28) becomes visible:[18]

non-mimetic:	proem:	poet speaks as poet
mimetic:	narrator-text:	poet speaks as narrator
	speeches:	poet speaks as character

If my interpretation of 60a 5-11 is correct, it was Aristotle who made the first step in distinguishing between author (poet) and narrator. The activity of narrating is more clearly defined as a *function* of the poet.

In his zeal to portray Homer as the most dramatic of epic poets, Aristotle ignores the fact that apart from the proems there are more personal passages in Homer. In this respect he stands at the beginning of a long line of critics who all claim that the Homeric narrative style is impersonal and objective.

Plutarch: De audiendis poetis 19a 6- 20c 25

In his busy life (± 50-125 A.D.) Plutarch of Chaeronea managed to combine political tasks and the office of priest in Delphi with an enormous activity as a lecturer and writer. The treatise *De audiendis poetis* (or, as translated from the Greek title: *How a young man should study poetry*) belongs to his pedagogical works: it is a practical guide[19] written with the son of a Roman acquaintance and his own son in mind as proto-types of the 'young men' of the title. According to Plutarch young people should not, as Plato had prescribed, be kept away from poetry, but, instead, use it as a pleasant stepping-stone on their way to philosophy (chapter I). How this goal can be reached is demonstrated in chapters II to XIII: proceeding from easy to difficult, from short quotations without context to complete books, Plutarch shows the young men how to evaluate the moral content of poetry and gradually acquire the ability to judge between virtues and vices. Having reached that stage, they have, in fact, already entered the realm of philosophy, which for Plutarch primarily means ethics (chapter XIV).[20]

In the passage 19a 6- 20c 25, belonging to chapter IV, Plutarch discusses examples of poets, who give *themselves* judgements:

(explicitly)[21]:	A. on words of one of their characters, either beforehand (A1) or afterwards (A2); B. on deeds, either beforehand (B1) or afterwards (B2);
(implicitly):	C. on words/deeds, by (afterwards) showing the reversal of fortune experienced by these characters.[22]

A, B, and C are illustrated with thirteen quotations, of which twelve are taken from Homer. This high percentage of Homeric examples, both here and elsewhere in *De audiendis poetis*, is no coincidence: Homer's reputation in the field of ethics (see above p. 2 and n. 1) made him most suited to Plutarch's pedagogical aims.[23] I concentrate on Plutarch's discussion of seven passages from the *Iliad*, following the outline given above.[24]

A1: according to Plutarch, Homer indicates e.g. in B 189 (ἀγανοῖς ἐπέεσσιν: 'with gentle words') that he favours, in A 24-5 (κακῶς ἀφίει: 'he sent away roughly') and A 223-4 (ἀταρτηροῖς ἐπέεσσιν: 'with baneful words') that he condemns the ensuing speeches. The lesson Homer teaches is, therefore, to avoid angry or harsh words.

A2: in Θ 198 Homer expresses his discontent with Hector's words (185-97) by qualifying them (afterwards) as 'boasting' (εὐχόμενος) and saying that Hera was indignant (νεμέσησε).

B1: in Ψ 24 the qualification ἀεικέα ('disgraceful') of Achilles' treatment of Hector's body (he plans to leave Hector's already mutilated body unburied, a prey for dogs) indicates criticism on the part of the poet.

B2: in Δ 104, Homer shows his contempt for Pandarus, who lets himself be per-suaded by Athena to shoot an arrow at Menelaus, by calling him ἄφρων ('a fool').

C: in O 32-3 Zeus severely rebukes Hera, who had just seduced him (in order to provide respite for the Greeks). According to Plutarch, these words teach that the favour women win through deceitful seductions does not last long and can also change into anger and enmity on the part of their husbands.

By now it will have become clear, I think, what is meant with a moralistic-didactic interpretation of the Homeric epics, which was current throughout an-tiquity and of which Plutarch is such a prominent representative. Whatever the merits of a moralistic *interpretation*, - which might be defended as a special form of *reception* - I disagree with Plutarch (and modern scholars) when they ascribe to the poet himself a didactical *intention*. Rather, I subscribe to Bowra's apodictic statement:

Homer wrote to please and not to secure crops or to avert disease. (1958: 69)[25]

Thus, the speech-introductions which Plutarch discusses in A1 and A2 can be interpreted differently, as will be shown in section 6.1. As regards the evaluative words Plutarch discusses in B1 and B2, here he is in good company, since, as we will see below, modern scholars also bring forward words like ἀεικέα and ἄφρων as (rare) subjective elements in the *Iliad*.

I conclude that the contribution Plutarch has made to the subject of the presentation of the story in the *Iliad* consists in his drawing attention to the presence of evaluative words in the narrator-text and to the possibility the poet has to express his judgement through emotional reactions of the characters (Hera in Θ, Zeus in O).[26] In other words, whereas Plato had considered the *diegesis haple* the natural domain of the poet, but had not given particulars as to how the poet manifests himself personally, where Aristotle had considered only the proems as personal, Plutarch now provides specific examples of the poet 'speaking in his own person' outside the proems.

Scholia

Scholia (diminutive of σχολή: 'learned discussion') are annotations written in the margins or between the lines of ancient texts. The Homeric scholia are of a very heterogeneous nature, both as to their origin and their content. Compiled during the time of the Byzantine renaissance (9th - 14th century A.D.), they also incorporate, in abbreviated and often distorted form, elements from much older scholarly material: commentaries or monographs from the Alexandrine, Hellenistic and Roman periods. Their content ranges from questions of the meaning of words (D-scholia); to interpunction, accentuation and textual criticism (A-scholia) and "aesthetisch-rhetorisch-moralische" interpretation (exegetical bT-scholia). It is in particular from these exegetical bT-scholia, coming closest to modern literary criticism, that I will draw my examples.[27] It should, however, be emphasized once more that we are not dealing with one uniform, full-fledged literary theory, but with dispersed fragments of several theories alternating with *ad hoc* observations. I have collected scholia[28] which have something to say about the presentation of the story in the *Iliad* and will discuss them under four headings:

     a. terminology used to refer to narrator-text and speeches

     b. the transition from narrator-text to speeches

     c. personal feelings of the poet

     d. speeches

a. terminology

At B 494-877 (lines 5-11) the scholia mention Plato's tripartite division (τρεῖς δέ φησιν ὁ Πλάτων λόγων ἰδέας),[29] referring to the narrator-text as ἀμίμητον, to the speeches as δραματικήν. The more usual terms are, however, διηγηματικόν[30] and μιμητικόν, e.g. in T 282-302, where the scholia praise the solemnity and graphic style of the narrator-text and the emotional force of the speech. Interestingly, the scholion on A 8-9 makes the διηγηματικόν start *after* the proem, which reminds one of Aristotle. As a matter of fact, scholars are divided on the question of whether the scholia make any direct use of Aristotle's *Poetics*.[31]

Another term we find in connection with the narrating activity of the poet in the narrator-text is (ἀπ)ἀγγελία, (ἀπ)ἀγγέλλειν ('report'), for which usage there are precedents in both Plato (*Republic* III 394c 2 and 396c 7) and Aristotle (*Poetics* 1448a 21 and 1449b 11,26). Thus, at Π 116b and P 605 the scholia draw attention to 'the rapid pace of the narrative' (τὸ τῆς ἀπαγγελίας τάχος); in I 212a and Σ 346 to Homer's ability to make 'the presentation of ordinary things' (ταπεινὴν ἀπαγγελίαν) like the heating of water solemn and forceful'.[32]

b. the transition from narrator-text to speeches

The bT-scholia on A 17, Δ 303b, Z 45-6, O 346.425-6 and Ψ 855b[33] comment on what they regard as abrupt transitions from narrator-text to speech: λείπει τὸ "τάδε λέγων" ('"with these words" is missing') and ἀπὸ τοῦ διηγηματικοῦ ἐπὶ τὸ μιμητικὸν μέτεισιν ('he passes (directly) from the narrator-text to the speech').[34] Now, in Δ 303 and Ψ 855 there is, indeed, a somewhat unexpected change from indirect speech to direct speech, which in Ψ 855 even takes place - a unique instance in the *Iliad* - within one and the same verse. In these cases, however, as in all the others just listed, there is a verb of speaking present to mark the transition from narrator-text to speech: λίσσετο ('he begged') in A 15 and Z 45, ἐπετέλλετο ('he gave orders') and ἀνώγει ('he urged') in Δ 301, ἐκέκλετο μακρὸν ἀΰσας ('shouting loudly he commanded') in O 346 and 424, ἀνώγει in Ψ 854. Apparently the scholia considered these verbs not to be proper verbs of speaking (λείπει τὸ "τάδε λέγων"). The effect of these sudden transitions has been analyzed by another ancient literary critic, the (unknown) author of *On the sublime* (27.1):

> 'Again sometimes a writer, while speaking of one of his characters, suddenly turns and changes into the actual character. A figure of this kind is a sort of outbreak of emotion: (O 346-9)
> Hector lifted his voice and cried afar to the Trojans
> To haste them back to the galleys and leave the blood-spattered booty.[35]
> Whomsoever I spy of his own will afar from the galleys, Death for him there will I plan.
> There the poet has assigned to himself the narrative as his proper share, and then suddenly without any warning attached the abrupt threat to the angry champion. To insert "Hector said so and so" would have been frigid.'
> (translation Hamilton Fyfe, Loeb-edition)

At A 105b,1 the bT-scholia contain a remark about the function of speech-introductions, which much improves on what Plutarch had said about this (see above p. 9):

> 'it should be observed that whenever the poet is about to introduce the words of one of his characters, he gives an indication beforehand (προσημαίνει) how the speech will be, e.g. when he says "and to him he spoke, looking from under his eyebrows" (A 148 and passim) the ensuing words will be insolent; or "and rebuking him" (9), one should look whether the words to be introduced contain reproaches; or "he spoke to them with good sense" (A 253 and passim) sensible words can be expected.'

c. personal feelings of the poet

In the first place, the numerous moralistic-didactic interpretations the bT-scholia contain can be mentioned under this heading. Thus, they comment on Δ 104 (cp. above Plutarch, p. 9) with: 'the poet teaches us (διδάσκει) not to obey a goddess who gives wicked advice.'[36]

Another sign of personal commitment of the poet which the bT-scholia bring forward is his nationalism (ἀεὶ γὰρ φιλέλλην ὁ ποιητής: Κ 14-6), e.g. ad Θ 131 (the Trojans are almost pent up in Troy like lamb):

> 'the poet exalts Diomedes' bravery and makes fun of the cowardice of the barbarians, if they, even when they are supported by Zeus, run the danger of being pent up like cattle, and that not even like adult cattle: for he says "lamb".'[37]

As in the case of Homer's alleged didacticism (see above p. 9), I am not convinced of his nationalism, at least not to the extreme degree the scholia (and some modern scholars) propose: a passage like Θ 131 can perfectly well make sense in terms of the story (see below section 3.3.2, p. 73) and, as Erbse (1978) has shown, a character like Hector, who according to the scholiasts is depicted by Homer as a despicable barbarian, does act in a consistent and defensible way.[38]

On a number of occasions the poet is said to show compassion or sympathy for his characters: e.g. scholion on Σ 17b (Antilochus is about to tell Achilles the news of Patroclus' death)":

> 'as if feeling sorrow himself (συναλγῶν) the poet says that to report Patroclus' death was a sorrowful message';

or scholion on Λ 243c¹ (the married state of Iphidamas, Agamemnon's first victim in his aristeia is twice mentioned in the text):

> 'those things (Λ 226-7) he had told in a dispassionate way (ψιλῶς),[39] but now he shows compassion (συμπαθῶν), because he says how much trouble Iphidamas had taken to gain his wife and how little he had been able to enjoy life with her.'

See further: Α 430a (τὴν ἰδίαν γνώμην).481 (συγχαίρων), Β 6c κατὰ συμπά-9ειαν), Κ 240 (ἐκ τοῦ ἰδίου προσώπου), Λ 262-3 (περιπα9ῶς), Π 796-7 (ἐμπαθῶς ... συνάχχεται), Τ 285 (συνάχχεσχαι), Χ 442-50 (συμπαθῶς).

A special group are the scholia commenting on the apostrophes (ἀποστροφὴ ἀπὸ προσώπου εἰς πρόσωπον), i.e. when the poet addresses a character (using the second person verb form) instead of talking about him (using the third person verb form).[40] Such an apostrophe betrays the emotions of the poet: Δ 127a: 'the poet feels compassion (προσπέπονθε) for Menelaus', Δ 146a (περιπαθῶς), Η 104-8 (φιλοστόργως), Ο 365b (περιπαθής), Π 692-3: 'in general the poet always feels compassion for (προσπάσχει) Patroclus'. The scholion on Π 787, containing an apostrophe itself, most elaborately describes the emotional power of an apostrophe:

> 'the apostrophe shows that (the poet) condoles (συναχθόμενον): with you, o Patroclus, who were loved so much by Achilles, who had exerted yourself to save your fellow Greeks, who had patiently endured Nestor's garrulity, who had lovingly tended Eurypylus, who had shed tears because of the (disaster of the) Greeks, who had persuaded unyielding Achilles, who had secured a way out (for the Greeks) at the cost of your own life. By relating all this to the apostrophe one can detect its highly pathetic meaning.'

d. speeches

The scholia frequently draw attention to the way in which speeches reveal the character of the person speaking, are 'fitting' to that person, e.g. on Θ 406-8:

> 'the words are fitting (ἁρμόζουσιν) to the character of Zeus, not to that of Iris (in Θ 420-2).'[41]

They also point out differences in vocabulary between poet and characters: Β 570a 1,2 (cp. Ζ 152b.210, Ν 301b), Η 422 (cp. Θ 485a, Λ 735a 1,2), Τ 114.[42]

At Γ 69, Ζ 377, Κ 220b, Λ 747a, Ο 739b, Π 7-8 and Φ 218 (Erbse V, p.98) we find puzzling remarks like the following: τοῦ ποιητοῦ τὸ ἐπίθετον, οὐ τοῦ προσώπου ('the epithet derives from the poet, not from the character speaking'); ἐκπέπτωκεν εἰς ποιητικὴν κατασκευὴν τὸ παρηγμένον ἡρωϊκὸν πρόσωπον ('the heroic character brought on to the stage has slipped into a poetical way of speaking'). The scholiasts do not say why a certain epithet is οὐ τοῦ προσώπου, but I think their argumentation can be reconstructed as follows.[43] In Γ 69 and Ο 739b they probably thought it improbable that Paris should call Menelaus ἀρηΐφιλον ('martial') and Ajax the Trojans πύκα θωρηκτάων ('with close-fitting breastplates'), in short, that he should speak in positive terms about the enemy. Hence, the epithets must derive from the poet. In other cases (Γ 352, Φ 331a,b and Ψ 581c) the scholia even go so far as to propose athetesis, on account of the epithets being 'inappropriate' (ἄκαιρος) or 'superfluous' (περισσόν) in the mouths of the characters speaking. In Κ 220b (θυμὸς ἀγήνωρ), Λ 747a (ἐπόρουσα κελαινῇ λαίλαπι ἴσος) and Φ 218 (ἐρατεινά), the scholiasts probably considered it unfitting that characters should speak in such overtly complimentary fashion about themselves. The remark on Π 7-8 may have been made on account of Π 46, where the poet in the narrator-text (also) calls Patroclus νήπιος ('foolish'). Z 377 can be explained along two lines: we find the epithet λευκώλενος ('white-armed') on two more occasions in direct speech, both times in connection with Hera (O 130: Athena speaking, Φ 512: Leto speaking), without the scholiasts commenting. They may have stumbled over it in Z 377 for the same reason as they stumble over ἀγήνωρ in K 220, etc.: it should not be Hector, who is talking in a complimentary fashion about his own wife. The second explanation runs parallel to that of Π 7-8: the poet had just before in the narrator-text (371) called Andromache λευκώλενος.

Taking (a), (b), (c) and (d) together, I summarize the contribution made by the scholiasts to the analysis of the presentation of the story in the *Iliad*. They are alert in distinguishing between narrator-text (διηγηματικόν) and speech (μιμητικόν), e.g. when they discuss differences in vocabulary between poet and heroic characters. They provide numerous examples of 'personal elements' in the narrator-text: passages where the poet teaches something (?, cp. Plutarch), where he displays nationalism (?), and, most importantly, where he shows sympathy or compassion for his characters. Finally, the scholia show a keen appreciation for the variety and subtlety of the speeches, which give expression to the nature or emotions of the speaking character. Whenever an epithet used in a speech is considered not fitting to the character speaking, the scholiasts athetize it or ascribe it to the poet.

1.2. Modern times

The vicissitudes of the Homeric text in the hands of its readers, in short the history of its reception, are recounted in Clarke (1981). I pick up the thread of my survey of opinions on the presentation of the story in the *Iliad* in 1795, the year of Wolf's *Prolegomena*, but also of Schiller's influential treatise *Über naive und sentimentalische Dichtung*. Here the narrative style of Homer is described as follows:

> Die trockene Wahrheit, womit er den Gegenstand behandelt erscheint nicht selten als Unempfindlichkeit ... Wie die Gottheit hinter dem Weltgebäude, so steht er hinter seinem Werk.[44]

This description, echoing Aristotle's dictum of *Poetics* 1460a 5-11, sets the tone for generations of scholars to come: as we shall see below, most classical scholars (1.2.1) and literary theorists (1.2.2) agree on the objectivity and impersonality of the Homeric epics.

1.2.1. Classical scholars

Objectivity
A clear definition of Homeric objectivity is given by Fränkel:

> Während sich die epischen Ereignisse sozusagen von selbst vorwärtstreiben, ..., berichtet der Dichter von ihnen mit souveräner Sachlichkeit und Gelassenheit, durch die er sich kräftig von den Vorgängen distanziert (1955: 4)

This definition can be split up in two elements:

a. the autonomy of the events, which "seem to tell themselves"[45]

b. the poet reports from a distance, without comment or emotion.

Both elements are also found in other scholars, cp. for (a):

> The words which transport us to the world of heroes come from a source so submerged from view that the heroic life seems to move of its own vitality (Bassett 1938: 27)

> We are aware of the poet's existence at the story's beginning ... Thereafter he disappears, simply the vehicle through whom the marvellously wrought tale is transmitted (Beye 1966: 75)

Cp. for (b):

> die mit gleichmässiger Objektivität auf das Hohe und Niedere hinblickende Ruhe des naiven Dichters (Schneidewin 1878: 13 and passim)

> Der Sänger berichtet, aber er reflektiert nicht. Als Person tritt er völlig hinter der Sache zurück. Er urteilt nicht über seine Gestalten und deutet nicht von sich aus ihre Charaktere; nur durch ihre Handlungen und Reden lehrt er sie uns kennen. Alle Problematik ist in der Erzählung stumm (Fränkel 1976: 41)

Jordan (1909: 27,28 and passim) considers the Homeric style objective, because events (e.g. woundings) are described from the outside and we do not hear about the feelings and emotions of the characters involved (cp. also Fränkel 1976: 41: "mit Zustandsschilderungen ist der Epiker sehr sparsam").

According to Bowra, objectivity is a general characteristic of all heroic poetry:

> Heroic poetry is essentially narrative and is nearly always remarkable for its objective character. It creates its own world of the imagination in which men act on easily understood principles and, though it celebrates great doings because of their greatness, it does so not overtly by praise but indirectly by making them speak for themselves and appeal to us in their own right. (1964: 4)

Subjectivity

Not all scholars have been convinced of the Homeric objectivity: the romantic critic John Keble applied to the Homeric text his biographical procedure and declared: "there is no writer known to us who more simply and openly exhibits, in almost every part of his poem, his real character and feeling" (see Abrams 1953: 256-62). Compare also the following statements:

> Die Ilias will nicht erzählen, sondern repräsentieren, nicht einmal Fakta will sie repräsentieren, sondern Leidenschaften, Stimmungen, Gefühle, nicht die gleich-mäßigen, sondern die heftig bewegten. Ein mächtiges Streben nach hallendem Pathos durchdringt die ganze Ilias. (Mülder 1910: 342)

> But quite apart from the express similes of feeling a study of some Homeric effects of emphasis, epithet, contrast, and the use of the particles would reveal him capable of expressing delicacies of sentiment which often escape the obser-vation of the very critics who harp on his limitations. (Shorey 1922: 250)

> What distinguishes the Ionian epic from most other narrative oral poetry ... is its preoccupation with motives and reactions; it is not only the objective event that counts, the duel of two chieftains or the insulting of the disguised Odysseus, it is the subjective effect of the event on its participants. (Kirk 1962: 380)

In point of fact, both scholars who adhere to the dogma of the Homeric objectivity and others who protest against this dogma or at least wish to see it put in a milder, more balanced form have pointed out subjective elements in the *Iliad*: Finsler (1914: 310-11), Rothe (1914: 231-2), Drerup (1921: 444-6), Bassett (1938: 81-113), Severyns (1948: 133-40), Gaunt (1976), Griffin (1976, 1980: 103-43), Effe (1983: 174-8).[46] Before listing these subjective elements, which I have grouped into 10 categories, I briefly introduce the scholars, indicating their position with regard to the dogma of the Homeric objectivity.

The first discussions by Homerists on Homeric objectivity are firmly en-trenched in the controversy between Analysts and Unitarians. The idea that Homer as a person is absent from his work was seen by the Analysts as a con-firmation of their thesis that the Homeric epics are not the creation of one poet. Accordingly, Unitarians saw it as part of their task to point out in the text traces of the personality of the poet. This search for subjectivity was under-taken along two lines:

- by collecting passages where the poet leaves aside his objective style and for a brief moment speaks in his own person;
- by trying to isolate individual traits of Homer as "künstlerische Persönlichkeit", as distinguished from his anonymous predecessors.

For my purpose only the first type of subjectivity is relevant.[47]

Finsler is an Analyst, but a special one: he considered the *Iliad* a unity, written by one poet, but not at one moment ("stufenweise Erweiterung"). He adheres to the dogma of Homeric objectivity and mentions subjective elements only as the exceptions that prove the rule.

Rothe, who is a Unitarian, maintains that the poet "gar nicht selten" leaves aside his objective style to show his own feelings.

Drerup is also a Unitarian. He brings forward more or less the same categories of subjective elements as Finsler and Rothe (categories 1-5 below), but considers these no real proof for Homeric subjectivity. This must be sought, according to him, in Homer as "bewußter Künstler", in other words along the second line of research (see note 47).

Bassett is a Unitarian. Following the lead of Käte Friedemann (see below p. 22) he opposes the close approximation of epic and drama, which ever since Aristotle had been standard, and, instead, calls attention to differences between the two genres: in drama "all exposition, description, motivation, and explanations" must be put into the mouths of the characters, whereas in epic this information can also be provided by the poet. Hence, "any tale worthy of the name cannot be by any means purely objective" (83). For the Homeric epics Bassett arrives at the following estimate:

> the impersonal narrative, chiefly the account of action, objectively presented, occupies one-fifth of the poem, the speeches three-fifths, and the direct personal utterance of the poet, or his interpretation or explanation which the objective narrative can not give, one-fifth (85)

Severyns is another scholar who brings forward subjective elements (categories 1-3 below) not as exceptions to the rule, but to challenge the dogma of Homeric objectivity:

> Le poète épique devrait se borner à raconter ou décrire sans jamais se démasquer dans ses récits ou descriptions. Homère ne garde pas cette passivité inhumaine. Souvent - plus souvent qu'on ne le croit d'ordinaire - il sort de sa réserve, tantôt pour révéler discrètement sa présence, tantôt pour se jeter résolument dans la mêlée. (1948: 133)

Gaunt and Griffin draw attention to more implicit forms of subjectivity, which, as they themselves readily admit, depend more heavily on the subjectivity of the observing scholar.[48] In the case of Griffin, this problem of what may be called "subjective subjectivity" is largely countered, I think, by his method, which consists of setting speech and narrator-text side by side. Thus, when certain motifs (e.g. "far from home", "bereaved parents" "lack of care after death") which in the mouths of characters have an unmistakably pathetic or emotional ring, occur in the narrator-text, it is legitimate to claim for these instances a similar effect.

The main purpose of Effe's article is to argue that the rules of objectivity and neutral omniscience, which have been claimed as general characteristics for *all* epic texts, hold true for the Homeric epics, but less for Hellenistic epic and Virgil, where one could speak of a subjective, authorial omniscience.[49] He mentions categories 1, 3, 4 and 8 as places where the Homeric text offered later authors starting-points for this move towards subjectivity. The majority of the authorial intrusions of the *Iliad* do not, according to Effe, so much reveal the poet's emotions as his "kritisch-überlegener Distanzierung" (178).[50]

Together, but as we have seen for different reasons, these eight scholars bring forward the following subjective elements in the *Iliad*.

Category 1: invocations of the Muses (e.g. A 1-7, B 484-93) and requests for information (e.g. E 703-4, Π 692). I return to this category in section 3.1.1.

Category 2: passages where an appeal is made to the audience in the form of second person optatives (e.g. Δ 223-5: 'there you would not have seen Agamemnon cowering ....') or rhetorical questions (e.g. P 260-1) or what can be called *if not*-situations (e.g. E 311: 'and now master of men Aeneas would have died, *if* Zeus' daughter Aphrodite had *not* watched sharply ...').[51] I return to this category in sections 3.2 and 3.3.

Category 3: passages where the emotions (mostly compassion) of the poet shine through (cp. the scholia, above pp. 12-3): the apostrophes;[52] the "obituaries" (Griffin 1980: 103-43), i.e. short biographical digressions made at the occasion of a (minor) warrior's death (e.g. Δ 474-9, E 51-4.59-64.153-8);[53] Σ 478-608 ("the shield is the best example in Homer of the introduction of extraneous material to enrich the objective narrative, particularly in its effect upon the emotions": Bassett 1938: 99); pathetic passages like Π 796-9 and P 51-2; passages introduced by emotional particles like ἦ, ἦτοι, μήν, μάν (Bassett 1938: 102).

Category 4: passages where we find the poet's explicit judgement (mostly critical) of characters' actions (cp. the didactic/moralistic interpretation of Plutarch and the scholia): in the form of evaluative adjectives, e.g. οὐλομένην (A 2: Achilles' 'accursed wrath'), ἐξαίσιον ἀρήν (O 598: Thetis' 'immoderate request'), ἀεικέα μήδετο ἔργα (X 395, Ψ 176), νήπιος (B 38, Π 46, etc.: 'foolish'); in the form of (longer) authorial intrusions, e.g. φρένας ἐξέλετο Ζεύς (Z 234: 'Zeus took away his [Glaucus'] good senses'), Π 684-91, Υ 264-6. I return to the question of the evaluative adjectives in section 4.3.

Category 5: passages which betray the historical perspective of the poet, e.g. M 3-35 (history of the wall around the Greek camp after the departure of the Greeks) and the οἷοι νῦν βροτοί-passages (e.g. E 304: 'such as are the people living now'). I return to these passages in sections 3.1 and 3.3.3.

Category 6: passages with present tense outside speeches, such as similes, descriptions of the gods and their attributes (e.g. Hera's chariot: E 726-8 or Hermes' wand: Ω 343-4). Here the poet speaks "directly to his audience of what is either a part of their own experience or is as true for them as for the story" (Bassett 1938: 87-8). I return to the similes in sections 3.3.4 and 4.2.

Category 7: "the substitution of indirect for direct presentation of action, feeling and thought" (Bassett 1938: 102). He distinguishes between:
- expression of cause, e.g. A 195-6, B 641-3, Ψ 137;
- expression of purpose (giving us "a glimpse into the minds of a character, which is one of the chief marks of the subjective narrative"), e.g. B 794, Δ 88, E 2.845, P 126-7;
- representation of words or thoughts (indirect speech), e.g. B 37.50-1, Z 240-1, Λ 646.
I return to this category in section 4.1.

Category 8: foreshadowing by the poet of events to come, e.g. B 38-40, K 336-7, Λ 604. Already the scholia comment on the effect - suspense, or, conversely, the removal of fear - these anticipations have on the audience, see Duckworth (1931). I return to this category in section 3.3.4.

Category 9: speeches:

> Die Zurückhaltung die sich der Epiker sonst auferlegt, gibt er preis in den zahlreichen Reden die er in die Erzählung einflicht ... In der Rolle einer epischen Gestalt darf und kann der Sänger reflektieren, er kann betrachten und deuten was geschieht, er kann eine Situation beschreiben und erklären, und er kann sogar die Individualität von Menschen meisterhaft kennzeichnen und bewerten. Überhaupt sind die Reden freier und reicher; der Stil, die Denkform, und der Gedankenablauf ist moderner als in der Erzählung, und nicht selten finden wir in den Reden Ansichten, Erwägungen und Verhaltungsweisen, die im Widerspruch zu denen stehen auf denen die Erzählung und Handlung beruht. (Fränkel 1976: 43-4)[54]

I return to the speeches in chapter 5.

Category 10: implied judgement (Gaunt 1976). Gaunt distinguishes between judgement implied through

- "the depiction of characters acting in a certain context", e.g. the embassy of Priam to Achilles in Ω,

> where various aspects of the heroic code (on the one hand hospitality and mercy towards a suppliant: on the other, the duty to avenge the death of a friend) are set against one another, and the resulting conflict of principles is resolved in favour of mercy;

- symbolism: e.g. the description of the night sky in Θ 553-65, where Homer reminds us of mortality;

- atmosphere: e.g. the frightening description of the river Scamander's pursuit of Achilles (Φ 233-71), which makes clear that, according to Homer, "Achilles should have accepted Scamander's appeal (to stop killing the Trojans) in deed and not in word only."

I must admit that I am not very convinced by Gaunt's examples, an extreme case of subjective subjectivity.

Dramatic style

The presentation in the *Iliad* is not only regularly called objective, but also dramatic. The roots for this affiliation of epic and drama lie, as we have seen, with Aristotle. With "dramatic", scholars refer either to the large quantity of direct speech (category 9 above) or to the content of the story, which Aristotle, *Poetics* 1459b, called παθητικόν ('full of calamities'): Hector and Achilles are "tragic rather than epic heroes"; the gods "comment on man's tragedy in the role of ideal spectators" (Tait 1943, and cp. Griffin 1978, 1980: 179-204); some heroes are aware of and accept their impending death, notably Achilles, others come to it unprepared (Müller 1978 and Rutherford 1982). A great number of the subjective passages mentioned above play a role in discussions of the tragic nature of the *Iliad* (compassion and criticism of the poet, foreshadowing) and I will not list them again here.

I save concluding remarks concerning the way in which Homeric scholars have approached the question of the presentation of the story in the *Iliad* for section 1.3.

1.2.2. Literary theorists

The Homeric epics, being among the oldest and most famous literary texts, have
naturally also attracted the attention of scholars outside the world of classics.
In this section I discuss the opinions of five literary theorists, Friedemann (1910),
Auerbach (1953: 3-23), Booth (1961: 3-6), Scholes & Kellogg (1966: 51-3) and
Delasanta (1967) on the presentation of the story in the *Iliad* (and *Odyssey*,
which they all take together).

Friedemann

In *Die Rolle des Erzählers in der Epik* K. Friedemann criticizes the rules of
"geistige Objektivität" (the poet disappears behind his work) and "formale Objektivität" (characters speak to us directly through their words and deeds) which
critics like Schiller and, one century later, Spielhagen[55] had projected from
drama into the epic. Instead, she asks attention for what distinguishes epic from
drama: the presence of a narrator, "der Bewertende, der Fühlende, der Schauende"
(34). In her discussion of "the role of the narrator" Friedemann touches upon
several of the 10 categories listed above in connection with Homeric subjectivity.
In fact, she sometimes even gives examples deriving from Homer - as a Germanist,
she bases herself primarily on German narrative texts -, thus using that very
text which her 'opponents' had mentioned time and again as a paragon of epic
objectivity.

Ad cat. 1: through his Muse-invocations Homer stresses the truth-value of his
narrative (85).

Ad cat. 2: an epic narrator can increase the illusion of reality "wenn er es für
möglich hält, dass der Gang der Ereignisse unter gewissen Bedingungen auch ein
anderer hätte sein können" (82), as in the Homeric *if not*-situations (not mentioned
by F.). For, by mentioning an alternative, the narrator stresses the authenticity
of the version actually presented by him.

Ad cat. 3: the "Anruf" (apostrophe) betrays the sympathy of the narrator (210),
who also can show his feelings in the similes, e.g. Δ 452-6 (234).

Ad cat. 4: attributive adjectives which have an evaluative meaning ("Werturteile"),
like 'beautiful' or 'good' (as opposed to descriptive ones like 'small', 'young'),
betray the presence of the narrator as "der Urteilende" (41-2).

Ad cat. 7: some epic narrators have the capacity to look inside their characters'
minds and read their thoughts, thus presenting these more directly to the reader

than when they are expressed by the characters themselves in direct speech (68-78). In the case of 'primitive naturalists' like Homer, she says, the epic narrator does not give his knowledge a rational background, by explaining its source (e.g. "from the look on his face one could gather that he was unhappy"), but "das Seelische bedeutet eine ebenso selbstverständliche Realität wie jede äussere Vorgang" (72). She also notes that in this kind of 'primitive' narrative feelings are not analyzed, but only reported as such, e.g. in α 323-4 ('and he, Telemachus, felt the change in his heart and was struck with awe, for he realized that it had been a god'). Incidentally, this observation of Friedemann's - though I would not accept it without modifications - offers an interesting alternative to Snell's theory (1955) that the lack of analytical reflection in the Homeric heroes originates in a 'primitive' stage of European thinking, preceding the "Entdeckung des Geistes". Avoiding the evolutional fallacy implied in this theory, one might consider the possibility that this unreflectiveness is not so much the result of a way of *thinking*, but of narrative *presentation*.

Ad cat. 8: "Hinweis auf Künftiges": the information about future events can be necessary and/or arouse emotions with the reader (119-22).

Throughout her book Friedemann stresses that we should distinguish the narrator from the historical author (24, 40, 69). Unfortunately she does not apply this important distinction to the Homeric epics, but continues to refer to "Homer" or "der Dichter". The reason for this becomes clear on p. 34, where she speaks of "der Urtypus des erzählenden Dichters: der Rhapsode". In other words, in the case of an oral performing poet, like Homer, she considers narrator and poet as one and the same. We will encounter this same - in my opinion wrong: see section 3.1.1 - line of reasoning below with Scholes & Kellogg.

On the whole, Friedemann's book might have enriched the analysis of the Homeric narrative style, but it has remained unnoticed by Homeric scholars, except Bassett, whose book, in its turn, has never had the influence which it deserves.

Auerbach

In the first chapter of his famous *Mimesis* E. Auerbach compares a passage from Homer (digression on Odysseus' scar: τ 393-466) and one from the Bible (Abraham and Isaac: *Genesis* 22:1) to illustrate his thesis that in Homer everything is "fully externalized", that there is no background, only "a uniformly illuminated, uniformly objective" foreground, whereas in the Bible many things remain mysterious and obscure. I concentrate on the Homeric part of this thesis. The situation in τ is as follows: while washing the feet of Odysseus, who is disguised as a beggar, his old nurse Eurycleia recognizes her master by a scar. At this highly dramatic moment a long digression tells us how Odysseus had got this scar in his youth. According to Auerbach, the digression is completely isolated from its context. Its function is "to relax the tension", to make the hearer/reader forget what has just taken place and although it might have been presented as a recollection of Odysseus (by inserting "the story two verses earlier at the first mention of the word scar"), this "subjectivistic-perspectivistic procedure, creating a foreground and background" was not chosen, being "entirely foreign to the Homeric style" (7).

Auerbach's book has in general been highly praised and his analysis of τ 393-466 is adopted by, among others, Genette.[56] His thesis on the Homeric narrative style has, however, not remained unchallenged. Austin (1966), Müller (1968: 33-4) and Sternberg (1978: 84-5) accept it as only partially true:

> (there are) two contrasting styles of narrative in Homer. The one is that which Auerbach has analyzed so well, in which all details, however trivial or incidental, are included and nothing is omitted or left unclarified. The other is a casual, allusive and elliptical way of presenting information. (Austin 1966: 297)

Both Austin and Sternberg also point out that digressions do not lessen, but heighten the emotional tension of the reader/hearer. Kirk (1976: 104-12) altogether rejects Auerbach's thesis, adducing counter-examples:

> Can it be true that there is nothing hidden, indirect or implicit in Homer, nothing mysterious? I waste no time on the answer; the passage about Odysseus asleep on the Phaeacian ship disproves it totally, and so do the deaths of Sarpedon, Patroclus and Hector in the *Iliad* or Priam's nocturnal journey in the last book of the same poem, to look no further. (105)

Köhnken (1976) goes one step further: instead of adducing counter-examples he attacks Auerbach's own example. He makes clear that the digression τ 393-466 is firmly anchored in the main story, that it is very effectively placed (after Odysseus' recognition by Eurycleia, but before its effect) and that the context is, therefore, certainly not forgotten by the hearer/reader. As part of his argument Köhnken draws attention to the prominent place Eurycleia takes in the digression and developing this idea I have argued elsewhere in detail (de Jong 1985c) that we should interpret the whole digression not as being told by the omniscient narrator (as Auerbach and Köhnken think), but as a flash-back taking place in the mind of Eurycleia at the moment she recognizes the scar.[57] If this interpretation is correct, we have here an example of that "subjectivistic-perspectivistic procedure", which Auerbach thought foreign to the Homeric style. In section 4.1 I will give more examples.

Booth

In *The Rhetoric of Fiction* W.C. Booth undertakes to demonstrate the means by which writers disclose their vision to the reader and persuade them of its validity. This, as Booth calls it, 'rhetoric' can be either ostentatious (e.g. in Fielding) or hidden (in "impersonal" writers like Flaubert or James). In his first chapter he discusses Homer and the Bible as typical representatives of "authoritative telling", i.e. narratives in which the author pronounces judgements or gives information concerning things which in real life would not be so open or clear-cut (e.g. what goes on in the mind of another person) and in which these judgements and information are accepted by the reader without question. Booth's description of the Homeric narrative style very much differs from all we have encountered so far:

> Homer scarcely writes a page without some kind of direct clarification of motives, of expectations, and of the relative importance of events ... we move through the Iliad with Homer constantly at our elbow, controlling rigorously our beliefs, our interests, and our sympathies ... (in the Odyssey) Homer "intrudes" deliberately and obviously to insure that our judgment of the "heroic", "resourceful", "admirable", "wise" Odysseus will be sufficiently favorable. (1961: 4-5)

Thus, Booth contends that Homer speaks personally far more often than Aristotle had suggested (93). He agrees that the Homeric style can be called impersonal and objective, but only in the sense that "the life of the real Homer cannot be discovered in his work". The "direct and authoritative rhetoric" of the Homeric text derives from what Booth later on in his book will call the "implied author", the author's "second-self" in the text.[58] Here he has shown the way, I think, out of the impasse of epic objectivity, which blocks an appreciation of the subtleties of the Homeric narrative style. His ideas have, however, never been picked up by Homerists. Although I will use concepts different from Booth's implied author, my approach is comparable to his (see esp. chapter 3).

Scholes & Kellogg

In *The Nature of Narrative* R. Scholes and R. Kellogg qualify Homer, once again placed on a par with the Bible, as an authoritative, reliable, omniscient, omnipresent, and objective narrator. With objective they mean that he

> does not talk about himself, but about the characters and actions of his story. Nor does he cultivate the intimacy of his audience at the expense of their sympathy with the story ... the omniscient narrator is very far from being 'objective' in that other sense of adopting a point of view resembling that of a neutral human observer of exclusively external events.

As the only "slight and highly stereotyped exception" to this authoritative and objective narrative style Scholes & Kellogg mention the Muse-invocations (category 1, p. 18), which they call "a movement in the direction of authorial self-consciousness".

Scholes & Kellogg, like Booth, point out that elimination by the author of his own personality need not automatically imply neutrality of the narrative style. However, as regards the distinction author vs. narrator, they confront us with a clear case of circularity:

> oral narrative invariably employs an authoritative and reliable narrator ... We are accustomed to identifying this omniscient narrator with the author ... He (the omniscient narrator) is objective in the senses ...that he is not "subjective" and that there is no ironic distance between himself and the author ... Since there is no ironic distance between the author and the teller of a traditional story we are not in the habit of distinguishing between them. (1966: 51-2)

Delasanta

In *The Epic Voice* R. Delasanta, like so many scholars before him, points to the scarcity of subjective elements in the Homeric epics. He is the first, however, to try to explain this phenomenon by comparing the Homeric epics with a literary epic like the *Aeneid*, where much more subjectivity is involved:

> In the oral epics, the poet's tone is literally present: in his, or the rhapsode's voice, his delivery, his very physical presence. The degree of explicitness necessary to the audience's appreciation of the story does not always need to be supplied by the narrated word. Approbation or disapprobation, tonal subtlety, irony can be supplied by a gesture, a vocal inflection, even a raised eyebrow. (40-1).

At first sight this suggestion seems to be corroborated by what is said by a specialist on oral poetry, R. Finnegan:

> a performer can inflect the message or atmosphere of a poem by his own dramatisation, speed, singing style, pauses, rhythmic movements, gestures, facial expression and so on. (1977: 125)

Even so, stress should be laid, I think, on the word "inflect" here: a performer can place his own accents, increase the impact of certain passages, but his performance cannot take the place of textual elements. It is instructive to remember what Taplin (1977: 2) has said about stage actions in Aeschylus' plays: "all, or at least most, stage actions of significance can be worked out from what we have" (sc. the text, IdJ). Applying this dictum to the Homeric texts, I submit that their performance or recitation can underline elements already present in the text, but never replace them.

Delasanta, who is primarily interested in "the story within the story" (Odysseus' story of his own adventures: ι - μ), makes two more general remarks on Homeric narrative style, which are worth mentioning here:

    1. the narrator can delegate narration to a character (thereby renouncing his omniscience), either to let him/her characterize him-/herself (e.g. the long speeches of Nestor) or others (e.g. Helen describing Greek leaders: Γ 161-244).

    2. whereas Scholes & Kellogg had connected omniscience to objectivity, Delasanta thinks that omniscience makes itself felt most clearly in those passages which have been called subjective: "in the area of interposition, intrusion, non-dramatic value-judgement"(40). As examples he mentions:

Ad cat. 1:   Ξ 508-10: the poet prays to the Muses for correct historical details;

Ad cat. 3:   the apostrophes: here Delasanta does not make clear why these vocatives express omniscience;

Ad cat. 4:   Z 234-6: "the poet's undramatic appraisal of a situation wedged into his otherwise objective account";   .

Ad cat. 8:   Π 46: Patroclus is called νήπιος, because the poet knows what will happen to him later.

We see that the picture developed by literary critics of the presentation of the story in the Homeric epics does not, except in the case of Booth, deviate sub-stantially from that of the Homerists. Does this mean that the matter is settled, that all has been said about the Homeric narrative style? Or do we allow Booth's short and probing remarks concerning the "rhetoric" of the *Iliad* to nag us, to provoke us into questioning the *communis opinio* of Homeric objectivity? In the next section I will indicate why a reopening of the question is indeed called for.

1.3. Conclusions

Let me first summarize the opinions on the presentation of the story in the *Iliad*, according to the three issues mentioned at the beginning of this chapter:

    1. according to the the majority of scholars the *Iliad* is presented by the poet, by Homer. Although Aristotle had made a first step towards distinguishing poet and narrator, this distinction, rediscovered and urgently prescribed by e.g. Friedemann, has not become generally established in the case of the Homeric epics;

    2. as a logical consequence of (1), the majority of scholars describe the presentator of the *Iliad* (the poet) as "imperceptible", disappearing behind his

work. Only Booth, who distinguishes between Homer as a person and Homer as an "implied author" claims that the latter is present everywhere. In emphasizing the open and authoritative rhetoric of *Iliad* and *Odyssey* Booth in fact revives in a modern fashion the approach of ancient interpretators like Plutarch and the scholiasts;

3. the Homeric narrative style is qualified by the adherents to the "invisible poet"-theory as objective, impersonal and dramatic, with only some occasional exceptions (the 10 categories of subjective elements). Both Booth and Scholes & Kellogg make the proviso that invisibility of the poet as a person need not necessarily imply a neutral narrative style. Booth even speaks of an authoritative style.

In several individual cases (Plutarch's and the scholiasts' views on Homer's didacticism and patriotism, Gaunt's examples of subjectivity, Auerbach's thesis) I have already expressed criticism, thus cutting short topics which will not further be pursued in this book. Surveying the totality of scholarship, I now wish to raise two general points of criticism, concerning systematics and terminology.

Systematics

The analysis of the presentation of the story in the *Iliad* has been superficial and far from comprehensive. These weaknesses are largely caused by a lack of analytic tools. As a consequence of the commonplace view of Homeric objectivity, almost all attention has been focused on the narrator-text, the question of the presence of the poet there, with neglect of the speeches as narrative components and the relation between narrator-text and speeches. This one-sidedness appears very clearly in the said verdict that the Homeric style is objective, whereas 45% of the text consists of speeches, which all do consider subjective. Scholars have been quick to use broad qualifications (objective, dramatic, impersonal, omniscient, authoritative) which are not always univocal (see below) and sometimes even mutually exclusive (authoritative vs. impersonal). Had more systematic analytic tools been used, such general statements would have been qualified, if not become altogether out of place.

Terminology

Largely as a consequence of this lack of systematic research the terms in which statements are couched are often ambiguous: when the Homeric narrative style is called *dramatic* this refers either to the large amount of direct speech (a formal criterion) and is then seen as a sign of the epic objectivity, or to the tragic stature of its main characters (a criterion pertaining to the content) and is then seen as a sign of subjectivity. *Subjectivity* is used both with reference to the characters (their speeches) and to the narrator (subjective elements in the narrator-text). The absence of the poet as a person and the neutral, distanced presentation are described in terms of *objectivity*. When feelings/thoughts of characters are represented in the narrator-text they reach us according to Friedemann more *directly*, according to Bassett and Genette more *indirectly* than when they are expressed in a speech. *Omniscience* is brought forward both as a mark of objectivity and of subjectivity.

In sum, although the question of the presentation of the story in the Iliad may at first sight seem a settled matter, because the same qualifications are found time and again, this uniformity is in fact deceptive: the very same terms have different meanings for different scholars and the research on which their application is based is shallow. This circumstance, and the puzzling incompatibility of "Homer being constantly at our elbow" (Booth, Plutarch, scholiasts) vs. "the story seems to tell itself" (the rest) make a renewed, systematic investigation imperative. The next chapter will provide the theoretical foundation for this investigation.

2. A NARRATOLOGICAL MODEL OF ANALYSIS

> "Hostility to theory usually means an opposition to other people's theories and an oblivion of one's own."
> (Terry Eagleton, *Literary Theory. An Introduction*)

In this chapter I set up the theoretical framework within which the systematic analysis of the presentation of the story in the *Iliad* will be undertaken (section 2.2). This framework is a narratological one. Although I will on occasion use concepts from other scholars also, I base myself essentially on the model of the Dutch narratologist Mieke Bal (1977 = 1983, 1985), which incorporates and partly refines that of Gérard Genette (1972 = 1980).[1] I start with a brief section on the concepts of *narrator* and *point of view*, which can be considered the historical antecedents of this model (2.1). The last section (2.3), on narrative situations, forms the transition to the main part of this book, which deals with the narrative situations of the *Iliad*.

2.1. Narrator and point of view

An important step in the analysis of the presentation of the story in a narrative text[2] was taken when scholars began to distinguish between the historical author and his fictional delegate in the text, the *narrator*. One example may make this distinction clear: the historical author of the famous Sherlock Holmes stories is

Sir Arthur Conan Doyle, the fictional narrator in the text, the "I" of the following passage, Dr. Watson:

> (1) When I glance over my records and notes of the Sherlock Holmes cases between the years '82 and '90, I am faced by so many which present strange and interesting features that it is no easy matter to know which to choose and which to leave.[3]

A second important, but highly elusive, concept is that of *point of view*, the position from which or angle of vision under which the narrator presents his story. My example here is the opening of Heliodorus' novel *Aethiopica*:

> (2) Day had begun to smile and the sun was shining upon the hilltops when a band of armed pirates scaled the mountain which extends to the mouth of the Nile called the Heracleot, where it empties into the sea. They halted for a little to survey the waters which stretched before them. Out at sea, where they first directed their attention, not a sail was stirring to whet the pirates' appetite for plunder; but when they turned to look at the coastline nearby their eyes encountered a strange spectacle. (transl. M. Hadas)

The narrator opens with a panoramic view of the scenery, providing geographical details. Then, having introduced a group of characters (the band of pirates), he continues his story from their point of view, describing what they see and what for them is "strange". In other words, the narrator restricts his knowledge to that of the characters.[4]

Ample scholarly interest in this aspect of the point of view has resulted in a multitude of typologies or classifications of narratives, which use criteria like the following: is the narrative told in 'I'- or 'he'-form; is the narrator a character in his own story or not; if he is a character, does he play an active role or is he merely an observer; if he is not a character, does he narrate from a great distance and with more knowledge than his characters or does he assume the point of view of one of them, restricting his knowledge to what they can possibly know, etc. Critical discussions of these typologies can be found in Romberg (1962: 11-26); Van Rossum-Guyon (1970); Genette (1972: 203-6 = 1980: 185-9) and Lanser (1981: 19-63). The most recent typologies, not discussed in these studies, are Stanzel (1979) and Lintvelt (1984).

It was Genette who pointed out that all typologies of point of view are based on the position of the narrator, whereas according to Genette the aspect of "who speaks" should be separated sharply from "who sees". Unfortunately, his own typology of point of view, or as he calls it *focalizations* (1972: 206-24 = 1980: 189-224),[5] which he set up to deal with the aspect of "who sees", falls into this same trap again or, as one critic put it: "the narrator creeps in again through the back door" (Rimmon 1976: 59).[6] It was to deal more radically with this problem of the distinction between "who speaks" and "who sees" that Bal (1977: 21-58 = 1983: 234-69) devised her model. This model forms the basis for the next section. The first part of the exposition to follow will be of a rather abstract nature, but I trust that gradually, as more examples from narratives are adduced as illustrations, the picture will become more concrete.

2.2. Presentation: narration and focalization

Bal approaches narrative texts semiotically, that is to say as a form of communication between an author sending a message and a hearer/reader receiving that message. The content of this message is a vision on a series of events caused or experienced by characters. To analyze and describe as precisely as possible the content of the message, "the particular effects which the text has upon its readers" (1985: 6), Bal distinguishes three layers (text, story, fabula). Semiotically speaking, each of these layers signifies the next. Thus, the text is the signifier of the story, which, itself the signified of the text, is in turn the signifier of the fabula.

The three layers: text, story, fabula
That which the hearer/reader hears/reads is a text (first layer). The *text*, consisting of a finite, structured whole of language signs, is the result of the narrating activity (narration) of a narrator. That which the narrator tells, the object of his[7] narration, is a story (second layer). The *story*, consisting of a fabula (see below) looked at from a certain, specific angle, is the result of the focalizing activity (focalization) of a focalizer. Focalization comprises not only "seeing", but ordering, interpreting, in short all mental activities. That which the focalizer focalizes, the object of his focalization, is a fabula (third layer). The *fabula*, consisting of a logically and chronologically related series of events, is the result of all kinds of activities by characters in a fictional world.[8]
The above may be graphically represented as follows:

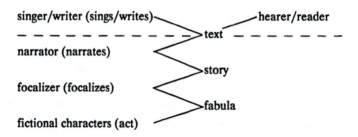

From this graphic representation of Bal's model two of its aspects become clear: in the first place, what I would like to call, the accordeon-nature of this model. For matters of analysis it is useful to 'pull out' (distinguish between) the three layers, but what we have, in fact, is only the text. It is through the text that we approach the story, through text and story, the fabula. Story and fabula are abstractions made on basis of the text. The second aspect concerns the double status of the text. A narrative text *de facto* derives from an author, but for purposes of a narratological analysis it is thought of as the result of a narrator's narrating activity. One could say that the text forms the hinge between the real, historical world of the author 'outside' and the fictional world of narrator and characters 'inside' (hence the broken line in the graphical representation).

I now resume the thread of my argument and return to the question of the analysis of the presentation of the story - whenever I use this expression, 'story' is to be understood as implying the fabula it represents. Presentation can now be described as comprising two activities: narration (by a narrator) and focalization (by a focalizer). Narrator and focalizer should not be thought of as persons: they are the indications of two different functions which have to be fulfilled in order for the fabula to become a story, the story to become a text. Formulated in this way it looks as if the fabula exists, as if it has an ontological status of its own, which, as I stated above, is not the case: both fabula and story are abstractions made by the hearer/reader on basis of the text. Yet, the *suggestion* in almost all narrative texts is that the events have at a certain time taken place (not necessarily as a historical, but as a fictional reality), and that they are now reported to us (cp. the use of (ἀπ)ἀγγέλλειν by Plato, Aristotle and the scholiasts).[9]

Every narrative must have a narrator and a focalizer, whether they become "perceptible" in the text or not.[10] We, the hearer/reader, are always confronted with a filtered view, i.e. selection and evaluation, of the events and this filtering is due to a focalizer. For this vision to become accessible to us, it must be put into words by a narrator. Thus, it is the narrator and the focalizer who together are responsible for what Booth called "the rhetoric of fiction".

Identity of narrator and focalizer

So far I have spoken of narrator and focalizer rather abstractly as functions. I now turn to the question of the *identity* of narrator and focalizer. The function of narrator (N) and focalizer (F) can be fulfilled by one of the characters (C) who plays a role in the story: in those cases I speak of an *internal* narrator (N=C) and *internal* focalizer (F=C). When narrator or focalizer do not coincide with one of the characters (N≠C, F≠C) I call them *external*. The functions of narrator and focalizer can be combined in one identity (N=F), which either coincides with one of the characters (N=F=C: an internal narrator-focalizer) or not (N=F≠C: an external narrator-focalizer).

An example of an internal narrator-focalizer is found in J.D. Salinger's *The Catcher in the Rye*:

> (3) The minute I went in, I was sorry I'd come. He was reading the Atlantic Monthly, and there were pills and medicine all over the place, and everything smelled like Vick's Nose Drops. It was pretty depressing.

The "I" who is narrating and focalizing here is Holden Caulfield, the main character of the narrative. "Pretty depressing" is *his* interpretation of the situation.

As we shall see in section 3.1, the *Iliad* is presented by an external narrator-focalizer, who has to invoke the help of the Muses to bridge the distance in time between himself and his story. However, the *Iliad* - as most narratives - has more than this one presenter. This is due to the fact that both narration and focalization allow embedding (Bal 1981).

Status of narrator and focalizer: embedding

It is in the nature of language that, whenever somebody tells anything he or she will of necessity and often unconsciously at the same time also give an interpretation of the thing told. This means that every narrator is also a focalizer:

NF: I narrate and focalize event/person x.

However, not every focalizer is also a narrator. Somebody may report the interpretation of someone else. A primary narrator-focalizer may embed the focalization of somebody else, a secondary focalizer:

$NF_1[F_2]$:   I narrate and focalize that person x sees event/person y;
person x focalizes event/person y.[11]

Or, a primary narrator-focalizer may embed focalization and narration of another, a secondary narrator-focalizer:

$NF_1[NF_2]$: I narrate and focalize that person x speaks;
person x narrates and focalizes event/person y.[12]

Let me illustrate these embeddings from E.M. Forster's *A Passage to India*:

(4) Except for the Marabar Caves - and they are twenty miles off - the city of Chandrapore presents nothing extraordinary.

(5) she went into the billiard-room, where she was greeted by 'I want to see the real India,' and her appropriate life came back with a rush. This was Adela Quested, the queer, cautious girl whom Ronny had commissioned her to bring from England.

In (4) a primary narrator-focalizer gives a description of Chandrapore as he "sees" it ("nothing extraordinary"), at the same time selecting a detail (the Marabar Caves), which will prove to play an important role in the story to come. In (5) the primary narrator-focalizer first embeds both narration and focalization: the sentence between inverted comma's are words spoken by Adela Quested and contain *her* focalization (*in casu*: a desire to see India). The words underlined are an example of the primary narrator-focalizer embedding the focalization of a secondary focalizer: they describe what goes on in the mind of the 'she' (= Mrs. Moore, the mother of Ronny). Though one can never with absolute certainty prove that the qualification of Adela Quested as "the queer, cautious girl" derives from this secondary focalizer and not from the primary narrator-focalizer, who, after all, is responsible for the verbal presentation, it is of heuristic-interpretative value to attribute it to Mrs. Moore. Indeed, this interpretation finds confirmation later on in the story, when Mrs. Moore, after the mysterious incident in the Marabar Caves, shows very little understanding or sympathy for the 'victim' Adela Quested (chapter XXII).[13]

Projecting this possibility of embedding into the three-layer stratification (text, story, fabula) we get the following picture:

TEXT 1 I narrate	STORY 1 and focalize	FABULA 1 person/event x		
"	"	person/event x= STORY 2 x focalizes	FABULA 2 person/event y	
"	"	person/event x= TEXT 2 x narrates	STORY 2 and focalizes	FABULA 2 person/event y

The number of embeddings is, in principle, indefinite, although too many embeddings will, for reasons of intelligibility, be avoided. A fairly complex example is *Odyssey* ι 511-12, which contains three embeddings: the primary narrator-focalizer (NF$_1$) narrates how Odysseus (as NF$_2$) narrates how the Cyclops (as NF$_3$) narrates the words of the seer Telemus (F$_4$).

We see that the presentation of the story is in the hands of at least one (primary) narrator-focalizer, but as a rule also of other (secondary, tertiary) focalizers and (secondary, tertiary) narrator-focalizers. The relation between these presentators is one of *subordination*: the primary narrator-focalizer decides when and for how long to let a secondary focalizer focalize or a secondary narrator-focalizer speak and he can also comment on their (secondary) stories and texts.

Presentation and reception

Narrative texts have been defined as a form of communication and their presentation consequently involves reception. Just as the author addresses a hearer/reader, the narrator addresses a *narratee* and the focalizer addresses a *focalizee*, the indirect object of focalization. The focalizer focalizes the fabula for the focalizee, the result being the story; the narrator tells the story to the narratee, the result being the text:

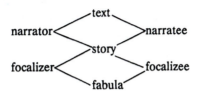

Identity (external, internal) and status (primary, secondary) of the narratee (Ne)

and focalizee (Fe) are in principle symmetrical to the status and identity of the narrator and focalizer to which they correspond:

external primary NF: external primary NeFe $\qquad$ (NF$_1$: NeFe$_1$)

internal primary NF: internal primary NeFe $\qquad$ (NF$_1$=C$_z$; NeFe$_1$=C$_y$)

internal secondary F: secondary Fe,internal/external $\qquad$ (F$_2$=C$_x$: Fe$_2$=C$_y$/≠C$_y$)[14]

internal secondary NF: internal secondary NeFe $\qquad$ (NF$_2$=C$_z$; NeFe$_2$=C$_y$)

I give two examples:

(6) D.H. Lawrence, *Lady Chatterley's Lover*:

> Ours is essentially a tragic age, so we refuse to take it tragically. The cataclysm has happened, we are among the ruins, we start to build up new little habitats, to have new little hopes ... We've got to live, no matter how many skies have fallen.

(7) *Odyssey* λ 333 = ν 1-2:

> Thus he (Odysseus) spoke and they (the Phaeacians) were all silent and were held in a spell in the shadowy palace.

In (6) an external primary NF uses "ours" to appeal to the experiences of his external primary NeFe. The ruined world he is referring to is the world after the first World War and this immediately makes clear that the NeFe is not the same as the historical reader of *Lady Chatterley's Lover*, who can be living, e.g., in 1987. In (7) the Phaeacians are the internal secondary NeFe to Odysseus, who, as internal secondary NF, recounts his adventures to them.

The historical hearer/reader can be invited to identify with the narratee(s) and focalizee(s), but just as the narrator-focalizers and focalizers are not the same as and do not necessarily represent the opinion of the author, similarly the hearer/reader need not necessarily share the feelings of the narratee-focalizee(s) and focalizee(s). Analysis of presentation and reception of the story inside the text is the domain of narratology, whereas the historical reception belongs to the domain of reception-esthetics (see also below ch. 3, p. 44).

2.3. Narrative situations

A convenient starting-point for a systematic analysis of the presentation of the story in a narrative is to make an inventory of types of presentation, or *narrative situations*. Criteria to define a narrative situation are identity and status of the presentators and of their recipients. Since many combinations are possible, the number of narrative situations actually displayed by narratives is considerable and I will here concentrate on the five narrative situations which are found in the narrative under consideration in this investigation, the *Iliad*. These five narrative situations are:

1. simple narrator-text: $NF_1 \rightarrow NeFe_1$.

An external narrator-focalizer presents the events/persons. Recipient is an external primary narratee-focalizee.

2. complex narrator-text (embedded focalization):

$NF_1[F_2=C_x \rightarrow Fe_2=/\neq C_y]NeFe_1$.

The external narrator-focalizer embeds in his narrator-text the focalization of one of the characters, who, thus, functions as an internal secondary focalizer. Recipients are a secondary focalizee, who is internal or external, and, ultimately, the external primary narratee-focalizee.

3. character-text (speeches): $NF_1[NF_2=C_x \rightarrow NeFe_2=C_y]NeFe_1$.

The external primary narrator-focalizer embeds in his narrator-text a character-text, presented by a character, who, thus, functions as an internal secondary narrator-focalizer. Recipients are an internal secondary narratee-focalizee and, ultimately, the external primary narratee-focalizee.

4. tertiary focalization:

$NF_1[NF_2=C_x[F_3=C_p \rightarrow Fe_3=C_q]NeFe_2=C_y]NeFe_1$.

The internal secondary narrator-focalizer embeds in his character-text the focalization of another character, who, thus, functions as a tertiary focalizer. Recipients are a tertiary focalizee, the internal secondary narratee-focalizee and, ultimately, the external primary narratee-focalizee.

5. embedded speech:

$NF_1[NF_2=C_x[NF_3=C_p \rightarrow NeFe_3=C_q]NeFe_2=C_y]NeFe_1$.

The internal secondary narrator-focalizer embeds in his character-text the speech of another character, who, thus, functions as a tertiary narrator-focalizer. Recipients are an internal tertiary narratee-focalizee, the internal secondary narratee-focalizee and, ultimately, the external primary narratee-focalizee.

If we now recall Plato's and Aristotle's analyses of narrative texts (above section 1.1), the descriptive refinement offered by the narratological model becomes clear. The *Iliad*, an epic narrative text, consists of:

PLATO	ARISTOTLE	NARRATOLOGICAL MODEL
diegesis haple	(non-mimetic) proem (mimetic) narrator-text	narrator-text simple complex

mimesis	(mimetic) speeches	character-text
		    tertiary focalization
		    embedded speech

To distinguish between *diegesis haple* and *mimesis* in a narrative text was an easy matter: mimesis is all the text between quotation-marks, often preceded or capped by a verb of saying. The remainder of the text is *diegesis haple*. But how do we recognize simple and complex narrator-text, etc.?

Sometimes simple narrator-text is marked as such by the NF$_1$ referring explicitly to his own activity as narrator (example 8) or focalizer (example 9):

(8) Chariton, *Chaereas and Callirhoe*:

I, Chariton of Aphrodisias, secretary to the advocate Athenagoras, <u>will narrate</u> a love-story, which has taken place in Syracuse.

(9) W. Somerset Maugham, *Virtue*

Unfortunately I cannot very well <u>remember</u> what he looked like ... I <u>forget</u> how long the road was, fifteen or twenty miles, I think, and I <u>forget</u> what purpose it was to serve.

In other cases, the presence of the NF$_1$ remains implicit, but it will, in practice, not be difficult to recognize the simple narrator-text. Complex narrator-text (embedded focalization) can roughly be divided into three kinds of passages:

    I   : those describing the content of perceptions
    II   : those describing the content of thoughts (memory), emotions, feelings
    III   : indirect speech.[15]

Accordingly, the transition from simple narrator-text to complex narrator-text can be marked explicitly by verbs of

    I   : seeing, hearing (example 10)
    II   : thinking, remembering, feeling (example 11)
    III   : speaking (example 12).

Examples:

(10) Th. Hardy, *Tess of the D'Urbervilles*:

> ... they could <u>see</u> over the stumps the spot on which Clare had followed her when he pressed her to be his wife; to the left the enclosure in which she had been fascinated by his harp and far away ... the mead which had been the scene of their first embrace. The gold of the summer picture was now *gray*, the colors *mean*, the rich soil *mud*, and the river *cold*.

(11) W. Somerset Maugham, *The vessel of wrath*:

> He <u>asked himself</u> *what the devil* his visitor could want. Evert Gruyter spoke English, Dutch, and Malay with equal facility, but he thought in Dutch. He liked to do this. It seemed to him a pleasantly ribald language.[16]

(12) E.M. Forster, *A Passage to India*:

> She accepted his escort back to the Club, and <u>said</u> at the gate that she wished she was a member, so that she could have asked him in.

In (10) the embedded focalization, triggered by "see", becomes very clear in the italicized words: the focalizing "they", who are at this moment very unhappy, see their unhappiness as it were reflected in the scenery surrounding them. In (11) the mimetic element "what the devil" in the embedded focalized passage triggered by "asked himself" also clearly points to focalization by the character "he".[17] Such explicit signals or markers as "see", "asked himself" or "said" may also be lacking, as e.g. in example (5) above. In that case I speak of *implicit* embedded focalization, which is the equivalent of what others call "erlebte Rede" or "free indirect discourse" (see McHale 1978). (12) is a case of indirect speech.

The transition from narrator-text to character-text, too, can be either implicit, as in example (5) above, - but note the helpful inverted commas - or explicit with the help of a verb of saying, e.g.

(13) W. Somerset Maugham, *The vessel of wrath*:

> 'I don't want your help,' she <u>said</u> coldly.
> 'You can go to hell,' he <u>answered</u>.

Such statements as "she said coldly" or "he answered" are known in narratology as *attributive discourse* (Prince 1978), a concept to which I will return in section 6.1.

The transitions to tertiary focalization and embedded speech, respectively, are either marked or unmarked, in the same way as the transitions to embedded focalization and character-text, respectively.

Preview

I have come to the end of the introductory part of this book. The historical context of the investigation has been sketched (ch. 1) and the analytical tools have been prepared for use (ch. 2). The next three chapters will deal with the five narrative situations of the *Iliad*:

Chapter 3:	simple narrator-text
Chapter 4:	complex narrator-text
Chapter 5:	character-text
	tertiary focalization
	embedded speech

I will primarily aim at a systematic description of these narrative situations. Secondly, I will try to show how such a systematic description can be helpful in solving problems of interpretation. The interpretative possibilities offered by the method result from the fact that it reveals the variety and the complexity of the presentation. If simple narrator-text presents one type of rather straight-forward presentation, character-text can offer different, more limited or even conflicting presentations, while complex narrator-text, as an intermediate form, blurs the otherwise seemingly unproblematic distinction between narrator-text and character-text. It is precisely that variation of narrative situations and the different effects they have, that raises our awareness of the devices of narrative.

3. SIMPLE NARRATOR-TEXT

> "With commentary ruled out, hundreds
> of devices remain for revealing judgment
> and moulding responses." (Wayne Booth,
> *The Rhetoric of Fiction*)

In this chapter the narrative situation of simple narrator-text - which takes up about 50% of the *Iliad*[1] - is central. Simple narrator-text involves a primary narrator-focalizer (NF_1) as presentator and a primary narratee-focalizee ($NeFe_1$) as recipient. These two poles of communication will be introduced in sections 3.1 and 3.2, through a discussion of passages where they are *explicitly* present.

Then, in section 3.3 I turn to cases where interaction between NF_1 and $NeFe_1$ *implicitly* reveals their presence.

3.1. The primary narrator-focalizer
3.1.1. Introduction

The simple narrator-text of the *Iliad* derives from a primary narrator-focalizer (NF_1) who only rarely refers explicitly to his own activity as narrator (example 1) and focalizer:

(1) B 493:
     ἀρχοὺς αὖ νηῶν ἐρέω νῆάς τε προπάσας.
     the leaders of the ships in their turn I will name and the
     total sum of their ships.

The NF$_1$ reflects on, and thereby explicitly reveals, his own activity as narrator and focalizer only when addressing the Muses. Before embarking on a discussion of the relation between NF$_1$ and Muses, I want to clear two points of a more theoretical nature. The first concerns the role of the NF$_1$ as focalizer: in chapter 2 it was set out that according to Bal's narratological model every narrative must have (at least) one narrator and focalizer. My claim at the opening of this chapter that the simple narrator-text of the *Iliad* is presented by a NF$_1$ is a theoretical postulate based on this model. Now, if the primary focalization remains implicit almost throughout, how can I 'prove', or rather convince the reader, that there is indeed such a primary focalizer at work? The second point is the relevance of the distinction author : narrator.

The primary focalizer

To show that there is a primary focalizer, an agent who orders and interprets the events of the fabula, I first take into consideration an aspect of the handling of 'time': *rhythm*.[2] It has been observed by many narratologists that the events of a fabula are presented in a certain rhythm, in Müller's (1947) terminology: the quantitative relation between "erzählte Zeit" and "Erzählzeit". Thus, some events are told scenically, others at a slow, again others at a rapid pace. In terms of Bal's model it is primarily the focalizer who determines the rhythm of presentation, since it is through him that a fabula is turned into a story. This rhythm is made clear by the narrator at the level of the text through his choice of verb-forms and time-indicators like 'once', 'regularly', etc.[3] Analysis of rhythm is one reliable way to detect a focalizer. I give four examples from the *Iliad*:

> (2) A 490-2 (Achilles is sitting idle near the ships, because of his wrath):
> οὔτε ποτ' εἰς ἀγορὴν πωλέσκετο κυδιάνειραν
> οὔτε ποτ' ἐς πόλεμον, ἀλλὰ φθινύθεσκε φίλον κῆρ
> αὖθι μένων, ποθέεσκε δ' ἀϋτήν τε πτόλεμόν τε.
> And he never went to the assembly bringing men fame nor to war, but he made his own heart to waste by staying where he was and he longed for the battle-cry and war.

Here, what can be reconstructed as a period of nine days in the fabula is condensed by the primary focalizer into a *summary*, which on the level of the text manifests itself through iterative verb-forms. In other words, the time of presentation is considerably shorter than the presented time.[4]

In Z 242-50 and Λ 33-40 we are dealing with a *pause*: the action of the fabula is frozen by the primary focalizer, while he focalizes Priam's palace and Agamemnon's shield, respectively. In other words, the presented time is zero: we are not dealing with an event, but with the description of an object. Whereas the object described belongs to the world of the fabula, the description itself exists in the story and text only.[5] On the level of the text we find imperfects of stative verbs ((ἔν)εσαν: Z 244.248, ἦσαν: Λ 33.34.39, (ἔ)ην: Λ 35.38) and pluperfects (ἐστεφάνωτο: Λ 36, ἐλέλικτο: 39), wedged in between aorists (ἵκανε: Z 242, ἤλυθε: 251; ἕλετ': Λ 32, θέτο: 41).

The primary focalizer can even skip over an event (*ellipsis*): the time of presentation is zero. This phenomenon was already known to the Homeric scholiasts as σχῆμα τῆς σιωπήσεως: 'the rhetorical figure of passing over in silence' (see Meinel 1915). E.g., in Π 432 Zeus speaks to Hera on Mount Ida. In O 79 we had been told that Hera went from Mount Ida to the Olympus, so the primary focalizer leaves out the event of Hera's return (somewhere between O 79 and Π 432) to Mount Ida.

As a second illustration of the implicit, but important focalizing activity of the NF₁ I take the war. War plays an important role both in the narrator-text and in the character-text. One of the ways in which a vision on war can be expressed is through attributive adjectives.[6] Characters indeed often use such attributive adjectives, as becomes clear from Appendix I (third column), where I have listed the adjectives appearing with the four main words for war/fighting: μάχη, π(τ)όλεμος, ὑσμίνη, φύλοπις. We also see, however, that such adjectives, and indeed often the same ones, are used by the NF₁ (first column) too: 40 times an adjective is found in a primarily focalized passage, as against 61 times in character-text (direct speech); 10 adjectives (of a total of 31) are used both by the NF₁ and the characters. This second phenomenon should, of course, first of all be explained genetically, in terms of the oral background of the *Iliad*. But, as section 4.3 will make clear, the distribution of adjectives is not always even over all three narrative situations and distribution-patterns may, therefore, be given a narratological significance. I conclude that the NF₁, by calling the war/fighting 'unabating', 'full of tears', 'destructive', 'bringing much woe', 'violent', 'forceful' and 'terrible', does in fact express his opinion on an important element of his story.

These two illustrations (rhythm and vision on war) must for the moment suffice to give an impression of the activity of the primary focalizer. Later on in this chapter more aspects will come to the fore.

The distinction author : narrator

As we have seen in section 1.2, the theoretical distinction between author and narrator was either not picked up by Homerists[7] or was considered not relevant for the *Iliad*. Taking the poem as orally composed, they identified the aoidos with the poet and the poet with the narrator. I submit that for a proper understanding of the presentation of the story this distinction is vital - regardless of whether the *Iliad* was composed orally or not - and forms the clue to the "puzzling incompatibility" (Homer is absent vs. Homer is constantly at our elbow) noted at the end of chapter 1 (p. 28). The historical author Homer - I assume that he existed and formed the last in a long succession of singers - is indeed absent from his own work as a person, i.e. he does not refer to himself. This does not mean, however, that

 1. nothing can be said about his intentions or standpoints, or

 2. that "the story tells itself".

<u>Ad 1</u>: investigation of the "Wirkungsabsichten" or "Rezeptionssteuerung" of an author belongs to the domain of reception esthetics ("Rezeptionsforschung/ -ästhetik") and for the *Iliad* I refer to Nicolai (1983).

<u>Ad 2</u>: the story does not tell itself, but is presented by a number of presentators. The hierarchically highest of these is the NF_1, who as such can be considered Homer's fictional representative inside the text. It is the NF_1 who is "constantly at our elbow".

 The NF_1 gives no biographical details about himself (name, place of origin, etc.), yet his identity as presentator can be defined. The NF_1 is *external*, i.e. he is not one of the characters who partake of the action of the fabula, and his presentation is *posterior*, i.e. follows *after* the events presented have taken place.[8] This can be inferred from the following indications:

 1. The οἶοι νῦν βροτοί-passages (E 302-4, M 378-85.445-9, Y 285-7), where the NF_1 says that the mortals 'of the present day' are less strong than the heroes of his story.[9]

 2. Two passages (Z 314, Ξ 287) where τότε ('then') does not refer to a specific moment in the story, but in general emphasizes the 'then' of the story vs. the 'now' of the moment of presentation, cp. the bT-scholion ad Ξ 287-8:

> καλῶς δὲ πρόσκειται τότε· νῦν γὰρ οὐ φύεται ἐκεῖ ἐλάτη. καὶ ὅτι
> μετὰ τὰ ἡρωϊκὰ ὁ ποιητής.
> "then" is rightly added, for now no fir grows there anymore. And (it also indicates) that the poet (lived/spoke) after the heroic events.

 3. The ἦν δέ τις-formula used to introduce certain characters (E 9, K 314,

N 663; and cp. P 575: ἔσκε δ' ἐνί Τρώεσσι Ποδῆς), which resembles the opening words of fairy-tales: Once upon a time there was ... Cp. also Häußler (1976: 26-7).

4. B 485-6, where the NF₁ says that his knowledge is based on 'report' (κλέος), not on autopsy. See further below pp. 51-2.

5. The description of the destruction of the Achaean wall after the return home of the Greeks (M 3-35) and the NF₁'s unique qualification there of the characters as ἡμιθέων γένος ἀνδρῶν (23: 'a race of semi-divine men'). For this passage see further below pp. 88-9.

6. The NF₁'s use of ἤματι κείνῳ ('on that (remote) day') in B 482 and Δ 543. In appendix II I argue this point more substantially.

Although the external NF₁ is not a character partaking of the action, has no name and no body (and strictly speaking no sex!)[10] he is not fully devoid of personality.[11] To begin with, there is his personality as a primary focalizer, i.e. as interpreter of the events before Troy, of which I have already spoken above. His personality can further be pinpointed through his relation with three different entities, all of which he occasionally addresses: the Muses (invocations), his addressee, the primary narratee-focalizee or NeFe₁ (passages with a second person verb-form) and the characters (apostrophes). Of these three relationships, two (with the Muses, with the NeFe₁) will be further investigated in this chapter. The third relationship (with the characters) I will not explore systematically in a separate section: the apostrophes have already been discussed satisfactorily by other scholars[12] and other aspects will be touched upon on several occasions throughout this chapter and the next.

To round off this introductory section on the NF₁: the presentation of the Iliadic simple narrator-text is in the hands of an external NF₁, whose activity as focalizer precludes a completely objective or impersonal narrative style: there is always a selection, arrangement, interpretation of events. As will appear from the next section, it is important to realize that this NF₁, as a fictional delegate of Homer, is after all a *creation* of the poet like the characters.

3.1.2. The primary narrator-focalizer and the Muses

The Homeric Muses have already received ample scholarly attention: Barmeyer (1968:34-48), Harriott (1969:41-5), who both also review older scholarship, but do not mention the interesting contribution of Klotz (1965). Recent contributions are Häussler (1973), Svenbro (1976: 11-45), Pucci (1978), Murray (1981) and Schmeling (1981). Since I consider the Muse-passages part of the fiction, i.e. the NF_1 addressing them and not the poet (pace Aristotle, see above p. 8), it is relevant to turn to these much discussed passages again.

In the *Iliad* the NF_1 addresses the Muse(s) on six occasions (A 1-7, B 484-93.761-2, Λ 218-20, Ξ 508-10, Π 112-3), referring in all cases but one (A 1-7) to himself (μοι: B 484 = Λ 218 = Π 112, B 489.490.761; first person singular and plural verb-forms: B 486.488.493). All these invocations contain either a request (ἄειδε: A 1; ἔννεπε: B 761) and/or a question (direct: B 761-2; indirect: B 484-487, Λ 218-20, Ξ 508-10, Π 112-3). On account of these requests and questions scholars have interpreted the relationship poet/NF_1-Muses primarily in terms of the former being *dependent* on the latter, with varying degrees of dependency. At one extreme is found e.g. Lenz, who, on account of ἄειδε in A 1, argues that the whole *Iliad* is in fact "die Äusserung der angerufenen Gottheit, die ihr Lied durch seinen (sc. des Dichters) Mund ertönen läßt" (1980: 27). In other words, we are to consider the NF_1 a mouthpiece of the Muse, a kind of 'musical instrument', so to speak. Others state that the NF_1 is dependent on the Muse only for his information: either specific information such as catalogues, which are difficult to memorize (Falter 1934: 7, Minton 1960: 293, Murray 1981: 90-1) or more in general the formulas and typical scenes (Notopoulos 1938, accepted in Harriott 1969: 45). This connection between Muses and the art of memorization has, of course, been emphasized and developed especially since the research initiated by Milman Parry. Redfield (1979: 98) also considers the Muses "a source of information", but adds an interesting suggestion: normally the Muse is asked by the NF_1 to tell him (ἔννεπε, ἔσπετε) certain facts, which he then in his turn tells to the audience. In the proem, containing ἄειδε instead of ἔννεπε/ ἔσπετε, this process is presented in a simplified form: the idea here seems to be that the Muse herself sings directly to the audience: "the bard in effect claims that his song is the authentic voice of the goddess". I think this idea of "claiming" can be elaborated upon: it will be argued that the NF_1 is not so much dependent on the Muses, but rather uses them to recommend his own activity as (primary) narrator and (primary) focalizer. In other words, the Muse-invocations portray the Iliadic NF_1 as a "self-conscious narrator" (Booth 1961: 155, 205-9), i.e. a narrator who is aware of and reflects on[13] his own role as narrator as against narrators "who seem unaware that they are writing, thinking, speaking, or "reflecting" a literary work" (e.g. in Camus' *L'Étranger*).

In the proem it is the NF₁ who takes the initiative, demands (with an imperative) the goddess to sing about a theme he has chosen (1) and for which he sets the tone (2-5), indicating also the starting-point of the story (6-7). The fulfilment of his demand follows from 9 onwards. It is left open whose voice is speaking, that of the Muse or of the NF₁, and this ambiguity ("die Verdunklung der Erzählinstanz": Klotz 1965: 14) becomes explicit in B 484-93, which opens with ἔσπετε and ends with ἐρέω.[14] Since the presentation of the narrator-text takes place implicitly almost throughout, a precise dividing line between NF₁ and Muse in this respect can hardly be drawn and, in my opinion, is not called for. I prefer this idea of an ambiguous (or, in terms of archaic Greek thinking, double, see below) presentation to a literal interpretation of ἄειδε in A 1, i.e., to taking the Muses as alone responsible for the presentation from 9 onwards. Not only would such a literal interpretation make the later Muse-invocations logically superfluous - why would the Muses be asked anything when they are supposed to be singing the entire poem anyhow? This argument derives from Bassett (1938: 13) -, but there are also a few positive indications which point to a human, rather than a divine presentator:[15]

(3) M 176:
     ἀργαλέον δέ με ταῦτα θεὸν ὡς πάντ' ἀγορεῦσαι
     but difficult would it be for me to narrate all these things
     like a god

The presupposition of the comparison θεὸν ὡς is that the speaking 'I' is *not* a god, ergo is not the Muse.[16]

(4) P 260-1:
     τῶν δ' ἄλλων τίς κεν ἧσι φρεσὶν οὐνόματ' εἴποι,
     ὅσσοι δὴ μετόπισθε μάχην ἤγειραν Ἀχαιῶν;
     But who could recount in his mind the names of the others,
     so many of the Greeks as aroused the battle behind them?

Here we find a rhetorical question, the pragmatic function of which is to indicate the large quantity of Greeks giving heed to Menelaos' adhortation (248-55), but which at the same time announces that the enumeration (257: πρῶτος, 258: τὸν δὲ μετ') is broken off.[17] I submit that the voice here is that of the NF₁,[18] on account of the similarity with:

48

(5) B 488-93:
πληθὺν δ' οὐκ ἂν ἐγὼ μυθήσομαι οὐδ' ὀνομήνω,
οὐδ' εἴ μοι δέκα μὲν γλῶσσαι, δέκα δὲ στόματ' εἶεν,
φωνὴ δ' ἄρρηκτος, χάλκεον δέ μοι ἦτορ ἐνείη,
εἰ μὴ ᾿Ολυμπιάδες Μοῦσαι, Διὸς αἰγιόχοιο
θυγατέρες, μνησαίαθ' ὅσοι ὑπὸ "Ἴλιον ἦλθον.
ἀρχοὺς αὖ νηῶν ἐρέω νῆάς τε προπάσας.
But the mass I will not describe nor mention by name-
(and I could not do so) even if I had ten tongues, ten mouths,
an unbreakable voice and a bronze heart, if not the Olympian
Muses, daughters of Zeus, called to mind how many came
to Troy. - The leaders of the ships, however, I will name
and the total sum of their ships.

The (syntactic) interpretation of this passage is difficult (see Krischer 1965,
Latacz 1977: 46, Lenz 1980: 29-30 and Kirk ad loc.). I take 488 as an emphatic
announcement[19] of the NF₁ that he will not, in the catalogue which is to follow,
mention the mass (in contrast to the ἡγεμόνες, κοίρανοι: 487) by name. The
hyperbolic verses 489-90 then serve to give an impression of the enormity of
this mass.[20] Since he is after all addressing the Muses, the NF₁ hastens to add
in 491-2 that even if he were physically able to mention all the names, he would
of course still need mental support from the Muses. After this digression on the
πληθύς, the NF₁ in 493 turns back again (αὖ)[21] to the ἀρχούς (= the
ἡγεμόνες, κοίρανοι of 487) and repeats his announcement to mention their
names (and their ships). The change from ἔσπετε (484) to ἐρέω (493) seems
due to the intervening (negative) statement οὐκ ... ἐγὼ μυθήσομαι οὐδ'
ὀνομήνω (488).

(6) B 781-3 (the Greek troops are marching out to battle)
γαῖα δ' ὑπεστενάχιζε Διὶ ὣς τερπικεραύνῳ
χωομένῳ, ὅτε τ' ἀμφὶ Τυφωέι γαῖαν ἱμάσσῃ
εἰν ᾿Αρίμοις, ὅθι φασὶ Τυφωέος ἔμμεναι εὐνάς
and the earth groaned beneath as under thunder-rejoicing
Zeus when angry, when he whips the earth around Typhoeus
in Arimae, where they say is the dwelling of Typhoeus

The presentator here (and in P 674) thinks it necessary to introduce anonymous
spokesmen ('they') to qualify his own statement - in B 781-3 φασί suggests that
the speaker is unable to check for himself, in P 674 it implies universal consent
-, which points to the NF₁ rather than the all-knowing Muses. In Appendix III
I discuss all φασί-passages in *Iliad* and *Odyssey*.

For a final indication I draw attention to the expression θαῦμα ἰδέσθαι ('a marvel to behold'). It is found twice in the mouth of *human* characters (K 439, Σ 83) and expresses their admiring focalization of divine objects (Rhesus' armour, which is more suited to be worn by gods than men: K 440-1; Achilles' armour, a gift of the gods: Σ 84-5). When this expression occurs in the narrator-text (E 725 and Σ 377) again in relation with divine objects (Hera's chariot and the tripods with golden wheels in Hephaestus' house), it is plausible to connect it with a human focalizer, the NF₁.[22] In a very similar way, the NF₁ in Σ 549 gives expression to his admiration for (part of) Achilles' armour as made by Hephaestus: τὸ δὴ περὶ θαῦμα τέτυκτο. He thereby is the first to fulfil Hephaestus' proud announcement of Σ 466-7:

ὥς οἱ τεύχεα καλὰ παρέσσεται, οἷά τις αὖτε
ἀνθρώπων πολέων θαυμάσσεται, ὃς κεν ἴδηται
for he will have beautiful armour, such as anyone of many
men will admire, when he looks at it

The upshot of the argumentation so far is that, whereas the NF₁ emphatically claims at the beginning of his story that it is the Muse who sings, it is he himself who in fact pulls the strings. He is unmistakably a mortal, for at certain points he gives expression to his admiration for divine objects or apologizes for his human limitations.

The five Muse-invocations apart from the proem remain to be considered: does the NF₁ really ask the Muses for information or for assistance of his memory, in other words is he unable to continue his story but for the help of the Muses? I take as point of departure for my discussion the passage P 260-1 (example 4 above). As we have seen the question is rhetorical (implied answer: "nobody") and together, question and implied answer are an expressive way to suggest a great mass of warriors. Comparable in this respect are E 703-4, Λ 299-300 and Π 692-3: Ἔνθα τίνα πρῶτον, τίνα δ' ὕστατον ἐξενάριξεν/-ον/-ας; ('There who first and who last did he/they/you kill?'). Although here an answer follows, the question can be said to be *posed* rather than *asked* (for this distinction see Lyons 1977: 755). In other words, the illocutionary force of the question-form is not so much a request for information as an expressive statement. Such an expressive formulation can "enhance the significance of a particular scene or the glory of a particular fighter" (Willcock 1978: ad E 703-4).[23] A shortened version of this 'who first-who last' type of question is found in

(7) Θ 273:

"Ενθα τίνα πρῶτον Τρώων ἕλε Τεῦκρος ἀμύμων;
There who of the Trojans did splendid Teucer kill first?

From this it is only a small step to the four short Muse-invocations (Β 761-2, Λ 218-20, Ξ 508-10, Π 112-3), of which I quote one

(8) Λ 218-20:

"Εσπετε νῦν μοι, Μοῦσαι, 'Ολύμπια δώματ' ἔχουσαι,
ὅς τις δὴ <u>πρῶτος</u> 'Αγαμέμνονος ἀντίον ἦλθεν
ἢ αὐτῶν Τρώων ἠὲ κλειτῶν ἐπικούρων.
Tell me now, Muses, that dwell in Olympian houses,
whoever came <u>first</u> against Agamemnon, either of the Trojans
themselves or of the illustrious allies.

In view of the close similarity with E 703-5 etc. and example (7) I interpret these short Muse-invocations also as questions posed.[24] What then, if not to ask for information, is the function of these invocations? According to Willcock (ad Λ 218): "An appeal to the Muses is a way of enhancing the importance of what is to follow, and so drawing attention to a critical moment in the story".[25] This is what can be called the classical interpretation, already voiced by the A and bT-scholia ad B 485-6. Its weakness, as Minton (1960: 294) has pointed out, is that it does not explain the absence of Muse-invocations at so many other critical points in the story of the *Iliad* (in the *Odyssey* they do not occur at all). While keeping the first part of the classical interpretation ("enhancing"), I propose the following alternative to its second part ("critical moment"). All four invocations contain a superlative, which in most cases returns in the answer: ὅχ' ἄριστος (Β 761): ἄρισται (763) and ἄριστος (768); πρῶτος (Λ 219, Ξ 509+511); πρῶτον (Π 113). I suggest that the appeal to the Muses increases the inherent force of the superlative: thus, in B 761 it is emphasized that Eumelus' horses and Ajax were 'by far the best'. As regards the three other cases (with πρῶτος/-ον), they seem to belong to a larger group of πρῶτος/-ον-passages, which have the form of a statement, not a question, e.g.

(9) Δ 456-7:

ὣς τῶν μισγομένων γένετο ἰαχή τε πόνος τε.
<u>πρῶτος</u> δ' 'Αντίλοχος Τρώων ἕλεν ἄνδρα κορυστήν
In like way there was a shouting and struggle of them en-
gaging in battle. And Antilochus was <u>the first</u> to kill a
helmeted man of the Trojans

The fighting books of the *Iliad* have 22 of such πρῶτος/-ον-passages, which always, as in example 9, follow after a general description of the battle.[26] Hence, the singling out of a character (most of the times the aggressor; in Λ 420, M 191, Π 399, P 597 the victim) has the effect of the NF₁ zooming in. I consider the three Muse-invocations containing πρῶτος/-ον as emphatic variants, but no more, of these πρῶτος/-ον-passages: in Λ 219 the NF₁ zooms in on Iphidamas, victim of Agamemnon; in Ξ 509/511 on Ajax as aggressor. Π 113, finally, is slightly different, since the question here is not 'who', but 'how' (ὅππως and note the concluding ὥς-clause in 124). Nor does a general battle description precede. Nevertheless, the effect of the Muse-invocation is the same, viz. to stress πρῶτον πῦρ: fire in the ships had been proclaimed by Achilles in I 650-3 as the signal which could incite him to action and as he sees it he spurs on his 'stand-in' Patroclus (126-9).

The last Muse-passage to be considered and the *locus classicus* for those scholars who maintain that the NF₁ is dependent on the Muses for his information is

(10) B 484-7:
> Ἔσπετε νῦν μοι, Μοῦσαι, Ὀλύμπια δώματ' ἔχουσαι
> - ὑμεῖς γὰρ θεαί ἐστε, πάρεστέ τε ἴστέ τε πάντα,
> ἡμεῖς δὲ κλέος οἶον ἀκούομεν οὐδέ τι ἴδμεν, -
> οἵ τινες ἡγεμόνες Δαναῶν καὶ κοίρανοι ἦσαν

commonly translated with (I quote Lesher 1981: 12):

> Tell me now, Muses that dwell in the palace of Olympus -
> for you are goddesses, you are at hand and know all things.
> But we hear only a rumour and know nothing -
> who were the captains and lords of the Danaans

As has been rightly remarked by Krischer (1965: 9) the value of κλέος when taken as 'rumour' is estimated far too low. Κλέος (lit. 'hearsay', from κλύω 'hear', cp. here ἀκούομεν) is one of the epic terms to express fame, fame consisting in the preliterate society of the Homeric heroes of 'being talked about', being remembered in story or song (see Steinkopf 1937: 4-16). The contrast described in 485-6, therefore, is not that between "knowledge and ignorance" (Murray 1981: 91),[27] but between two different degrees or kinds of knowledge of the past:[28] *human* (ἡμεῖς in 486 is 'we humans' as opposed to ὑμεῖς 485 'you goddesses'), based on hearing (oral reports), and *divine*, based on seeing (autopsy).[29] In terms of my narratological model, what the NF₁ in B 484-7 reflects on is the focalization: how are the events of the fabula, which belong to the past, 'perceived'? They are heard of by himself and remembered by the Muses, who have witnessed them.[30]

I submit that the NF₁, by invoking the Muses here and in A 1-7, far from belittling his own activity as presentator,[31] adds a divine dimension to both his focalization (the reliability of his narrative) and his narration (the aesthetic perfection of his narrative). The form in which he does so is typical for archaic religiosity. I refer to Lesky's principle of the "Doppelte Motivation" (1961): in the Homeric epics an activity is often ascribed to a human and a divine cause *at the same time*, which in the archaic Greek way of thinking does not mean that the human factor is overshadowed by the divine one, but rather that it is placed in the spotlight precisely because of that divine patronage. So far this pattern of thought has been recognized by scholars only in relation to the characters of the story, but since the NF₁ is after all, like those characters, a creation of the poet, it can also be applied to his case. The NF₁ of the *Iliad* describes the presentation as being now in the Muses' hands, then in his own, the overall suggestion being that they are *both* involved. The intended effect of this 'double presentation' is an indirect and unobtrusive self-recommendation of the NF₁, who, as the Thamyris digression in B 595-600 makes clear, is only too aware of the dangers of an open rivalry with the Muses.

Conclusion

In the two long Muse-invocations the NF₁ portrays himself as a self-conscious narrator, or as I prefer to say, presentator. Not seldom self-conscious presentators are given the shape of writers: one could think of the presentators of Sterne's *Tristram Shandy*, Proust's *A la recherche du temps perdu*, Gide's *Paludes* and Mann's *Dr. Faustus*. In the case of the Iliadic NF₁, his relation with the Muses (and the verb 'sing' with which the narrative opens) suggests that we are dealing with a self-conscious presentator in the shape of a professional aoidos like Phemius and Demodocus in the *Odyssey*.[32] Just as the art of these two singers is described as due to personal initiative and at the same time as a gift of the gods, in other words as being 'doubly motivated' (see Lesky 1961: 30-1),[33] the NF₁ claims a double presentation by himself and the Muses without a sharp division of labour.

The function of the four shorter Muse-invocations is slightly different, viz. to strengthen the force of the superlative they all contain, the effect being that of a close-up, either literally (after general battle descriptions) or figuratively (a special quality or important event being highlighted).

A common element in the interpretations given above of the six Muse-passages is that all are shown to aim at a certain *effect*. This effect or rhetoric is directed at the NeFe$_1$, to which I now turn.

3.2. The primary narratee-focalizee

The addressee of the Iliadic NF$_1$ is the primary narratee-focalizee (NeFe$_1$), who like the NF$_1$ is *external* and for the greater part remains imperceptible. Nowhere do we find such direct addresses to 'the reader' as e.g. in:

(11) H. Fielding, *Tom Jones* (ch. 2)

> Reader, I think proper, before we proceed any further together, to acquaint thee that I intend to digress through this whole history as often as I see occasion ...

Yet, there are certain passages where it is possible to track down the NeFe$_1$ more or less explicitly and I do not agree with Griffin (1986: 39) that in the *Iliad* we have "an audience whose presence is never acknowledged". The pioneering work of Prince (1973, 1982: 16-24) and Piwowarczyk (1976) on the "narrataire"/"narratee" is especially helpful to recognize signs of the 'you'. Before presenting the results of my "pursuit of signs" I want, just as in the case of the primary focalizer, to go into a theoretical question, viz. the relevance of this narratological category of fictional addressees.

In chapter 2 it was stated that we should distinguish the text-internal recipients NeFe$_1$, NeFe$_2$ (characters listening to the words of other characters) from the external, historical hearer/reader. Investigation of the historical reception of literary works belongs once again (cp. above p. 44) to the domain of the "Rezeptionsforschung" and for the Homeric epics I call to mind Clarke (1981), already mentioned in chapter 1. An important function, however, of the NeFe$_1$, and NeFe$_2$ is to *mediate* (to form a "relais entre narrateur et lecteur" Prince 1973: 95), to provide the hearer/reader with clues as to how to interpret the events presented. Thus, when we are told that Thetis, functioning as NeFe$_2$ of Achilles' speech (A 365-412), starts weeping (413), we are invited - though not compelled - to share her emotion and pity Achilles. Macleod (1983: 3) has suggested very much the same in the case of characters in the *Odyssey* reacting to "songs within the song"

> can the reactions of people involved in the events narrated suggest what reactions poetry would normally be taken to elicit? The answer, I think, is 'yes'. The responses of the people concerned are distinguished from other responses, so we can see them for what they are. But they also *cannot but affect our own responses; because they are in the poem they come to form part of the hearer's reaction to it* (my italics).

In the remainder of this chapter I hope to show the mediating function of the NeFe$_1$ in the Iliadic simple narrator-text.

Signs of the 'you'

In its most elementary form the addressee of the NF$_1$ (the 'I' of the presentation) is a 'you' and five times we find a second person verb-form in the simple narrator-text:

(12) Δ 223-5:
"Ενθ' οὐκ ἂν βρίζοντα ἴδοις 'Αγαμέμνονα δῖον,
οὐδὲ καταπτώσσοντ', οὐδ' οὐκ ἐθέλοντα μάχεσθαι,
ἀλλὰ μάλα σπεύδοντα μάχην ἐς κυδιάνειραν.
Then you would not have seen divine Agamemnon slumbering nor cowering, nor being unwilling to fight, but driving eagerly towards the fighting which brings men glory.

(13) Δ 429-31:
οἱ δ' ἄλλοι ἀκὴν ἴσαν, οὐδέ κε φαίης
τόσσον λαὸν ἕπεσθαι ἔχοντ' ἐν στήθεσιν αὐδήν,
σιγῇ δειδιότες σημάντορας
And the others went silently, and you would not have said/thought that so numerous an army followed, having the power of speech in their breast, silently in fear of their commanders

(14) Ε 85-6:
Τυδεΐδην δ' οὐκ ἂν γνοίης ποτέροισι μετείη,
ἠὲ μετὰ Τρώεσσιν ὁμιλέοι ἦ μετ' 'Αχαιοῖς.
And of Tydeus' son you would not have been able to discern with whom he was, whether he mingled with the Trojans or with the Greeks.

(15) Ο 697-8:
φαίης κ' ἀκμῆτας καὶ ἀτειρέας ἀλλήλοισιν
ἄντεσθ' ἐν πολέμῳ, ὡς ἐσσυμένως ἐμάχοντο.
You would have said/thought that fresh and unwearied they faced each other in fighting, from the vehemence with which they fought.

(16) P 366-7:
"Ὣς οἱ μὲν μάρναντο δέμας πυρός, <u>οὐδέ κε φαίης</u>
οὔτε ποτ' ἠέλιον σῶν ἔμμεναι οὔτε σελήνην
So they fought on like fire, and <u>you would not have</u>
<u>thought/said</u> that the sun was secure at all nor the moon

All five passages contain an optative with ἄν/κεν, which I analyze as follows:
I, NF_1, tell you, $NeFe_1$, that you certainly would (not) have seen, thought/said
x, (if you had yourself been present at that moment and at that place).[34] The
implicit elements I have added between brackets are found in full in

(17) Euripides *Supplices* 764:
φαίης ἄν εἰ παρῆσθ' ὅτ' ...
you would have said so, if you had been present when ...[35]

Now the external $NeFe_1$, of course, has not been present, but the effect of
these five passages is to turn him temporarily into an eyewitness: in fact, the
focalizee here functions as focalizer, yet, of course, as a focalizer who is
instructed by the NF_1 what to see, think.[36] This effect has been already observed
by the anonymous author of *On the sublime* (26.1), giving as a Homeric example
O 697-8

> Change of person gives an equally vivid effect, and often makes the audience
> feel themselves set in the thick of the danger.
> (transl. Hamilton Fyfe)

This technique of involving a $NeFe_1$ as an eyewitness is found in other narrative
texts too, e.g.:

(18) Virgil *Aeneid* IV 401:

> migrantis <u>cernas</u> totaque ex urbe ruentis
> And <u>you could see</u> them moving away and streaming forth
> from every part of the city[37]

(19) *La Chanson de Roland* 349:

> Là, <u>vous auriez vu</u> pleurer tant de chevaliers

(20) W. Somerset Maugham, *Lord Mountdrago*:

> His eyes remained fixed on the other's face, but they were
> so empty of expression that <u>you might have thought</u> he did
> not even see him.

Some NF₁'s are even more demanding of their NeFe₁'s, asking them not to transport themselves mentally in time, but 'really' in place:

(21) W.M. Thackeray, *Vanity Fair*:

> The astonished reader must be called upon to transport himself ten thousand miles to the military station of Bundlegunge ...

A remarkable feature of the Iliadic second person-passages is that they all, except (15), contain a negation. In (12) this negation takes the form of a *litotes* or *negatio contrarii*: negation of the opposite, which results in a strong expression. Agamemnon was not unwilling to fight, which amounts to: he was very eager to fight (the positive pendant is expressed explicitly in 225). In other words, the NeFe₁ is invited by the NF₁ to admire Agamemnon's fighting spirit. Two cases of φαίης κε found in direct speech are comparable to examples (13), (15) and (16):

(22) Γ 392-4 (Aphrodite speaks to Helen about Paris):
>   "<u>οὐδέ κε φαίης</u>
> ἀνδρὶ μαχεσσάμενον τόν γ' ἐλθεῖν, ἀλλὰ χορόνδε
> ἔρχεσθ', ἠὲ χοροῖο νέον λήγοντα καθίζειν."
> "And <u>you would not say/think</u> that he had just come back from a duel with a man, but rather that he was going to a dance, or having just stopped dancing, had sat down."

(23) Γ 220 (Antenor speaks to Helen and Trojans about Odysseus):
> "<u>φαίης κε</u> ζάκοτόν τέ τιν' ἔμμεναι ἄφρονά τ' αὔτως."
> "<u>You would have said/thought</u> him to be a surly man and simply devoid of reason."

In the 5 passages containing φαίης ἄν/κε a contrast is indicated between what you would expect and what was really the case. This contrast can take the form of either

1. you would not have said/thought x (which was, in fact, the case), but y (not always expressed explicitly) or

2. you would have said/thought x (something negative or negated through alpha privative), but y (not always expressed explicitly) was, in fact, the case.

To the first category belong examples (13), (16) and (22). In (13) the silence of the Greek soldiers is presented as something remarkable and, as the contrast with the noisy Trojans (Δ 433-8) seems to imply, laudable. In the same vein, the silence and discipline of the Greek troops had been stressed at the beginning of book Γ (8-9), again in contrast to the clamorous Trojans (2-7). In (16) the NeFe₁ is meant to place himself in the situation of the warriors fighting in complete darkness - in P 268-70 Zeus sent a cloud - over Patroclus' body. In P 643-6 one of these warriors will describe the handicap caused by this darkness. In (22) Aphrodite tries to reinforce Helen's desire for Paris by describing his splendid appearance (392: στίλβων), which rather resembles that of someone dressed up for dancing than of someone exhausted by fighting. The contrast (with the untrue alternative, Paris as a dancer, explicitly formulated) is, of course, very appropriate to Paris' situation in the *Iliad*: he is repeatedly described as being more interested in song, dance, his looks and women than in fighting (see esp. Hector's words Γ 39-57).

To the second category belong examples (15) and (23). In (15) the fervour with which Greeks and Trojans are fighting would induce one to think that they had only just begun fighting, whereas, in fact, they have already been fighting the whole day (from Λ 1 on). Again, as in (13), the formulation aims at eliciting a positive (admiring) reaction from the NeFe₁. In (23) the Trojan Antenor describes how he has once seen Odysseus perform as an orator: as Odysseus had stood there with his eyes fixed to the ground and holding his stick stiffly, he at first seemed to be an unskilled speaker and you (which here refers both to those present at that occasion, Antenor included, and those now addressed, the Trojans and Helen, who are supposed to visualize the scene) would not have expected him to be an able orator. This impression, however, was proved wrong as soon as Odysseus started speaking: the true alternative y is described in 221-3.

Example (14) remains to be discussed. Comparable to this passage are

(24) Ξ 58-60 (Nestor speaks to Agamemnon: the strategic position of the Greeks is bad):
οὐδ' ἂν ἔτι γνοίης μάλα περ σκοπιάζων
ὁπποτέρωθεν 'Αχαιοὶ ὀρινόμενοι κλονέονται
And you could not distinguish anymore, even when looking sharply, from which side the Achaeans, brought into confusion, are routed

and

(25) Π 638-40 (simple narrator-text):
οὐδ' ἂν ἔτι φράδμων περ ἀνὴρ Σαρπηδόνα δῖον
ἔγνω, ἐπεὶ βελέεσσι καὶ αἵματι καὶ κονίησιν
ἐκ κεφαλῆς εἴλυτο διαμπερὲς ἐς πόδας ἄκρους.
And even an observant man would not have been able anymore to recognize divine Sarpedon, because he was completely covered from his head to his toes with spears, blood and dust.

In these three cases (14, 24, 25) an eyewitness is invoked by the NF$_1$ (14,25) or by a speaking character (24) to see what in fact is very difficult to see (note μάλα περ: Ξ 58, περ: Π 638). The intended effect of (14) is for the NeFe$_1$ to admire Diomedes' impetuosity, who single-handedly puts the mass of Trojans to flight (93-4). Example (25) is somewhat different from the previous ones, because here we are not dealing with a 'you', but with an indefinite ἀνήρ ('a man') and also with a secondary indicative with ἄν.[38] One could compare

(26) *Nibelungenlied* 282:

> An ihrem Kleid erstrakten viel Edelsteine. Die rosige Farbe ihrer Haut schimmerte lieblich. Selbst ein Mann der sich irgend etwas hätte wünschen dürfen, hätte nicht sagen können, dass er auf dieser Welt irgend etwas Schöneres erblickt hatte.

and

(27) Th. Hardy, *Tess of the D'Urbervilles*:

> (description of Tess and another woman working in the fields) ... their movements showed a mechanical regularity ... the pensive character which the curtained hood lent to their bent heads would have reminded the observer of some early Italian conception of the two Marys.

There are three other places in the *Iliad* where we meet such an "imaginary spectator" (Leaf ad N 343-4) or, as I would prefer to call him, *anonymous focalizer*,[39] i.e. an observer who is neither the NF$_1$, nor NeFe$_1$ nor one of the named characters. The anonymous focalizer makes his longest appearance in

(28) Δ 539-42 (many Greeks and Trojans have been killed):
> Ἔνϑα κεν οὐκέτι ἔργον ἀνὴρ ὀνόσαιτο μετελϑών,
> ὅς τις ἔτ᾽ ἄβλητος καὶ ἀνούτατος ὀξέϊ χαλκῷ
> δινεύοι κατὰ μέσσον, ἄγοι δέ ἑ Παλλὰς Ἀϑήνη
> χειρὸς ἑλοῦσ᾽, αὐτὰρ βελέων ἀπερύκοι ἐρωήν
> And there no more could a man, having entered the field, have made little of the fighting, (a man) who, still unhit and unpierced by sharp bronze, would rove around in the middle (of the fighting), and him Pallas Athene would lead, having taken him by the hand, and she would avert from him the rush of the spears.

This passage is an interesting variant of what we find in

(29) P 398-9 ≅ N 127-8 (a fierce battle is fought around Patroclus' body):

οὐδέ κ' ῎Αρης λαοσσόος οὐδέ κ' ᾿Αθήνη
τόν γ' ἰδοῦσ' ὀνόσαιτ', οὐδ' εἰ μάλα μιν χόλος ἵκοι

And seeing that (battle) neither Ares, urger of hosts, nor
Athene could have made little of it, not even if anger had
strongly invaded them

Instead of the two gods of war, Ares and Athena, in (28) an anonymous *human* observer is introduced. His appearance is given such a realistic form that the NF₁ even bothers to describe how Athena would protect this man. The bT-scholia (ad Δ 541) suggest that

θεατὴν ἑαυτῷ ἀνέπλασε τῆς μάχης, ὑπὸ θεῶν ὁδηγούμενον,
ἵνα ἀθορύβως σκοπῇ καὶ ἐν μέσοις τοῖς μαχομένοις, καὶ ἵνα
ἀκριβῶς θεῷτο.

(the poet) has created a spectator of the battle <u>for himself</u>, who is
guided by the gods, in order that he might take an undisturbed look
even amidst the fighting and to behold (everything) in detail.

Rather than with the poet, I prefer to connect this θεατής, this anonymous focalizer, with the NeFe₁, a suggestion which is already found in Eustathius (506, 6-8):

τοιοῦτος δ' ἂν εἴη θεατὴς ὁ <u>τοῦ ποιητοῦ ἀκροατής</u>, ὃς οὐ τῶν
τοῦ πολέμου κακῶν μετέχει, ἀλλὰ τοῦ τῶν πολεμικῶν διηγήσεων
κατὰ νοῦν ἀπολαύει καλοῦ θεάματος

Such a spectator might have been <u>the hearer of the poet</u>, who does
not partake in the misery of the war, but who enjoys in his mind the
splendid spectacle of these war stories ...

The anonymity of the focalizer in (28) invites the NeFe₁ (and through him the historical hearer/reader) to identify himself with him and to share his feelings of awe - my evaluation is different from that of Eustathius - about the intensity and fierceness of the battle. The anonymous focalizer turns up again in

(30) N 343-4:

μάλα κεν θρασυκάρδιος εἴη
ὃς τότε γηθήσειεν ἰδὼν πόνον οὐδ' ἀκάχοιτο.

And very stout-hearted would be the man, who could then,
seeing their toil, rejoice and not feel sorrow.

and

(31) Δ 421: (Diomedes' armour makes a terrible noise):

ὑπό κεν ταλασίφρονά περ δέος εἷλεν.

Even a steadfast man would have been gripped by fear.

It is made clear that the NeFe₁ and therefore we, the historical hearer/reader, must feel sorrow (30) or must be impressed by the fearful noise of Diomedes' armour (31).

With these two passages I have come to the end of my investigation of explicit traces of the NeFe$_1$. According to Block (1982: 13) the function of the second person addresses is "to mark crucial passages". This interpretation (and cp. Kirk "a dramatic turn of speech") labours under the same disadvantage as the classical interpretation of the short Muse-invocations (above p. 50), viz. that there are so many crucial moments which are not marked by second person verb-forms. Secondly, what is so crucial about Agamemnon in Δ? His aristeia takes place in Λ. Therefore, I suggest that the function of these anonymously focalized passages is to involve the NeFe$_1$ more directly into the story: he is made to listen (13, 31), see (12, 14, 15, 16, 25, 30) for himself and even to 'visit' (28) the actual battlefield. At the same time he is instructed as to how to react emotionally to what is told: with admiration (12, 13, 14, 15), awe (28), pity (25), sorrow (30), and fear (31).[40] It is only rarely that the NF$_1$ addresses his recipient so directly, his usual rhetoric being more subtle or implicit, as we shall see in the next section.

3.3. Interaction between primary narrator-focalizer and primary narratee-focalizee

In the previous sections the (scarce) explicit references to NF$_1$ and NeFe$_1$ have been discussed. It turned out that the Muse-invocations, though formally addresses by the NF$_1$ to these goddesses, were, as far as their effect is concerned, directed towards the NeFe$_1$. A similar conclusion has been reached by Block (1982: 9) with regard to the apostrophes, which are formally addressed to characters, but in fact meant for the NeFe$_1$

> Apostrophe, overtly verbalizing emotion toward either a real or imagined object, asks the audience to respond ideally *as the narrator responds to the situations or evaluations that he introduces* (my italics)

The direct addresses to the NeFe$_1$ (in the form of second person verb-forms) and indirect ones (through the anonymous focalizer) are an even clearer indication that the NF$_1$ does not just produce his story, regardless of his recipient, but instead takes heed of that recipient, steering the latter's reception. I therefore propose to describe the communicative process between NF$_1$ and NeFe$_1$ as *inter-action*: although the NeFe$_1$ nowhere speaks himself, his very evocation as recipient nevertheless conditions the presentation of the NF$_1$. Let me give one example: in A 46-9 the NF$_1$ gives a frightening description of Apollo descending from the

Olympus. His arrows rattle on his shoulders (46: ἔκλαγξαν), he resembles dark night (47: νυκτὶ ἐοικώς) and when he shoots his disastrous arrow it makes 'a fearful twang' (49: δεινὴ κλαγγή). All these audio-visual effects are clearly directed towards the NeFe₁, because at that moment (Apollo is sitting at some distance from the Greek camp) the characters are still unaware of the danger that lies ahead.

In this section four aspects of the interaction between NF₁ and NeFe₁ will be discussed.

3.3.1. Presentation through negation

When hearing/reading a narrative text one will normally not pay much attention to the presence of negations in the non-dialogue parts, the narrator-text. Negative statements like

(32) Λ 255:
    ἀλλ' οὐδ' ὣς ἀπέληγε μάχης ἠδὲ πτολέμοιο
    but all the same he (Agamemnon) did <u>not</u> stop fighting

or

(33) Π 140:
    ἔγχος δ' οὐχ ἕλετ' οἶον ἀμύμονος Αἰακίδαο
    but only the spear of the excellent grandson of Aeacus he
    (Patroclus) did <u>not</u> take

are accepted as relevant information just like any positive statement. Yet, on reflection, the fact that the NF₁ chooses to tell something that is *not the case*, must strike one as curious. The examples (32) and (33) represent two different types of negative statements. In (32) the negation belongs to a *binary* taxonomy ("not male but female"): 'Agamemnon did not stop fighting' means 'Agamemnon continued fighting'. In (33) the negation belongs to a *multiple* taxonomy ("not green, not red, not blue, etc."): a statement like 'Patroclus did not take Achilles' spear' could theoretically be replaced by: 'Patroclus did not take Achilles' belt', 'Patroclus did not put on Achilles' greaves', etc.[41] Now what motivates the NF₁ in (32) to present an event ('Agamemnon continued fighting') in a negative form and in (33) to present a non-event, of which there is in principle an indefinite number? An answer is provided by Stierle (1975: 242-3):

> Im Hinblick auf das, was der Fall ist, gibt es unendlich Vieles, was nicht der Fall ist. Das bedeutet daß eine Negation Sinn nur hat wenn sie einer Ökonomie der Negation folgt ... Negation ist sinnvoll dann, wenn das Negierte eine Erwartung, Absicht, Befürchtung, Hoffnung etc. des 'Empfängers' oder des 'Senders' artikuliert;

and Prince (1982: 18):

> (Negations) contradict the beliefs of a narratee; they correct his mistakes; they put an end to his questions. The narrator of *Les Faux-Monnayeurs* vigorously denies the theory constructed by his audience to explain Vincent's escapades: "No, it was not to see his mistress, that Vincent Molinier went out every night".

In other words, the choice of the NF$_1$ to present an event in a negative form has to do with the *expectation* of the NeFe$_1$. The expectation (or "Vorinformation", "Erwartungshorizont")[42] can be extracted from the negative statement itself, on account of what has been called the "explizite Einbeziehung (Mitformulierung) des Gegensatzes" (Weiss 1969: 270-3): the statement 'Agamemnon did not stop fighting' in itself contains the alternative 'Agamemnon stopped fighting' and this is what the NeFe$_1$ (having just been told that Agamemnon was wounded) evidently expected.

Most of the times the scope of the negation is *retrospective*, i.e., it negates an expectation the NeFe$_1$ has on account of what he has been told earlier (e.g. in example 32). But sometimes the scope of the negation is (also) *prospective* and an expectation is created. This can be illustrated by example (33): the fact that Patroclus, putting on Achilles' armour, does not take his spear first of all means a departure from custom (cp. e.g. Paris in Γ 338) and this strikes the NeFe$_1$. At the same time the negation has a prospective scope, since it suggests that the spear will later play a role in the story. And indeed it is with this spear that Achilles will kill Hector in X 326-7 and avenge the death of his friend Patroclus.[43]

My suggestion to explain the use of negations in connection with the expectations of the NeFe$_1$ is corroborated by the fact that negative statements are often followed by a γάρ-clause: having contradicted the expectation of his addressee, the NF$_1$ hastens to explain *why* what is (normally or on account of the context) to be expected does not happen now or is not the case. E.g.

(34) Π 789-90 (Patroclus meets Apollo on the battlefield):
ὁ μὲν τὸν ἰόντα κατὰ κλόνον οὐκ ἐνόησεν·
ἠέρι γὰρ πολλῇ κεκαλυμμένος ἀντεβόλησε
He (Patr.) did not notice him (Ap.) going through the battle.
For covered up in thick mist he (Ap.) came against him

Patroclus and Apollo had met not long before this passage (Π 698-711) and one might have expected Patroclus to notice Apollo (and keep clear of him). The γάρ-clause explains why Patroclus failed to see his dangerous opponent.[44] In the following, 13 more examples of presentation through negation will be discussed, which must serve as a sample of what is in fact a vast corpus.[45]

Negations with retrospective scope
The expectation contained in:

(35) B 170-1:
    οὐδ' ὅ γε νηὸς ἐϋσσέλμοιο μελαίνης
    ἅπτετ', ἐπεί μιν ἄχος κραδίην καὶ θυμὸν ἵκανεν.
    And he (Odysseus) did not take hold of (his) black ship
    with good rowing benches, since grief touched his heart
    and his spirit.

is that Odysseus would take hold of his ship. The expectation is based on 151-2, where it was told that the Greeks encouraged each other to take hold of the ships (ἀλλήλοισι κέλευον ἅπτεσθαι νηῶν).[46] In other words, the NeFe₁'s expectation is based here on *contextual* knowledge. In the following three examples it is based on *general knowledge of the world* (36, 37) and *'historical'* knowledge (38):

(36) A 331-2 (two heralds come to Achilles and the NeFe₁ expects
    them to deliver their message):
    τὼ μὲν ταρβήσαντε καὶ αἰδομένω βασιλῆα
    στήτην, οὐδέ τί μιν προσεφώνεον οὐδ' ἐρέοντο
    the two stood still, confused and in awe of the king, and
    they did not address or question him[47]

(37) B 753 (the river Titaressus pours its waters in the Peneus
    and one expects the water of the two rivers to merge):
    οὐδ' ὅ γε Πηνειῷ συμμίσγεται ἀργυροδίνῃ
    but he does not mingle with the silver-eddied Peneus[48]

(38) B 641-2 (Thoas is mentioned as the leader of the Aetolian
    contingent and apparently this was not the name the NeFe₁
    expected:
    οὐ γὰρ ἔτ' Οἰνῆος μεγαλήτορος υἱέες ἦσαν,
    οὐδ' ἄρ' ἔτ' αὐτὸς ἔην, θάνε δὲ ξανθὸς Μελέαγρος
    for the sons of great-hearted Oineus were not alive anymore,
    nor was he himself alive, and fair Meleager had died

Notice that in (38) the particle ἄρ' emphasizes the unexpected nature of what is told. Indeed, ἄρα, ἄρ, ῥ', ῥα is found very often in combination with a negation: 49 times in the narrator-text.[49]

Finally, the expectation of the NeFe₁ can be based on knowledge of the *heroic code*:

> (39) Δ 532 (Thoas has killed Peiroos and one expects him to
> strip off his victim's armour):
> τεύχεα δ' οὐκ ἀπέδυσε· περίστησαν γὰρ ἑταῖροι
> but the armour he did not take off, for his (Peiroos') com-
> panions came and stood around him[50]

One could hesitate here whether to qualify knowledge of the heroic code as a special kind of contextual knowledge or as 'historical' knowledge.

The argument or contextual element on which the NeFe₁'s expectation is based is sometimes expressed within the negative statement itself (often in the form of a participle + περ), e.g.

> (40) N 417-9:
> Ἀργείοισι δ' ἄχος γένετ' εὐξαμένοιο,
> Ἀντιλόχῳ δὲ μάλιστα δαΐφρονι θυμὸν ὄρινεν·
> ἀλλ' οὐδ' ἀχνύμενός περ ἑοῦ ἀμέλησεν ἑταίρου
> And grief came upon the Greeks on account of his boasting
> and he moved especially the heart of courageous Antilochus.
> Yet, grieved as he (Antil.) was, he did not neglect his com-
> panion[51]

There is a whole group of negative statements following an announcement by the NF₁ that someone is hit, e.g.

> (41) N 161-2 (Meriones throws a spear against Deïphobus' shield):
> τῆς δ' οὔ τι διήλασεν, ἀλλὰ πολὺ πρὶν
> ἐν καυλῷ ἐάγη δολιχὸν δόρυ
> but he did not at all pierce it (the shield), but long before
> that the long spear was broken at its head[52]

The use of negative statements in this context seems to be due to the fact that the NeFe₁ may expect that normally when somebody is hit the spear enters body or armour (cp. e.g. Γ 357-8) and that he is curious to know whether the hit is fatal or not. In E 95-106 this expectation or maybe even anxiety on the part of the NeFe₁ is subtly played with by the NF₁: Pandarus hits Diomedes with an arrow (98-9), Diomedes' corslet is stained with blood (100) and Pandarus proclaims him mortally wounded (103-5). Only after Pandarus' triumphant speech does the NF$_1$ tell that the projectile did not kill Diomedes (106: τὸν δ' οὐ βέλος ὠκὺ δάμασσεν). The manipulation of the NF$_1$ exists in postponing the negative statement, which normally follows immediately after the announcement that somebody is hit (see example 41 and those given in note 52).[53]

This last example shows that the expectation of the NeFe$_1$ sometimes coincides with, maybe even is triggered by, that of a character (here Pandarus). Two more examples are:

(42) Z 371:
οὐδ' εὗρ' ' Ανδρομάχην λευκώλενον ἐν μεγάροισιν
but he (Hector) did not find white-armed Andromache in the house

(43) K 181-2:
οὐδὲ μὲν εὕδοντας φυλάκων ἡγήτορας εὗρον
ἀλλ' ἐγρηγορτὶ σὺν τεύχεσιν εἴατο πάντες.
And they (Agamemnon and other Greek leaders) did not find the leaders of the pickets asleep, but they all sat wide awake by their weapons.[54]

In (42) Hector clearly had expected to find his wife at home (cp. his words in 365-6) and in (43) the negative statement can be seen as a reaction to Agamemnon's words in K 98-9, where he said that he feared that the pickets might have fallen asleep.

Negations with prospective scope
In the following example (44) a non-event is narrated, the relevance of which becomes clear only afterwards:

(44) Ψ 862-4 (Teucer has the first shot in the archery-contest):
αὐτίκα δ' ἰὸν
ἧκεν ἐπικρατέως, οὐδ' ἠπείλησεν ἄνακτι
ἀρνῶν πρωτογόνων ῥέξειν κλειτὴν ἑκατόμβην.
And immediately he forcefully shot an arrow, but he had not vowed to sacrifice a celebrated hecatomb of firstling lambs to the lord (= Apollo).

Teucer misses his target, 'for Apollo begrudged it to him' (865), in other words precisely because he had not vowed a sacrifice. This becomes especially clear when Meriones, who shoots after him and does make the vow (872-3 ≅ 863-4), is successful. From Δ 119-21, where the archer Pandarus (following the advice of Athena: 101-3) also promises Apollo a hecatomb, it might be deduced that in situations where success was particularly asked for, it was normal to make such a vow. The negation in Ψ 863-4 then also has a retrospective scope.

A great number of the NF₁'s *prolepses* or foreshadowings (see below section 3.3.3) are in a negated form, e.g.

> (45) K 336-7 (the Trojan spy Dolon has left for the Greek camp)
> οὐδ' ἄρ' ἔμελλεν
> ἐλθὼν ἐκ νηῶν ἄψ "Εκτορι μῦθον ἀποίσειν.
> but he was not destined to come back again from the ships and bring news to Hector.[55]

Just before, Dolon had expressed his confidence in the success of his mission (329-31) and the negative statement (communicated by the NF₁ to the NeFe₁ only!) unmasks this confidence as mere illusion. In other words, the NeFe₁ is given an advantage in knowledge in comparison to the character involved, which results in dramatic irony and suspense.

In the last example of presentation through negation to be discussed the ignorance of a character stands in contrast not only to knowledge of the NeFe₁, but to that of all other characters involved:

> (46) X 437-46 (Hector has been killed by Achilles):
> ἄλοχος δ' οὔ πώ τι πέπυστο
> "Εκτορος· οὐ γάρ οἵ τις ἐτήτυμος ἄγγελος ἐλθὼν
> ἤγγειλ' ὅττι ῥά οἱ πόσις ἔκτοθι μίμνε πυλάων,
> 440 ἀλλ' ἥ γ' ἱστὸν ὕφαινε μυχῷ δόμου ὑψηλοῖο
> δίπλακα πορφυρέην, ἐν δὲ θρόνα ποικίλ' ἔπασσε.
> κέκλετο δ' ἀμφιπόλοισιν ἐϋπλοκάμοις κατὰ δῶμα
> ἀμφὶ πυρὶ στῆσαι τρίποδα μέγαν, ὄφρα πέλοιτο
> "Εκτορι θερμὰ λοετρὰ μάχης ἐκ νοστήσαντι,
> 445 νηπίη, οὐδ' ἐνόησεν ὅ μιν μάλα τῆλε λοετρῶν
> χερσὶν 'Αχιλλῆος δάμασε γλαυκῶπις 'Αθήνη.
> but Hector's wife had not yet heard anything. For no faithful messenger had informed her that her husband had remained outside the walls, but she was busy weaving a web in a remote corner of the lofty house, a double purple one, and on it she inserted colourful designs. And she ordered her fair-haired maids in the house to place a big tripod around the fire, in order that there would be warm bath water for Hector when he returned from the battle, foolish woman, for she did not know that, far away from bath water, owl-eyed Athena had subdued him by the hands of Achilles.[56]

The passage opens and closes with a negative statement, the content of the closing one (445-6) describing a later stage (Hector's death) than the opening one (437-9: Hector staying alone outside Troy). Line 439 recalls X 5-6 ('deadly fate held Hector shackled in front of Troy and the Scaean gates') and 440-4 therefore contain a description of Andromache's activities during Hector's fatal confrontation with Achilles (cp. T scholia ad 437a), which was watched from the walls by his parents and the other Trojan citizens. The unmistakable dramatic impact of the whole passage[57] results in the first place from the fact that the one person most concerned, Hector's wife (note that the name Andromache is not mentioned, but is replaced by the telling denomination ἄλοχος) is the only one who does not yet know of the death of her husband (note again the denomination πόσις). Her ignorance is then made even more pathetic by the description of her activities: first, she is weaving deep inside the palace just as Hector had ordered her to do in Z 490-3. The colourful pattern of her web suggests her (forced?) optimism.[58] This optimism, a joyful and loving expectation of Hector's return, becomes evident when she orders bath water to be prepared. The scope of the negations in 437.438, and 445 is both retrospective and prospective: they set Andromache apart from all other characters and prepare for her delayed and all the more dramatic recognition of Hector's death. First she *hears* the wailing coming from the walls (447), then *sees* Hector's body being dragged around the city (463-4). Thus, whereas in tragedy a messenger would have reported the bad tidings to her, a narrative text allows a character to go and find out through his/her own perceptions (focalization).

This last example has demonstrated once again that the effect of the negative presentation is meant for the NeFe$_1$: the characters, notably Hector's parents, do not know, at least are not presented as knowing or worrying about Andromache's ignorance. Andromache in her turn is of course unaware of her own ignorance. It is only the NeFe$_1$ who, through the two negative statements, knows of and pities Andromache's ignorance.

Conclusion

Negative statements are an indication of the activity of the NF$_1$: on the level of the fabula only events exist and when these events appear in the text in a negative form this must be explained as due to the focalizing and narrating activity of the NF$_1$. This holds a fortiori for non-events: they exist *only* on the levels of story and text.

The NF$_1$ uses negative statements in interaction with his addressee, the

NeFe$_1$, contradicting the latter's expectations (based on contextual knowledge, general knowledge of the world, 'historical' knowledge, or knowledge of the heroic code) and/or creating expectations (suspense). Sometimes the negative statement contradicts expectations of characters in the story.

Two linguistic observations have been adduced to corroborate this analysis of negations in connection with the NeFe$_1$: (1) the frequent combination of negation + the particle ἄρα, expressing surprise or lively interest, and (2) the high percentage of γάρ-clauses following upon negative statements, in which the NF$_1$ explains to the NeFe$_1$ why something did not take place.

3.3.2. *If not*-situations

In the *Iliad* we find 38 passages of the type: 'and now x would have happened, if somebody had not done y'. I call these passages *if not*-situations[59] and consider them a special type of *counterfactuals*. A normal counterfactual is e.g.

(47) Ψ 526-7:
    εἰ δέ κ' ἔτι προτέρω γένετο δρόμος ἀμφοτέροισι,
    τῶ κέν μιν παρέλασσ' οὐδ' ἀμφήριστον ἔθηκεν.
    and if the course had been even longer for both, he then
    would have driven past him and not made (the victory)
    doubtful

An example of an *if not*-situation is:

(48) Θ 90-1:
    καί νύ κεν ἔνθ' ὁ γέρων ἀπὸ θυμὸν ὄλεσσεν,
    εἰ μὴ ἄρ' ὀξὺ νόησε βοὴν ἀγαθὸς Διομήδης
    And there the old man would have lost his life, if Diomedes,
    good at the battle-shout, had not watched sharply

The main differences between normal counterfactuals and *if not*-situations are

1. that in the latter the normal order of conditional clause *preceding* main clause (Greenberg 1966: 84) is reversed. A pragmatic explanation for this reversal is that event x represents the logical consequence of what precedes, y the unexpected new course of events.

2. that only the main clause of the *if not*-situation is counterfactual: in (47) both main clause and conditional subordinate clause are purely hypothetical,

but in (48) the εἰ μή-clause describes a real event, which triggers a new series of events (Diomedes comes to the rescue of Nestor).

If not-situations are found also in other narrative texts:

(49) J. Diderot, *Jacques le Fataliste*:

"(Jacques) Je perdais tout mon sang, et j'étais un homme mort si notre charrette, ..., ne se fût arrêtée devant une chaumière".

(50) H. Fielding, *Joseph Andrews*:

nor would it probably have been a sufficient excuse for his wife, had not ...

The corpus of Iliadic *if not*-situations consists of:
(in <u>narrator-text</u>) B 155-6, Γ 373-5, E 22-4.311-3.679-80, Z 73-6, H 104-8, 273-6, Θ 90-1.130-2.217-9, Λ 310-2.504-7, M 290-3, N 723-5, O 121-7.459-64, Π 698-701, P 70-3.319-25.530-2.613-4, Σ 151-2/165-8, Y 288-91, Φ 211-3.544-6, X 202-4, Ψ 154-5.382-4.490-1.540-2.733-4, Ω 713-5;
(in <u>character-text</u>) E 388-90, Λ 750-2, Ξ 258-9, Σ 397-9.454-6.
The main clause contains an aorist (31 times) or imperfect indicative (4 times: H 273-6, Λ 504-7, Ψ 733-4, Ω 713-5) + ἄν/κεν, seldom optative + ἄν/κεν (E 311-7.388-90, P 70-3). The subordinate clause always contains an aorist indicative.[60] In E 22-4, O 459-64 and P 319-25 we find ἀλλά instead of εἰ μή.

If *not*-situations have been discussed by Bassett (1938: 100-2), Kullmann (1956: 42-8), Reinhardt (1961: 107-10) and Fenik (1968: 154, 175-7, 221). Bassett gives them a function in connection with the listener ("to mark the critical situation" for him: 101), whereas Kullmann and Reinhardt see them as a way for the poet to organize his plot, or more specifically to change the course of events. In my opinion, *if not*-situations involve both "poet" and "listener" and should be analyzed in terms of the interaction between NF_1 and $NeFe_1$. A first indication for this is the high percentage of ἄρα after εἰ μή (Γ 374, E 312.680, Θ 91.132, Y 291, Ψ 541, Ω 715) or in the nearby relative clause (O 461, P 72.532, Ψ 384), as was noted by Ruijgh (1971: 436).

Since the complete dossier of *if not*-situations has as yet never been interpreted in detail - the four scholars mentioned above only discuss random examples -, I depart from my usual method of discussing a sample and start with interpreting them all. After this I proceed with my narratological analysis of this form of presentation.

Interpretation of if not-situations in the narrator-text

Speaking broadly, the *if not*-situations of the narrator-text describe

    1. the near death of a hero (11 x)

    2. the near defeat of either Greeks or Trojans (11 x)

    3. less dramatic situations (11 x)

The near death of a hero

I start with five cases where a god saves the life of a hero.

Γ 373-5: Aphrodite snaps the strap of Paris' helmet, by which action she prevents him from choking and Menelaus from dragging him to the Greek side (the aorist εἴρυσσεν (373) would have meant the completion of the imperfect εἷλκε (370)). Aphrodite's rescue-action is preceded, or triggered by her 'watching sharply'. The same formula εἰ μὴ ἄρ' ὀξὺ νόησε recurs in E 312.680, Θ 91.132 and Υ 291, the character watching being a god except in Θ 91. One could compare the expression οὐδ' ἀλαοσκοπιὴν εἶχε: '(god x) did not keep blind man's watch' (K 515, N 10 and Ξ 135) and these instances of gods watching human events form part of the larger concept of the "divine audience", for which see Kullmann (1956: 83-7) and Griffin (1978, 1980: 179-240). The *if not*-situation emphasizes Menelaus' lost chance to glory (κῦδος) rather than Paris' critical situation (just as in E 311-7 it might also have run: 'and there Paris would have died'). This is in tune with the whole context of the duel between Paris and Menelaus, where from beginning to end emphasis is put on Menelaus' eagerness to revenge himself on Paris (cp. Γ 21-9.97-110.351-4.365-8.379-80.449-50).

E 311-3: Aphrodite protects her son Aeneas, who is about to be killed by Diomedes. As in Γ 373-5 this divine first aid is followed by a final removal of the hero from the battlefield. In both cases there is a clear motive for Aphrodite's intervention: as regards Paris, her position as benefactress; as regards Aeneas, her position as his mother (notice the denomination μήτηρ (313) and υἱόν (314)).

Υ 288-91: Aeneas is saved once more. The *if not*-situation consists of two elements, which together form a kind of compressed battle-scene:[61] Aeneas would have hit Achilles with the stone he had just picked up, but Achilles (protected by his divine armour) would have hit him with the sword he had just drawn, if not ... This time Aeneas is not saved by his mother, but by Poseidon. Poseidon's intervention comes somewhat unexpectedly in view of the fact that he is a pro-Greek god. His motive becomes clear in the dialogue (293-317), which takes place between the moment of his perception of Aeneas' critical situation (291 and cp.

in his speech: 293-4) and his actual rescue of that hero (321-9). Similar divine discussions on whether or not to save a hero's life take place in Π 433-57 and X 168-85. The heroes involved there, Sarpedon and Hector, were destined to die and Zeus' proposal to rescue them both times meets with severe criticism from Hera and Athena, respectively. Aeneas, however, is destined by Zeus to stay alive (302 and cp. 336 and 339) and Poseidon proposes to save him, fearing Zeus' anger. Hera in this case declares herself indifferent as to whether the mortal hero stays alive or not (see Van der Ben 1980: 69-70).

O 459-64: Hector's life is saved by Zeus, who breaks Teucer's bowstring while he is aiming at Hector. This is one of the two instances (the other being O 694-5, cp. Groß 1970) where Zeus himself directly intervenes, rather than through Hera, Athena or some other god. The motive for his intervention is that he has to protect Hector as the main instrument of his Will. See further below section 5.1, pp. 157-9.

E 22-4: Hephaestus saves the Trojan Idaeus before he is killed by Diomedes like his brother. The motive for Hephaestus' intervention is presented in the form of embedded focalization (the final ὡς-clause : 'in order that the old man would not be too much grieved'). The 'old man' is the father of the two brothers, a priest of Hephaestus (9-10). This individual relationship between man and god explains why Hephaestus, a pro-Greek god, saves the life of a Trojan.

A special case is X 202-4, where the intervening god does not so much save a hero's life as postpone his death. The *if not*-situation has the form of a rhetorical question, which amounts to: Hector would never have escaped death for so long, if Apollo had not helped him for the last time. The *if not*-situation reflects and answers a question which must have arisen with the NeFe₁ after 201 (οὐ δύνατο μάρψαι ποσίν), viz. how was it possible that Achilles, famous for the speed of his feet, could not overtake Hector, to whom never any special ability to run quickly had been attributed? As often (cp. Γ 375, O 461, P 72.352, Ψ 384), a relative clause further specifies the intervention: Apollo gave Hector fresh energy and made his knees light (204).

The life-saving agent can also be human.

Θ 90-1: Diomedes rescues Nestor.[62] The *if not*-situation forms the climax of the whole scene Θ 78-114: Zeus has thundered in support of the Trojans and many Greek leaders have turned to flight with the exception of Nestor, who must stay behind against his will, because one of his horses has been shot. The structure of 78-80 (οὔτ' ... τλῆ μίμνειν οὔτ' ... οὔτε ... μενέτην) already creates a certain tension, which is then heightened by the ὄφρ' ... τόφρ' passage (87-90): while the old man is frantically trying to free his entangled horses, Hector (note the menacing effect of the polyptoton Ἕκτορος ... Ἕκτορα: 88, 90) draws closer and closer and by now we are convinced that the old man certainly would have got the worst of it, if Diomedes had not noticed his critical situation. Having unsuccessfully asked Odysseus to join him in coming to the old man's rescue (93-6),[63] Diomedes finally does so on his own. Throughout this passage Nestor is referred to as ὁ γέρων, 'the old man', both by the NF₁ (87, 90, 100) and Diomedes (96, 102). The denomination seems to underscore Nestor's vulnerable position.[64]

P 613-4: Idomeneus, fighting on foot, is saved by Meriones' charioteer Coeranus, who, driving near his master's chariot, picks up the older commander. Coeranus, however, pays with his own life for this intervention, since the spear aimed at Idomeneus hits him. Through the combination with an *if not*-situation the common "charioteer slaying" motif (Fenik 1968: 204) gets a pathetic ring (cp. bT-scholia ad 615-6).

H 104-8: after some hesitation Menelaus has accepted Hector's challenge for a duel. This would, according to the NF₁, surely have led to his death, if the Greek kings and especially Agamemnon had not withheld him. The NF₁'s conviction that Menelaus would have stood no chance against Hector, because the latter is much stronger (105: πολὺ φέρτερος) is shared by Agamemnon in his speech (111: σεῦ ἀμείνονι). The motive for Agamemnon's intervention is, apart from brotherly love (bT-scholia), the fact that Menelaus forms the major reason for the Greek enterprise. His death would rob it of its purpose (H 155-82 and cp. Antilochus' considerations in E 566-7, presented in the form of embedded focalization).

The last two passages follow a catalogue of slain warriors (Φ 209-10 and E 677-8) and describe not the rescue of one named hero, but of an unknown number.

Φ 211-3: Achilles would have killed many more Paeonians, but for the intervention of the rivergod Scamander.

E 679-80: Hector stops Odysseus from killing more Lycians.

The near defeat of either Trojans or Greeks

Z 73-6: the Trojans would have been driven back into the city, but for the seer Helenus' strategic and religious advice to Aeneas and Hector: 77-101, his πρίν-clause (81-2) mirrors 73-4. A divine motivation for Helenus' intervention is not given (contrast H 44-5), but might be implied in his qualification in 76 as οἰωνοπόλων ὄχ' ἄριστος ('by far the best of the bird-augurs'), which he shares with Calchas only (A 69).

Θ 130-2: the Trojans almost became pent up like lambs in Troy, if Zeus had not thundered and lightened to frighten off the Greeks. The *if not*-situation comes somewhat as a surprise, since only some verses ago almost all Greek leaders had turned to flight (78-9). Apparently Diomedes' counter-attack, together with Nestor, was considered by Zeus a serious enough threat to thunder again (cp. 75-6): "Diomedes erscheint an dieser Stelle ganz und gar im selben Glanz wie in seiner Aristie" (Andersen 1978: 115). In an ancient variant the *if not*-situation is longer and even more dramatic, Hector being almost killed by Diomedes (131 a,b).

N 723-5: the *if not*-situation forms a kind of recommendatory introduction to Polydamas' following speech (726-47). But for Polydamas' speech (in which he advises Hector to hold a council) the Trojans would have retreated λευγαλέως ('miserably', 'with great losses'). Through the contrast between this λευγαλέως in the narrator-text (723) and ἀπήμονες ('unharmed') in Polydamas' speech (744) the NF₁ subtly indicates that he favours Polydamas' suggestion.[65]

Π 698-701: the Greeks, led by Patroclus, almost captured Troy, but for Apollo's intervention. The whole passage Π 698-711, of which this *if not*-situation forms part, was rejected by some scholars, "probably rightly", according to Leaf, "as the idea of an actual assault upon the walls is quite unprepared and seems hardly consistent with the attitude of Hector in 713". I think that the very improbability of the assault fits in well with Patroclus' situation shortly before his death. In Π 647-55 (embedded focalization) Zeus decides to prolong Patroclus' life a little, in order to inflict even more losses upon the Trojans. In this period of 'extra time' Patroclus comes to 'deserve' his death by acting through infatuation (μέγ' ἀάσθη: 685), which exists in not giving heed to Achilles' warning (686-7). His assault upon the Trojan walls (which is doomed to be unsuccessful, as Apollo points out: 707-9) is a clear sign, indeed the climax, of this infatuation. Exactly as Achilles had predicted in 91-4, Patroclus incurs with it the enmity of a god (Apollo), who in 804 will prepare the way for Euphorbus and Hector to kill him.[66]

P 319-25: the *if not*-situation consists of two complementary elements: the retreat of the Trojans into the city (P 319-20 = Z 73-4) would have meant the acquisition of glory by the Greeks 'even beyond Zeus' fate, relying on their own force and strength'. Apollo intervenes, exhorting Aeneas (327-32), who on his turn exhorts the Trojans to keep firm (335-41). In their speeches, both Apollo and Aeneas

74

refer to the situation as described in 319-22: Apollo, wishing to provoke Aeneas' fighting spirit, asks him how the Tròjans would defend the city 'even against a god', since they are not fighting now while a god (Zeus) is on their side. His example of other men fighting against all odds 'relying on their own force' mirrors (unconsciously or consciously) the behaviour of the Greeks at that moment: 329-30 ≅ 322. Aeneas, addressing his compatriots, (dis)qualifies their impending retreat 'overpowered by lack of resistance' (ἀναλκείησι δαμέντας: 337 = 320) as 'a shame' (αἰδώς: 336).[67]

Φ 544-6 recalls Π 698-701, but this time the threat that Troy will be captured by the Greeks is much more real: the Trojans are routed by Achilles and Priam has ordered the gates to be opened for them to get into the safety of the city. However, Achilles is in such a rage that he would certainly have continued his pursuit even within the walls, if Apollo had not placed Agenor before him as a kind of bait. Achilles concentrates on the pursuit (away from the city) of this one man and thus the other Trojans can safely enter the city (606-7).[68]

Let us now turn to the Greeks and their camp.

B 155-6 form the climax of the Diapeira-scene. Zeus, planning the fulfilment of his Will, sends a 'baneful' Dream to Agamemnon and orders him to get his men under arms. In the execution of this order Agamemnon adds a rather unexpected element of his own, viz. to test the morale of his troops, by suggesting to them to return home. His plan fails because the soldiers react so enthusiastically that they have already started making preparations for the return before any of the leaders has got the opportunity to hold a counter-speech as planned.[69] It is only the intervention of Hera - spurring on Athena, who in her turn spurs on Odysseus - which prevents a premature (ὑπέρμορα: 'beyond fate') return home of the Greeks (155-6). The bT-scholia (ad 156) praise Homer for the invention of the *deus ex machina*:

εἰς τοσοῦτον προάγει τὰς περιπετείας ὡς δύνασθαι θεὸν μόνον αὐτὰς
μεταθεῖναι. πρῶτος δὲ καὶ τοῖς τραγικοῖς μηχανὰς εἰσηγήσατο.
he brings the danger to such a height that only a god can put it right again.
And he was the first to introduce to the playwrights the *deus ex machina*.

Θ 217-8: Hector would have put the Greek ships on fire, if Hera had not spurred on Agamemnon. Ameis-H. consider "die den Höhepunkt der Gefahr bezeichnende Wendung übertrieben". The danger of Hector putting the ships on fire, however, is not so imaginary if we recall his threatening words in 181-2 (πυρὶ νῆας ἐνιπρήσω: 'I will burn the ships with fire'). And Agamemnon, addressing his troops, also considers the danger to be real: ὃς τάχα νῆας ἐνιπρήσει πυρὶ κηλέῳ (235: (Hector) 'who will soon burn the ships with destroying fire').

In a very similar situation, Λ 310-2 ('the Greeks, in flight, would have tumbled into their ships'), there is no divine intervention, but it is Odysseus who adhorts Diomedes to make a stand together. Again, the danger described in the *if not*-situation is realized by the characters as well: καί νύ κεν νήεσσι πέσον φεύ-γοντες ᾿Αχαιοί (311) is mirrored in Odysseus' speech: ἔλεγχος ἔσσεται εἴ κεν νῆας ἔλῃ κορυθαίολος ῞Εκτωρ (314-5: 'it will be a shame, if Hector with glancing helm captures the ships').

Twice we find a special variant of the *if not*-situation, viz. 'event x would <u>not yet</u> (οὐ ... πω)[70] have taken place, if somebody had not done y'. In other words, here x does in fact take place.

Λ 504-7: the Greeks would not yet have retreated, if Paris had not wounded the physician Machaon. The presentation of the Greek retreat in the form of an *if not*-situation almost seems to excuse them: it was the loss of such an important man (cp. Idomeneus' words in 514-5) which caused it.

M 290-3: Hector and the Trojans would not yet have broken through the Greek gate, if Zeus had not spurred on Sarpedon. Leaf comments: "These lines are practically meaningless ... for the ineffective attack on the wall has in the end no bearing whatever on Hector's successful assault on the gate". I do not agree with this dismissal of the lines: Sarpedon's assault on the Greek wall is presented by the NF$_1$ as important and menacing (note the pair of similes 293 and 299-306, Moulton 1977: 20) and also felt as such by the Greeks (330-2). As a result of the pressure exercized by Sarpedon, the main defender of the Greek wall, Ajax, is forced to leave his position opposite Hector, thus giving the latter a chance to break through (459-62 brings the fulfilment of 290-1). The importance of Sarpedon's role is later acknowledged by Patroclus (addressing the two Ajaxes): κεῖται ἀνὴρ ὃς πρῶτος ἐσήλατο τεῖχος ᾿Αχαιῶν, Σαρπηδών (Π 558-9 ≅ M 438, there said by the NF$_1$ of Hector).

Less dramatic situations

Σ 151-2/165-8 is a complex *if not*-situation, since it consists of two *protaseis* and one *apodosis*: the Greeks would not have been able to drag Patroclus' body from under the missiles ... Hector would have dragged the body (to the Trojan side), if Hera had not incited Achilles (through Iris) to make an appearance. Iris' words in 173 and 174-6 mirror the *if not*-situation of 151-22 and 165.

In Ψ 540-2 Achilles' spontaneous decision to grant Eumelus (who, though he had the best horses, came in last) the second prize, is kept from being executed by protests from Antilochus, the real winner of the second prize. Whereas the NF_1 stressed the generosity of Achilles' gesture (approved of by all the other Greeks), Antilochus' focalization of that same gesture results in a different formulation: ἀφαιρήσεσθαι (544: 'take away') instead of πόρεν (540 'give').

In two cases gods do not, as they do usually, help, but thwart human characters.

P 70-3: Apollo begrudges (ἀγάσσατο)[71] Menelaus the acquisition of Euphorbus' armour and therefore rouses Hector against him. As a result Menelaus will lose not only Euphorbus' but also Patroclus' armour. It is not indicated what the motive was for Apollo's intervention here. Ameis-H. (ad 71) refer to Apollo's habitually favouring the Trojans, but a more specific reason might be the circumstance that Euphorbus had cooperated with Apollo in the execution of Patroclus (Π 804-13).

Ψ 382-4: Apollo 'became enraged' (κοτέσσατο) with Diomedes and made him drop his whip, thus preventing him from overtaking Eumelus in the horse-race. Apollo's motive is not only that he had himself bred Eumelus' horses (Β 766), but also, as Andersen (1978: 142-3) has pointed out, the fact that Diomedes is driving horses which he in Ε 323-7 had captured from Aeneas. Apollo's intervention is counteracted by Athena, who breaks the axle of Eumelus' chariot (392-7), which enables Diomedes to win the race after all. She also acts under the impulse of anger (383: κοτέουσα). Such divine anger (see in general Irmscher 1950) and (unfair) interventions might to us seem slightly odd, but the bT-scholia remark that the participation of gods in the race makes it more 'elevated': σεμνοποιῆσαι θέλων τὸν ἀγῶνα καὶ θεοὺς συμφιλονεικοῦντας εἰσάγει.

Only once does an if not-situation describe a god intervening in activities of another god:

O 121-7: Zeus would again, and even more terribly, have become angry at the other Olympians, if Athena had not withheld Ares from revenging the death of his son Ascalaphus. In Θ 5-27 Zeus had forbidden all gods to interfere in the war and this command had already been transgressed by Poseidon (from Ν 17 onwards) and Hera (the Διὸς ἀπατή: Ξ 153-Ο 4). In her speech (128-41) Athena sets out her motive for withholding Ares: fear for reprisals from the side of Zeus not only upon Ares himself (132-3, Ares had declared himself ready to face them: 117-8), but upon all the gods (134-7). Thus, her speech elaborates on what had been indicated summarily in the if not-situation: πᾶσι περιδείσασα

9εοῖσιν.

Finally, there are six cases where *if not*-situations describe how a series of connected events or a process is cut short.

H 273-6: having exchanged words, spears and stones Ajax and Hector are about to attack each other with swords, when heralds put an end to the duel. Hector had already been wounded twice by Ajax: 260-2, 268-72[72] and as the bT-scholiasts (ad 274-5) say: οἰκονομικῶς σῶσαι 9έλων τὸν Ἑκτορα τῇ ποιήσει διαλύει τὴν μάχην ('for reasons of economy, viz. wanting to save Hector for his poem, the poet puts an end to the duel'). In fact, we already knew from Helenus' words in 52 that it was not Hector's destiny to die in this duel.

P 530-2: the Ajaxes, having been called to help (532: ἑταίρου κικλήσκοντος, sc. Automedon in 508-15), intervene when Automedon and Hector are about to attack each other with swords.

Ψ 490-1: Achilles puts an end to a quarrel between Idomeneus and Ajax which threatened to escalate. μηκέτι in Achilles' speech (492) corresponds to προτέρω ἔτ' (490).

Achilles again intervenes in Ψ 733-4 and stops the wrestling-game between Odysseus and Ajax before the decisive third round (each hero having won one): he declares both victor and they receive equal prizes (735-7).

In Ψ 154-5 and Ω 713-5 (verbal) interventions of Achilles and Priam, respectively, put an end to the mourning of their men, which otherwise would have continued (ὀδυρομένοισιν: present participle) until sunset, i.e. endlessly. Both Achilles and Priam motivate their intervention with the argument that there is a point of saturation as regards weeping (Ψ 157: γόοιο μὲν ἔστι καὶ ἆσαι and Ω 717: ἄσεσθε κλαυθμοῖο).

Interpretation of if not-situations in character-text (direct speech)

Λ 750-2: Nestor, telling Patroclus by way of paradigm about his own youthful exploits, relates how he had once almost killed the Actoriones, who were saved in the last minute by their father Poseidon.

E 388-90: Dione, wanting to comfort the wounded Aphrodite, tells her about other gods who have suffered physical pain. Her first example concerns Ares who had almost gone to pieces, being shut up in a bronze pot for 13 months, if Eeriboea had not informed Hermes, who stole him from the pot. In view of the immortality of the Homeric gods, which is stressed throughout the epics, it seems best to take κεν ... ἀπόλοιτο as hyperbolical and not literal: Ares was suffering physical inconvenience (391: τειρόμενον ... δεσμὸς ἔδαμνα), to which, as a god, he was not used.[73]

Ξ 258-9: Hypnus, addressing Hera, motivates his hesitation to help her by recounting an earlier occasion when he put Zeus to sleep according to her orders and would have been thrown from heaven into the sea, if Night (his mother, according to Hesiod, *Theogony* 758) had not saved him.

Σ 397-9: Hephaestus, addressing Thetis, recalls how his mother had thrown him down from the Olympus: 'and I would have suffered pains in my heart, if Eurynome and Thetis had not received me at their breast'. It is the memory of this help which makes him prepared to grant Thetis any wish she might have.

Σ 454-6: the *if not*-situation (the Greeks would have taken Troy, if Apollo and Hector had not killed Patroclus) forms the dramatic climax of the resumé Thetis gives to Hephaestus of the events before Troy as described in the *Iliad* so far (444-56). As such it leads up to her request to him to provide Achilles with new armour (see also below section 6.2, pp. 216-8).

Narratological analysis: why if not-situations?

If not-situations seem a congenial feature of story-telling. An indication for this is that all five *if not*-situations occurring in character-text form part of a narrative (cp. also example 49, where Jacques is telling his master one of his adventures). To mention something even if it did in the end not take place, is effectful, either because the counterfactual event x in itself contains relevant information (even if Nestor did not kill the Actoriones, the fact that he almost did adds to his heroic stature) or because it places event y in a special light (Hephaestus' plight increases the value of Thetis' assistance to him).

Thus, characters use *if not*-situations as a rhetorical instrument to

1. bring home a critical situation: Dione in E, Hypnus in Ξ;
2. eulogize: Nestor himself in Λ, Hephaestus Thetis in Σ;
3. incite pathos: Thetis in Σ.

In my interpretation of these five passages I have already tried to indicate how the rhetorical effect of the *if not*-situation enhances in its turn the effect of the embedded narrative as a whole: Nestor stressing his own prowess in order to increase the paradigmatic function of the narrative Λ 671-761, etc.

How does the NF$_1$ exploit this rhetorical instrument in *his* narrative? He uses it to

1. bring home a critical situation: B 155-6, E 22-4.311-3, Θ 90-1.217-8, O 121-7, Σ 151-2/165-8, Y 288-91, Ψ 490-1;

2. eulogize: Z 73-6 (the seer Helenus), Λ 310-2 (steadfast Odysseus), M 290-3 (wall breaker Sarpedon), N 723-5 (sage counsellor Polydamas); or excuse: Λ 504-7 (the Greeks).

3. incite pathos: P 613-4, Ψ 154-5, Ω 713-5;

4. characterize a character or his situation: Γ 373-5 (Menelaus' frustration), Θ 130-2 (Diomedes' prowess), O 459-64 (Hector as Zeus' instrument), Π 698-701 (Patroclus' fateful infatuation), P 319-25 (Trojan despondency vs. Greek energy), Φ 211-3 (Achilles' lust for revenge).544-6 (Achilles' rage), Ψ 540-2 (Antilochus' youthful temper);

5. indicate that y was different from what the NeFe₁ might have expected: E 679-80 (Odysseus intends to take the lives of many Lycians), H 273-6 (after throwing spears it was normal to continue the fight with swords), P 70-3 (no human character dared come against Menelaus).530-3 (see ad H 273-6), X 202-4 (Achilles could be expected to overtake Hector), Ψ 382-4 (Eumelus already feels the hot breath of Diomedes' horses down his neck).733-4 (a third decisive round was to be expected).

All this rhetoric is aimed at the NeFe₁, as was noted also by the scholia (ad Θ 217-9):

εἰς ἄκρον τοὺς κινδύνους εἴωθεν ἐξάγειν ἀεί, καὶ ἐναγώνιαν ποιήσας τὸν ἀκροατὴν τῷ προσδοκίᾳ, εὐθὺς τὴν ἴασιν ἐπιφέρει.
(the poet) is wont to bring his story to a summit of danger and having made his hearer full of anguish through expectation he immediately brings relief.

Similar remarks are found ad B 156, H 104-8 and Σ 151-2.

Very often the intervention described in an *if not*-situation consists of or entails a speech: B 157-65, Z 77-101, H 109-19.279-82, Θ 93-6.140-2.228-42, Λ 313-5, N 726-47, O 128-41, Π 707-9, P 75-81.327-32, Σ 170-80, Y 293-308, Φ 214-21, Ψ 156-60.492-8.543-54.735-7, Ω 716-7. We have seen that in these speeches characters refer to the 'almost event' x, which for them has reality as a thing to fear, to be ashamed or angry about etc.: B 158-9 and 174-5 (refer back to 155), Z 81-2 (73-4), H 111 (104-5), Θ 96 and 102-3 (90). 235 (217), Λ 314-5 (311), N 743-4 (723-4), O 134 (121-2), Π 707-8 (698-9), P 336-7 (319-20), Σ 173 and 174-6 (151-2 and 165), Y 294 (290), Ψ 157 (154).492 (490).544 (540), Ω 717 (713).

After relating *if not*-situations to the NeFe₁ and to the characters, I now turn to their producer, the NF₁. Here it is interesting to compare a discussion by Füger (1978: 206-8) of *if not*-situations or as he calls them "alternativ Verläufe" in Fielding's *Joseph Andrews*. Füger draws attention to the presence of modifications like "probably" (cp. above example 50) or "very likely" in the counterfactual main clause. He suggests that through these modifications the narrator of *Joseph Andrews*, who presents himself as a reliable biographer, indicates that he can only speculate about events which have not really taken place. I have found two comparable cases of modification in the Iliadic *if not*-situations: in Υ 289 (Aeneas would have hit Achilles *either* on his helmet *or* on his shield) and in Ψ 382 (Diomedes would have *either* overtaken Eumelus *or* have made the victory disputed, i.e. have ended *èx aequo*). Notwithstanding these modifications, Füger continues, the "alternativ Verläufe" of *Joseph Andrews* are, in the end, "Fiktionssignale"

> es geht dabei um eine indirekte Selbstcharakterisierung des kreativen Prozesses, diesmal in dem Sinne, daß der Erzähler deutlich zu erkennen gibt, daß er die Geschichte durchaus anders hätte verlaufen lassen können, wenn er nur gewollt hätte ... Allen gegenteiligen Beteuerungen zum Trotz läßt der Erzähler den Leser nie im unklaren darüber, daß die Erzählung sein eigenes Konstrukt ist, Resultat seiner souveräner Entscheidungsakte.

One is reminded here of what Genette (1969: 92-3) has called "l'arbitraire du récit": in principle, a narrator at every point of his story has a limitless number of ways to continue his story. Genette makes a subdivision between "arbitraire de direction" and "arbitraire d'expansion". Both categories can be illustrated from Diderot's *Jacques le Fataliste*:

> (51) Que cette aventure ne deviendrait-elle pas entre mes mains, s'il me prenait en fantaisie de vous désespérer. Je donnerais de l'importance à cette femme; j'en ferais la nièce d'un curé du village voisin; j'ameuterais les paysans de ce village ... etc.

> (52) Vous concevez, lecteur, jusqu'où je pourrais pousser cette conversation sur un sujet dont on a tant parlé, tant écrit depuis deux mille ans, sans en être d'un pas plus avancé.

Are the Iliadic *if not*-situations also an expression of "l'arbitraire de direction", are they "Fiktionssignale"? At this point it must be realized that both Fielding and Diderot are novelists who deliberately play with, in fact, expose the tricks of narrative fiction. Their narrators are extreme cases of self-conscious narrators (above pp. 46-7), in the sense that they are not only aware of their own narrating activity, but in fact make clear that they are inventing their very story. Thus, not only we, the historical readers, are aware that the story is fictitious, but also the narrator and his narratee. The situation in the *Iliad* is different and more complex: for us, the historical readers (and most probably for the ancient Greek hearers/readers) the *Iliad* represents what I would call *semi-fiction*. It tells of events, which at least partly were given by tradition - it is difficult to assess exactly what is traditional and what is invention in the *Iliad*, but I myself am convinced that a rather large part of it is invention - a tradition, which again partly - how much? - covers historical facts.[74] The NF₁, however, claims to present, with the help of the Muses, a reliable account of the heroic past. For him and for the NeFe₁ the events are not fictitious. This claim precludes any overt "arbitraire de direction". In other words, the (counterfactual) event x of an *if not*-situation is not a real, but only an imaginary alternative.[75] This becomes very clear in those cases where it is indicated (by the NF₁ or by speaking characters) that event x would have run counter to fate, fate representing the traditional or 'historical' course of events:[76] B 155 (ὑπέρμορα), H 52 (οὐ ... μοῖρα), Π 707-8 (οὐ ... αἶσα), P 321 (ὑπὲρ Διὸς αἶσαν), Υ 302 (μόριμον).336 (ὑπὲρ μοῖραν). The implication here is that the real course of events y is according to fate and I conclude that *if not*-situations are yet another way for the NF₁ - the other being his invocation of the Muses as eyewitnesses in B 485 - to confirm his status as a reliable presentator, a presentator of what really happened.

3.3.3. Prolepses and analepses

An important aspect of the interaction between NF₁ and NeFe₁ is the anticipation of events still to be told ("Vorauswendungen", "foreshadowings", "prolepses") and the retroversion to events already told ("Rückwendungen", "flash-backs", "analepses"). The subject of *order*, i.e. the way in which the chronological order of events in the fabula is changed on the levels of story and text, has always been of great interest both to narratologists (Lämmert 1955, Genette 1972: 77-121 = 1980: 33-85, the terms prolepsis and analepsis, here adopted, derive from him, Sternberg 1978, Bal 1985: 51-68) and to Homeric scholars (Kraut 1863, Wieniewski 1924, Duckworth 1933, Schadewaldt 1938, Balensiefen 1955, Hellwig 1964 and Kullmann 1968).

In view of this abundant and in my opinion excellent scholarship on the 156 prolepses and 388 analepses of the *Iliad* (figures according to Balensiefen 1955: 19), I will not repeat this investigation here. What does seem to be needed, however, is a frame of reference, which coherently and systematically describes all the various passages belonging to this corpus. This desideratum will become clear from the inventory of labels and definitions under which scholars have discussed (parts of) this corpus, with which I begin this section. After this inventory I set out a frame of reference, based on Genette and encompassing all types of analepses and prolepses, including those occurring in character-text. This means that I will cross the boundaries of this chapter, which in principle deals with simple narrator-text only. In the end, however, I return to my initial point of departure, the interaction between NF_1 and $NeFe_1$, and analyze a number of prolepses and analepses by the NF_1.

Labels and definitions

Epische Prolepsis: as defined by Kraut (1863: 2) "den dem Gang des Epos vorgreifenden Aufschluß über den Verlauf im ganzen oder Begebenheiten im einzelnen, durch welchen der epische Dichter beurkundet, daß er von Anfang an die Entwicklung der epischen Handlung bis zu ihrem Ende übersieht". Kraut distinguishes between prolepsis of events inside and outside the *Iliad*.

Foreshadowing (Duckworth 1933): he distinguishes between exact forecasts and more vague foreshadowings, between the forecasting of events inside and outside the epic and between forecasts which reach the reader only or which reach both a character and the reader.

Annonces: as defined by Wieniewski (1924: 115) "on est en présence d'une annonce toutes les fois que le poète nous prévient directement d'un événement futur; on ne l'est pas nécessairement toujours, quand le poète est remplacé dans ce rôle par un des personnages de l'action." (125) "nombre d'annonces se rapportent aux événements qui restent au delà des limites de l'un des deux poèmes".

Vorausdeutung as defined by Hellwig (1964: 54) "eine Wendung in die erzählte Zukunft, die sich in kurzen Hinweisen - Vorhersagen, Wünschen usw. - kundtut"; "vorausdeutend sprechen ... Figuren und der Dichter selbst."

Rück- und Vorverweisungen as defined by Balensiefen (1955:19) "die ausdrückliche Erzählung eines von gegenwärtigen Zeitpunkt der Handlung aus gesehenen vergangenen oder künftigen Ereignisses, wobei ihr Umfang zunächst gleichgültig ist ... versteckte Andeutungen sind nicht unter die Verweisungen gezählt"; he distinguishes between (20) "Verweisungen auf Geschehnisse die außerhalb des Zeitverlaufs der Ilias liegen" and "Ereignisse, die noch in der Handlungsgang der Ilias fallen" and between "Verweisungen im epischen Bericht" und "in direkten

Reden".

Rückverweis: as defined by Hellwig (1968: 46) "eine flüchtige Erwähnung früherer Ereignisse, der den ganzen sukzessiven Erzählgang nicht anhält ... Dabei ist es gänzlich gleichgültig, ob ein angedeuteter Vorgang schon dargestellt worden ist oder nicht, und weiter, ob er überhaupt der erzählten (oder nicht erzählten) Vergangenheit oder aber Vorvergangenheit des Geschehens angehört."

Digressions: as defined by
- Austin (1966: 300) "anecdotes which describe action outside the time of the poem";
- Gaisser (1969a: 2) "the tales and episodes that interrupt the flow of the action to tell of events unconnected with the main story and to give background information";
- Braswell (1971: 16) "stories that have only incidental relevance to the main narrative".

Paradeigma: as defined by Willcock (1964: 142) "a myth introduced for exhortation or consolation" (sc. by a speaking character).

Wiedererzählungen as defined by Hebel (1970: 5) "Erzählungen, die der Dichter als eigentlicher Erzähler des ganzen Epos einer handelnden Person innerhalb der Dichtung überträgt; diese Wiedererzählungen berichten Vergangenes, sei es, daß es aus dem unmittelbar zum Epos gehörenden Geschehen genommen, sei es, daß es von außen herangebracht ist".

Mirror-stories as defined by
- Létoublon (1983a: 27) "récit spéculaire (prospectif ou rétrospectif) renvoyant au récit/ à l'histoire (réelle/fictive)";
- de Jong (1985a: 5): prospective or retrospective stories, which refer to something told in the main story and which are either true or fictitious relative to the facts of the main story.

Time-order in the Iliad: a frame of reference
The frame of reference set out below takes into account the following three criteria:

    1. the direction of the change in order: forward (prolepses) or backward (analepses)

    2. the narrative situation in which the prolepses and analepses occur: simple narrator-text, complex narrator-text, character-text

    3. the relation of the prolepses and analepses to the time-span covered by

the primary fabula[77] (which in the Iliad runs from the arrival of Chryses in the Greek camp to Hector's burial): when they refer to events within that time-span they are internal, outside that time-span they are external.

It remains a matter of choice whether one includes in the corpus of analepses/ prolepses also indirect or covert backward/forward references, as e.g. in the case of a simile with anticipatory elements like N 137-42. As we have seen, Balensiefen excludes such "versteckte Andeutungen", but the majority of scholars include them and the definition Genette (1972: 82 = 1980: 40) gives of prolepsis and analepsis also seems to point in that direction:

> toute manoeuvre narrative consistant à raconter *ou évoquer* d'avance un événe-ment ultérieur ... toute *évocation* après coup d'un événement antérieur au point de l'histoire où l'on se trouve (my italics).

	PROLEPSES		ANALEPSES	
	internal	**external**	**internal**	**external**
simple narrator-text	Φ 47-8 death of Lycaon: Φ 116-9	M 3-35 destruction of the Greek wall	E 795 wounding of Diomedes: E 95-100	B 101-8 history of Agamemnon's sceptre
complex narrator-text	Π 646-55 Zeus meditating on Patroclus' death: Π 787-857	P 406-7 Achilles' expectations concerning fall of Troy	E 319-20 Sthenelus recalls orders: E 261-4	Ω 27-30 Athena and Hera are angry on account of Paris' judge-ment
character-text	Π 851-4 Patroclus prophesies Hector's death: X 326-63	X 358-60 Hector prophesies Achilles' death	A 366-92 Achilles recounts events of A 6-349	I 529-99 Meleager-story told by Phoenix

The advantages of this frame of reference are that it uses a consistent termino-logy and that it takes into account the narrative situation in which the prolep-sis/analepsis occurs. Thus, it is important to realize, especially in the case of prolepses, who receives the information: the $NeFe_1$ (in all three narrative situ-ations), one character (the F_2 in the case of embedded focalization), two or more characters (NF_2 and $NeFe_2$ in the case of direct speech).

I wish to draw attention to two more points. The first concerns external analepses by characters in their speeches. Andersen (1987) has suggested that "mythological paradigms" can have two functions: a primary or *argument* function on the level of the communication between characters and a secondary or *key* function on the level of the communication between poet and reader. If one accepts this suggestion, as I am inclined to do, this means that external analepses, in fact, allow *two* analyses: first, in relation to their argument function, as external analepses, and second, in relation to their key function, as internal prolepses. Thus, the Meleager-story, told by Phoenix to Achilles as a paradigm (argument function), is for these characters an external analepsis, since it recounts events which have taken place long before the *Iliad*: Phoenix himself introduces the story as τόδε ἔργον πάλαι, οὔ τι νέον γε (Ι 527: 'this work of old, not at all recent'). At the same time, the story contains certain signs for the NeFe$_1$ with regard to Achilles' subsequent behaviour in the *Iliad* (key function): he will not give up his wrath and will resume fighting only when circumstances force him to do so. As such the passage also is an internal prolepsis, not for the characters involved, but for the NeFe$_1$.

My second point concerns the relation between order and another aspect of the handling of time, frequency. *Frequency* is the numerical relationship between the events of the fabula and those of story and text, or how often is an event presented? This concept was first developed by Genette (1972: 145-82 = 1980: 113-60). One of the more obvious categories of frequency is *repetition*, i.e. one event being presented more than once. Internal analepses and prolepses, in so far as they do not fill in an ellipsis (above p. 43), belong to this category (cp. Genette 1972: 95-100, 110-2 = 1980: 54-61, 73-4). An example is the death of Patroclus, which takes place in Π 787-857, but is

predicted by the NF$_1$ (Λ 604, Π 46-7.251-2.686-7.692-3); meditated upon by Zeus as F$_2$ (Π 646-55); announced by Zeus as NF$_2$ (Θ 476, Ο 65-7);	INTERNAL PROLEPSES
not expected by Achilles as F$_2$ (Ρ 404-7); fearfully anticipated by Achilles as NF$_2$ (Σ 6-14) remorsefully recalled by Achilles as NF$_2$ (Σ 80-2)[78]	INTERNAL ANALEPSES

As this example shows, such repetitious internal prolepses and analepses form an indication for the NeFe$_1$ of the importance of an event and also confront him with its various aspects.

Prolepses and analepses in the simple narrator-text

In the following I analyze a number of prolepses and analepses by the NF_1 to show what kind of effect(s) they are meant to have on the $NeFe_1$.

Internal prolepses

Except for omens, which are perceived by the characters too,[79] internal prolepses in the simple narrator-text reach the $NeFe_1$ only and the characters remain ignorant of what lies ahead of them. Internal prolepses, therefore, in the first place create *dramatic irony*, defined by Sedgewick (1935: 49) as "the sense of contradiction felt by spectators of a drama who see a character acting in ignorance of his condition".[80] Above (p. 66) I discussed K 336-7 as an example of a prolepsis in negative form: the NF_1 announces that Dolon will not return from his spying mission. It is against the background of this information that the $NeFe_1$ experiences the ensuing scene of the confrontation between Dolon and Diomedes + Odysseus (339-468). Sometimes the NF_1 stresses the ignorance of the characters involved by calling them νήπιος (lit. 'childish', hence 'blind or poor fool'), e.g.

> (53) Π 46-7 (Patroclus has just asked Achilles for his armour)
> "Ὣς φάτο λισσόμενος μέγα νήπιος· ἦ γὰρ ἔμελλεν
> οἱ αὐτῷ θάνατόν τε κακὸν καὶ κῆρα λιτέσθαι.
> Thus he pleaded, greatly foolish: for indeed it would turn
> out that he supplicated evil death for himself.[81]

Scholars have given the following interpretations of νήπιος

- Duckworth (1933: 11): "it expresses the poet's scorn that they have no realization of fate in store for them"

- Fränkel (1962: 41, n. 31): it does not imply a judgement of the poet, "die Torheit ist eine objektive Qualität, denn sie ist identisch mit der Erfolgwidrigkeit seines (sc. des Menschens) Handelns"

- Griffin (1980: 126): "always said by the poet with emotion, whether pity or derision".

In my opinion, with νήπιος the NF_1 refers to the limitations of the human race, its restricted knowledge of the true nature of things or course of events, its inability to determine its own fate. Thus, when Achilles in Y 262-3 fears that Aeneas' spear will pierce his shield he is called νήπιος, because he does not realize the divine super-quality of his own armour. When the Trojan Nastes goes to war with golden armour, this does not prevent him from being killed by Achilles

(B 872-5). Except for Υ 264, νήπιος is mostly found wedged in between mention of a character's *optimistic* expectations[82] and the NF₁'s description (often prediction) of the true (disastrous) course of events. Signalling the contrast between hope and delusion, it expresses and elicits pity, despite the fact that the delusion is often brought about by the character's own tragic error (for νήπιος and ἄτη see Bremer 1969: 101-4). Virgilian *infelix*, which also "foreshadows future tragedy",[83] is clearer in this respect.

Apart from νήπιος, example (53) contains another word which asks for discussion, viz. ἔμελλεν. The verb μέλλω occurs 26 times in narrator-text, of which 18 times as part of a prolepsis. The prolepses are focalized by the NF₁ in B 36.694.724, K 336, M 3.34.113, Π 46, P 278.497, Υ 466, Φ 47; by characters, notably Zeus, in B 39, Λ 54, O 601 (cp. character-text O 69-71).612, Π 460, Ω 85.[84]

A second effect of internal prolepses is *suspense*, described by the master of suspense himself, Alfred Hitchcock, as: "the audience is provided with information the characters in the picture don't know about. Because of this knowledge the tension is heightened as the audience tries to figure out what is going to happen next".[85] Thus, the NeFe₁ from Λ 604 on knows that evil will befall Patroclus and he waits with anxiety for Damocles' sword to fall.

Internal analepses

I give two examples:

Υ 270-2: The NF₁ recalls that Hephaestus had constructed Achilles' new shield in five layers (Σ 481). This information now is very relevant, since the spear thrown by Aeneas, remains stuck in the third, golden, layer and therefore is not fatal. The extra details given in Υ 271-2, as compared with Σ 481, concerning the material of which the layers are made, serve to underline the tension inherent in the situation.[86]

X 323: at the dramatic moment when Achilles is looking for a weak spot in Hector's armour to strike, his armour is described (in a relative clause) as 'beautiful, which Hector had taken from Patroclus after he had killed him'. Scholars so far have failed to remark on this small, but highly effectful analepsis (Leaf only states that the line is "obviously open to suspicion"): it recapitulates the very reason why Achilles is so eager to kill Hector.[87] I am even inclined to analyze the analepsis as focalized by Achilles as F₂, i.e. as representing Achilles' thoughts at the moment he is intently looking (εἰσορόων: 321, φαίνετο: 324) at Hector's = Patroclus' = his own armour.

External prolepses

There are only two external prolepses in the simple narrator-text, the characters anticipating mostly on events to come:[88] B 724-5 and M 3-35. I discuss the latter.

M 3-35: the passage describes the destruction of the wall around the Greek camp by the joint efforts of Poseidon, Apollo and Zeus, as it will take place after Troy has fallen and the Greeks have departed. This external analepsis is the farthest reaching of all analepses, since those by characters reach no further than Achilles' death and the fall of Troy. Yet, it tells of events which for the NF₁ and NeFe₁ already belong to the past, as is indicated through ἡμιθέων. What is the function of this long external prolepsis? So far, two interpretations have been brought forward:

1. the poet had to explain to his audience why no remains of the wall were to be seen anymore in the Troad and

2. the poet wanted to incorporate in his *Iliad* elements of another tradition, according to which Zeus' will encompassed the destruction of a whole generation of heroes. The destruction of the wall reflects and at the same time replaces this other tradition.

The second interpretation was defended by Scodel (1981), who in her note 2 also discusses the first one, which was already current in antiquity. Both interpretations find their origin in extra-textual arguments and I would venture to add a third, intra-textual interpretation: the Greek wall is going to be the centre of the events in book M (which was called τειχομαχία in antiquity). Normally, the NF₁ underlines the importance of an object by telling its *history*, i.e. through an external analepsis, e.g. concerning Agamemnon's scepter in B 101-8. Since the Greek wall had only recently been built the NF₁ here turns to another device, telling the *future* of the object involved. The effect is to illustrate to the NeFe₁ the fragility of human existence, the tininess - yet not insignificance[89] - of human enterprises, even those of semi-divine men, when set against the eternity of nature and the immortal gods. Clues for this interpretation are H 442-63, where Zeus prophesies the destruction of the Greek wall and says that the κλέος ('fame') of the wall around Troy, built by Poseidon and Apollo, will last longer than the κλέος of this wall built by the Greeks, and especially O 361-6, where Apollo pulls down part of the Greek wall. The ease (362: ῥεῖα μάλ') and detachment with which the god destroys the result of hard work by the Greeks (365: πολὺν κάματον καὶ ὀϊζύν and cp. in M 29: μογέοντες Ἀχαιοί) is illustrated in the simile of a child, playing near the sea and playfully trampling down its own sand-castle (362-4).[90] The NF₁, apostrophizing Apollo in 365, almost seems to be indignant with him, because of this 'playful' attitude. In M 3-35 the NF₁, having come halfway his story, shows how the scene of so many bloody struggles will some day look as if nothing has happened (notice λεῖα and αὖτις).[91]

External analepses

External analepses by the NF_1 can be divided into two categories:
1. those describing the origin of objects and
2. those providing biographical details about characters.

The effects of these analepses have for the greater part already been analyzed by Griffin (1980: 1-50 on "significant objects"[92] and 1976, 1980: 103-43 on "obituaries"). There is, however, one subgroup of 2 which has so far not received much attention: external analepses which provide information on characters that is necessary for the $NeFe_1$ to understand or fully appreciate their speeches. I discuss two examples.[93]

Λ 122-5: the NF_1 tells that Peisander and Hippolochus, who have just been caught by Agamemnon, are the sons of Antimachus, a very rich Trojan who had been bribed by Paris into opposing the surrender of Helen to Menelaus. These elements play a role in the speeches which follow: the two brothers promise Agamemnon that their father will give a huge ransom in return for their lives (131-5). A similar promise is made by two other suppliants (Z 46-50, K 378-81), but the two brothers are the only ones to mention their father's name (Λ 132: ἐν 'Αντιμάχοιο δόμοις, as opposed to Z 47: ἐν ἀφνειοῦ πατρός and K 378: ἔνδον). Unintentiously, they thus trigger Agamemnon's memory and sign their own death sentence. For Agamemnon, remembering the role their father had played, sternly rejects their plea (138-42). His version of Antimachus' role (141: A. had urged the Trojans to kill Menelaus) differs from that of the NF_1 (125: A. had not allowed Helen to be given back to Menelaus). Are the two versions complementary (Antimachus having suggested not to give back H. and, on top of that, to kill M.) or is Agamemnon exaggerating? We will never know, especially since our only other witness of Menelaus' (and Odysseus') visit to Troy, the Trojan Antenor, does not refer to Antimachus at all (Γ 205-24).

Φ 34-46: Lycaon meets Achilles on the battlefield and the NF_1 informs the $NeFe_1$ about an earlier confrontation between the two. Achilles had taken Lycaon captive 'from the garden of his father', had sold him to a man on Lemnus - to this same event the NF_1 refers in Ψ 746-7 - from whom Lycaon had been ransomed by a guest-friend and transported to Arisbe. Having fled from this place of refuge, he had for only eleven days enjoyed his freedom at home when a god again put him in the hands of Achilles. This time the encounter with Achilles will end fatally for him (46-7: internal prolepsis). Both Achilles and Lycaon refer to these events in their speeches. Achilles is surprised how Lycaon could have escaped from Lemnus (54-9). The perfect participle πεπερημένος (58: contrast the aorists in 40 and 78) reveals his conviction (now contradicted) that Lycaon had been sold there *once and for all*. Lycaon stresses his bad luck of being confronted with Achilles again, having just safely returned home. His emphatic mention of the height of his ransom (τρὶς τόσσα: 80, cp. in the NF_1's version a more vague πολλά: 42) seems aimed at whetting Achilles' mercantile instinct and thus persuading him to spare his life once more. Achilles' revengeful spirit, however, this time precludes such a merciful settlement. The external analepsis of 34-46 has provided the $NeFe_1$ with the necessary information to follow the exchange of speeches, understand Achilles' surprise, sympathize with Lycaon's bad luck, and all the more to notice Achilles' present bloodthirstiness. In fact, the $NeFe_1$ is better informed than the characters, knowing (in contrast to Achilles) what happened to Lycaon after he had been sold on Lemnus and (in contrast to Lycaon) that he will not survive his second encounter with Achilles.

Conclusion

Analepses and prolepses found in the simple narrator-text can be considered *surplus*-passages in comparison to the primary fabula: internal pro- and analepses present events also presented elsewhere and external pro- and analepses present information which lies outside the temporal boundaries of that primary fabula. This surplus status might account for the fact that so many of these passages have been athetized or, in the case of digressions, have been considered purely ornamental element characteristic for the "epische Breite". However, in this section I hope to have demonstrated that analepses and prolepses find their *raison d'être* in the interaction between NF_1 and $NeFe_1$: they create dramatic irony and suspense, incite pathos, elicit pity, signal the importance or symbolical value of objects, recall important information and provide background information necessary for the appreciation of following speeches.

3.3.4. Motivation and presupposition

The greater part of the interaction between NF₁ and NeFe₁ consists of the NF₁ providing his addressee with information. In this section I want to draw attention to two aspects of this process of transference of information: motivation and presupposition. By *motivation* I mean the NF₁ adding information to explain what he has just told. The term *presupposition* is used here to refer to cases where the NF₁ assumes that his addressee has certain information at his disposal.[94] On the level of the text, this assumption can manifest itself either by information being presented as knowledge shared (by NF₁ and NeFe₁) or by information being left out by the NF₁.

Motivation

One of the rare occasions where the NeFe₁ almost seems to speak, i.e. to have an active part in the interaction, is when the NF₁ asks a question which represents a question the NeFe₁ might have asked. Prince (1973: 184) gives as example from Balzac's *Le Père Goriot*:

> (54) Ce qu'il avait été? Mais peut-être avait il été employé au ministère de
> la Justice ...?

The *Iliad* offers one certain and one possible example. The certain example is X 202-4, discussed above, p. 71. The possible one is

> (55) A 8:
> τίς τ' ἄρ σφωε θεῶν ἔριδι ξυνέηκε μάχεσθαι;
> Which then of the gods brought these two together to contend
> in quarrel?

According to Ameis-H. this is "eine Frage aus der Seele des Hörers", which is triggered by ἐρίσαντε in the proem (6). I find this interpretation more attractive than to take the question as being put by the poet to the Muses (so e.g. Minton 1960: 295) or as a rhetorical question (Kirk).

Much more frequently, we find that the NF₁ anticipates a question from his addressee by providing an explanation for something just told, in the form of a γάρ-clause.[95] In these cases we are dealing with what Genette (1969: 97) aptly called "le parce que chargé de faire oublier le pourquoi".[96] Above (pp. 62-3 and n. 44) we have already seen that often a negative statement is followed by a γάρ-clause. Thus, the NF₁ anticipates the question from his NeFe₁, "*why is such or such not the case?*". Two other examples of motivating γάρ are:

(56) A 54-5 (the plague sent by Apollo has been raging for nine days):
τῇ δεκάτῃ δ' ἀγορήνδε καλέσσατο λαὸν 'Αχιλλεύς·
τῷ γὰρ ἐπὶ φρεσὶ θῆκε θεὰ λευκώλενος "Ηρη
But on the tenth day Achilles called the men to assembly,
for white-armed Hera had put it in his mind (to do so).

(57) Ψ 450-1 (the Greeks are watching a horse-race):
πρῶτος δ' 'Ιδομενεὺς Κρητῶν ἀγὸς ἐφράσαθ' ἵππους·
ἧστο γὰρ ἐκτὸς ἀγῶνος ὑπέρτατος ἐν περιωπῇ
And Idomeneus, leader of the Cretans, first spotted the
horses: for he sat outside the place of contest, very high,
at a place where he could see all round.

In (56) the question anticipated by the NF₁ is "why did Achilles rather than Agamemnon, the leader of the expedition, take the initiative for calling together the meeting?"[97] The answer given in the γάρ-clause both legitimizes and accentuates this initiative of Achilles, whose active role at this point will prove to be of decisive importance in the future course of events (see Van Erp Taalman Kip 1971: 10). In (57) the γάρ-clause answers the implied question "how could Idomeneus see the horses before the other Greeks?" Both in (56) and (57) the story might have continued after A 54 and Ψ 540, respectively, but through the addition of A 55 and Ψ 451 the NF₁, as it were halting and retracing his steps, motivates his story.[98] Often the explanation of the NF₁ does not concern the whole of the previous sentence, but only one specific element of it, e.g.

(58) B 408-9:
αὐτόματος δέ οἱ ἦλθε βοὴν ἀγαθὸς Μενέλαος·
ᾔδεε γὰρ κατὰ θυμὸν ἀδελφεὸν, ὡς ἐπονεῖτο.
and Menelaus, good at the battle-cry, came to him on his
own accord, for he knew in his heart that his brother was
in trouble.[99]

where the γάρ-clause explains αὐτόματος.

In those cases where the explanation concerns the deliberate and conscious act of a character, the motivation given *now* by the NF₁ can be said to coincide with the motivation *then* of the character itself, e.g.

(59) B 665-6 (Tlepolemus has killed a relative):
βῆ φεύγων ἐπὶ πόντον· ἀπείλησαν γὰρ οἱ ἄλλοι
υἱέες υἱωνοί τε βίης ῾Ηρακληείης.
he went away in exile over the sea: for the other sons and
grand-sons of mighty Heracles had threatened him.

Below, in section 4.1, I will go into this question more deeply.

For my conclusion I turn to a typology developed by Genette (1969: 98-9)

> Soient distingués trois types de récit:
> a) le récit vraisemblable, ou à motivation implicite, exemple: "La marquise
> demanda sa voiture et alla se promener".
> b) le récit motivé, exemple: "La marquise demanda sa voiture et se mit au
> lit, car elle était fort capricieuse" (motivation du premier degré ou motivation
> restreinte), ou encore " ... car, comme toutes les marquises, elle était fort
> capricieuse" (motivation du second degré, ou motivation généralisante).
> c) le récit arbitraire, exemple: "La marquise demanda sa voiture et se mit
> au lit".

In view of the many motivating γάρ-clauses in the Iliadic narrator-text - and I have not even taken into account causal connections through δέ as e.g. in B 589-90 or causal participles as e.g. in Δ 23 - I conclude that the *Iliad* can be qualified as a "récit motivé". This same conclusion had been reached by Braswell (1971: 25) on account of his analysis of Iliadic digressions

> ... the whole *Iliad* is a long catena of causes, so that at any stage of the action
> we can almost always find an immediate cause for a given event ... the poet
> constantly supplies reasons, because he has to tell a story and his audience
> will expect to know why a given character acts as he does in a particular
> situation. The source of Homer's causal reasoning lies then in the demands of
> his narrative art.

In my conclusion to this section as a whole I will go into the relevance of this status of the *Iliad* as a "récit motivé".

Presupposition

Above in section 3.3.1 I have on occasion mentioned the NeFe₁'s general knowledge of the world and 'historical' knowledge. These two categories of knowledge can be called extra-textual in contradistinction to contextual or intra-textual knowledge. Whereas intra-textual knowledge is based on information provided by the NF₁, extra-textual knowledge is presupposed by the NF₁ to be there and is at times reactivated. I will now discuss some more examples of presupposition by the NF₁, starting with cases of *shared knowledge*.

The most important group in this category consists of the similes. Broadly speaking, similes are inserted by the NF₁ to help the NeFe₁ to visualize what is told (for a more precise analysis of the function(s) of similes see below section

5.2). As such, they must refer to things which are familiar to the $NeFe_1$:

Neben den heroischen Gegenstand tritt hier (sc. in the similes, IdJ) ergänzend
sein Widerspiel in der Welt des Alltags: neben das einzigartig fremde Geschehen
die Folie eines gewohnten und vertrauten Vorgangs ... (Fränkel 1976: 44)

More specifically, the familiarity of the Homeric similes takes the form of permanent facts, i.e. the similes refer to things which take place and have taken
place repeatedly and, therefore, can be expected to be known to the $NeFe_1$. This
permanent or recurrent character of the facts expressed in the Homeric similes
is marked syntactically by:

1. the presence of the particle τε, and/or

2. (in those cases where the simile contains a finite verb-form) the use of
present (seldom perfect) indicative, gnomic aorist and/or distributive-iterative
subjunctive.[100]

At this point it ought to be realized, once again, that there is a fundamental
difference between NF_1 and $NeFe_1$ on the one hand and historical poet and
hearer/reader on the other. Through the syntactical features just mentioned
(most of) the Homeric similes are characterized as permanent or *omnitemporal*
(Lyons 1977: 680), i.e. without exact temporal deixis. Within the world of NF_1
and $NeFe_1$ (which is itself not clearly fixed in time) the things referred to in
the similes are familiar, because known to have taken place repeatedly. To what
extent the similes reflect the world of the historical poet remains, to me, a
matter of conjecture.[101] As regards the historical hearer/reader, finally, here we
are dealing with a constantly changing factor. Natural phenomena, animal behaviour or psychological facts (e.g. the experience of a dreamer: X 199-201) are as
familiar to us, 20th century readers, as they were to the historical hearer of
Homer's time and similes describing these phenomena are for us also omnitemporal.
However, technical procedures (e.g. women weighing wool for spinning: M 433-5
or the process of tanning: P 389-93) for us belong to a historical past and similes
describing these procedures are for us *not* omnitemporal.

There are still other passages in the simple narrator-text, apart from the
similes, which describe permanent facts: 'typical' descriptions (i.e. descriptions
which furnish general or characteristic details), general truths and geographic
or ethnographic facts.[102] e.g.

(60) Φ 264:
       θεοὶ δέ τε φέρτεροι ἀνδρῶν
       for gods are more powerful than men

(61) Ψ 655 (Achilles offers as a prize a mule)
ἑξετέ᾽ ἀδμήτην, ἥ τ᾽ ἀλγίστη δαμάσασθαι
six years old, unbroken, which is most difficult to be tamed.

As last category of shared knowledge one could think of the four passages where the NF₁ gives an alternative name for a part of the body (E 305-6), constellations (Σ 487, Χ 29) and a bird (Ω 315-6). As in the case of the φασί-passages (see Appendix III), the NF₁ here invokes anonymous spokesmen (καλέουσι 'they call it'). Rank (1951: 109) has suggested that the alternative names are added as clarifications and possibly derive from popular speech (according to Kleinlogel 1981: 267 from "Fachterminologie"). If they really are supposed to function as clarifications, they must refer to names familiar to the NeFe₁, in short to knowledge shared.

In other cases the assumption of the NF₁ that the NeFe₁ knows certain facts, leads to the *suppression* in the text of information. The NF₁ presupposes the main characters to be familiar to the NeFe₁. They are nowhere introduced nor is their biographical background filled in[103] - this in contrast to the minor characters or "kleine Kämpfer" who do receive an introduction, or, rather, an epilogue. Occasionally main characters are given some sort of introduction, but then always as a preparation for an important speech they are going to make, e.g. Nestor in Α 247-52 (see further below section 6.1). In the same way the NeFe₁ is supposed to be informed about the main events concerning the Trojan war, its cause, main events and ending. This presupposed knowledge of the NeFe₁ about characters and events is unusual ("le narrataire ne sait absolument rien des événements ou des personnages dont on lui parle", Prince 1973: 181) and is to be considered 'historical' knowledge, acquired through hearing traditional stories or songs. Just as the NF₁ has been given the shape of a professional singer, his addressee is given the shape of a regular recipient of traditional songs.

We may ask whether the NeFe₁ really always has the knowledge the NF₁ presupposes him to have: already Aristotle (*Poetics* 1451b) said τὰ γνώριμα ὀλίγοις γνώριμά ἐστιν ('the known things are only known to a few'). A clear example of knowledge the NF₁ presupposes, but which his NeFe₁ simply can not have concerns the Iliadic scenery. Both Elliger (1975: 29-102) and Andersson (1976: 15-37) reached the same conclusion

> fast immer tut der Dichter so, als sei dem Hörer die Gegend bereits vertraut, als brauche er nur auf Bekanntes hinzuweisen ... (Elliger 1975: 52).

and

> Homer's method is to provide the reader with a large, blank canvas, on which,
> as time goes on, he enters a few items here and there, more or less at random.
> There is no general design on which we may rely in following the progress of
> the narrative. As a result, we are occasionally confronted with the presupposition
> of knowledge we do not have (Andersson 1976: 24).[104]

According to Latacz (1985: 69-70), what the poet does is not so much presuppose
knowledge as stimulate the hearer/reader's imagination.[105] A third possibility (cp.
Vivante 1970: 16-8) is that the NF_1 purposefully restricts himself to "a few essen-
tial outlines", wanting to concentrate on the action rather than on the surrounding
scenery. Recently, Thornton (1984: 150-63) has made yet another suggestion,
which I consider most attractive, viz. that "most of the landmarks are constantly
associated with a particular sort of situation or with a particular party or person
in the poem". Thus the landmarks have a symbolic, associative function and certainly are not used "more or less at random" as Andersson suggested. To give
one of Thornton's examples: the oak-tree near the Scaean gates (mentioned by
the NF_1 in E 693, Z 237, H 22.60, Λ 170, Φ 549, by Achilles in I 354) is "associated with safety for the Trojan troops, but also with a foreboding of evil
for Hector" (152).

Conclusion

The aspects of transference of information discussed in this section in a way
are in tension with each other: motivation means that the NF_1 adds, presupposition
that he suppresses information. It appears that the information suppressed by
the NF_1 concerns the main characters and the general outline of the story (which
is supposed to be known to the $NeFe_1$ from tradition), but that many other
events, details of his own story and actions of characters are motivated. This is
not only yet another indication for the high degree of rhetoric exercized by the
NF_1, but also seems to confirm at a narratological level the innovative power of
the poet of the *Iliad*, as described e.g. by Heubeck (1978: 13)

> It is not enough to say that Homer further developed traditional epic and excelled
> his predecessors in the art of it. He confronted traditional epic with his own
> new work - the realization of a fundamentally and completely different conception
> of epic poetry.

3.4. Summary

Ɪn this chapter we became acquainted with one of the presentators of the Homeric *Iliad*, the NF_1, and his addressee, the $NeFe_1$. It has turned out that they are both external, i.e. do not belong to the world of the characters: the presentation of the story follows after the events have taken place. Despite this temporal gap between moment of presentation and events presented, the NF_1 claims to give a reliable account by invoking the Muses as eyewitnesses. The analysis of the relationship between NF_1 and Muses in terms of "doppelte Motivation" has further revealed him to be a self-conscious presentator in the shape of a professional singer. It has been shown that the $NeFe_1$ is supposed to have traditional/ 'historical' knowledge concerning main events and characters and, therefore, to be a regular listener to traditional songs.

Apart from introducing and defining the Iliadic NF_1 and $NeFe_1$, this chapter has largely been devoted to the analysis of the interaction between these two poles of communication in the simple narrator-text. This interaction takes place implicitly most of the time, viz. with the NF_1 and $NeFe_1$ remaining 'imperceptible'. Here the narratological model set out in chapter 2, with its ternary structure, has proved to be a valuable analytical tool: for it is in particular the discrepancies between the fabula and story layers which bring to light (on the level of the text) the rhetoric of the NF_1: internal pro- and analepses mean that the order of the fabula is changed; negative statements present a (positive) event of the fabula in a negative form; non-events, *if not*-situations and external pro- and analepses involve extra narrative information in comparison to the fabula; presupposition discloses gaps in the fabula. I submit that enough examples have been adduced to disprove that in the *Iliad* "the story tells itself" and to argue Booth's point - which was merely stated by him, not argued - that this narrative is a clear instance of the rhetoric of fiction.

Now what about this Homeric rhetoric, what is it aimed at? Partly it concerns the presentator himself: the NF_1 claims to be a reliable (Muse-invocation B 484-93, *if not*-situations which describe the real, i.e. not against fate, course of events), accomplished (Muse-invocation A 1-7) and fascinating presentator. Manifestations of this last skill are: *if not*-situations describing near death or defeat, suspense created through negations with prospective scope, internal prolepses, external analepses describing the origin of objects, negative statements contradicting the expectations of the $NeFe_1$.

Most of the NF₁'s rhetoric, however, concerns the characters. The NF₁ aims at arousing certain emotions in his addressee concerning these characters. Which are these emotions? Let me start with quoting Plato on this subject, who himself must many times have heard the Homeric poems recited and who makes one of his characters, the rhapsode Ion, say

> Plato *Ion* 535 C + E:
> ... when I relate a tale of woe, my eyes are filled with tears; and when it is of fear or awe, my hair stands on end with terror, and my heart leaps ... at such moments I see them (audience) crying and turning awe-struck eyes upon me and yielding to the amazement of my tale. (transl. L.R.M. Lamb)

Recently Macleod mentioned (1983: 12) "(1) glory, (2) pity, and (3) consolation" as "three of the major themes of Homer's poetics." Drawing on the results of the narratological analyses carried out in this chapter - which dealt with the simple narrator-text only, not with the poem as a whole, on which Ion and Macleod's remarks are based - I arrive at more or less the same emotions: 1) admiration and 2) pity.

Ad 1: the emphasis put in recent times on "tragic form and feeling in the *Iliad*" somewhat distracts from the *encomiastic* nature of the Homeric epics. The NF₁ tells of, and thereby celebrates, the glorious deeds of heroes of the past, who are superior to the people of his own and the NeFe₁'s time (cp. Bowra 1964: 4, Fränkel 1976: 38). Thus, we have seen how the short Muse-invocations, stressing the force of the superlative they all contain, certain second person verb-forms, passages with an anonymous focalizer and certain *if not*-situations are meant to arouse the NeFe₁'s admiration. Sometimes this admiration mingles with fear and becomes awe. All the same, I think that fear is a less dominant factor in the *Iliad* than in tragedy (cp. Aristotle, *Poetics* 1449b, 1453b, who mentions 'fear' and 'pity' as the main emotions of drama). There is, of course, suspense, but this means that one fears for a character, not for oneself.

Ad 2. Aristotle's qualification of the *Iliad* as παθητικόν (*Poetics* 1459b) has been amply illustrated by other scholars (see above section 1.2.1., p. 20) and I restrict myself here to summing up passages discussed in this chapter which create pathos, dramatic irony, in short are meant to elicit pity: (certain) passages with second person verb-forms, (certain) non-events, (certain) *if not*-situations and internal prolepses.

Although this chapter mainly concerned the NF₁ and NeFe₁, I have at times also paid attention to the characters: their expectations (contradicted by negative statements of the NF₁), anxieties (expressed in speeches occurring in the context of *if not*-situations) and (unjustified) optimism (νήπιος-passages). Here we have traced an important difference between NF_1 and $NeFe_1$ on the one hand and characters on the other: the latter are actively and emotionally engaged in the events, which for them are real, whereas the NF_1 and $NeFe_1$ are ultimately 'onlookers' (focalizers and focalizees), who at the most are emotionally moved - and here I think of the $NeFe_1$ rather than the NF_1, who does not necessarily have himself to feel the emotions he elicits - , but are not directly engaged. This difference will be further elaborated on in the following chapters.

4. COMPLEX NARRATOR-TEXT (EMBEDDED FOCALIZATION)

> "Homer reveals the thoughts of his
> characters indirectly, that is, in other
> ways than by the *ipsissima verba*, more
> than is generally recognized" (Bassett,
> *The Poetry of Homer*)

This chapter is devoted to the narrative situation of complex narrator-text or embedded focalization, $NF_1[F_2C_x]$. There is embedded (or secondary) focalization when the NF_1 represents in the narrator-text the focalization of one of the characters. In other words, the NF_1 temporarily hands over focalization (but not narration) to one of the characters, who functions as F_2 and, thereby, takes a share in the presentation of the story. Recipient of the F_2's focalization is a secondary focalizee (Fe_2). One example may illustrate right away the relevance of distinguishing this narrative situation of embedded focalization:

(1) H 311-2:
Αἴαντ' αὖθ' ἑτέρωθεν ἐϋκνήμιδες ᾿Αχαιοὶ
εἰς Ἀγαμέμνονα δῖον ἄγον, κεχαρηότα <u>νίκη</u>
On the other side the well-greaved Greeks led Ajax, happy
on account of his <u>victory</u>, to illustrious Agamemnon

At first sight νίκη in H 312 is problematic, since heralds had in 274-5 ended the duel between Hector and Ajax before one of the two had won. Commentators have tried to explain νίκη by pointing out that Hector had already been hit twice by Ajax and had been the first to suggest a peaceful settlement (bT-scholia,

Ameis-H.), in other words that Ajax "had certainly been superior, if not strictly victorious" (Willcock). I suggest that νίκη, as object of κεχαρηότα, represents the focalization of Ajax, who rejoices about what he *interprets* as a victory.

In the first section of this chapter (4.1) a general survey will be given of complex narrator-text in the *Iliad*. I start (4.1.1) with cases of *explicit* embedded focalization, viz. those introduced by verbs of 1) perceiving, 2) thinking/feeling etc. 3) speaking (for these three main categories of embedded focalization see above chapter 2, p. 38). In 4.1.2 examples of *implicit* embedded focalization, i.e. cases where an introductory verb is lacking, are discussed. The other two sections contain two special studies involving embedded focalization: in 4.2 I discuss what I call *assimilated* comparisons and similes: whereas comparisons and similes normally are the domain of NF_1 and $NeFe_1$ alone, in this group of comparisons and similes emotions of characters who function in the context of the comparison or simile as F_2, are (also) represented. In 4.3 I return to a problem which we have met in chapter 1, viz. the interpretation of evaluative or affective words. Here the distinction between NF_1 on the one hand and characters functioning as F_2 on the other will prove to be useful from a methodological point of view.

4.1. Explicit and implicit embedded focalization
4.1.1. Explicit: perceptions, thoughts/emotions, indirect speech

Perceptions[1]
Explicit embedded focalization involving the perceptions of characters can be triggered off in the *Iliad* by the following verbs: (see, look at) νοέω, ὁράω, δέρκομαι, σκέπτομαι, λεύσσω, δοκεύω, φράζομαι, γιγνώσκω; (look with wonder, admire) θηέομαι, θαυμάζω; (appear) φαίνομαι, ἰνδάλλομαι, εἴδομαι; (hear) ἀΐω, ἀκούω, πεύθομαι; (not remain unnoticed) οὐ λανθάνειν.[2]

The content of the embedded focalization is formed by the syntactic object of these verbs of perceiving, sometimes also by a subsequent main clause (example 4), e.g.

(2) H 444:
　　　　θηεῦντο μέγα ἔργον Ἀχαιῶν χαλκοχιτώνων.
　　　　they (the gods) looked in wonder/with admiration at the
　　　　great work of the bronze-clad Greeks.

(3) H 307-9:

τοὶ δ' ἐχάρησαν,
ὡς εἶδον ζωόν τε καὶ ἀρτεμέα προσιόντα
Αἴαντος προφυγόντα μένος καὶ χεῖρας ἀάπτους·

And they (the Trojans) rejoiced, when they saw him (Hector)
approach, alive and unharmed, having escaped the vigour
and the irresistible hands of Ajax.

(4) X 463-5:

τὸν δὲ νόησεν
ἑλκόμενον πρόσθεν πόλιος· ταχέες δέ μιν ἵπποι
ἕλκον ἀκηδέστως κοίλας ἐπὶ νῆας 'Αχαιῶν.

And she (Andromache) saw him (Hector) being dragged along
before the city: and fast horses dragged him ruthlessly to
the hollow ships of the Greeks.

In (2) the admiration/wonder of the gods is reflected in μέγα;[3] in (3) the influence of the Trojans as F_2 on the presentation of the story appears from an
emotionally coloured word like ἀάπτους ('irresistible'), just as in (4) ἀκηδέστως
('ruthlessly') reflects Andromache's interpretation of what she sees.[4]

Another influence of a F_2 on the presentation is when we find an indirect
reference instead of a proper name, e.g.

(5) K 524-5:

θηεῦντο δὲ μέρμερα ἔργα,
ὅσσ' <u>ἄνδρες</u> ῥέξαντες ἔβαν κοίλας ἐπὶ νῆας.

And they looked in amazament at all the baneful deeds
which <u>the men</u> had perpetrated before returning to the
hollow ships.

(6) O 422-3:

Ἕκτωρ δ' ὡς ἐνόησεν <u>ἀνεψιὸν</u> ὀφθαλμοῖσιν
ἐν κονίῃσι πεσόντα νεὸς προπάροιθε μελαίνης

And as Hector saw <u>his nephew</u> fallen in the dust in front
of the black ship

In (5) the NF₁ uses 'the men' instead of the proper names 'Odysseus' and
'Diomedes', because the Trojans (F_2) do not know who are responsible for the
massacre. In (6) the use of 'nephew' rather than the proper name (Kaletor) marks
the fact that it is Hector who is focalizing. The effect is to stress the kinship-
relation between him and the victim (cp. Y 419-20 where κασίγνητον ('his
brother') is added to the name Polydorus).[5] It was Uspenskij (1975: 29-41) who
called attention to the relevance of denomination for the analysis of point of
view. One of the examples he gives is from Dostojevski's *Brothers Karamazov*:
the character Dmitrij Karamazov is alternately referred to as "brother

Dmitrij", "brother Dmitrij Fedorovich", "Mitja", "Dmitrij", "Miten'ka" and "Dmitrij Fedorovich", depending on who is speaking or focalizing. Three more Iliadic examples of interesting denomination in embedded focalization are: βασιλῆα (Π 660: 'their king') instead of 'Sarpedon', with the Lycians as F_2,[6] ἡνιόχοιο (P 427: 'their driver') instead of Patroclus, with Achilles' horses (!) as F_2, and τὸν (Ω 702: 'him') instead of 'Hector', with Cassandra as F_2.[7] Occasionally we find the reversed situation, viz. a proper name where an indefinite pronoun would be expected:

(7) Γ 191-2 (cp. 225-6):
Δεύτερον αὖτ' Ὀδυσῆα ἰδὼν ἐρέειν' ὁ γεραιός·
"εἴπ' ἄγε μοι καὶ τόνδε, φίλον τέκος, ὅς τις ὅδ' ἐστί"
Secondly, seeing <u>Odysseus</u>, the old man (Priam) asked: "Come
on, tell me also about this man, dear child, who he is"

In Γ 191 (≅ 225) the NF_1 can be said to 'intrude upon' Priam's embedded focalization (ἰδὼν), since from 192 it appears that Priam does not know whom he is seeing. The NF_1 inserts Odysseus' (in Γ 225 Ajax') name, in order to enable the $NeFe_1$ to appreciate more fully Priam's descriptions of these two Greeks in the following speeches (Γ 193-8 and 226-7). A comparable but somewhat more complicated case is

(8) Π 278-82:
Τρῶες δ' ὡς εἴδοντο <u>Μενοιτίου ἄλκιμον υἱόν</u>,
..., πᾶσιν ὀρίνθη θυμός, ἐκίνηθεν δὲ φάλαγγες,
ἐλπόμενοι παρὰ ναῦφι ποδώκεα Πηλεΐωνα
μηνιθμὸν μὲν ἀπορρῖψαι, φιλότητα δ' ἑλέσθαι
But when the Trojans saw <u>the valiant son of Menoetius</u>
(Patroclus), ..., the mind of all began to waver, thinking
that by the ships the swift-footed son of Peleus (Achilles)
had renounced his wrath and opted for friendship.

In Λ 796-801 (≅ Π 40-3) Nestor had suggested to Patroclus that he put on Achilles' armour, in order that the Trojans, taking him to be Achilles, would stop fighting. The panic-stricken reaction of the Trojans in Π 280 suggests that the trick is successful and that the Trojans really think Patroclus is Achilles.[8] The mention of Patroclus instead of Achilles in 278 is then due to the intervention of the NF_1 and meant solely for the communication with the $NeFe_1$. The $NeFe_1$ knew about the trick from the beginning and in his presentation of the event the NF_1 does not need to maintain the same charade as that taking place in the story itself.[9] Again, in Π 420 the proper name Πατρόκλοιο derives from the NF₁ and not from the F₂ Sarpedon, who in the speech following upon his perception says that he does not know the identity of 'this man' (τοῦδ' ἀνέρος: 423-5).[10] Note that Sarpedon does not take the man to be Achilles: in other words, we are already half-way towards Patroclus' démasqué, which is completed when Glaucus and Hector in their speeches refer to him with his own name (Π 543 and 859).

The perception-passages are all very short (rarely longer than two verses) and mostly do not contain new information, but repeat information already given by the NF₁, e.g.

(9) Λ 581-3:
   τὸν δ' ὡς οὖν ἐνόησεν 'Αλέξανδρος θεοειδὴς
   τεῦχε' ἀπαινύμενον 'Απισάονος, αὐτίκα τόξον
   ἕλκετ' ἐπ' Εὐρυπύλῳ
   But as soon as godlike Alexander saw him (Eurypylus) stripping off the
   armour of Apisaon, he immediately bent his bow against Eurypylus

which repeats

(10) 580:
   Εὐρύπυλος δ' ἐπόρουσε καὶ αἴνυτο τεύχε' ἀπ' ὤμων
   Eurypylus rushed at him and stripped the armour from his
   (Apisaon's) shoulders[11]

I draw attention to the presence in (9) and in many other perception-passages of the (backward-referring) particle οὖν.[12]
Sometimes the perception-passage does contain new information, e.g.

(11) Φ 49-51:
   τὸν δ' ὡς οὖν ἐνόησε ποδάρκης δῖος 'Αχιλλεὺς
   γυμνόν, ἄτερ κόρυθός τε καὶ ἀσπίδος, οὐδ' ἔχεν ἔγχος,
   ἀλλὰ τὰ μέν ῥ' ἀπὸ πάντα χαμαὶ βάλε
   And when Achilles saw him (Lycaon) unarmed, without his
   helmet and shield, nor did he hold his spear in his hands,
   but he had dropped all these things on the ground

which describes more than the NF₁ had said about Lycaon in 35: ἐκ ποταμοῦ φεύγοντι.[13]

The importance of perception-passages seems to lie not so much in making clear *what* a character sees, but in signalling *that* a character perceives something. An analysis of a longer passage may illustrate this:

Δ 134-40: the NF₁ tells how the arrow shot by Pandarus penetrates Menelaus' girdle, corslet and mitra, scratches his skin, and how blood streams out of the wound.

149-50: Agamemnon (F₂) and Menelaus (F₂) see the blood stream out of the wound (149 repeats information of 140) and shiver.

151-2 : Menelaus (F₂) sees that the arrow's string and the barb are outside his body (151 contains the same information as 139, but expressed differently)[14] and he regains his composure.

155-82: Agamemnon (NF₂) holds a pessimistic speech.

184-7 : Menelaus (NF₂) now tells what he has seen in 151 and what the NF₁ had told the NeFe₁ in 134-9, viz. that his girdle, corslet and mitra have sufficiently slowed down the arrow so as not to become fatal to him.

We see how perceptions form the hinges of the story: something happens, characters perceive it, react emotionally and evaluate what they have seen in a speech. Taking into account all perception-passages I have found that they fulfil one or more of the following three functions with regard to the NeFe₁:

1. to signify the emotional effect of events on characters.[15] The emotions are either mentioned in the nearby simple narrator-text (e.g. ῥίγησεν in Δ 148.150)[16] and/or expressed in the complex narrator-text itself (e.g. ἀκηδέστως in example 4).

2. to indicate what induces a character to come into action: in example (9) the sight of Eurypylus stripping off a compatriot's armour makes Paris tend his bow at him.[17] Also, three important phases in Patroclus' existence as an Iliadic character are triggered by a perception: Λ 599 (Achilles spots Nestor and Machaon), O 395 (Patroclus sees the Trojans rush at the Greek walls) and Π 127 (Achilles sees that Trojan fire has reached the Greek ships). Again, the majority of divine interventions follows upon a perception of human affairs, e.g. Π 17-20 and numerous *if not*-situations.

3. often the action of a character brought about by a perception is of a verbal nature (direct speech). Since the narrative situation of complex narrator-text can be considered an intermediary stage between simple narrator-text and character-text, it is eminently suited to form the transition from one narrative situation to another, as e.g. in Ε 239-50:

Ε 239-40	simple narrator-text:	the NF₁ tells how Pandarus and Aeneas head for Diomedes.
241	complex narrator-text:	(the NF₁ tells how) Sthenelus (F₂) spots Pandarus and Aeneas.
243-50	character-text:	(the NF₁ tells how) Sthenelus (NF₂) describes to Diomedes the two heroes he sees and advises him to retreat.[18]

The close relationship between perception-passage and direct speech is confirmed by the fact that very often the character refers in his/her speech with a demonstrative pronoun (ὅδε, οὗτος, seldom ἐκεῖνος) to the person s/he has just seen, e.g.

> (12) Λ 347 (Diomedes has perceived Hector and says to Odysseus):
> "νῶϊν δὴ <u>τόδε</u> πῆμα κυλίνδεται, ὄβριμος Ἕκτωρ"
> "Towards the two of us now rolls <u>this</u> evil, the mighty Hector"[19]

Apart from these functions pertaining to the NeFe₁, the perception-passages also offer the NF₁ a handy expedient

4. to bring on stage characters necessary for the story:[20] e.g. in Γ 16-20 Paris steps forward and is seen by Menelaus, who jumps from his chariot. When Paris, seeing Menelaus appear in the front line, retraces his steps, this is seen by Hector, who rebukes him. In this way three important characters are introduced by seeing each other.[21] This is one of the Homeric devices which show a considerable subtlety in the art of story-telling. The characters are not only introduced as individuals, but more importantly, in their relationship to, and relevance for each other.

It is to be noted that it is the character who sees who is (re)introduced, whereas the character who is seen is already there. This is in accordance with the principle mentioned above, viz. that perception-passages seldom contain new information. The usual procedure in drama or novels is the other way around: persons already on the stage see another person approach and thus announce his/her entrance on the stage, e.g.

> (13) Aristophanes, *Lysistrata* 831 (Lysistrata speaks):
> Ἄνδρ', ἄνδρ' ὁρῶ προσιόντα παραπεπληγμένον
> a man, I see a man approach, stricken with desire

The entrance of the man follows in 845.[22]

Another type of embedded focalization, closely related to the perception-passages, which occurs with some frequency in the *Iliad* is that triggered off by verbs of <u>finding</u>: εὑρίσκω, κιχάνω, ἔτετμε, ἦλθε ἐπί. These find-passages form part of arrival-scenes and although a verb of perceiving is lacking, it is clearly to be understood that what follows is described as seen by the character who is arriving: "Der Dichter begleitet den Ankommenden, von diesem her ist alles gesehen" (Arend 1933: 28-34).[23] An example:

(14) Ω 472-6:

ἐν δέ μιν αὐτὸν
εὖρ', ἕταροι δ' ἀπάνευϑε καϑῆατο· τὼ δὲ δύ' οἴω,
ἥρως Αὐτομέδων τε καὶ Ἄλκιμος, ὄζος Ἄρηος,
ποίπνυον παρεόντε· νέον δ' ἀπέληγεν ἐδωδῆς
ἔσϑων καὶ πίνων· ἔτι καὶ παρέκειτο τράπεζα.

And he (Priam) found him (Achilles) inside (his tent), but
his friends sat apart. Two alone, hero Automedon and Alcimus,
scion of Ares, were bustling around in his presence. And
he had only just stopped eating and drinking: and the table
still stood by.

The find-passage describes what Priam sees when he enters Achilles' tent. Especially the detail of the table still standing there, is, I think, an indication of
Priam's perception: this 'tells' him that Achilles has just stopped eating.[24]

An important difference between perception-passages and find-passages is
that the former describe events, the latter situations: on average find-passages
are longer, they often contain a main clause with its verb(s) in the imperfect
and/or pluperfect, e.g.

(15) Ζ 321-4:

τὸν δ' εὖρ' ἐν ϑαλάμῳ περικαλλέα τεύχε' ἕποντα,
ἀσπίδα καὶ ϑώρηκα, καὶ ἀγκύλα τόξ' ἀφόωντα·
'Αργείη δ' 'Ελένη μετ' ἄρα δμωῇσι γυναιξὶν
ἧστο καὶ ἀμφιπόλοισιν περικλυτὰ ἔργα κέλευε.

And he (Hector) found him (Paris) in his bedroom busy
with his very beautiful armour, his shield and corslet, and
turning in his hands his curved bow. Argive Helen was sitting
amongst her servant women and giving them instructions
for their illustrious works.[25]

As a consequence of their greater length, the embedded focalization in find-
passages is not always maintained consistently throughout the whole passage. In
example (14) the proper names of Achilles' servants (Automedon and Alcimus),
which are not likely to be known to the focalizer Priam, must derive from the
NF$_1$, who intervenes as in examples (7) and (8) above. In the following two
examples the NF$_1$ adds information for the sake of his addressee, which is either
irrelevant (16) or imperceptible (17) to the characters who are focalizing:

(16) Ι 186-8:
τὸν δ' εὗρον φρένα τερπόμενον φόρμιγγι λιγείη,
καλῇ δαιδαλέῃ, ἐπὶ δ' ἀργύρεον ζυγὸν ἦεν,
τὴν ἄρετ' ἐξ ἐνάρων, πόλιν Ἠετίωνος ὀλέσσας
And they found him (Achilles) delighting his mind with his
clear-toned lyre, beautiful, artfully wrought, and upon it
was a silver bridge. This lyre he had taken from the spoils,
after destroying the city of Eetion

(17) Ω 166-8 (Iris found the whole household of Priam weeping):
θυγατέρες δ' ἀνὰ δώματ' ἰδὲ νυοὶ ὠδύροντο,
τῶν μιμνησκόμεναι, οἳ δὴ πολέες τε καὶ ἐσθλοὶ
χερσὶν ὑπ' Ἀργείων κέατο ψυχὰς ὀλέσαντες.
the daughters and daughters-in-law were lamenting in the
palace, remembering those who, many and brave, lay dead
having lost their lives at the hands of the Greeks.[26]

The phenomenon that a NF₁ adds elements of his own or intrudes upon embedded focalization is not restricted to the Homeric epics. Here is an example from a novel:

(18) Th. Hardy, *Tess of the D'Urbervilles* (Tess is F₂):

The warm red-brick lodge came first in sight ... Far behind the bright-hued corner of the house, ..., stretched the soft azure landscape of the Chase, a truly venerable track of forestland, one of the few remaining woodlands in England, of almost primeval date, wherein Druidical mistletoe was still found on aged oaks...

The information contained in the underlined passage cannot derive from the uneducated country-girl Tess, who had never before left home. It must have been added by the NF₁, who also on other occasions displays an antiquarian interest.

I return to the Iliadic find-passages: what is their function? They do not serve any of the four functions mentioned above for the perception-passages: they do not in themselves cause some new action to start and when they are followed by direct speech, the speaking character only rarely refers to the situation s/he has found.[27] Occasionally there is even a discrepancy between situation and speech: e.g. in Ε 794-5 Athena finds Diomedes 'cooling his wound', but in the ensuing speech (800-13) she asks why he is not fighting, without mentioning the wound at all. Yet, find-passages do contain - in contradistinction to perception-passages - new, at least for the NeFe₁, information and their functions seem to be to describe the setting or background for the ensuing scene (example

110

14 and cp. Macleod ad Ω 472-6), to evoke an atmosphere (example 16, 17) or to characterize a character (womanizer Paris in 15).

Thoughts/emotions

Explicit embedded focalization involving the thoughts/emotions of characters can be triggered off in the *Iliad* by the following verbs: (know, recognize) οἶδα, γιγνώσκω; (remember, think of) μιμνήσκομαι, οὐ λήθομαι; (think, deem, plan) φημί, φρονέω, μήδομαι, μητιάω, οἴομαι; (ponder, consider) μερμηρίζω, ὁρμαίνω, δίζω; (seem) εἴδομαι, φαίνομαι, δοάσσατο; (be angry) ἐπιμηνίω, χολόομαι, χώομαι; (be glad) χαίρω, γηθέω; (feel sorrow) ἄχνυμαι, ἄχθομαι, ἄχος πύκασε/γένετο; (want, aspire, be eager) ἐθέλω, βούλομαι, ἵεμαι, λιλαίομαι, μέμονα, μενοινάω, μενεαίνω, λελίημαι, τιτύσκομαι, θυμὸς ἀνῆκε, ἀνώγει; (fear) περιδείδω, ἔχε τρόμος; (hate) μισέω; (miss) ποθέω; (think, hope) ἔλπομαι; (regard, honour) αἰδέομαι, τίω; (shrink from doing) ὀκνέω; (dare) τολμάω, ἔτλην.

The content of the embedded focalization is formed by the syntactic object of these verbs, e.g.

(19) N 386-7: ὁ δὲ ἵετο θυμῷ ᾿Ιδομενῆα βαλεῖν
And he longed in his heart to hit Idomeneus

(20) E 433 (Diomedes attacked Aeneas):
γινώσκων, ὃ οἱ αὐτὸς ὑπείρεχε χεῖρας ᾿Απόλλων.
(although) knowing that Apollo himself was holding his hands above him (Aeneas).

(21) E 298 (Aeneas rushes at Pandarus' body):
δείσας μή πώς οἱ ἐρυσαίατο νεκρὸν ᾿Αχαιοί.
afraid that the Greeks might anyhow drag the body away from him.

(22) N 455-7:
Δηΐφοβος δὲ διάνδιχα μερμήριξεν,
ἤ τινά που Τρώων ἑταρίσσαιτο μεγαθύμων
ἂψ ἀναχωρήσας, ἤ πειρήσαιτο καὶ οἶος.
And Deiphobus hesitated between two alternatives, whether he should go back and seek the company of one of the other great-hearted Trojans or whether he should make a try on his own.[28]

Like the perception-passages discussed above, most thoughts/emotions-passages are very short. Only occasionally do we find a longer passage, e.g.

(23) Ω 4-9:

κλαῖε φίλου ἑτάρου μεμνημένος, ...
Πατρόκλου ποθέων ἀνδροτῆτά τε καὶ μένος ἠΰ,
ἠδ' ὁπόσα τολύπευσε σὺν αὐτῷ καὶ πάθεν ἄλγεα,
ἀνδρῶν τε πτολέμους ἀλεγεινά τε κύματα πείρων

But Achilles continued weeping, remembering his dear companion ... yearning for the manliness and valiant vigour of Patroclus, and all the actions he had seen to the end and the hardships he had suffered with him, experiencing wars with men and grievous waves.

The influence of Achilles as F_2 on the presentation emerges from emotional expressions like τολύπευσε, πάθεν ἄλγεα, ἀλεγεινά.[29] Whereas here Achilles' grief over the loss of Patroclus is presented in embedded focalization, in Τ 315-32 Achilles had expressed it himself in character-text (cp. Τ 315: φίλταθ' ἑτάρων and 321: σῇ ποθῇ).

Embedded focalization can also take the form of final clauses (24) and certain indirect (deliberative) questions (25), e.g.

(24) Τ 39 (Thetis poured ambrosia and nectar through Patroclus' nostrils):

ἵνα οἱ χρὼς ἔμπεδος εἴη.

in order that his flesh would remain intact.[30]

(25) Γ 316-7:

κλήρους ἐν κυνέῃ χαλκήρεϊ πάλλον ἑλόντες,
ὁππότερος δὴ πρόσθεν ἀφείη χάλκεον ἔγχος.

having taken the lots, they shook them in the bronze helmet (to decide) which one of the two would hurl his bronze spear first.[31]

In the case of example (24) Thetis herself had just before declared that she intended to preserve Patroclus' body:

(26) Τ 33:

αἰεὶ τῷ γ' ἔσται χρὼς ἔμπεδος, ἢ καὶ ἀρείων.

and forever his flesh will remain intact, or even better.[32]

Causal clauses (introduced by γάρ, ἐπεί, ὅτι, οὕνεκα, ὅ)[33] are more difficult to analyze as regards their presentation. In section 3.3.4 I discussed γάρ-clauses containing explanations given by the NF_1 to his addressee. We saw that in certain cases the explanation of the NF_1 *now* (at the moment of narration) coincides with the motive of the character *then* (at the moment of action). I now go into this question in more detail:

(27) Ψ 137 (Achilles held Patroclus' head):
ἀχνύμενος· ἕταρον γὰρ ἀμύμονα πέμπ᾽ Ἄϊδόσδε.
grieving, for he was accompanying his excellent companion
on his way to Hades' house.

(28) N 460-1:
αἰεὶ γὰρ Πριάμῳ ἐπεμήνιε δίῳ,
οὕνεκ᾽ ἄρ᾽ ἐσθλὸν ἐόντα μετ᾽ ἀνδράσιν οὔ τι τίεσκεν.
for he (Aeneas) was always wroth at illustrious Priam, because
he did not honour him, though outstanding amongst men.

(29) N 352-3 (Poseidon helped the Greeks):
ἤχθετο γάρ ῥα
Τρωσὶν δαμναμένους
for it grieved him that they were at present being overcome
by the Trojans.

(30) P 603-4 (Leïtus, wounded by Hector, shrank back):
ἐπεὶ οὐκέτι ἔλπετο θυμῷ
ἔγχος ἔχων ἐν χειρὶ μαχήσεσθαι Τρώεσσιν
because he had no more hope of fighting with his spear in
his hand against the Trojans.

(31) Λ 626-7:
ἥν οἱ Ἀχαιοὶ
ἔξελον, οὕνεκα βουλῇ ἀριστεύεσκεν ἁπάντων.
(Hecamede), whom the Greeks had picked out for him (Nestor),
because he excelled all in counsel.

In (27) and (28) the γάρ- and οὕνεκ᾽-clause follow closely after a verb of emotion and as they describe the content of that emotion they are best analyzed as embedded focalization.[34] In (29) and (30) the verbs of emotion, triggering off embedded focalization, are found within the γάρ- and ἐπεί-clause itself. Since the causal clauses explain a deliberate and conscious action of a character ('helped', 'shrank back'), they may be said to represent the character's reasons for acting as he or she does and, at the same time, an explanation of the NF_1 for his addressee. In other words, they are focalized *doubly* (see Bal 1985: 113).[35] The same holds true for example (31), where a verb of thinking/feeling is altogether lacking: the NF_1 shares the conviction of his characters that Nestor excelled all in counsel and takes over their motive in the form of an explanation.[36]

As for the function of thoughts/emotions-passages: they stand in between the presentation by the NF_1 of a thought/emotion as an event only (e.g. Γ 418:

ἔδεισεν δ᾽ Ἑλένη: 'Helen was frightened') and the expression of such thoughts/ emotions by the characters themselves in direct speech. As a result of the presence of such thoughts/emotions-passages the narrator-text does not consist of a succession of events only, but is interspersed with short 'peeps' into the minds of the characters participating in those events. In this way the story is motivated (see above section 3.3.4, p. 93 for the *Iliad* as "récit motivé") and at the same time the hearer/reader (through Fe_2 and $NeFe_1$) is drawn into the story more fully.

There are even two groups of characters whose feelings and opinions the hearer/reader gets to know *only* through embedded focalization: the mass of warriors and women as a collective, which are never quoted in direct speech by the NF_1. I have discussed these two categories of "silent characters" elsewhere (de Jong 1987a) and will give only one example here:

(32) Ο 699-702:
    τοῖσι δὲ μαρναμένοισιν ὅδ᾽ ἦν νόος· ἤτοι ᾽Αχαιοὶ
    οὐκ ἔφασαν φεύξεσθαι ὑπὲκ κακοῦ, ἀλλ᾽ ὀλέεσθαι,
    Τρωσὶν δ᾽ ἔλπετο θυμὸς ἐνὶ στήθεσσιν ἑκάστου
    νῆας ἐνιπρήσειν κτενέειν θ᾽ ἥρωας ᾽Αχαιούς.
    And for them, while fighting, their thought was as follows: the Greeks thought that they would not escape destruction but were going to perish, whereas for the Trojans, the heart in each man's breast hoped that they would set fire to the ships and slay the Greek heroes.[37]

Here we may say that the choice of the narrative situation is conditioned by the social status of the characters involved: just as the NF_1 refrains from giving the names of the πληθύς (Β 488-92), he does not - except for an occasional tis-speech: see De Jong (1987b) - deem the mass of warriors important enough to let them express their feelings in speech.

Sometimes the presentation of thoughts/emotions in the form of embedded focalization is conditioned by the situation, e.g.

(33) Ε 563-4:
    τοῦ δ᾽ ὤτρυνεν μένος ᾽Αρης,
    τὰ φρονέων, ἵνα χερσὶν ὑπ᾽ Αἰνείαο δαμείη.
    his (Menelaus') fighting spirit Ares stimulated, minded that he might be subdued under Aeneas' hands

Ares' real intention (death of Menelaus through Aeneas) is different from what his action seems to imply (support of Menelaus) and it is only logical that it is kept from all those involved, except, of course, the NeFe₁.[38] An interesting case in this respect is the passage Ω 582-6: Achilles orders Hector's body to be washed out of Priam' sight, lest the old man become angry and thus infuriate Achilles, who might then be unable to restrain himself and kill him against Zeus' injunctions. The narrative situation of the whole passage is complex narrator-text (embedded focalization), but do the verses 583-6 (from ὡς μή onwards) form part of Achilles' indirect speech (582: λοῦσαι κέλετ᾽) or are they his *unspoken* thoughts?[39] Commentators have paid no attention to this question. Lattimore in his translation chooses the first alternative, even translating 583-6 as direct speech ("but take it first aside ..."). I prefer the second alternative: it seems improbable that Achilles would speak thus openly about his own violent temper in front of female servants (δμῳάς). It is interesting to observe that some verses before, when Achilles speaks to Priam about his irritability (568-70), he had not mentioned the possibility of his killing Priam, as we find in 586. Whichever alternative one chooses, analyzing Ω 582-6 as embedded focalization informs us that Achilles is himself very much aware of his irascible temper, just as his best friend Patroclus is (Λ 653-4). Later authors will exploit to a maximum the technique of juxtaposing a character's unspoken thoughts to his spoken words. I am thinking here in particular of a short story called *The Waltz* by Dorothy Parker (where a woman *says* she enjoys waltzing, whereas from her hidden thoughts we learn that in fact she abhors dancing and loathes her dancing partner) and Forster's *A Room with a View*, where the presentation of the story is brilliantly adapted to the theme of the novel, viz. the suppression of one's real feelings in favour of impeccable social behaviour.

Indirect speech[40]

Explicit embedded focalization involving indirect speech of characters can be triggered off in the *Iliad* by the following verbs: (say, declare) ἔειπον, φημί, στεῦμαι; (report) ἀγγέλλω; (ask, bid) εἴρομαι, λιτανεύω, λίσσομαι; (promise, vow) ὑπίσχομαι, ἀπειλέω; (refuse) ἀναίνομαι; (assent) ἐπευφημέω; (pray, boast) εὔχομαι, εὐχετάομαι, ἀράομαι; (blame) αἰτιάομαι; (challenge) προκαλίζομαι; (order, exhort) κελεύω, κέλομαι, ἐπιτέλλω, ἄνωγα, (ἐπ)ὀτρύνω, ὄρνυμι.

Indirect speech belongs to the complex which is known in narratology as *speech representation*: the words of a character can be mentioned as an event (I call this 'speech-act mention'), can be represented in indirect speech or can be quoted directly as direct speech:[41]

(34) Λ 165:
'Ατρεΐδης δ' ἕπετο σφεδανὸν Δαναοῖσι κελεύων.
And Agamemnon followed, impetuously exhorting the Greeks

(35) Β 151-2:
τοὶ δ' ἀλλήλοισι κέλευον
ἅπτεσθαι νηῶν ἠδ' ἑλκέμεν εἰς ἅλα δῖαν
And they exhorted each other to take hold of the ships
and drag them to the bright sea

(36) Ε 528-32:
'Ατρεΐδης δ' ἀν' ὅμιλον ἐφοίτα πολλὰ κελεύων·
"ὦ φίλοι, ἀνέρες ἕστε ..."
And Agamemnon went to and fro among the host, exhorting
much: "friends, be men ..."

In (34) Agamemnon's activity of exhorting is only mentioned as an event, in
(35) the gist (not the actual form) of the exhortations is represented in the
infinitives dependent on κέλευον (these infinitives form the content of the embedded focalization) and finally, in (36) Agamemnon's exhortations are quoted in
direct speech.

Of these three modes of speech representation the third one (direct speech)
is by far the most frequent in the *Iliad*: there are 677 speeches as against 88
cases of indirect speech (rarely longer than two verses) and 39 of speech-act
mention. We might say that indirect speech forms the exception to the rule of
direct speech[42] and the question arises in which circumstances the NF$_1$ chooses
to represent words of characters indirectly instead of directly. A first indication
is given by Bassett (1936: 104-6), who suggests that the indirect method was
chosen when the poet was interested to give the bare facts, not the emotions.
In the following I will argue that indirect speech is found mainly:

1. when the NF$_1$ wishes to summarize speeches;

2. when he wants to incorporate speeches which belong to a period before
that covered by the primary fabula of the *Iliad*.

Ad 1. The need to summarize words spoken by characters arises in the first
place when several speeches are involved which can be supposed to have more
or less the same content, as e.g. in:

(37) Τ 303-4:
αὐτὸν δ᾽ ἀμφὶ γέροντες ᾽Αχαιῶν ἠγερέϑοντο
λισσόμενοι δειπνῆσαι
And around him (Achilles) the elders of the Greeks gathered,
entreating him to eat[43]

Here we see several speeches of the Greek elders reduced to one infinitive dependent on λισσόμενοι. Note that Achilles' single, resolute answer, in which he
declines to eat, is quoted in direct speech: 305-8.

A second ground for summarizing is when the speaking characters are not
deemed important enough to be quoted directly, e.g.

(38) Β 400-1:
ἄλλος δ᾽ ἄλλῳ ἔρεζε ϑεῶν αἰειγενετάων,
εὐχόμενος ϑάνατόν τε φυγεῖν καὶ μῶλον ῎Αρηος.
and each (of the soldiers) made a sacrifice to one or other
of the everliving gods, praying to escape death and the
contest of war.

The private prayers of the soldiers are represented in indirect speech, both
because here, as in (37), several speeches with identical content are involved,
but, more importantly, because here the NF_1 is again dealing with the πληϑύς
(cp. above, p. 48). As if to drive home the difference in status between mass
and individual leaders, in 412-8 the NF_1 quotes Agamemnon's official prayer
directly. Or, as Race (1982: 33, n.5) remarks: "the summary priamel (ἄλλος δ᾽
ἄλλῳ) serves as foil for the introduction of the subject of interest" (sc.
Agamemnon). Yet, here and in Α 22-3,[44] Β 151-2, Θ 346-7 = Ο 368-9 and Ψ 823
the mass of soldiers for once partakes of the presentation of the story, albeit
merely as F_2's.

A third ground for summarizing arises when the content of the speech is
not deemed important enough to be quoted in full. This is especially the case
when *orders* are involved, e.g.

(39) Β 50-1:
αὐτὰρ ὁ κηρύκεσσι λιγυφϑόγγοισι κέλευσε
κηρύσσειν ἀγορήνδε κάρη κομόωντας ᾽Αχαιούς
But he ordered the clear-voiced heralds to summon the
long-haired Greeks to the assembly

(40) Θ 318-9:
Κεβριόνην δ' ἐκέλευσεν ἀδελφεὸν ἐγγὺς ἐόντα
ἵππων ἡνί' ἑλεῖν
And he ordered his brother Kebriones, who was near to
him, to take the reins of his horses[45]

What counts here is not so much the actual verbal form of the orders, but the
fact that they are given and executed. Thus, very often we are told immediately
afterwards that the order is executed, e.g. B 50-1 (example 39) is followed in 52
by ἐκήρυσσον ('they summoned').[46]

A fourth (not very frequent) use of indirect speech is to prepare for a
speech, e.g.

(41) Υ 364-5:
Τρώεσσι δὲ φαίδιμος "Εκτωρ
κέκλεθ' ὁμοκλήσας, φάτο δ' ἴμεναι ἄντ' 'Αχιλῆος
but illustrious Hector urged on the Trojans, shouting en-
couragements and he declared that he <u>would go and confront</u>
<u>Achilles</u>

Here ἴμεναι ... 'Αχιλῆος gives a summary of the speech following (366-72, cp.
especially 371: τοῦ δ' ἐγὼ ἀντίος εἰμι: 'and I will go and confront him').[47]
In other words, the indirect speech forms part of the attributive discourse (see
below ch. 6.1)

Ad 2. An example of indirect speech representing speech which has taken place
before the time-period covered by the primary fabula of the *Iliad* is

(42) Ν 365-9 (Idomeneus kills Othryoneus, who had only recently
come to Troy):
ἤτεε δὲ Πριάμοιο θυγατρῶν εἶδος ἀρίστην
Κασσάνδρην ἀνάεδνον, ὑπέσχετο δὲ μέγα ἔργον,
ἐκ Τροίης ἀέκοντας ἀπωσέμεν υἷας 'Αχαιῶν.
τῷ δ' ὁ γέρων Πρίαμος ὑπό τ' ἔσχετο καὶ κατένευσε
δωσέμεναι.
And he (Othryoneus) had asked for the hand of the most
beautiful of Priam's daughters, Cassandra, without bride
price, but he had promised a mighty deed, viz. to drive the
Greeks away from Troy against their will. And to him the
old man Priam had promised and consented that he would
give (her).[48]

It remains the prerogative of the characters to include in their character-texts

118

speeches which lie outside the time-boundaries of the *Iliad*. For this see further below section 5.3.

My last example concerns a very special case of indirect speech which does not belong to either of the two categories discussed so far. It is found in the description of Achilles' shield:

> (43) Σ 499-500 (two men are depicted as disputing about a blood price):
>   ὁ μὲν εὔχετο πάντ᾽ ἀποδοῦναι,
> δήμῳ πιφαύσκων, ὁ δ᾽ ἀναίνετο μηδὲν ἑλέσθαι.
> the one claimed to have given everything due, stating his case to the people, and the other denied having received anything.

It is a well-known (and admired) feature of the description of Achilles' shield (Σ 478-608) that it is not static but dynamic, both in that it follows Hephaestus while making the shield and in that some of the images described come alive, are dramatized as scenes.[49] The inclusion of indirect speech as part of the description can be considered the highest possible degree of this dramatization: direct speech would have turned the shield into a kind of speaking machine (cp. also the indication of sounds, e.g. in 569-72, 580, 586 and the representation of thoughts: 510-2).

4.1.2. Implicit embedded focalization

Implicit embedded focalization is embedded focalization *not* marked by a verb of perceiving, thinking/feeling or speaking. In fact, the previous section already contained some examples of implicit embedded focalization: final clauses, (some) causal clauses and indirect (deliberative) questions. The suggestion to analyze these passages as embedded focalization is based on their *semantic* value: final clauses express the intentions, indirect questions the questions and (certain) causal clauses the motives of characters. In the following I present a number of other passages which, I think, can be analyzed as embedded focalization:

> (44) Θ 487-8:
> Τρωσὶν μέν ῥ᾽ ἀέκουσιν ἔδυ φάος, αὐτὰρ Ἀχαιοῖς
> ἀσπασίη τρίλλιστος ἐπήλυθε νὺξ ἐρεβεννή.
> For the Trojans daylight went down against their will, but to the Greeks welcome and thrice supplicated was the coming on of night.

Here an event (nightfall) is focalized by Trojans and Greeks, respectively, resulting in two different evaluations. The focalizing characters appear in the text in the dative. One of these focalizers, Hector, will somewhat later himself verbalize in character-text these evaluations: "I had expected to defeat the Greeks, but before that darkness came and saved them" (498-501). There are more of these datives indicating who is focalizing:[50] Thersites was ἔχθιστος ('most hateful') to Achilles and Odysseus (Β 220); Nestor' speech was ἑαδότα ('pleasing') to all Greeks (Ι 173); Zeus was στυγερός ('hateful') to Hera (Ξ 158); of all his guest-friends Phaenops was 'most dear' to Hector (Ρ 584). It is important to pay attention to the narrative situation in these cases, because it makes one aware that the qualification of an event or person is not necessarily universal (not all characters consider Zeus hateful or nightfall thrice asked for) or true, but may represent the opinion (focalization) of one character.

(45)   Φ 28 (Achilles took captive twelve Trojans):
       ποινὴν Πατρόκλοιο Μενοιτιάδαο θανόντος.
       as payment for the death of Patroclus.[51]

(46)   Π 144 (Cheiron gave Peleus the Pelian lance):
       φόνον ἔμμεναι ἡρώεσσιν
       to be death for heroes.[52]

(47)   Τ 312-3 (Greek leaders try to cheer up Achilles):
       οὐδέ τι θυμῷ
       τέρπετο πρὶν πολέμου στόμα δύμεναι αἱματόεντος
       but he would not let himself be comforted before entering
       the jaw of bloody war.[53]

In (45) we have a substantive used in predicative apposition and with a final nuance, in (46) an infinitive used as final clause, and in (47) a πρίν-clause with a final nuance. All three passages express the intentions of the characters who are subject of the main verb. Hence I suggest to analyze them, just like regular final clauses, as complex narrator-text. In the case of (45) one could compare Achilles' words in Σ 336-7 and Ψ 22-5.

(48)   Ω 479 (Priam kisses Achilles' hands):
       δεινὰς ἀνδροφόνους, αἵ οἱ πολέας κτάνον υἷας.
       dreadful, man-slaughtering, <u>which had slain many of his sons.</u>

The relative clause forms a kind of epexegesis of the epithet ἀνδροφόνους and gives expression to what must flash through Priam's head at the moment he kisses

Achilles' hands.[54] One could compare Hecabe's words in Ω 204-5 (and Achilles' in Ω 519-21!): why do you want to face the man 'who has killed many brave sons of yours?' (see also below section 5.4, p. 189). There are more relative clauses which can be interpreted as embedded focalization, e.g. Z 294-5 (note the superlatives, which are rare outside direct speech and cp. Z 271-2 where Hecabe is explicitly indicated as focalizer: τοι (2 x) and αὐτῇ), Π 460-1 (cp. Λ 54-5, where in a very similar context we find a οὔνεκα-clause), X 323 (see above, p. 87), Ω 29-30.85-6. I draw attention to the so-called sympathetic dative, stressing the emotional engagement of the focalizing subject, in Π 460, Ω 85 and 479. An intriguing case is

(49) Γ 126-8 (Iris finds Helen weaving a web, on which she depicts):
                                 ἀέθλους
Τρώων θ' ἱπποδάμων καὶ 'Αχαιῶν χαλκοχιτώνων,
οὓς ἕθεν εἵνεκ' ἔπασχον ὑπ' Ἄρηος παλαμάων
the struggles of horse-taming Trojans and bronze-clad Greeks,
which they were suffering because of her under the hands
of Ares.

In my opinion the relative clause should be analyzed as focalized by Helen (not by the NF₁, nor by Iris who since Γ 125 εὗρ' is F₂): she projects her own feelings of guilt into the motifs of her weaving, signs as powerful as her self-incriminating words in Γ 173-6 and Z 344-8.[55] Arguments in favour of this analysis are

1. that the NF₁ nowhere speaks negatively about Helen
2. the resemblance between Γ 128 and

(50) K 27-8 (Menelaus cannot sleep, fearing for the Greeks):
           τοὶ δὴ ἕθεν εἵνεκα πουλὺν ἐφ' ὑγρὴν
ἤλυθον ἐς Τροίην πόλεμον θρασὺν ὁρμαίνοντες.
who because of him had come over much water to Troy,
waging fierce war.

where we are dealing with explicit embedded focalization (ἔχε τρόμος ... μή: 25-6)

3. the presence both in Γ 128 and K 28 of accented ἕθεν, which according to most modern grammarians is an indirect reflexive rather than an anaphoric personal pronoun[56] and of εἵνεκα, which except for Ω 28 (implicit embedded focalization) and Σ 498 (simple narrator-text) occurs (48x) in character-text only.

(51) Ω 328 (Priam's friends and relatives accompany him on the
first part of his mission to Achilles):
πόλλ' ὀλοφυρόμενοι ὡς εἰ θάνατόνδε κιόντα
weeping much for him as if he were going to his death.

Here the NF₁ through the addition of ὡς εἰ ('as if') makes clear that the
interpretation of Priam's mission as suicidal is the characters'.

(52) Ψ 252-3:
κλαίοντες δ' ἑτάροιο <u>ἐνηέος</u> ὀστέα λευκὰ ἄλλεγον
weeping, they (the Greeks) collected the white bones of
their <u>gentle</u> companion Patroclus

The unique presence outside direct speech of ἐνηής may be explained as due
to implicit embedded focalization by Patroclus' companions.

(53) Η 216-8 (Ajax has accepted Hector's challenge for a duel. The
Trojans, seeing him in full armour, are frightened):
Ἕκτορί τ' αὐτῷ θυμὸς ἐνὶ στήθεσσι πάτασσεν·
ἀλλ' οὔ πως ἔτι εἶχεν ὑποτρέσαι οὐδ' ἀναδῦναι
ἄψ λαῶν ἐς ὅμιλον, ἐπεὶ προκαλέσσατο χάρμῃ.
and also for Hector himself his heart beat in his breast:
but he could not in any way retreat or retire back into
the crowd of the people, after he had issued the challenge
by reason of his fighting spirit.

I would consider analyzing the ἀλλά-clause (217-8) as embedded focalization:
these are Hector's considerations at the moment he perceives 'enormous' (πελώριος) Ajax.[57] When Paris in Γ had first stepped forward challenging the Greeks
and then retreated at the sight of Menelaus, Hector had fiercely rebuked him
and he feels he cannot now do what he then reproached Paris for doing. A comparable case is

(54) Σ 237-8 (Achilles weeps, looking at the lacerated body of
Patroclus):
τόν ῥ' ἤτοι μὲν ἔπεμπε σὺν ἵπποισιν καὶ ὄχεσφιν
ἐς πόλεμον, οὐδ' αὖτις ἐδέξατο νοστήσαντα.
him he had sent out to war with his horses and chariot,
but he had not welcomed him back again.

Ameis-H. perceptively remark: "die beide Versen geben eine schmerzliche Betrach-
tung aus den Gedanken Achills". Examples (53) and (54) are the only two passages
in the *Iliad* which come close to the "stream of consciousness" passages, found

so frequently in modern novels (see Cohn 1978). Once again we see confirmed that in the *Iliad* direct speech is the preferred narrative situation for the expression of thoughts/emotions of characters.

4.1.3. Conclusion

In this section I have tried first of all to convey an impression of the different ways in which embedded focalization in the *Iliad* manifest itself: perception-passages, find-passages, thoughts/emotions- passages, indirect speech, final clauses, indirect questions, (certain) causal and relative clauses. Whereas modern novels often contain long passages of embedded focalization, the secondarily focalized passages of the *Iliad* are short and in comparison to direct speech far less frequent: character-text is clearly the preferred mode of presentation of the words and thereby of the thoughts/emotions of characters. Yet, the narrative situation of complex narrator-text (embedded focalization) has been shown to fulfil several important functions. It can

- enliven and motivate the events told by revealing the fears, expectations, intentions, hopes etc. of the characters involved in these events. Presentation of these thoughts/emotions in embedded focalization instead of in character-text can be due to 1) the wish of the NF_1 not to interrupt his story too much (cp. Page 1973: 31: "indirect speech can offer a gain of pace and economy"); 2) the status of the characters involved, either as speaker or as addressee; 3) the situation in the story.

- bring on stage characters necessary for the story.

- indicate for the $NeFe_1$ the setting, atmosphere of a scene, characterize a character.

- summarize the content of several identical speeches or speeches which are not of enough interest to be given in full (esp. orders) or speeches which have been spoken in the time-period before that covered by the *Iliad*.

The intermediary position of complex narrator-text between simple narrator-text on the one hand and character-text on the other makes it preeminently suited to

- prepare for an ensuing direct speech, either by making clear *why* a character speaks (on account of a perception and/or emotion) or *what* s/he will say (indirect speech as summary content).

- give to the mass of anonymous soldiers and women as a collective, who are only rarely allowed to speak, a way to express themselves.

On the whole I submit that there is enough significant embedded focalization in the *Iliad* to challenge the following statement of Redfield (1975: 20), which reminds one of Auerbach (above section 1.1.2, pp. 22-3)

> Homeric man, being objective, has no innerness ... He has no hidden depths or
> secret motives: he says and does what he is.

We have seen that there is more between saying and doing than dreamt of by Homerists, viz. focalizing.

I conclude this section with one final remark concerning method. The observation that in a number of cases (examples 7, 8, 14, 16, 17) the boundaries between primary and secondary focalization turned out to be not as clear-cut as the theory of the model 'predicts' them to be, should not induce one to reject the model. Rather, such 'deviations' can help to detect the idiosyncracies of a narrative style. In the case of the *Iliad* we see that the NF_1 gives high priority to his $NeFe_1$ being well informed. For this purpose he sometimes intrudes upon the embedded focalization of his characters and substitutes proper names or adds information which he considers relevant for a proper understanding of what follows.

4.2. Assimilated comparisons and similes[58]

The Homeric comparisons and similes[59] have been the subject of many investigations. As for the literary investigations[60] the attention of scholars has concentrated on:

    1. the question of the "Vergleichspunkt" or *tertium comparationis*.

    2. the function of the simile.

Ad 1. In 1921 H. Fränkel furiously attacked the idea that the tertium comparationis is the only point of interest for an interpreter, everything else in the simile being ornamental or even illogical extension by a garrulous narrator. As replacement of the, in his eyes, too restricted concept of *tertium comparationis* he suggested "Bildähnlichkeit" and "Stimmungsgleichheit" (16). His suggestion has found approval e.g. with Kamerbeek (1962), but was attacked by Shorey (1922), Jachmann (1958: 269-326), who spoke of a "symbolistisch-allegorisierende Umdeutung", De Vries (1962) and Lee (1964: esp. 47-9).

Ad 2. Also in 1921, Bassett offered a survey of scholarship, ancient and modern, on the functions of similes. To mention some: similes serve to make the story more vivid, to bring variety, to mark crises in the action. Bassett himself maintains that similes, detached from their context, are the "chief lyrical κόσμος of the epic". Coffey (1957) made the useful suggestion to distinguish between the *primary* function of a simile, viz. its function in relation to the immediate context, and its *secondary* function, viz. in relation to the wider context. Examples of convincing analyses of such secondary functions are Moulton (1977), which is "concerned to set out a detailed demonstration of the relationship of major similes to narrative structure, characterization and themes" (13)[61] and Krischer (1971: 13-89).

In this section I will discuss a special group of comparisons and similes, viz. those in which the NF_1 assimilates his own focalization to that of one of the characters. Since my investigation has relevance for both points just mentioned, I will first set out my own assumptions concerning status and function of the Homeric comparison and simile.

Status and function of comparison and simile

342 comparisons and similes occur in the *Iliad*[62], of which 39 are found in speeches, i.e. are produced by characters. The comparisons and similes of the narrator-text are all narrated and almost all focalized - for exceptions see below category III, pp. 134-5 - by the NF_1 and they find their origin in his wish to illustrate for his addressee, the $NeFe_1$, visual, auditory or psychological aspects of what goes on in the story. For instance, if he wants to give an impression of the noise produced by a mass of soldiers rushing from one place to another, he introduces a simile of waves crashing on a shore (Β 209-10). To this primary (illustrating) function may be added another, secondary one: to express "Stimmungsgleichheit", to add pathos or to confer emphasis, e.g.

(55) Ε 559-60:
> τοίω τὼ χείρεσσιν ὑπ' Αἰνείαο δαμέντε
> καππεσέτην ἐλάτῃσιν ἐοικότε ὑψηλῇσι.
> as such did these two, subdued by the hands of Aeneas,
> crash to the ground like lofty firs.

The comparison serves in the first place to illustrate the crashing down of the two warriors, the suggestion being that the firs are felled (cp. the more elaborate simile of Ν 389-93). But as Griffin has pointed out (1980: 105), the comparison also suggests pathos. Other secondary functions are: to structure the story, to support characterization and development of themes. An example is N 137-42, where the NF$_1$ compares Hector with a boulder rolling down a slope. The primary function of the simile is to illustrate Hector's impetuous and eager attack. However, the NF1 adds the information that the boulder, having reached the plain, stops rolling. This anticipates what is going to happen in the story: Hector's attack, which seemed to bring him victoriously to the sea, will come to a halt when he encounters the phalanxes around the two Ajaxes. Of course, not every comparison or simile has such an extra function, and, conversely, one comparison or simile can fulfil more than one extra function.

Now one has to keep in mind that comparisons and similes produced by the NF$_1$ reach the NeFe$_1$ only, the characters remaining unaware of the fact that they are compared to, say, a lion.[63] In other words, comparisons and similes are no events on the level of the fabula, they are *interpretations* of events, belonging to story and text only. This important feature will be illustrated by two examples.

The simile Δ 141-7 has been brought forward by Porter (1972: 12) as a striking example of "violent juxta-position" of simile and context: Menelaus has just been wounded by Pandarus. The visual effect of the dark blood flowing over his legs is compared to a Phoenician woman colouring a piece of ivory with purple. The beauty, preciousness and prestige of the piece of art she is making are described at leisure and the almost festive tone of the simile (cp. κόσμος and κῦδος: 145) stands in clear contrast to the grim reality of the story, which is soon after put into words by Agamemnon (155-82). Fränkel (1921: 54) called the simile one of the "merkwürdigsten in Ilias und Odyssee", because he had expected Agamemnon's panic to be represented in it. If the NF$_1$ had done so, this would have resulted in an assimilated simile. However, the NF$_1$ chooses not to do so and his reasons become clear if we recall the structure of the whole passage Δ 134-87, which I analyzed above, section 4.1.1, p. 106. The NeFe$_1$ at this stage already knows that Pandarus' shot is not fatal and, therefore, can take pleasure in the detailed simile of 141-7. For Agamemnon and Menelaus the tension will not be relieved until later. To call this simile "detached from its context" means to neglect its true recipient, the NeFe$_1$, and incorrectly taking the characters as criterion, who do not 'receive' the simile at all.

My second example concerns the passage Π 2-11: Patroclus, who is weeping because of the distressing situation in which the Greeks find themselves, is compared by the NF$_1$ to a dark-watered spring (3-4).[64] In all likelihood, the tenor of the simile is the steady flow of water/tears.[65] This same event of Patroclus weeping induces Achilles to use a very different picture: that of a crying little girl, who wants to be picked up and carried by her mother (7-10). The friendship between himself and Patroclus allows Achilles to use a teasing tone, and at the same time reveals itself in the underlying tenderness of the imagery he chooses. Both the NF_1 and Achilles, functioning as NF_2, comment on Patroclus' weeping with a simile, the difference in relationship resulting in two very different pictures.[66]

We can conclude from these examples that, in principle, comparisons and similes in the narrator-text are a matter between NF_1 and $NeFe_1$. Yet, characters are sometimes involved too. This is the case when the NF_1 *assimilates* his focalization to that of a character, i.e. illustrates in the comparison or simile an event as it is seen, experienced by a character. The NF_1 is still focalizing, but his focalization comes close to that of a character, which often in the context of the comparison or simile functions as F_2. An illustrative example is X 26-32: all the Trojans have fled into the city and Hector remains alone outside the walls to face Achilles, who is on his way back from his pursuit of Agenor/Apollo. Priam, who since Φ 526 is standing on top of the Trojan walls, is the first to see Achilles approaching: Achilles, running at full speed in his splendid new, divine armour is compared to the star Orion, brightest of all, but also a κακὸν σῆμα (30: 'a bad portent'), because it brings fever δειλοῖσι βροτοῖσιν (31: 'to wretched mortals'). The primary function of the simile is, of course, to illustrate Achilles' swift and dazzling appearance.[67] Yet, it's secondary function is to express Priam's feelings (who in the context is secondary focalizer: ἴδεν ὀφθαλ-μοῖσι: 25) at seeing Achilles running straight towards his son.[68] For him this is a threatening sight and the simile forms an effective prelude to the emotional outbreak in 33-5 and his speech 38-76 (note in particular the repetition of δειλοῖσι βροτοῖσι: 76). It is instructive to compare this star-simile to another one, found in X 317-20: the gleaming of Achilles' spear, with which he is soon to kill Hector, is compared to the splendid appearance of the evening-star. This simile does not stand in a secondarily focalized context and the star is called κάλλιστος ἐν οὐρανῷ (318: 'most beautiful in the sky'). Here the NF_1 has chosen to focus attention on Achilles and his supreme heroism (see Moulton 1974: 394), not on Hector as its victim.

The following investigation of assimilated comparisons and similes aims to provide an antidote to Bassett's idea of the complete "detachment" of the Homeric similes on the one hand,[69] and to support (but also restrict) Fränkel's concept of "Stimmungsgleichheit" on the other.

Assimilated comparisons and similes

I first give an inventory of all assimilated comparisons and similes, distinguishing between:

    I. Comparisons and similes appearing in a context with explicit embedded focalization (the verbs marking the embedded focalization are given in brackets).[70]

    II. Comparisons and similes which do not appear in a context with explicit embedded focalization, but which all the same contain elements referring to the feelings of one of the characters (these elements are given in brackets).[71]

I add as a third, closely related, category:

    III. Comparisons and similes which are focalized by one of the characters.

Category I:

Γ 23-8 (21: ἐνόησεν, 27: ἐχάρη, 28: ἰδών)[72].33-7 (30: ἐνόησεν ... φανέντα, 31: κατεπλήγη φίλον ἦτορ, 37: δείσας), Δ 275-82[73], Ε 597-600 (596: ἰδὼν ῥίγησε), Η 4-7 (7: φανήτην).63-6 (61: ἀνδράσι τερπόμενοι)[74].208-11 (214: ἐγήθεον εἰσορόωντες, 215: τρόμος, 216: θυμὸς ... πάτασσεν), Λ 62-5 (64: φάνεσκεν)[75].113-21 (121: ὑπ' Ἀργείοισι φέβοντο), Μ 299-308 (307-8: θυμὸς ἀνῆκε + two infinitives and cp. in Sarpedon's speech 328, which corresponds to 305-6), Ν 471-7 (470: οὐκ ... φόβος λάβε, 476-7: μένεν Αἰνείαν ἐπιόντα)[76].492-5 (494-5: γεγήθει, ὡς ἴδε),[77] Ο 271-8 (279: ἴδον ... τάρβησαν). 586-9 (585: οὐ μεῖνε).618-22 (622: Τρῶας μένον).624-9 (629: ἐδαΐζετο θυμὸς)[78].630-6 (637: ἐφόβηθεν ὑφ' Ἕκτορι καὶ Διὶ πατρὶ)[79], Ρ 61-9 (68-9: οὐ ... ἐτόλμα ἀντίον ἐλθέμεναι).755-9 (758-9: ὑπ' Αἰνείᾳ τε καὶ Ἕκτορι), Σ 219-21 (222: ἄϊον, 223: ὀρίνθη θυμός)[80], Υ 164-75 (174-5: ὤτρυνε + inf.), Φ 573-82 (571: Ἀχιλῆα μένεν, 571-2: ἦτορ ἄλκιμον ὡρμᾶτο + inf., 580: οὐκ ἔθελεν φεύγειν, πρὶν πειρήσαιτ' Ἀχιλῆος), Χ 26-32 (25: ἴδεν ὀφθαλμοῖσι).93-7 (92: μίμν' Ἀχιλῆα ἄσσον ἰόντα).132-5 (136: ἐνόησεν, ἕλε τρόμος).162-6 (166: ὁρῶντο).

Category II:

Γ 2-7 (6: φόνον καὶ κῆρα φέρουσαι, 7: κακὴν ἔριδα), Θ 555-61 (559: γέγηθε δέ τε φρένα ποιμήν), Κ 485-8 (486: κακὰ φρονέων), Λ 324-6 (325: μέγα φρονέοντε), Ρ 109-13 (112: ἀέκων), Σ 318-23 (322: δριμὺς χόλος αἱρεῖ, cp. in Achilles' speech 337: χολωθείς), Φ 22-6 (24: δειδιότες).346-9 (348: χαίρει), Χ 410-1.

128

Category III:
Δ 75-80, E 864-6, Λ 129, M 130, N 330, Y 45-6, Ω 328.

I have selected the following passages for discussion: (category I:) E 597-600, H 4-7, X 93-7.162-6; (category II:) Θ 555-61, X 410-11; (category III:) all passages.

Category I

E 597-600. The position of this simile in its context is as follows:

E 590-5	:	(simple narrator-text)	: Hector, Enyo and Ares, followed by the Trojans, attack the Greeks.
596	:	(complex narrator-text)	: Diomedes perceives Ares and shudders.
597-600	:	(simple narrator-text)	: Diomedes steps back like a man spotting a swift-flowing river.
601-6	:	(character-text)	: Diomedes addresses the Greeks, refers to (Hector and) Ares and advises to retreat.

The primary function of the simile is to illustrate Diomedes stepping back (599: ἀνά τ' ἔδραμ' ὀπίσσω; 600: ἀνεχάζετο), its secondary function to express Diomedes' feelings at seeing Ares: for him the war god is as frightening as a swift-flowing and foaming river for a traveller. Thus the simile prepares the way for the speech, which follows (see also above X 26-32 preparing for Priam's speech).[81] A detail like ἀπάλαμνος (the traveller is 'helpless', i.e. at a loss, because he does not know how to cross the river) gives the NeFe₁ a clue as to why Diomedes advises his troops to retreat: he sees no possibility to oppose such formidable enemies as Ares (and Hector).

H 4-7. Paris and Hector return to the battlefield, from which they both have been absent for a long time (Paris since Γ 373 and Hector since Z 116-8). For the Trojan soldiers their appearance means the same as a favourable wind, sent by a god to sailors exhausted with rowing. Both sailors and Trojans had longed for a long time (present participle ἐελδομένοισι: 4 and 7) for the wind/their leaders to come. Fränkel (1921: 9) is right in arguing that more is expressed in this simile than just "Befriedigung eines sehnsüchtigen Verlangens" (Ameis-H. ad 4), yet in his own interpretation he is inconsistent (on p. 9 he suggests that the Trojans are exhausted from their "schwerer Kampfsarbeit", whereas on p. 31 he speaks of a "Windstille" during Paris' and Hector's absence) and too short (the simile is supposed to "explain itself"). In fact, the four verses contain more than might be realized at first. Instead of describing the arrival of Hector and

Paris on the battlefield, the NF₁ immediately turns to the *effect* of their arrival on the Trojans.[82] It is to be noted that there is no introductory sentence leading up to the simile, which strengthens the impression of a quick 'camera-turn' from Hector and Paris, bursting with fresh energy (cp. Z 506-29, H 2-3), to the Trojans. The god mentioned at the beginning of the simile already is an indication that the NF₁ assimilates his focalization to that of the Trojans, since the Trojans 'reverenced Hector like a god'.[83] The simile also suggests what has happened during Hector's absence: he had left his troops at a critical moment, adhorting them to keep firm during the time he himself would have to be in the city. The exhaustion of the sailors in the simile (5: κάμωσιν; 6: καμάτῳ) implies that the soldiers have indeed been fighting with the utmost exertion, have reached the end of their reserves and have been wishing all the time for Hector to return.

X 93-7. Hector is alone awaiting Achilles, who draws nearer to him. His father and mother had begged him to come inside the walls, but they had not persuaded him. At this point the NF₁ inserts the simile X 93-7, in which Hector is compared to a snake coiled up in front of his lair, awaiting a man. The primary function of this simile is to illustrate the fact that Hector is staying at his post (92: μίμν', 93: μένῃσι, 96: οὐχ ὑπεχώρει) and also his unquenchable fighting-spirit (94: χόλος αἰνός, 96: ἄσβεστον μένος). But how are we to see this simile in the light of the monologue which follows (99-130)? There Hector shows himself far less determined to fight and is, in fact, considering several ways to evade a confrontation with Achilles: "Das Selbstgespräch Hektors, ..., setzt einen *ganz unvermittelten Umschwung seiner Stimmung* voraus" (Ameis-H. ad 99, my italics). And this is not all: although in his monologue he decides to stay, his perception of Achilles and all the details of his armour (131-6) suffices to put him to flight.[84] Fenik (1978), comparing this monologue with three others in the *Iliad* (Λ 404-10, P 91-105, Φ 553-70), has suggested that both the place of the simile (*before* rather than, as in the three other cases, *after* the monologue) and the choice of the snake as vehicle of comparison ("not an intrepid beast, hard to dislodge") already are indications that Hector will soon flee. I agree with Fenik that the choice of the snake here is significant for what follows, but not in the way he suggests. His association of snake and flight is not warranted by any other instance where snakes occur in the *Iliad*.[85] And also in X 94-5 it is clear that the snake is determined to defend itself as well as possible. Conversely, even "noble beasts of prey" like those of the other three similes, can be forced to withdraw:

P 109-13 (!) and see further e.g. Λ 546-557 and P 657-66. There is also the primary function of the simile as set out above, which precludes the association with Hector's flight already at this moment. Instead, I propose to explain the choice of the snake here in combination with πελώριον in 92: just as for a snake a man is many times bigger than himself, Achilles in the eyes of Hector takes on 'gigantic' proportions. Of the 25 times πελώριος occurs in *Iliad* and *Odyssey* it is 22 times in a secondarily focalized context (embedded focalization and direct speech)[86] and the adjective seems to denote not objective measuring of size but rather the subjective impressions and emotions of someone who is scared by the enormity of what he perceives (especially illuminating in this respect is the repeated use of this adjective by Odysseus when he describes the Cyclops: ι 187.190.257). In other words, the secondary function of the simile is to transport the NeFe₁ into the local (at the foot of the walls, outside the city and not, like Hecuba and Priam on top of the walls, inside the city) and psychological position of Hector: he feels overpowered by Achilles, but is at the same time determined to fight. Thus the assimilated simile prepares for the monologue which follows: the NeFe₁ gets a first inkling of Hector's *real* feelings at this moment (as opposed to his outward appearance).[87] These feelings are then further set out by Hector himself in the monologue. It will be the sight of Achilles' Pelian spear (131-6) which breaks his last resistance.

X 162-6. Achilles and Hector are running around Troy and, as the NF₁ says, their running was not an athletic contest where prizes are to be gained, but a deadly serious race where Hector's life is at stake. After this priamel (see Race 1982: 39-40, 42) the passage X 162-6, in which Achilles and Hector are compared to race-horses running for a prize, comes somewhat as a surprise. Moulton (1974: 396 and cp. 1977: 83 n. 59) offers the following solution for this "puzzling inconsistency"

> ... two different aspects of the scene are being stressed by the poet: first the gravity of the race (not for prizes but for life), and next its swiftness (as with race-horses who compete for prizes). A linear progression is the only method available for these emphases.

This interpretation suffices to account for the primary function of X 162-6. But the simile expresses more. Assimilating his focalization to that of the gods (X 166: θεοὶ δ' ἐς πάντες ὁρῶντο: 'and all the gods watched'),[88] the NF₁ indicates that for them, although they show their concern for their 'favourite heroes' (see Zeus' speech: 168-76), the life-and-death race between Hector and Achilles is, after all a *spectacle*.[89] In Griffin's (1980: 139) interpretation X 158-61 and 162-6 are taken together: "It almost was an athletic spectacle of the conventional sort - except that the gods were the audience and the stake was the life of Hector". It might be preferable to keep the contrast between the two passages: in 158-61 the NF$_1$ instructs his addressee how he should interpret the scene presented to him. Immediately afterwards he contrasts this human focalization with the divine one (162-6). The juxtaposition of the two interpretations of the scene (human and divine) suggests that the historical hearer/reader is meant to adopt the first rather than the second one. The net result is that the mortality of man is placed against the background of the immortality of the gods, for whom human misery is like a tragic play, which they watch, but in which they themselves are not directly involved. Taken in this way, both priamel and simile prepare for the theme of human mortality as discussed by Zeus and Athena in X 168-85.

Category II

Θ 555-61. The Trojans are bivouacking outside the city and the mass of their camp-fires is compared to the multitude of stars at a bright heaven, watched by a shepherd, who is pleased with the comforting light they spread. This simile has been interpreted very differently by two scholars in the course of different argumentations. The first scholar is Fränkel (1921: 5-6) and the context is his polemic with those scholars who want to look at the tertium comparationis only (see above p. 123):

> ... wird man zunächst glauben dürfen, es komme alles oder doch fast alles auf die Fülle, die Menge an. Aber ist es auch nicht möglich, daß zwar die Fülle gemeint ist, daß aber vieles andere außerdem auch gilt? Z.B. gleich das Leuchten? Und die fröhliche Empfindung, die man beim Anblick so vieler heller Lichter aufsteigen fühlt? Und wenn es nun ... heißt "der Hirte freut sich ..."; und wenn auch diese troischen Feuer, die zum ersten Mal in der befreiten Ebene erstrahlen, als Zeichen des Sieges gelten dürfen; wenn uns der Dichter eben selbst erzählt hat, die Stimmung der Troer, als sie draußen bivackieren, sei stolz und fröhlich gewesen - wer wagt da unserm natürlichen Empfinden halt zu gebieten und zu sagen: die Fülle - ja, sie ist urkündlich bezeugt; aber das übrige - nein, davon steht nichts im Text!

The other scholar is Adam Parry (1956: 2) and the context the establishment of the oral, formulaic theory of the Homeric epics. After showing that Θ 555-61 is "almost entirely made up of formulaic elements", Parry uses this fact as an argument to explain why at this moment of the story, "when the situation of the Achaeans is for the first time obviously perilous", Homer represents in the simile "not the horror of the fires, but their glory": there was only one way to describe a multitude of fires and Homer did not consider adapting this given description to the special needs of the occasion. It turns out that Parry, in his zeal to prove his point of the formulaic nature of the text, has overlooked the possibility of connecting the simile with the situation of the Trojans, as Fränkel (1921: 34), Austin (1966: 263, n. 48), Latacz (1966: 148) and Moulton (1977: 104) do. Yet, it is not as easy as that: "Die Schau, aus der das Bild genommen ist, ist diesmal sicher eine "Götterperspektive" ... *Für wen sonst als für einen Olympier* ... kann das troische Land in dieser Nacht den Sternenhimmel wiederzuspiegeln scheinen" (Fränkel 1921: 34, my italics). This same point about the perspective has brought Friedrich (1982: 118-9) to adopt the strict *tertium comparationis*-approach, so much despised by Fränkel

> Was da miteinander verglichen wird, ist, wie längst beobachtet, lediglich die Unzahl der Lichter hier auf dem troischen Blachfeld und dort am Firmament. Sonst finden wir nichts gemeinsames. *Wer könnte denn von weitem auf all die Lagerfeuer schauen* und sich ihrer freuen wie der Schäfer sich des Mond- und Sternhimmels freut? (my italics).

Friedrich mentions (and rejects) three possible answers to his own rhetorical question: the Greeks have the desired distanced position, but they are not glad to see the fires; Hector? But he is sitting amidst the fires, i.e., he is to be compared with the moon (555: σελήνην) rather than the shepherd; spectators from the Trojan wall? But the poet places us between the two camps, giving an impression of both the Trojan and the Greek (cp. I 1-8) side.

It seems worthwhile to have another close look at the larger context. In 485-8 night falls after the second day of fighting, which has ended very successfully for the Trojans. In an optimistic and boastful speech (497-541) Hector announces that the night will be spent outside the walls. He orders to kindle many fires, to prevent the Greeks from fleeing in the dark of the night (509-16). His orders are executed and the Trojans are in high spirits (553: μέγα φρονέοντες). In view of this context it seems natural to connect the shepherd and his joy in the simile (559) with the Trojans,[90] in other words to consider the simile assimilated to the Trojans and to give it as secondary function to represent their present optimistic mood. To this more or less intuitive argument (Hector or the Trojans are not explicitly marked as secondary focalizers of the fires in the context) two others can be added. In the first place, there is the so-called sympathetic dative σφισι in 554, which underlines the connection between the fires and the Trojans. The fires are not just burning, they are burning *for them*. In the same way, the stars are not just bright, but their brightness has value for the shepherd, because it means that he can have a quiet night. In the second place, there is the negative reaction of the Greeks to these fires, which, by contrast, also points to a connection between the fires and the Trojan mood of the moment. Friedrich already mentioned the passage I 1-8, but the following three passages are even more revealing:

(56) I 76-7 (Nestor is speaking: the Greeks need good advice):
"ὅτι δήϊοι ἐγγύθι νηῶν
καίουσιν πυρὰ πολλά· τίς ἂν τάδε γηθήσειε;"
"because the enemies are burning many fires near the ships: who would be glad about these?"

The answer to Nestor's rhetorical question is, of course: nobody, that is to say, nobody of the Greeks, for the formulation in itself also bears a suggestion of the opposite, viz. the joy of the enemies.[91]

(57) K 11-3 (Agamemnon is nervous and unable to sleep):
ἤτοι ὅτ' ἐς πεδίον τὸ Τρωϊκὸν ἀθρήσειε,
θαύμαζεν πυρὰ πολλά, τὰ καίετο Ἰλιόθι πρό,
αὐλῶν συρίγγων τ' ἐνοπὴν ὅμαδόν τ' ἀνθρώπων.
Whenever he gazed toward the Trojan plain, he wondered at the many fires that burned before Troy and at the sound of flutes and pipes, and the noise of men.

Again, the focalization of the fires by a Greek is joined by an emotion (wonder as opposed to grief when looking at the Greek camp: 14-6).

(58) I 232-5 (Odysseus to Achilles: the situation is critical):
"Ἐγγὺς γὰρ νηῶν καὶ τείχεος αὖλιν ἔθεντο
Τρῶες ὑπέρθυμοι τηλεκλειτοί τ' ἐπίκουροι,
κηάμενοι πυρὰ πολλὰ κατὰ στρατόν, οὐδ' ἔτι φασὶ
σχήσεσθ', ἀλλ' ἐν νηυσὶ μελαίνῃσιν πεσέεσθαι"
"For the overbearing Trojans and far-famed allies have set their bivouac near the ships and the wall, having kindled many fires throughout the host, and they think that they will no longer be stopped, but will fall upon the black ships"

It is significant that in this short description of the critical situation (meant to persuade Achilles to return to the battlefield) the Trojan fires again figure prominently: in the darkness of the night they are of course the only visible sign of the Trojan presence, but they also constantly remind the Greeks of the threat of fire to their ships (cp. I 241-2.347.435-6.601-2.653), and above all they symbolize to them the victorious mood of the Trojans, as reconstructed by Odysseus in 234-5. In view of these three passages it seems obvious to suppose that the simile Θ 555-61 should indeed be interpreted in connection with the joy of the Trojans. The point of the "Götterperspektive" remains to be discussed. On this point, both Fränkel and Friedrich make the mistake of not distinguishing between simile and context: in the simile there is no "Götterperspektive", but the position the NF₁ chooses is that of the shepherd. Only *after* the simile does the NF₁ give a bird's-eye view, receding as it were from the field of action, just as in other cases (e.g. the opening lines of Γ and Z) he starts from a position of overview and then zooms in on the actors.[92]

X 410-11. Hector has been killed by Achilles and is now dragged around the city behind his chariot. Seeing this, Priam, Hecabe and with them the whole Trojan population start weeping and lamenting 'and it resembled most this, as if the whole of mountain-built Troy was ablaze top to bottom with fire'.[93] The simile-like passage forms the climax to a whole series of similes dealing with besieged cities (Σ 207-14.219-21, Φ 522-5), since here an explicit reference to Troy is made. I suggest that this remarkable specification is the result of the NF₁'s assimilating his focalization to Hector's parents and the Trojans. For them Hector's death, indeed, means the same as the fall of Troy: the Trojans call Hector's son Astyanax, because Hector alone protects Troy (Z 402-3, X 506-7); Priam in X 56-76 automatically associates Hector's (imminent) death with Troy's destruction; and even Achilles, on his part, confirms Hector's position as supreme defender of Troy, when he considers the question whether the Trojans will continue fighting after Hector's death (X 382-4).

Category III

Δ 75-80. Athena, hurrying down from Olympus, is compared to a shooting star. From 79-80 (θάμβος δ' ἔχεν εἰσορόωντας: 'and wonder took hold of them as they watched') it appears that her descent is also focalized by the Greek and Trojan soldiers, and the question arises: what do they see? Is Athena really transformed into a shooting star?[94] Another simile, P 547-52, may be of help: here it is obvious that Athena does not change into a rainbow, but only *resembles* one in her outward appearance (551: πορφυρέη νεφέλη πυκάσασα ἐ αὐτήν: 'having enveloped herself with a purple cloud', the rainbow was called 'purple' in 547). The same holds true, I think, for Δ 75-80: Athena is not transformed into a shooting star, but resembles one. The complication here is that this resemblance is noted not only by the NF₁, who uses it to illustrate for the NeFe₁

Athena's quick descent, but also by the characters (the Greek and Trojan soldiers): as appears from the tis-speech 82-4 (see also De Jong forth.), they interpret what they see as an omen from Zeus, which implies that they (think they) have seen a shooting star, just as the NF_1 'predicted' they would in 76 τέρας ... στρατῷ εὐρέϊ λαῶν: (a shooting star) 'an omen for a broad army of men'. In other words, the passage Δ 75-80 is focalized *doubly* (see above p. 112): what for the NF_1 and his addressee has the status of a simile only, is reality for the soldiers as F_2.

E 864-7. Ares, going up to heaven, appears to Diomedes (866-7: Διομήδεϊ ... φαίνεθ') like a dark cloud. I consider the close correlation between simile and context (οἵη ... τοῖος) and the explicit reference to Diomedes in the dative to be arguments to analyze E 864-5 as focalized by him. This suggestion seems to be borne out by the following comment of the bT-scholia (ad 866-7): γραφικῶς ἔχει Διομήδης τὴν ἄνοδον θεώμενος Ἄρεος ('Diomedes is imaginative in his perception of Ares going upwards').

Λ 129. Two young Trojans had just lost control over the reins of their chariot and then Agamemnon, 'in front of them, rose like a lion'. I analyze the comparison as focalized by the two Trojans on account of ἐναντίον, which describes "wer im Gesichtskreis ist" (*LfgrE* s.v. ἀντίος B, col. 945).

N 330. The Trojans 'saw him (Idomeneus), resembling a flame as regards his force'. The Trojans compare Idomeneus to a flame, because of the glittering of his armour (331: σὺν ἔντεσι δαιδαλέοισι).

Y 45-6. The Trojans were gripped with fear, 'when they saw swift-footed Achilles, glittering in his armour like man-slaughtering Ares'. Except for this instance and M 130[95] all comparisons of warriors with Ares are focalized by the NF_1.[96]

Ω 328. This passage has been analyzed already on p. 121.

Conclusion

Of the 342 Iliadic comparisons and similes ca. 10% occur in character-text, 90% in narrator-text. Of the 303 comparisons and similes occurring in narrator-text, 296 are focalized by the NF_1, 6 (E 864-7, Λ 129, M 130, N 330, Y 45-6, Ω 328) by characters and 1 (Δ 75-80) by both NF_1 and characters. All 303 are narrated by the NF_1. Whether produced by NF_1 or characters, comparisons and similes are *interpretations* of events or persons, belonging to the levels of story and text only. In about 12% of the comparisons and similes focalized by the NF_1, the NF_1 assimilates his focalization to that of a character - who in the context of comparison or simile often functions as F_2. The comparison or simile, thereby, acquires as a secondary function the expression of the emotions of characters. I suggest to reserve Fränkel's "Stimmungsgleichheit" for the three categories of assimilated and secondarily focalized comparisons and similes only. Their number is large enough to warrant a modification of Bassett's idea that similes are "detached from" their context, and merely serve as decoration.

As a result of the assimilation or "Stimmungsgleichheit", the $NeFe_1$ (and through him the historical hearer/reader) is more involved in the story and stimulated to respond directly to the emotions of the characters. The only exception is X 162-6, where the juxtaposition with 159-61 seems to invite the hearer/reader not to identify with the Fe_2 and therefore to adopt the human, not the divine focalization of Achilles' life-and-death pursuit of Hector. In a great number of cases the assimilated simile prepares for a speech and the following subtle sequence of narrative situations can be observed:

event	: simple narrator-text
perception of event	: complex narrator-text
illustration of event	: assimilated simile in simple narrator-text
evaluation of event	: character-text

This section has shown how, just as the NF_1 sometimes intrudes upon the focalization of his characters, the emotions of characters sometimes invade a domain which, in principle, is reserved for NF_1 and $NeFe_1$ only: comparison and simile.

4.3. Evaluative and affective words/expressions in the narrator-text

In chapter 1 (category 4, p. 18) we have seen how certain adjectives were repeatedly brought forward as subjective elements, i.e. elements which betray (in the narrator-text) the presence of the otherwise invisible poet: ἀεικέα, κακά, νήπιος, etc. In the preceding sections of this chapter I have on a number of occasions spoken of "emotionally coloured words", which point to the presence (in the narrator-text) of a character as secondary focalizer: ἀκηδέστως.

ἀάπτους and see notes 4, 29. In this section I will look more systematically at these evaluative and affective words/expressions.

There are already two studies of Homeric "Gefühlswörter": Opelt (1978) and Griffin (1986).[97] Both studies argue that evaluative and affective words are found almost exclusively in the speeches of characters

> Die Tendenz des Dichters zur objektiven Erzählhaltung verbietet ihm - ... - deutliche Parteinahme am Schicksal seiner Gestalten. Affektivische, also nicht objektiv beschreibende Sprache hat folglich nur in den Reden ihre Berechtigung (Opelt 1978: 170)

In her zeal to show that affective speech is "justified" in the speeches only, Opelt passes over in silence the occurrences of affective words outside the speeches. Thus, when she discusses νήπιος she does not refer at all to the 20 occurrences of this word in narrator-text. In this respect Griffin is more candid and duly mentions the exceptions, i.e. evaluative and affective words found outside direct speech. It is mainly in such exceptions that I am interested in the following.[98]

Before starting the discussion I want to raise a problem of method. Which words are to be considered evaluative or affective in the first place? Neither Opelt nor Griffin indicate according to which criteria they have selected their corpus of "Gefühlswörter". Are we to take words like πολύδακρυς ('with many tears': epithet of war) or πολύμητις ('of many devices': epithet of Odysseus) as descriptive or affective/evaluative? This question must be seen separately from that raised by M. Parry, viz. whether fixed epithets have a *particular* (= relevant to the context) or *generic* (= irrespective of the context) meaning: even when πολύμητις is an epithet with generic meaning, one might ask whether it is descriptive or evaluative/affective. It will be understood that the decision is vital to the whole question of the so-called Homeric objectivity. As most scholars, Opelt and Griffin (see esp. 1986: 36, 40, 46) included, qualify the Homeric style as objective and impersonal, they apparently consider a word like πολύμητις purely descriptive. It will have become clear from my discussion of the adjectives of war/fighting (above section 3.1.1, p. 43), that I am inclined - in the wake of Booth: above chapter 1, pp. 24 - to think that even fixed epithets can have an evaluative or affective nuance and that general semantic definitions of evaluative and affective can be applied to them too.[99] Calling Odysseus πολύμητις the NF₁ does evaluate that character or at least *induces the NeFe₁ to admire* clever Odysseus. Indeed, the continual repetition of epithets seems one of the most powerful rhetorical instruments of the NF₁. I will not further pursue this question here but, confining myself to the more obvious or well-known cases of evaluative and affective words/expressions in the narrator-text, return to the subject proper of this section: their narratological analysis.

I begin with three much debated cases:

(59) X 395 = Ψ 24:
καὶ ῞Εκτορα δῖον <u>ἀεικέα</u> μήδετο ἔργα.
and he (Achilles) planned <u>dishonouring</u> deeds for divine Hector.

(60) Ψ 176 (Achilles kills twelve Trojans at Patroclus' pyre)
<u>κακὰ</u> δὲ φρεσὶ μήδετο ἔργα.
and he devised <u>bad</u> deeds in his mind.[100]

Do these words imply moral judgement on the part of the NF$_1$? In favour of this moralistic interpretation are: Ameis-H. (ad Ψ 176) and Segal (1971a: 13-6). Contra: Leaf (ad Ψ 176), Bassett (1933) and Griffin (1977: 45 n. 36). I side with the latter, since ἀεικέα and κακά, as syntactic objects of μήδετο, refer to the thoughts of *Achilles* as F$_2$: thus, he had himself voiced his intention to dishonour Hector's body in X 345-54.[101] Observe also that in the majority of cases a dative or accusative indicates the person for/to whom something is bad or dishonouring.[102] This also suggests that ἀεικέα, κακά should be interpreted from the point of view of the characters involved (one as *agens*, the other as *patiens*) and not from that of the NF$_1$. An exceptional case is

(61) Σ 312:
῞Εκτορι μὲν γὰρ ἐπήνησαν κακὰ μητιόωντι
for (the Trojans) agreed with Hector, who was giving bad counsel

It is certainly not Hector's intention to give bad counsel. Here it is the NF$_1$ who indicates that Hector's advice (set out in the speech 285-309) will turn out to be disastrous for the Trojans and for himself. What the NF$_1$ is doing here is not so much criticizing Hector as emphasizing the dramatic mistake (note νήπιοι in 311) he and the Trojans make in not giving heed to Polydamas' 'good advice' (313: ἐσθλὴν βουλήν). This point brings me back to example (59): although I do not think that ἀεικέα implies moral condemnation of Achilles' behaviour by the NF$_1$,[103] it does seem to create (especially through the collocation with δῖον) an effect of pathos.[104]

The third debated case is ἐξαίσιον in

(62) Ο 597-9 (Zeus wanted to give glory to Hector):
ἵνα νηυσὶ κορωνίσι θεσπιδαὲς πῦρ
ἐμβάλῃ ἀκάματον, Θέτιδος δ' ἐξαίσιον ἀρὴν
πᾶσαν ἐπικρήνειε
in order that he (Hector) would throw on the curved ships
consuming, tireless fire, and bring to full completion Thetis'
immoderate request

The whole passage Ο 596-602 is focalized by Zeus (596: ἐβούλετο ... 603: τὰ φρονέων) and the qualification of Thetis' request as 'immoderate'[105] may derive from him as F_2 rather than from the NF_1. Zeus seems to display a certain impatience to fulfil his promise to Thetis: having supported Hector for so long (according to this promise), he now wishes to give the Greeks their due share of glory (note the repetition 596: Ἕκτορι γάρ ... ἐβούλετο κῦδος ὀρέξαι, 602: Δαναοῖσι δὲ κῦδος ὀρέξειν).

The following passage has never been brought forward as a subjective element, but does contain a remarkably direct evaluation:

(63) Γ 28:
φάτο γὰρ τείσεσθαι ἀλείτην.
for he (Menelaus) thought to himself that he would take
revenge upon the <u>sinner</u> (Paris).

The explanation is again that we are dealing with Menelaus' focalization (φάτο) of Paris and that the qualification ἀλείτην is therefore best attributed to this character (cp. also Γ 366) rather than to the NF_1.[106] Like Helen, Paris is nowhere explicitly condemned by the NF_1.

These four examples have made it sufficiently clear, I think, that when dealing with an evaluative or affective word/expression in the narrator-text it is very important to take into account *who is focalizing*: the NF_1 or a character as F_2. Due to the ambiguity inherent in the narrative situation of embedded focalization (it is after all the NF_1 who verbalizes the focalization of the character) it is not always possible to decide with certainty that a certain word should be ascribed to the F_2. Here it can be helpful to look at the distribution of a word over the narrative situations. Certain evaluative or affective words/expressions appear in all three narrative situations (see also appendix I on the adjectives of war/fighting), e.g.[107]

Fig.I

	simple narrator-t.	complex narrator-t.	character-text
δεινός ('terrible')	37	11	10
ὑπέρθυμος ('great-hearted, 'overweening')	8	3	8

In the case of such an even distribution pattern, the ambiguity of embedded focalization remains insoluble. One example may illustrate the problem. Macleod remarks on

(64) Ω 483:
ὣς ᾿Αχιλεὺς θάμβησεν ἰδὼν Πρίαμον θεοειδέα
Thus Achilles was surprised at seeing godlike Priam

"it (the epithet 'godlike) corresponds to Achilles' wonder and it makes Priam his equal (cf. 629-32)". However, if we take the distribution of θεοειδὴς Πρίαμος into account, it appears that (apart from this place) the epithet is always found in simple narrator-text[108] and it is therefore not self-evident to attribute it to Achilles as F_2 in (64). The situation is different in

(65) X 370 (Greek soldiers assemble around Hector's corpse):
οἳ καὶ θηήσαντο φυὴν καὶ εἶδος ἀγητόν
who also admired his stature and admirable appearance

The word ἀγητός is further found in direct speech only (Ε 787, Θ 228, Ω 376), i.e. is used by characters only, and on account of this distribution pattern it seems justified to ascribe it in (65) to the focalizing characters (the Greek soldiers).[109] Let me give an example from a modern novel:

(66) E.M. Forster, A Room with a View

(Lucy) "What does a girl do when she comes across a cad?"
(Miss Bartlett) "I always said he was a cad, dear." She moved feebly to the window, and tried to detect the cad's white flannels among the laurels.

On account of the fact that the (depreciatory) word "cad" is first used twice by speaking characters, its third occurrence in embedded focalization (Miss B. is focalizing) may be ascribed to that focalizing character. Indeed, the NF₁ throughout gives a favourable account of the "cad", George Emerson.

In figure II evaluative and affective words from the *Iliad* are listed which are found mainly in direct speech. When such a word occurs in complex narrator-text, I suggest it should be ascribed to the focalizing character, rather than to the NF₁:

Fig.II

	simple narrator-t.	complex narrator-t.	character-text
ἄαπτος ('irresistible')	2	1 H 309	8
ἀγητός ('admirable')	-	1 X 370	3
ἀεικής ('unseemly', 'shameful')	2	4 M 435, Ξ 13, X 395 = Ψ 24	15
αἰδοῖος ('respectful/-able')	3	1 Δ 402	10
αἰδώς ('shame')	-	1 O 657	15
ἀκηδής, ἀκηδέστως ('without care')	-	1 X 465	5
ἀλαπάζω ('destroy')	1	1 E 166	7
δειλός ('wretched')	4	1 Ψ 221	19
μήστωρα φόβοιο ('causer of flight')	-	2 M 39, Ψ 16	2
μέρμερος ('baneful')	2	1 K 524	4
ὀϊζυρός ('wretched')	1	1 N 569	2 (+10 x *Od.*)

	simple narrator-t.	complex narrator-t.	character-text
ὀλοός,-οιός ('destructive')	3	6 Λ 71 = Π 771, Ν 665, Π 567. 568.701	16
πελώριος ('monstrously big')	3	5 Η 208.211, Ε 594, Φ 527, Χ 92	8

I discuss one example:

(67) Δ 401-2 (Agamemnon has critized Diomedes):
ὣς φάτο, τὸν δ᾽ οὔ τι προσέφη κρατερὸς Διομήδης,
αἰδεσθεὶς βασιλῆος ἐνιπὴν αἰδοίοιο.
Thus he spoke and him valiant Diomedes did not answer,
reverencing the rebuke of the king, worthy to be held in
reverence.

Kirk remarks: "not a standard epithet with βασιλεύς, αἰδοῖος is evidently selected to emphasize the point Diomedes is making." To this I would add that
the distribution pattern of αἰδοῖος confirms that one should ascribe it to
Diomedes: for him Agamemnon (as leader of the expedition) is a person he feels
he should respect.

Occasionally the very distribution pattern of a word can even provide a clue
that it has an affective colouring. Thus, the adjective αἰπύς is found in its
literal sense ('steep') in all narrative situations, but in its figurative sense
('difficult', 'hard') only in embedded focalization (e.g. example 68) or direct speech:

(68) Λ 601 (Achilles stands on the stern of his ship):
εἰσορόων πόνον αἰπὺν ἰῶκά τε δακρυόεσσαν.
watching the sheer toil of war and the lamentable rout'[110]

Another way in which evaluation or affection can be expressed is through *inten-*
sifiers (among which I also count superlatives), and again investigation of distribution patterns can result in interesting observations:[111]

Fig.III

	simple narrator-t.	complex narrator-t.	character-text
διακριδόν ('eminently')	-	1 M 103	1
ὅττι τάχιστα ('as quickly as possible')	-	1 I 659	6
πάγχυ ('altogether', 'entirely')	-	3 E 24, M 268, Π 120	11
ἔχθιστος ('most hateful')	-	1 B 220	3
νεώτατος ('youngest')	-	1 Υ 409	3
φίλτατος ('dearest')	-	3 P 411.584, Υ 410	20

I give two examples:

(69) E 24 (Hephaestus saved the son of Dares):
ὡς δή οἱ μὴ πάγχυ γέρων ἀκαχήμενος εἴη.
in order that the old man (Dares) would not be <u>entirely</u> brought to grief.

(70) P 411 (Thetis did not tell Achilles)
ὅττι ῥά οἱ πολὺ φίλτατος ὤλεθ' ἑταῖρος.
that his <u>dearest</u> companion by far (Patroclus) had died.

For (70) compare in direct speech P 655.

So far I have argued that evaluative and affective words/expressions occurring in embedded focalization should preferably be interpreted in connection with the focalizing character and not be ascribed automatically to the NF_1. In certain cases this analysis could be made more plausible on the basis of the distribution pattern of the word involved. Thus, it has turned out that many of the exceptions recorded by Griffin, viz. evaluative and affective words found outside direct speech, are not really exceptions, since they can be analyzed as focalized by characters. I now turn to the real exceptions, evaluative and affective words which are found mainly in direct speech, but also occasionally occur in simple narrator-text. Again I begin with a much debated word: οὐλομένην ('accursed') as qualification of Achilles' wrath (A 2). The word does indeed seem to reveal personal engagement of the NF_1, if we take into consideration that apart from here it is found only in direct speech.[112] Exactly what sentiment is conveyed by οὐλομένην remains a matter of debate: most commentators[113] take it as a sign of criticism. I do not think this is likely: to criticize Achilles' wrath would mean to criticize Zeus' will (5), which is the "divine extension and intensification" (de Jong 1985a: 10) of that wrath. Rather, through οὐλομένην and the ensuing relative clause ὅ ... πᾶσι the NF_1 announces to the $NeFe_1$ the substance of the narrative to come.

The exceptional use of the particle ἦ in Π 46 seems expressive of the NF_1's sentiments when he first announces Patroclus' death.[114]

An exception which has as yet not been commented upon is

(71) X 403-4:
τότε δὲ Ζεὺς δυσμενέεσσι
δῶκεν ἀεικίσσασθαι ἑῇ ἐν πατρίδι γαίῃ.
and then Zeus granted his (Hector's) enemies
to dishonour him in his own fatherland.

The word δυσμενέεσσι seems to be affective and to underline the pathos which is inherent in the whole passage X 401-4 (see note 104), since it is found, apart from here, in direct speech only. In general, the NF_1 never speaks of 'enemies': for him neither Trojans nor Greeks are enemies. It is the characters who focalize or speak of each other as enemies, as the following figure illustrates:

Fig. IV

	simple narrator-t.	complex narrator-t.	character-text
ἀνάρσιος ('strange')	-	-	1
δήϊος ('destructive')	-	13[115]	13
δυσμενής ('bearing ill-will')	1	-	16

Likewise, most of the instances appearing in the first column of figures II and III turn out to have a pathetic colouring:[116]

ἄαπτος: used by the NF_1 in Λ 169 and Υ 503 to underline the grimness of the massacre brought about by Agamemnon and Achilles.[117]

ἀεικής: used in K 483≅ Φ 20 in combination with στόνος ('groaning' of men being butchered) and then meaning 'miserable'.

ἀλαπάζω: see below on μέρμερος.

δειλός: in E 574 the combination of τὼ ... δειλώ and ἐν χερσὶν ἑταίρων strengthens the pathos inherent in this type of scene (cp. Griffin 1980: 112-5 on the 'near to friends' motif). For X 31 see above p. 126. In Ψ 65 the expression ψυχὴ Πατροκλῆος δειλοῖο ('the soul of wretched Patroclus') anticipates on Achilles' words in Ψ 105-6.

μέρμερος: both μέρμερος and ἀλαπάζω are used by the NF₁ only in the passage Λ 502-3 and call attention to Hector's destructive aristeia.

ὀϊζυρός: in N 569 the combination ἀλεγεινὸς ὀϊζυροῖσι βροτοῖσιν ('painful for wretched humans') emphasizes (note also μάλιστα 'most' in 568) the extreme painfulness of the wound Adamas receives.

ὀλοός, ὀλοιός: in O 605 and Σ 535 the adjective describes the intrinsic des-tructive quality of fire and of the goddess Ker, respectively. But in X 5 the NF₁ through ὀλοιὴ μοῖρα ('baneful fate') anticipates Hector's death with sym-pathy.

Conclusion

In this section I have tried to analyze as precisely as possible to whom (certain) evaluative or affective words/expressions found in the narrator-text are to be ascribed, to the NF₁ or to characters functioning as F₂. So far scholars had distinguished between narrative parts and direct speech only and, therefore, had ascribed all evaluative or affective words occurring in the narrative parts to the poet (the NF₁). These instances were considered the (rare) exceptions to the rule of objectivity, evaluative and affective words occurring mainly in the speeches. Having expressed my doubt as to whether there are indeed so few evaluative or affective words in the narrator-text, i.e. whether scholars do not-by implication: they do not specify their criteria - consider too many words as simply descriptive, I have confined myself to a discussion of the more obvious or well-known cases, which were either brought forward by others as subjective elements or 'exceptions', or collected by myself.

The distinction between simple narrator-text and complex narrator-text has provided us with an important refinement. Many of the subjective elements or 'exceptions' occur in complex narrator-text (embedded focalization) and can therefore be ascribed to the characters. The inherent ambiguity of embedded focalization (it is the NF₁ who verbalizes the focalization of a character) makes it difficult to ascribe with certainty a certain word or expression to the character focalizing. Here investigation of the distribution pattern of a word over the three narrative situations has proved a helpful criterion. If a word is found mainly in character-text, i.e. is used mainly by characters, it seems warranted to ascribe it, when occurring in complex narrator-text, to the character focalizing. Evaluative or affective words/expressions which exhibit such a significant distribution pattern are: ἄαπτος, ἀγητός, ἀεικής, αἰδοῖος, αἰδώς, ἀκηδής, ἀκήδεστως, ἀλαπάζω, ἀνάρσιος, δειλός, δήϊος, διακριδόν, δυσμενής, ἔχθιστος, μήστωρα φόβοιο, μέρμερος, νεώτατος, ὀϊζυρός, ὀλοός, ὀλοιός, ὅττι τάχιστα, πάγχυ, πέλωριος, φίλτατος. Again, when a word is found mainly in embedded focalization and direct speech, its occurrence in simple narrator-text can often be argued to convey to the passage a pathetic colouring.

It is to be expected that further research will reveal more significant distribution patterns. I am thinking in particular of particles, comparatives, and pronouns (e.g. the so-called sympathetic and ethic datives). Another branch of Homeric research which might benefit from the distinction between simple and complex narrator-text is that initiated by Austin (1975: 11-80, and cp. Vivante 1982: 205-7), who shows that different characters (and the NF_1) use different epithets (e.g. for Odysseus).

4.4. Summary

The heroes of this chapter were characters functioning as secondary focalizers in the narrator-text and the main result of my investigations may be summed up in the statement that the characters' influence on, or participation in, the presentation of the story reaches further than the speeches alone, the domain traditionally assigned to them. Their perceptions, emotions, and speeches can be represented by the NF_1 as embedded (secondary) focalization. It will now have become clear why I have chosen the term 'complex narrator-text'. Through 'complex' it is indicated that the presentation is in the hands of more than one presentator: NF_1 *and* F_2. This complexity of presentation brings about its own problems - the NF_1 intruding upon the focalization of an F_2; uncertainty as to whether an evaluative or affective word is to be ascribed to the NF_1 or to the F_2 - yet also has its own advantages, to be summarized below.

Though not as frequent nor as long as the narrative situations of simple narrator-text and character-text, complex narrator-text manifests itself in the *Iliad* in a surprising variety of forms. Explicit embedded focalization is found after verbs of perceiving, finding, feeling (etc.) and speaking. Implicit embedded focalization can take the form of final, (certain) causal or relative clauses and indirect (deliberative) questions. Sometimes it is simply the addition of a dative which indicates that what is told represents the focalization of one character. All these forms of complex narrator-text often contain evaluative or affective words/expressions, which then correspond or give expression to the emotions of the focalizing character. In a considerable number of cases investigation of the distribution pattern of these words has confirmed their interpretation in connection with the focalizing character rather than the verbalizing NF_1.

The main advantage of embedded focalization as a mode of presentation is exactly its intermediate position between simple narrator-text and character-text:

simple narrator-text	: NF_1
complex narrator-text	: $NF_1[F_2C_x]$
character-text	: $NF_1[NF_2C_x]$

It allows the NF_1

- to include what is not deemed worth quoting nor meant to be quoted in direct speech (orders, feelings of women or soldiers, a character's private thoughts);
- to enliven and motivate the events presented in the simple narrator-text. Especially, it gives clues as to why a character comes into action: actions are triggered by perceptions or by perceptions and emotions. Very often embedded focalization forms the transition to a speech, in which a character, promoted from F_2 to NF_2, narrates what he or she has seen, how he or she feels and what he or she intends or suggests to do.

Perhaps the most unexpected extension of the character's influence on the presentation of the story illustrated in this chapter is formed by the assimilated comparisons and similes. In these comparisons or similes the NF_1 illustrates not just an event, but an event as experienced by one of the characters. Thus, though himself remaining focalizer, the NF_1 assimilates his focalization to one of the characters. This character often in the context functions as F_2, which helps to detect this type of assimilated comparison and simile. There are even a few comparisons and similes in the narrator-text which are actually focalized by characters.

If one acknowledges the validity of the narrative situation of complex narrator-text in the *Iliad* as analyzed in this chapter, one acknowledges a considerable degree of sophistication in the Homeric narrative style. Moreover, embedded focalization offers us brief, but maybe more liberal (all social and sexual classes are represented) and uninhibited (thoughts rather not pronounced aloud) access to the characters' minds than the speeches do.

5. CHARACTER-TEXT (SPEECHES)

> "Die Personen des Dichters sagen nicht nur, was der Vers fordert, sondern auch was sie wollen." (Ø. Andersen, *Der Diomedes-Gestalt in der Ilias*)

In this chapter the narrative situation of character-text (direct speech) - which takes up 45% of the *Iliad*[1] - is central. In their speeches characters themselves verbalize (as N_2) their perceptions, emotions, interpretations, in short their focalization (as F_2) of events, persons, objects etc. The recipients of their words are other characters, functioning as secondary narratee-focalizee, $NeFe_2$. When characters speak, this is an event on the level of the (primary) fabula just like all other actions by characters. However, speeches are a special type of events in that they result in texts, which are embedded in the primary text. The events of the secondary fabula can belong to the same period of time as that covered by the primary fabula, but they can also, and this is a special characteristic of character-text, belong to a period preceding or following that covered by the primary fabula.[2]

The fact that character-text is embedded in the narrator-text has two consequences:

1. the NF_1 can exercize influence, e.g. by determining how long a character is allowed to speak

2. the $NeFe_1$ also receives the message of the speaking character.

Especially this second point is a factor of importance in the *Iliad*. For instance, it explains the working of a form of *dramatic irony*, viz. when words spoken by characters have a different meaning for the NeFe$_1$ than they have for the characters who speak and hear.[3] The NeFe$_1$ is privileged compared to the NeFe$_2$, since he receives *all* speeches as well as, of course, the information of the narrator-text. Again, as we will see in section 5.4, the repetition of verse clusters in different speeches can often be noticed and savoured by the NeFe$_1$ only.

Since character-text occupies almost half of the *Iliad*, it will be clear that in this chapter only some aspects of this narrative situation can be discussed. Before announcing which these will be, I give a short (systematical, not chronological) inventory of scholarship on the Iliadic speeches.[4] Scholars have investigated:

1. the different types of speeches (monologue, dialogue, prayers, adhortations etc.): see Fingerle (1939) on the "Typik" of Homeric speeches, Beckmann (1932) on prayers, Petersmann (1973, 1974) on monologues and Latacz (1977) on "Kampfparänesen".

2. the distribution of the speeches over the poem: see Myres (1954).

3. the formal structure of the speeches: see Lohmann (1970: 12-94) on "Innere Komposition".

4. the relations between speeches: see Lohmann (1970: 95-156) on "Äußere Komposition", i.e. relations between speeches which follow closely upon another and (157-82) on "Übergreifende Komposition", i.e. relations between speeches which stand at a distance from each other.

5. speech as a "personality symbol": already an old topic (see Lohmann 1970: 1 n. 3), it has been pursued with new energy since the emergence of the oral-formulaic theory: see A. Parry (1956), Reeve (1973, against Parry), Claus (1975), Friedrich & Redfield (1978), Schein (1980, against Reeve), Messing (1981), Friedrich & Redfield (1981, against Messing), Scully (1984) and Griffin (1986: 50-7).

In view of the main orientation of my study, I will concentrate on aspects of the presentation of the story in speeches. I begin (5.1) with a discussion of cases where different speakers describe the same event, because these are straightforward illustrations of the way in which characters function as NF$_2$'s. In 5.2 the presentation by a character of an *external analepsis* is analyzed. In 5.3 I discuss the way in which speaking characters represent the words of other characters. In 5.4 a typically Homeric feature is tackled: the verbatim repetition of verse clusters in speeches (repeated speech).

5.1. Different speakers referring to the same event

Speeches are the verbal expression by characters of their own focalization. One example will suffice to illustrate this: N 620-39, which typologically belongs to the category of triumph speeches, contains Menelaus' focalization of the Trojan war. In the *Iliad* Menelaus operates for the greater part in the shadow of other heroes like Agamemnon, Achilles or Odysseus.[5] Only in N 620-39 does he get the chance to express fully - it his longest speech in the *Iliad* - his feelings concerning the Trojans:[6] for him the fighting is not just a heroic undertaking where fame is achieved and booty gained (as it is, for example, for Achilles), but he is personally taking revenge on the Trojans for the 'outrage' (λώβης: 622, λωβή-σασθε: 623) they have inflicted on him in the past (by taking away Helen and many of his possessions) and are still inflicting in the present (by continuing to fight instead of making amends).[7]

Due to the fact that the speaking characters are themselves closely involved in the events they refer to in their speeches, the narrative situation of character-text contains many emotional words (cp. Menelaus' use of λώβη, λωβήσασθε) and expressive particles. E.g. δυσάμμορος, δύσμορος ('very miserable'), λοίγιος ('baneful'), σχέτλιος ('tough', 'merciless'), ἐτέον ('truly'), θην ('in truth'), που ('methinks') are found in direct speech only. For this see further section 4.3.

By putting their emotions and opinions into words, characters communicate them to other characters.[8] This presence of an audience can influence the presentation of the speaking character, i.e. his/her selection, interpretation and verbalization of events. He or she can choose to leave out or, conversely, emphasize certain elements, strive for rhetorical effects or even purposefully give false information. Both principles, viz. 1) that in their speeches characters are the narrators of their own focalization and 2) that they can adapt their presentation according to the person(s) they are addressing, become very clear when *different* speakers refer to the *same* event/person[9] or when *one* speaker addresses *different* persons on account of the *same* event/person. For example, compare the following three references to Sarpedon:

(1) Π 521-2 (Glaucus: Apollo):
                "ἀνὴρ δ' ὥριστος ὄλωλε,
Σαρπηδών, Διὸς υἱός"
"our best man is dead, Sarpedon, son of Zeus"

(2) Π 541-2 (Glaucus: Hector)
"κεῖται Σαρπηδών, Λυκίων ἀγὸς ἀσπιστάων,
ὃς Λυκίην εἴρυτο δίκῃσί τε καὶ σθένεϊ ᾧ"
"Sarpedon lies low, leader of the shield-bearing Lycians,
who protected Lycia by his right judgments and by his valour"

(3) Π 558-9 (Patroclus: Ajaxes):
"κεῖται ἀνὴρ ὃς πρῶτος ἐσήλατο τεῖχος Ἀχαιῶν,
Σαρπηδών"
"dead lies the man who first scaled the wall of the Greeks,
Sarpedon"

When addressing Apollo, Sarpedon's compatriot Glaucus refers to him as 'son of Zeus' (example 1); when addressing Hector (example 2), the same character stresses Sarpedon's status as an ally and a man honoured by his compatriots. Patroclus, opponent of Sarpedon, adhorts the Ajaxes by reminding them of the important role Sarpedon played in destroying the Greek wall (example 3).[10] In the remainder of this section seven more examples of different speeches referring to the same event/person will be discussed.

Second example
The event of Thetis' supplication to Zeus (to honour her son Achilles) is referred to both by Hera (4) and Athena (5):

(4) A 557 (Hera: Zeus)
"ἠερίη γὰρ σοί γε παρέζετο καὶ <u>λάβε</u> γούνων"
"for in the morning she (Thetis) sat herself next to you
and <u>took</u> your knees"

(5) Θ 371 (Athena: Hera):
"ἥ οἱ γούνατ' <u>ἔκυσσε</u> καὶ ἔλλαβε χειρὶ γενείου"
"(Thetis) who <u>kissed</u> his knees and took his chin with her
hand"

Hera's version is accurate - it resembles that of the NF₁ (A 500: λάβε γούνων and 512: ἥψατο γούνων) and of Zeus himself (Ο 76: ἥψατο γούνων). She is bent on provoking Zeus (κερτομίοισι: A 539) and lets him feel that she knows perfectly well that something has been contrived by him and Thetis.[11] Athena in (5) is very angry with Zeus and, conversing privately with Hera, she turns to a "malicious exaggeration" (Edwards 1980: 25).

Third example

In the following two passages a difference in focalization between gods and human beings is nicely brought out by their (partly) using the same formulation, in connection to a similar event, viz. breaking off war/a duel:

(6) H 29-32 (Apollo: Athena):
"νῦν μὲν παύσωμεν πόλεμον καὶ δηϊοτῆτα
σήμερον· ὕστερον αὖτε μαχήσοντ᾽, εἰς ὅ κε τέκμωρ
Ἰλίου εὕρωσιν, ἐπεὶ ὣς φίλον ἔπλετο θυμῷ
ὑμῖν ἀθανάτῃσι, διαπραθέειν τόδε ἄστυ."
"But let us now put an end to the fighting, today: tomorrow they will fight again <u>until they reach the end of Troy, for this pleases you goddesses, to destroy this city</u>"

(7) H 290-2 (Hector: Ajax) ≅ 375-8 (Priam: Trojans) ≅ 394-7 (Idaeus: Greeks):
"νῦν μὲν παύσωμεν πόλεμον καὶ δηϊοτῆτα
σήμερον· ὕστερον αὖτε μαχησόμεθ᾽, εἰς ὅ κε δαίμων
ἄμμε διακρίνη, δώῃ δ᾽ ἑτέροισί γε νίκην"
"But let us now cease fighting, today: tomorrow we will fight again, <u>until a god separates us, and gives one of us victory</u>"

The gods (6) know what the future will bring (the destruction of Troy) and are themselves executers of that future, whereas the Trojan focalizers (7) put their individual (Hector) and collective (Priam and Idaeus) fate into the hands of the gods and still give themselves 50% chance to win.

Fourth example

In H 337-43 Nestor suggests to the Greek leaders that they construct a wall and a ditch[12] around the camp as 'protection for our ships and ourselves' (H 338: εἶλαρ νηῶν τε καὶ αὐτῶν). The first reaction to this wall comes from the side of the gods: Poseidon, who correctly assesses its defensive function (449: νεῶν ὕπερ) is angry, because the Greeks have not brought the proper offerings and even more so because he fears that the fame of this wall will surpass that of the one around Troy, built by himself and Apollo. Zeus (455-63) reassures him that he will be allowed to destroy the wall of the the Greeks once they have returned home (cp. M 3-35, discussed above section 3.3.3, pp. 88-9). This already warns us that the wall may not the indestructible bulwark the Greeks hope it to be. And indeed, the one who should have been impressed by it, Hector, is not: confident on account of Zeus' support (Θ 170-1), he (dis)qualifies it in front of the Trojans as 'weak and nobody's care' (Θ 178: ἀβλήχρ᾽ οὐδενόσωρα).

He declares that it will not retain his might and that his horses will 'easily' (179: ῥέα) jump over the ditch. His low opinion of the wall is shared by Achilles (Ι 349-52), who observes sarcastically that Agamemnon[13] has even built a wall and a ditch, 'wide and great' (350: εὐρεῖαν μεγάλην), to compensate for his, Achilles', absence from the battlefield. But even so, he warns Odysseus, he will not be able to halt Hector. And indeed, Hector breaks through the wall in Μ 457-66. Nestor (8) and Agamemnon (9) look back in

(8)   Ξ 55-6:
"τεῖχος μὲν γὰρ δὴ κατερήριπεν, ᾧ ἐπέπιθμεν
<u>ἄρρηκτον</u> νηῶν τε καὶ αὐτῶν εἶλαρ ἔσεσθαι"
"for the wall lies destroyed on which we relied, to be a protection <u>not to be broken through</u> for the ships and for ourselves"

(9)   Ξ 66-8:
"τεῖχος δ' οὐκ ἔχραισμε τετυγμένον, οὐδέ τι τάφρος,
ᾗ ἔπι πόλλ' ἔπαθον Δαναοί, ἔλποντο δὲ θυμῷ
<u>ἄρρηκτον</u> νηῶν τε καὶ αὐτῶν εἶλαρ ἔσεσθαι"
"the wall built has not availed us, nor the ditch, at which the Greeks suffered much, and they hoped it to be a protection <u>not to be broken through</u> for the ships and for themselves"

If we compare Ξ 56 and 68 to Η 338 we see that Nestor and Agamemnon now add the qualification 'not to be broken through', emphasizing exactly that quality of the wall which has proved disappointing.

Fifth example
Having killed Patroclus, Hector decides not only to rob him of his (in fact, Achilles') armour, but actually to put it on himself. Hector calls the armour beautiful (καλά: Ρ 187) and for him it has an additional attraction in being 'the famous armour of Peleus' son' (κλυτὰ τεύχεα Πηλεΐονος: 191). Zeus condemns Hector's act of putting on Achilles' 'divine' (ἄμβροτα: 202) armour. With 'divine' he alludes to the fact that the gods had given the armour to Achilles' father Peleus, information which just before (194-6) had been provided to the NeFe$_1$ by the NF$_1$. The armour is for the last time referred to by Achilles himself in Σ 82-5: he calls it 'impressively big' (πελώρια: 83), 'a marvel to behold' (θαῦμα ἰδέσθαι: 83), 'beautiful' (καλά: 84) and recalls that it had been a divine wedding present (84-5).

Sixth example

This example illustrates the adaptation by a speaker of his presentation in accordance to his addressee. Poseidon, exhorting the Greek leaders (N 95-124), emphatically states that Agamemnon is 'entirely and truly to blame' (πάμπαν ἐτήτυμον αἴτιος: 111) for the present misery of the Greeks, because he 'dishonoured' (ἀπητίμησε: 113) Achilles. In Ξ 139-46, however, when the same god addresses (and exhorts) Agamemnon himself, he puts the blame for the Greek losses entirely with Achilles, whom he considers heartless (οὗ οἱ ἔνι φρένες οὐδ' ἠβαιαί: 141) and whom he curses in rather aggressive terms (142).[14] Both in N and in Ξ Poseidon does not speak *in propria persona*, but in human disguise. The difference in mask (in N he assumes the shape of Calchas, in Ξ that of an anonymous old man) seems to symbolize the difference between the opinions he voices. We can only guess at Poseidon's personal opinion concerning the conflict between Agamemnon and Achilles.

Seventh example

In their speeches characters can tell stories (*internal or external analepses*: see above section 3.3.3). The subject of these analepses belongs to the next section (5.2), but at this point I want to draw attention to an external analepsis which is presented by different speakers: the story of Tydeus' embassy to Thebes.[15] It is presented by Agamemnon (Δ 372-98), Athena (E 802-8), and Diomedes (K 285-90).[16]

Agamemnon's version is by far the most elaborate one. He addresses (Tydeus' son) Diomedes and accuses him of not displaying the same fighting spirit as his famous father. The ensuing story of Tydeus' embassy serves therefore as a hortatory paradigm.[17] Agamemnon's account runs as follows: Tydeus and Polynices come to Mycenae to gather military support for their expedition against Thebes (where Polynices' brother Eteocles is reigning). At first they seem to be successful, but then a portent sent by Zeus detains the Mycenaeans from joining the expedition. Therefore, the expedition sets out without them and when they have reached the river Asopus, Tydeus is sent alone as an ambassador to Thebes. At the court of Eteocles, Tydeus challenges the Thebans to meet him in an athletic contest and with the support of Athena he is victorious on all points. In revenge, the Thebans lay an ambush for him on his way back, but again he defeats them all, sparing one man to report the defeat in Thebes.

One reason why Agamemnon's version is longer than those of Athena and

Diomedes, is that he starts with a prelude about Tydeus' stay at Mycenae (Δ 376-81). Since, in the end, Tydeus' activities there remain without result and have no consequences for the events to follow, one might ask why this episode is mentioned at all. I suggest that here the identity of the speaker, the NF₂, is relevant: it is Agamemnon, *king of Mycenae*, who is speaking and through the Mycenae-episode he indicates that there has been contact between his family and the famous Tydeus. More in particular, as Andersen (1978: 35) has suggested, Agamemnon subtly reminds Diomedes that at that time the Mycenaeans had shown themselves prepared tò help Tydeus. Therefore, Diomedes should now fight with all his might to help Agamemnon.[18] Since he intends the external analepsis to function as a hortatory paradigm, Agamemnon stresses in particular the bravery of Tydeus, who alone twice faced (and beat) a majority of opponents: πολέας ... Καδμείωνας: 385; μοῦνος ἐὼν πολέσιν μετὰ Καδμείοισιν: 388; πάντα: 389; πάντας: 397.

In <u>Athena</u>'s version the addressee (NeFe₂) is again Diomedes, and again the external analepsis serves as a hortatory paradigm. Yet, there are some significant differences, due to the fact that Athena is now the focalizer: she concentrates on the episode of the athletic contest and adds that at first she had not allowed Tydeus to provoke the Thebans and had ordered him to sit down at dinner and keep quiet (E 802-5) - this is information Agamemnon could not have. The rhetorical reason for this extra information is to give her introductory remark (801: 'Tydeus was small of stature, but a real fighter') more relief: the hero's fighting spirit was so exuberant, that in spite of her advice, he challenged (and defeated) the Thebans. The goddess pays tribute to his courage by assisting him.[19]

The last version is that of <u>Diomedes</u> himself, addressing Athena in prayer. Of the whole story of Tydeus' embassy, Diomedes only tells that Tydeus went alone to Thebes, leaving the other Greeks behind near the river Asopus. He adds the detail that Tydeus went with a conciliatory message (K 288) and stresses in particular Athena's assistance (290), which he mentions in connection with the ambush and not - as Agamemnon and Athena had done - with the athletic contest. The emphasis put on Athena's assistance is of course to be understood in the light of the fact that he is praying for help to that goddess now (παρέστης: 290, παρίστασο: 291)[20] and the change from 'help during contest' into 'help on way back' might be the result of the situation Diomedes finds himself in: he is on his way, together with Odysseus, to spy on the Trojans and hopes for a safe return (cp. earlier Odysseus' prayer: 281-2).

Taking all three versions together, I conclude that the presentation of an external analepsis in character-text is conditioned by

a. who is speaking

b. to whom and

c. in what situation, i.e. for what purpose.[21]

Thus, we have seen how

- the identity of the speaker can explain the *addition* of certain elements (in the case of Agamemnon: the prelude about Tydeus in Mycenae; in the case of Athena: her advice to Tydeus to keep quiet);

- the rhetorical function of the embedded story can explain the *emphasis* put on certain aspects of the story (Agamemnon and Athena stressing Tydeus' prowess, Diomedes Athena's assistance);

- the identity of the addressee conditions the *selection* of information. Twice the addressee is Diomedes, once Athena, who can both be expected to be familiar with the story and therefore need not be told details which are irrelevant for the point to be made.

Eighth example

My last example concerns the passage O 458-493, where one event, the breaking of Teucer's bowstring, is successively presented by the NF_1 (458-65), Teucer himself (467-70), his brother Ajax (472-3) and Hector (486-93).

The presentation by the <u>NF_1</u> runs as follows: in 437-41 Ajax had adhorted his brother Teucer to shoot arrows at the Trojans, in order to avenge a companion killed by Hector. With his first shot Teucer indeed kills a Trojan and in 458-9, taking another arrow, he aims at Hector. The NF_1 emphasizes the danger of the situation by pointing out in the form of an *if not*-situation that, had Teucer killed Hector, an end would have come to the fighting near the Greek ships.[22] In other words, the Διὸς βουλή would have come to a premature end. It is, therefore, no surprise that Zeus himself intervenes and saves the life of Hector by breaking Teucer's 'well-twisted' string on his 'perfect' bow at the moment he is pulling it. As a result the arrow 'heavy with bronze' swerves astray and the bow drops from Teucer's hand. The crucial passage 462-5, describing Zeus' intervention, is highlighted by an abundance of epithets,[23] all in unique combination with their noun: ἐϋστρεφέα νευρήν, ἀμύμονι τόξῳ, ἰὸς χαλκοβαρής. The epithets emphasize the excellence of Teucer's equipment, and thereby foreground all the more the abruptness of Zeus' intervention.

The 'victim' of Zeus' intervention, the one who is robbed of his εὖχος ('triumph': 462) is <u>Teucer</u>. He shudders and immediately expresses to his brother Ajax his surprise (note 467: ὢ πόποι) about what has happened: the string was 'newly twisted' (νεόστροφον: 469, a *hapax*) and had been adjusted only that morning. To see it broken so quickly suggests to him that a god must have wished to frustrate their plan (to avenge their fallen companion). There are some interesting changes in comparison to the version of the NF₁: instead of ἔκπεσε (465: the bow 'fell out of' his hand) Teucer claims that the god has 'smashed it' (468: ἔκβαλε) from his hand. Instead of ῥῆξ' (464: 'snapped'), we find the more expressive ἐξέρρηξε (469: 'snapped asunder'). Most interesting, however, is his use of δαίμων (468: 'a god'), to which I shall return presently.

In his answer, <u>Ajax</u> suggests to his brother to let the bow and numerous arrows lie and to continue fighting with his spear, 'because a god (θεός) has confounded them, begrudging the Greeks' (473). As he is trying to calm his brother and also is not the direct victim of the divine intervention, Ajax shows a certain distance in his interpretation of the event: whereas Teucer had connected the divine intervention only with the two of them (467-8: μάχης ... μήδεα ... ἡμετέρης), Ajax sees it in a wider perspective: all Greeks are suffering from it. In contrast to the omniscient NF₁, neither Teucer nor Ajax know that it is Zeus who has broken Teucer's bowstring. The unexpected nature of the event, however, induces both speakers to explain it in terms of divine intervention. The question arises why Teucer uses δαίμων and Ajax θεός. According to most scholars, the words are synonyms: together with θεοί or Ζεύς, they are used by characters whenever they do not know or do not wish to say whoever of the individual gods is responsible. Other scholars claim that there is an ontological difference between (Olympic) gods and daimones. I have argued elsewhere, together with N. van der Ben, that there is a functional difference between δαίμων and θεός.[24] In Appendix IV I have collected the observations and figures on which our interpretation is based. Both δ. and θ. can refer to Olympic gods, but δ. (which occurs far less often than θ.) is almost exclusively used by *human* speakers, whenever they feel that a god interferes for a *short* time, *directly* and *concretely* in their life; θ. is used both by *human and divine* speakers, often in reference to situations and qualities, i.e. to divine influence over a *longer* perod, or in *general* contexts. Accordingly, the direct victim Teucer, voicing his individual disappointment, uses δ. (a parallel is Φ 93), whereas Ajax, having a more distanced and general perspective, uses θ. (a parallel is P 688).

He who profits from Zeus' intervention, and the last speaker in the succession, is <u>Hector</u>. His speech is preceded by embedded focalization:

(10) O 484:
"Εκτωρ δ' ὡς εἰδεν Τεύκρου βλαφθέντα βέλεμνα
And Hector, as soon as he saw <u>that Teucer's projectiles
were baffled</u> (adhorted his men)

Hector immediately grasps the psychological advantage to be gained from this event - he does not seem to be aware that he himself has only just escaped death - and tells his men what he has seen (489 ≅ 484), adding the significant detail that the projectiles were baffled 'by Zeus' (Διόθεν). Of course, he has not actually seen Zeus intervene, but like Teucer and Ajax he infers from the unexpectedness of the event that a god must have had a hand in it. For rhetorical purposes, and also because since Λ 207-9 he knows himself continually supported by Zeus, he mentions that god, unwittingly telling the truth. With this confident statement of Hector's the circle is complete and we have returned to where we started: an intervention by Zeus. All four presentators have given their interpretation of the event of Teucer's bowstring breaking. The NF_1 mentions the individual good luck (of Hector) and bad luck (of Teucer), Teucer curses his own bad luck, Ajax, broadening the perspective, speaks of the plight of all the Greeks, and Hector (ignorant of his own individual good luck) tells his men that Zeus is thwarting the Greeks and helping the Trojans. The differences in focalization are neatly matched on the level of the text: Ζεύς - δαίμων - θεός-Ζεύς.

Conclusion
Analysis of cases where different speakers (or one speaker addressing different persons) refer to the same event/person has seemed the best method to illustrate some aspects of the presentation of the story by characters in character-text.
Two basic facts are
    1. that in comparison to the one NF_1 (and $NeFe_1$) there is a multitude of NF_2's (and $NeFe_2$'s) and
    2. that the speaking (and hearing) characters are personally involved in the events they refer to in their speeches. In fact, their speeches themselves constitute events on the level of the primary fabula and can exercize a considerable influence on the course of events. This explains why in many cases

the characters' focalization is of an emotional nature and why their presentation (even of external analepses) is always functional and aimed at achieving certain effects (persuasion or dissuasion).

More specifically, we have seen how the

3. nationality (Trojan-Greek) of a speaker, cp. examples 1, 4, 8

4. nature (divine-human) of speaker or addressee, cp. examples 1, 3, 4, 5, and 7

5. identity of speaker, cp. examples 4 (Hector, Achilles, Nestor, Agamemnon), 5 (Hector, Achilles), 7 (Agamemnon, Diomedes), 8 (Teucer, Ajax, Hector)

6. identity of addressee, cp. examples 2 (Zeus-Hera), 6 (Greek leaders, Agamemnon)

7. purpose of the speech (exhortation, prayer), cp. examples 1, 6, 7, 8.

all are factors which determine the focalization and narration by characters. As a result, speeches offer a richly varied, often emotionally coloured spectre of interpretations, evaluations and verbalizations. One character may even voice two different opinions. Interpretators of the Homeric texts should acknowledge, indeed profit from, this diversity of opinions, instead of flattening them out, either by athetesis or interpolation. It is one of the *Iliad*'s attractions that it is, in epic terminology, πολύφημος: 'many-voiced'.

5.2. External analepses told by characters

The investigation of digressions, exempla, paradigms or, as I prefer to label them *external analepses*, occurring in character-text is certainly not a neglected field of Homeric scholarship: see Oehler (1925), Kakridis (1949: 111-42, 96-105), Willcock (1964), Austin (1966), Gaisser (1969a), Hebel (1970), Braswell (1971), Lang (1983) and Andersen (1987). In view of the large number of external ana-lepses told by characters and the abundant scholarly attention they have already received, I restrict myself in this section to the discussion of some general char-acteristics and then the analysis of one example, the Bellerophontes-story (Z 155-95).

General characteristics

Characteristic for all external analepses is the "casual, allusive and elliptical way" in which they are presented (Austin 1966: 297, and cp. Kirk 1962: 164-6:

"the abbreviated-reference style"). The speaking character presupposes the stories, especially those of the remote past, which we call myths, to be known to his addressee, just as the NF_1 presupposes them to be known to the $NeFe_1$, and, ultimately, the poet to his public. The speaker concentrates on those details which he or she considers relevant for the present context. In the story about Ares being shut up in a bronze pot by Otus and Ephialtes (E 385-91), for example, we do not hear why the two did so nor what happened to them afterwards. The character speaking is Dione, who tries to console her wounded daughter Aphrodite, the $NeFe_2$. Accordingly, she concentrates on Ares' suffering and stresses the fact that he endured the pain.

External analepses told by characters differ from those told by the NF_1 as regards their function: as we have seen above (pp. 89-90), the latter serve to provide background information or to confer pathos. The former are told for a variety of reasons, always in subservience to the rhetorical purpose of the speech as a whole:[25] through them characters exhort (e.g. Phoenix in I 529-99), console (e.g. Dione in E 385-404) their addressees or recommend (e.g. Diomedes in Ξ 119-25), excuse (e.g. Agamemnon in T 95-133) themselves. Besides this *argument* function, an external analepsis can have a *key* function, when it contains a sign for the $NeFe_1$ (see Andersen 1987 and above, section 3.3.3, p. 85).

A last general point which deserves attention is the question how the speaking characters know what they are telling. In a great number of cases they have themselves witnessed (e.g. Antenor in Γ 205-24)[26] or even actively participated in the events (e.g. Nestor's reminiscences from his youth: A 260-73, H 132-57, Λ 670-762, Ψ 629-43). Sometimes both speaker and addressee have played a role in the events and the speaker can draw on common memory, e.g.

(11) O 18 (Zeus to Hera):
"ἦ οὐ μέμνῃ ὅτε τε κρέμω ὑψόθεν ...;"
"Or do you not remember the time when you were suspended from above ...?"[27]

When they have not themselves been present at the events they narrate, speaking characters often qualify their information as generally known (example 12) or deriving from hearsay (13), which in an oral society (as depicted in the *Iliad*) was a positive, rather than a negative qualification (cp. above section 3.1.1., p. 51):

(12) Υ 214 (Aeneas is about to tell his genealogy):
      "πολλοὶ δέ μιν ἄνδρες ἴσασι"
      "and many people know it"[28]

(13) Δ 374-5 (Agamemnon to Diomedes: Tydeus always fought
      before the others):
      "ὣς φάσαν οἵ μιν ἴδοντο πονεύμενον· οὐ γὰρ ἔγωγε
      ἤντησ' οὐδὲ ἴδον· περὶ δ' ἄλλων φασὶ γενέσθαι."
      "thus said those who had seen him fighting: I for my part
      have never met nor seen him, but they say that he surpassed
      all others."[29]

With statements like these speaking characters authorize their stories, just as
the NF₁ does by invoking *his* eyewitnesses, the Muses.

The Bellerophontes-story
The external analepsis of the Bellerophontes-story is told by Glaucus to Diomedes
in Z 155-95. I have chosen this example because existent interpretations, with
one exception,[30] are of a genetic nature. Scholars have compared the Homeric
version of the story to others - either later, Greek ones (Radermacher 1938:
96-117, Gaisser 1969b), or a (hypothetical) earlier one (Peppermüller 1962) or
Near Eastern parallels (Strömberg 1961, White 1982) - and drawn up inventories
of fairy-tale motifs, adaptations of traditional material and omissions. Especially
the numerous omissions (e.g. of the famous winged horse Pegasus)[31] have bothered
scholars, who offered the following explanations:

   1. Homer did not know certain details (Radermacher)

   2. knowledge of this suppressed information could be presupposed with the
audience (Strömberg, Peppermüller)

   3. the speaking character Glaucus wishes to gloss over negative points
concerning his ancestor (Radermacher, Hebel, Gaisser 1969b)

   4. by leaving out the crimes of B. (killing of Bellerus, flying too high with
Pegasus), but mentioning the divine curses which befall him, Homer gives a picture
of B. as a man prone to mysterious and unexplicable vicissitudes of life. Thus,
he adapts the B.-narrative to illustrate the simile concerning the alternations of
glory and decay in human life (Z 146-9) with which Glaucus opens his speech
(Gaisser 1969b).
Of these four explanations, the first is gratuitous (exactly what Homer knew or
did not know is now very difficult, if not impossible, to retrace); the second
too general; the third valid (but not sufficient), the fourth attractive. However,
what is still lacking is an interpretation of the story as it stands: is it coherent

enough to be understood by Diomedes, *to* whom it is told in the first place, and can its particular form be explained from Glaucus' individual situation, *by* whom it is told in the first place?

Let us first have a look at the context of Glaucus' speech, of which the story forms a part. In Z 119-236 an encounter on the battlefield between the Lycian Glaucus and the Greek Diomedes is described. The scene, which is supposed to take place in the time during which Hector walks from the battlefield to the Trojan gates, consists of a short introduction by the NF₁ (119-22),[32] three speeches (by Diomedes: 123-43, Glaucus: 145-211 and Diomedes: 215-31) and a conclusion by the NF₁ (232-6). Diomedes opens the verbal exchange[33] by asking his opponent 'who he is of the mortal humans', announcing that, if he is human, he will fight with him, but if he is a god, he will not. Glaucus at first seems unwilling to answer Diomedes' question: why should he bother to tell his ancestry, when the generations of men are as fleeting as those of leaves (145-9)? Yet, by implication this simile does provide an answer: he is a human being, not a god.[34] Glaucus proceeds to present his genealogy *ab ovo* (152-210), dwelling at length on his grandfather Bellerophontes (155-95) and ending with the proud conclusion: 'of such ancestry and blood I claim to be' (211). Events then take a somewhat unexpected turn, since instead of a fight, there follows a third speech, in which Diomedes announces that they are guest-friends by inheritance: his grandfather Oineus once entertained Glaucus' grandfather Bellerophontes, at which occasion the two exchanged gifts. Accordingly, Diomedes suggests that they do not fight, but instead also exchange gifts, specifically (parts of) their armour. Glaucus agrees and thus the encounter comes to a peaceful end.[35] Already from this broad sketch it appears that the B.-story plays an important role in the encounter: it can be said to be triggered by Diomedes' question and in its turn to cause Diomedes' second speech and, in fact, to provide the key to the peaceful settlement.

When taking a closer look at Glaucus' speech itself, the immediate context of the B.-story, it is instructive to compare Φ 149-61, where a very similar question-answer exchange takes place between Achilles and Asteropaeus. Achilles asks Asteropaeus: 'who and whereof are you of men, who *dare* to come against me? *Unhappy* are the parents whose children meet my might' (Φ 150-1). From the italicized words it becomes clear that Achilles' question is not so much a request for information as a way to intimidate his opponent. Although Diomedes asks the same question (Z 123, Φ 150) and adds the same threatening words (Z 127 = Φ 151), his tone is not aggressive (note the vocative φέριστε, 'my dear' in 123) and, as his reference to the fate of Lycurgus (130-41) indicates, he is really anxious to know whom he faces. Here we should recall that in E 127-31 Athena had instructed Diomedes not to fight with gods. Only at the end of his speech (143) does he show an aggressive confidence similar to Achilles'. In their answers, both Glaucus and Asteropaeus

- show that they know only too well the identity of their opponent (Τυδεΐδη μεγάθυμε: Z 145; Πηλεΐδη μεγάθυμε: Φ 153);

- start with what appears to be a refusal to answer (rhetorical question τίη γενεὴν ἐρεείνεις: 'why do you ask my ancestry?': Z 145 ≅ Φ 153);

- then proceed to give the answer all the same: the genealogies Z 150-211 and Φ 154-60. In the case of Asteropaeus the rhetorical question seems to spring from a certain impatience: he wishes to fight rather than talk (160). Glaucus explains his question by the ensuing simile - simile and rhetorical question are connected by asyndeton explicativum -, which sets a different tone. I postpone a discussion of the nature of this tone until after my analysis of the Bellerophontes-story.

B. was born in Ephyra, a city in the Argolid, as son of Glaucus (a namesake of the Glaucus who is speaking) and grandson of Sisyphus. The gods gave him 'beauty and charming valour' (156), but king Proetus, to whom Zeus had made B. subject,[36] plotted against him and expelled him from the Argive people. The reason for Proetus' behaviour and the precise content of the evils is explained in what follows (160-70). Proetus' wife Anteia had fallen in love with B. (whom, as we have just heard, was very beautiful) and desired to have a secret affair with him. However, she had not been able to persuade 'righteous', 'valorous'/ 'shrewd'[37] B. and, hurt in her feminine pride, told her husband a lie, viz. that B. had tried to seduce her against her will. As expected, her husband became angry, but instead of killing B. (as Anteia had asked) he sent him abroad, to Lycia. He gave B. a tablet, on which 'many baneful ... death-bringing signs' (σήματα λυγρά ... θυμοφθόρα πολλά: 168-9) were written and ordered him to show these to his father-in-law (the king of Lycia), 'in order that he might die'. Under divine protection, B. safely reached Lycia and for nine days was entertained 'heartily' (προφρονέως: 173) by the king of Lycia (171-4). Then, on the tenth day, the king asked B. to see the sign 'which he carried with him from his son-in-law Proetus.' As is indicated by the indefinite pronoun ὅττι (177), the king was at that moment still ignorant of the nature of the sign. Only when he had received it from B. did he find out that it was in fact κακόν ('evil-bringing'), viz. to its bearer. Accordingly, the Lycian king, who like Proetus seems loath to kill B. himself, sent him on dangerous missions. A detail deserves attention here: scholars (starting with the scholia ad 170 b,c) have remarked that the name of the king of Lycia is never mentioned, which is one of the many omissions. It is relevant to note, however, that what is stressed by Glaucus is the *relation* between Proetus and the king of Lycia: 'son-in-law' (γαμβρός: 177, 178) and 'father-in-law' (πενθερός: 170). This relation is of primary importance for the story: Proetus, wanting to get rid of an (alleged) seducer of his wife, sent him to her father (his father-in-law), whom he could expect to help him accomplish his goal. And indeed the king of Lycia obliged his son-in-law by sending his guest, whom he had just before treated with great respect (slaughtering nine oxen: 174), on three dangerous missions.

B. (still supported by the gods: 183) was successful in all three trials: he killed the Chimaera and defeated the Amazones and the Solymoi (179-86). A small detail in

(14) Z 185:
   "καρτίστην δὴ τήν γε μάχην <u>φάτο</u> δύμεναι ἀνδρῶν."
   "that fight (sc. with the Solymoi) was, <u>he (B.) said</u>, the
   fiercest he had ever entered with men."

is of interest.[38] The verse as a whole serves to emphasize the heroic nature of B.'s second 'labour', but through φάτο ('he said') we are informed of the fact that B. himself must on numerous occasions have told the story of his adventures: on his return, but also later to his son or maybe even to his grandson Glaucus. Thus, the latter may be said to have grown up with this 'family-story', a point which will prove to be of importance later.

The king of Lycia once more tried to dispose of B., now by laying an ambush for him on his way back from his third mission. Again B. proved victorious (187-90). The invincibility of B. was then interpreted by the king as a sign of divine parentage and he gave up: he married B. to another of his daughters and gave him half of his royal honours (191-3). According to Gaisser (1969b: 173, and cp. also Leaf ad loc.), Homer alludes in

(15) Z 191:
   "ἀλλ᾿ ὅτε δὴ γίγνωσκε θεοῦ γόνον ἠὺν ἐόντα"
   "but when he (the Lycian king) gradually began to realize
   that he (B.) was the valiant son of a god"

to another version of the B.-story (told e.g. by Hesiod, *fragment* 43a, 81-3), in which B.'s real father is Poseidon. This relation between B. and Poseidon is carefully suppressed by Homer (one of the many omissions) and only here does he "forget to do so". This may be true, but one should be cautious: we are dealing with Glaucus' presentation of the Lycian king's focalization. As the A-scholia say: ὅτι ἐκ τῶν πραττομένων τοῦτο συνέβαλεν ('he has come to that conclusion on account of the feats accomplished.'). In other words, B.'s divine parentage as mentioned in 191 may be no more than the inference of one character (the Lycian king), adopted only too willingly by another character (Glaucus), who thus augments the glory of his family.

The Lycians, who had profited from B.'s defeat of Chimaera, Solymoi and Amazones, gave B. a 'fine piece of land' (194-5). At this point, the B.-story having come to a happy end, Glaucus resumes the thread of his genealogy (196-9). In 200-2, however, he interrupts it again and adds a short epilogue on B.: even such a favourite of the gods as B.[39] incurred their wrath (how, Glaucus does not tell) and he became a lonely wanderer in the land Aleion, avoiding all contact with men. One might wonder what the function of this epilogue is. I suggest that the divine wrath incurred by B. affects (part of) his offspring also: his son Isander is killed by Ares and his daughter Laodameia by Artemis. I base this suggestion on the fact that ἤτοι in Homer functions more or less as μέν (see Ruijgh 1981): thus we get the sequence ἤτοι ὅ (201: B.), ῎Ισανδρον δέ (203) and τὴν δέ (205: Laodameia). The reason why Glaucus mentions the unhappy fate of his family seems to be to indicate that his own father Hippolochus is the *only* surviving son of B. Now his father had exhorted him at the moment he left for Troy to fight bravely and not to bring shame to his forefathers, 'who had been the best both in Ephyra and broad Lycia' (206-10). In other words, his father Hippolochus had exhorted him exactly by referring to the illustrious ancestry which he, Glaucus, has just told Diomedes. It is up to him and his nephew Sarpedon (199), who in peaceful times enjoy the *privileges* of having inherited B.'s position of honour - they cultivate the 'fine piece of land' given to B. by the Lycians: M 313-4 -, to maintain the honour of the family.

After this analysis of the B.-story, the question of the tone of the simile 146-9 and of Glaucus' speech as a whole is easier to address. Opinions diverge widely on this point. According to Craig (1967) and Gaisser (1969b), Glaucus is afraid of Diomedes and does not expect to survive the encounter: "what more natural than that he would visualize *sadly* in that moment the common lot of men in their fleeting generations" (Craig 1967: 243, my italics). As we have seen (above p. 162), Gaisser goes further than this and suggests that the whole B.-story, with its ups and downs, was adapted so as to form an illustration to the simile, and in a wider sense "a comment on the tragic nature of the poem as a whole" (179). A completely opposite opinion is voiced by Hebel (1970: 124-5): Glaucus is proud of his ancestry and "großzügig und ein wenig herablassend" he tells Diomedes what in fact everybody knows. Well-balanced is the interpretation given by Griffin (1980: 72): "Glaukos begins on a *subdued* note", but "the man who declined to give his ancestry at the beginning *boasts* of it at the end. Only such complexity can do justice to the Homeric conception of heroism: family pride and social obligation uplift and compel the hero, who yet remains aware of inevitable death" (my italics). This interpretation of Glaucus' speech in terms of the heroic code can, I think, be made more specific and adapted to Glaucus' personal situation. Although I would not go as far as Fränkel, who considered the simile a "Fremd-körper", its impact seems to be restricted to the very beginning of the speech. *Pace* Craig and Gaisser, it is not inspired by fear. Rather, Glaucus wishes to remind Diomedes of the 'condition humaine' pertaining to them both, thereby also implicitly answering Diomedes' question and asserting that he is human and not a god. The ensuing presentation of his genealogy serves a double function: with respect to his addressee, to show that he, Glaucus, is of equal birth and heroic stature as Diomedes; with respect to himself, to remind himself of the heroic burden resting on his shoulders, a burden of which his father had reminded him before leaving. For both purposes, the B.-story is relevant: B. was an outstanding hero and just because of his sad end and the death of the greater part of his offspring Glaucus must try to bring new life to the fame of the family.

Conclusion

The Bellerophontes-story, analyzed as an example of an external analepsis told by a character, has displayed the three general characteristics of its group, mentioned at the beginning of this section:

    1. it is told allusively

    2. it fulfils an important function within the speech

    3. the speaking character indicates how he knows the story.

<u>Ad 1</u>: when speaking characters turn into narrators of external analepses they tend to present their information with great economy, leaving out irrelevant details and emphasizing relevant ones, the relevancy being determined by the

rhetorical goal they are aiming at. Thus, Glaucus leaves out the proper name of the king of Lycia, but refers to him in his quality of father-in-law. Again, he does not tell why B. became hated to all gods, but focuses on the important point that his family tree, through the misfortunes of B. and two of his children, has narrowed down to himself (and Sarpedon).

Ad 2: the Bellerophontes-story forms part of a genealogy, which in its turn forms part of a speech preceding a duel. Story, genealogy and speech are functional on the one hand as propaganda (towards the addressee Diomedes, who needs to be impressed), on the other hand as pep-talk (for the speaker Glaucus, who needs to reassure himself, facing a formidable opponent). An unexpected (positive) effect of Glaucus' telling this particular story is that it brings about a peaceful settlement of his meeting with Diomedes.

Ad 3: two small details indicate how the story has reached Glaucus: from φάτο (185) we may gather that B. himself told about his adventures and from 207-10 (Hippolochus exhorts his son not to bring shame to his illustrious forefathers) it seems reasonable to infer that on the occasion of Glaucus' departure for Troy, Hippolochus reminded him of his ancestry and in particular of his illustrious ancestor Bellerophontes. Similarly, Peleus adhorts his son Achilles when he leaves for Troy (l 254-8).

All in all the embedded story as presented by Glaucus forms a coherent whole and makes sense as it stands, both to Diomedes and to us, the historical hearer/reader. This positive conclusion, reached after a narratological approach to the text, forms a welcome complement to the results of genetic and comparatistic investigations which, apart from yielding many interesting and valid observations, paid too much attention to all that is lacking in the Homeric version.

5.3. Embedded speech

Speaking characters may in their speeches report (as indirect speech) or even quote (as direct speech) the words of other characters. I call these passages *embedded speech*. In terms of narrative situation, embedded speech is to be analyzed as follows:

embedded *indirect* speech is tertiary focalization:

$$NF_1[NF_2C_x[F_3C_y]]$$

embedded *direct* speech is tertiary narration-focalization:

$$NF_1[NF_2C_x[NF_3C_y]].$$

From this analysis it appears that the two types of embedded speech each belong to a narrative situation which is different from that of character-text: $NF_1[NF_2C_x]$. From a systematical point of view they should be discussed in separate chapters, but there are good reasons for discussing them in close connection with character-text and, therefore, in this chapter. To argue this point I shall start by taking a close look at forms of tertiary focalization other than embedded indirect speech.

Tertiary focalization

The examples discussed in the first two sections of this chapter all showed us direct speech as the verbal expression by speaking characters of their *own* focalization. Speaking characters may, however, also choose to embed the focalization of *other* characters, who thereby function as tertiary focalizers (F_3). I give four examples:

(16) I 359-61 (Achilles announces to Odysseus that he will return home):
"ὄψεαι, αἴ κ' ἐθέλησθα καὶ αἴ κέν τοι τὰ μεμήλῃ,
ἦρι μάλ' Ἑλλήσποντον ἐπ' ἰχθυόεντα πλεούσας
νῆας ἐμάς, ἐν δ' ἄνδρας ἐρεσσέμεναι μεμαῶτας"
'and you will see, if you care to watch and if these things are of any concern to you, my ships very early in the morning sailing on the fishy Hellespont and on them my men, eager to row"

(17) Σ 175-7 (Iris spurs on Achilles to defend Patroclus' body, which the Trojans long to drag to Troy):
"μάλιστα δὲ φαίδιμος Ἕκτωρ
ἑλκέμεναι μέμονεν· κεφαλὴν δέ ἑ θυμὸς ἄνωγε
πῆξαι ἀνὰ σκολόπεσσι ταμόνθ' ἁπαλῆς ἀπὸ δειρῆς."
'and above all illustrious Hector is eager to drag it: and his spirit urges him to fix his (Patroclus') head upon stakes, having cut it from his tender neck."

(18) Π 17-8 (Achilles: Patroclus):
"ἦε σύ γ' Ἀργείων ὀλοφύρεαι, ὡς ὀλέκονται
νηυσὶν ἔπι γλαφυρῇσιν ὑπερβασίης ἕνεκα σφῆς;"
'or are you weeping for the Greeks, how they are perishing near the hollow ships as a result of their own transgression?"

(19) Γ 241-2 (Helen: Priam):
"νῦν αὖτ' οὐκ ἐθέλουσι μάχην καταδύμεναι ἀνδρῶν,
αἴσχεα δειδιότες καὶ ὀνείδεα πόλλ', ἅ μοί ἐστιν."
'but now they (her brothers Castor and Pollux) do not want to enter the fight of men, because they fear insults and many reproaches, which are mine."

In (16) Achilles changes within one sentence from his own focalization (358: προερύσσῳ and cp. again in 363: ἱκοίμην) to that of Odysseus (ὄψεαι) and describes his own departure as seen by someone standing ashore, i.e. remaining behind in the Troad.[40] He thus effectively reinforces the point he has just made: Agamemnon's insulting behaviour, resulting in his (Achilles') absence from the fighting, has disastrous consequences for the other Greeks (346-55). When he, Achilles, leaves altogether, the consequences will be all the worse for those remaining behind. The sarcastic hypothetical clause ('if you care to watch ...') also drives this point home: of course, Odysseus and the other Greeks very much care for Achilles to remain.[41]

In (17) Iris describes to Achilles emotions and aspirations of Hector, partly correctly (μάλιστα ... μέμονεν = Σ 155-6 Ἕκτωρ ἑλκέμεναι μεμαώς), partly in exaggerated form: from P 125-6 (Ἕκτωρ ... Πάτροκλον ἕλχ', ἵν' ἀπ' ὤμοιιν κεφαλὴν τάμοι) we know that Hector, indeed, wants to cut off Patroclus' head, but the gruesome detail of fixing the head on a stake here seems to be invented and added by Iris to make her appeal to Achilles all the more forceful.[42] This example makes clear that speaking characters, even gods, may not be entirely "reliable narrators" when representing the focalization of other characters and that the content of embedded speech is not always to be taken at face value.

In (18) Achilles tries to read Patroclus' mind and offers four suggestions as to why he is weeping. The first three of these (Π 12-6), referring to the situation at home in Phthia, can be considered serious, even if or maybe precisely because they are discarded immediately by Achilles himself. Coming to speak of the Greeks (17-8), however, he can not suppress his own feelings and turns to irony.[43] Especially a word like ὑπερβασίης (18) betrays Achilles' own focalization, showing through that of Patroclus, who as subject of ὀλοφύρεαι is supposed to be focalizing. The fact that the Greeks had not opposed Agamemnon when he took Briseis away from him forms a 'transgression' in Achilles' eyes and he does not feel sorry for them in their present plight.[44]

In (19), which I analyze as *implicit* tertiary focalization, Helen projekts her own feelings of guilt and shame onto her brothers, suggesting that they do not fight because they fear reproaches from their comrades. As if to indicate that Helen is here substituting her own focalization (as NF$_2$) for that of her brothers, the NF$_1$, immediately after the speech, gives the real reason for Castor's and Pollux' absence: they are dead.

These four passages show that speaking characters, when they embed the (tertiary) focalization of other characters

1. aim to achieve rhetorical effects (examples 16, 17)

2. intrude considerably with their own feelings, interpretations etc. upon the tertiary focalization (example 18)

3. so that, as a result of 1 and 2, the content of tertiary focalization need not be true (examples 17, 19).

The important conclusion to be drawn is that, at least in the *Iliad*, the relation between secondary narration-focalization and tertiary focalization is of a different nature than that between primary narration-focalization and secondary focalization: whereas the NF_1 in cases of embedded focalization does indeed hand over focalization to the characters and only seldom intrudes (and then only to provide factual information to the $NeFe_1$), speaking characters (functioning as NF_2) to a far greater degree interfere with tertiary focalization, exploiting it for the purposes of their own speech. In short, the level of secondary narration-focalization *dominates* the (hierarchically lower) level of tertiary focalization. These close ties between the levels of secondary narration-focalization and tertiary focalization warrant a discussion of embedded indirect speech in this chapter on character-text.

As regards embedded *direct* speech, both the expectation that here too the secondary level of narrration-focalization dominates the tertiary level of narration-focalization and its similarity to embedded indirect speech justify a discussion in this section and this chapter.

Embedded speeches

In the *Iliad* we find 20 cases of embedded direct speech and about four times as many cases of embedded indirect speech.[45] The only scholar who has dealt in some detail with embedded speeches is Willcock (1977). Although he approached the subject from a genetical point of view - he investigates Homer's *ad hoc* invention in comparison to tradition - his conclusions very much resemble mine, viz. that assertions found in speeches "are directly related to the occasion at which they are made and to the particular circumstances of the person who is being addressed" (1977: 45). In the following I will discuss a number of representative examples.[46]

Embedded speech forms a congenial part of external analepses told by characters. For example, the Bellerophontes-story analyzed in the previous section contains one instance of embedded direct speech (Z 164-5) and four instances of embedded indirect speech (170.176-7.179-80.185). It is not difficult to see why Glaucus chooses to quote Anteia's words directly in

(20) Z 164-5:
"τεθναίης, ὦ Προῖτ', ἢ κάκτανε Βελλεροφόντην
ὅς μ' ἔθελεν φιλότητι μιγήμεναι οὐκ ἐθελούσῃ."
"may you perish, Proetus, or kill Bellerophontes, who wanted
to mingle with me in love against my will."

Her denouncement of Bellerophontes is a crucial point in the story, changing the entire course of his life. Further, the pressure put on Proetus and the perfidy of Anteia's denouncement (accusing Bellerophontes exactly of that which she herself had wanted: φιλότητι μιγήμεναι: 161 en 165) are thus brought out with dramatic vividness. In 170 and 179-80 we are dealing with cases of embedded indirect speech which are to be explained along the same lines as most cases of indirect speech in the narrator-text: they describe orders and what counts is that these orders are given and executed (note the confirmation κατέπεφνε after ἐκέλευσε πεφνέμεν). The effective juxtaposition in 170 of words said and real intentions kept silent (ὄφρ' ἀπόλοιτο) calls to mind Ω 583-6, discussed above, section 4.1.1, p. 114. For the importance of 185 see above p. 165.

An external analepsis which consists almost completely of embedded direct speech is the Zeus-Ate story: T 95-133. It is told by Agamemnon by way of apologetic paradigm:[47] even Zeus once fell victim to Ate (the personification of ἄτη: 'delusion, which one comes to regret').[48] On the day Alcmene is about to give birth to Heracles, Zeus proudly announces amidst the gods that the man born on this day will reign over many neighbours (embedded direct speech: 101-5). Hera challenges him to turn this statement into an oath (embedded direct speech: 107-11), which he does. She then halts Heracles' birth and speeds up that of Eurystheus. She triumphantly reports the birth of Eurystheus to Zeus (embedded direct speech: 121-4) and he, realizing that he has been the victim of Ate, throws her, his own daughter, from the Olympus. He adds the solemn oath that she will never return there (embedded indirect speech: 128-9). On the whole, the role of Ate is remarkably subordinate to that of Hera, who is the one actively deceiving Zeus (97, 112: δολοφροσύνης, -ην; 97: ἀπάτησεν; 106: δολοφρονέουσα). Indeed, if one compares this version of Heracles' delayed birth with that found in Diodorus Siculus (iv. 9.4-5), it appears that there Ate is not mentioned at all. The introduction of Ate into the story of Heracles' birth seems to be an *ad hoc* invention of Agamemnon (in the end of course of Homer, who 'invents' Agamemnon).[49] His reason is clear enough: by depicting Zeus as a fellow-victim of Ate, he creates an analogy between what has happened to himself and what has happened to that god. By comparing himself with the king of gods and, in fact, a far more innocent victim than he himself is, Agamemnon tries to regain the respect and sympathy of his audience.[50] The embedded speeches serve this rhetorical purpose: we, and the Greeks listening to Agamemnon, see for ourselves how Zeus' formulation (ὃς [sc. Heracles] ... ἀνάξει, τῶν ἀνδρῶν γενεῆς οἳ θ’ αἵματος ἐξ ἐμεῦ εἰσι: 104) is cunningly exploited by Hera (ἀνάξειν ὃς κεν ... πέσῃ: 109-10) with the result that in 122 she can proclaim ἀνήρ (sc. Eurystheus) γέγον’ ..., ὃς ... ἀνάξει. Zeus is pictured as a victim of his own words and this is another point of analogy with Agamemnon's case: it was the vehement words exchanged between himself and Achilles in A (to which Agamemnon explicitly refers in T 88: εἰν ἀγορῇ) which led to his fatal decision to take away Briseis from Achilles.

We see that embedded speech can increase the rhetorical impact of an external analepsis told by a character. This effect is cleverly exploited by Odysseus in B 323-9: wishing to revive the fighting-spirit of his men, he reminds them of an omen they had received in Aulis, at the very start of the expedition. At first, the soldiers had been startled by the omen, but a favourable interpretation by Calchas, who prophesied victory, had taken away their fear. By quoting verbatim the words spoken by Calchas on that occasion, Odysseus maximally reactivates the memory of the soldiers and also reckons that these words will again have a positive and stimulating effect. More in particular, by recalling that Calchas had prophesied nine years of war - which have now passed - and victory in the tenth, Odysseus seeks to counterbalance the defeatism of Agamemnon (134-8), who had interpreted the nine years as a sign of the failure of the whole expedition. That Odysseus' rhetoric is indeed effective appears from the enthusiastic reaction of the soldiers in B 333-5.

A special group of embedded speeches is constituted by the admonitions of fathers to their sons, when they leave for the war. I take as examples the words of Peleus and Menoetius spoken at Phthia.[51]

174

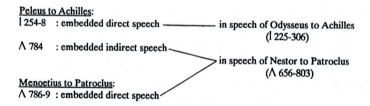

Peleus to Achilles:
I 254-8   : embedded direct speech ——————— in speech of Odysseus to Achilles
(I 225-306)

Λ 784   : embedded indirect speech
in speech of Nestor to Patroclus
(Λ 656-803)

Menoetius to Patroclus:
Λ 786-9 : embedded direct speech

In I 225-306 Odysseus is trying to persuade Achilles to give up his wrath and resume fighting; Nestor in Λ 656-803 brings home to Patroclus that he is the only person who could try and persuade Achilles to resume fighting. Both speakers, Odysseus and Nestor, use embedded speech with a view to strengthening the hortatory effect of their own speeches. More in particular, they hope to achieve this by quoting words of those persons who for their addressees have greatest authority, their own fathers.[52] Although it appears from Λ 767-8 that *both* Odysseus and Nestor were present in Phthia at the moment Peleus and Menoetius adhorted their sons and, therefore, must have heard the *same* speeches, they each pick out those elements which are best suited to context and addressee. Thus Nestor, addressing Patroclus, directly quotes Menoetius as saying (to Patroclus) that, whereas Achilles is the stronger of the two, he, Patroclus, is older and therefore in the right position to offer wise advice to and guide his friend. This is exactly what Nestor now wants Patroclus to do (note πείσεται: 789 and πίθηται: 791). Of Peleus' admonition (to Achilles), Nestor only reports (as embedded indirect speech) the general heroic maxim 'always to be the best and to surpass the others'.[53] Odysseus, in his turn, addressing Achilles, quotes directly more of Peleus' admonition, viz. that part in which he warns Achilles for his own heroic temper and advises him to be friendly to others and to refrain from quarreling. This, again, is exactly what Odysseus now asks from Achilles. Due to the fact that the NF₁ does not provide us with the words of Peleus and Menoetius themselves, it is difficult to assess to what extent Nestor and Odysseus are faithfully quoting them. A rather extreme position is taken by Willcock (1977: 46-7), who implies that the conversation in Phthia never took place and that Nestor and Odysseus simply invent the embedded speeches themselves. Hebel (1970: 51-2) is more cautious: "Es ist gewiß nicht der Eindruck beabsichtigt, Odysseus erfinde hier die ganze Mahnung, vielmehr interpretiert er die Worte des Vaters, indem er sie umformt und so zitiert, daß sie für die augenblickliche Lage größtes Gewicht bekommen." I have myself chosen to speak of "each picks out ...", because Nestor and Odysseus can hardly invent a conversation which their present addressees are supposed to have heard and for their words to have the authoritative ring they intend them to have, they can not deviate too much from what Peleus and Menoetius really said. Indeed, in Λ 768 Nestor strongly emphasizes that he (and Odysseus) has heard 'exactly everything' (πάντα μάλ') that Menoetius said to Patroclus.

Another rhetorical use of embedded speech is to remind one's addressee(s) of words (mostly threats or boasts) spoken by him-/themselves in the past, e.g.

> (21) Υ 83-5 (Apollo: Aeneas):
> "Αἰνεία, Τρώων βουληφόρε, ποῦ τοι ἀπειλαί,
> ἃς Τρώων βασιλεῦσιν ὑπίσχεο οἰνοποτάζων,
> Πηλεΐδα Ἀχιλῆος ἐναντίβιον πολεμίξειν;"
> "Aeneas, leader of the Trojans, where are the boastful pledges, which you, drinking wine, made to the leaders of the Trojans, that you would fight against Achilles, son of Peleus?"[54]

Apollo's intention here is to incite Aeneas against Achilles (cp. 79-80) and he challenges him to put into practice what he had once announced, in a situation of security (and under the influence of wine).

The embedded speeches discussed so far all concerned utterances which also for the speaking character belong to a relatively distant past. Thus he/she can represent them in a more or less neutral, unemotional fashion, selecting those elements which are best suited for his/her present rhetorical purposes. As soon as embedded speeches concern words spoken *recently*, viz. within the confines of the primary fabula, the emotional involvement of the NF_2 and therefore his meddling with the tertiary level of focalization (in the case of embedded indirect speech) or narration-focalization (in the case of embedded direct speech) can be expected to increase: the embedded speeches now refer to events which are of immediate concern to the speaker and in which he/she plays a role. A good example is

> (22) Α 109-13 (Agamemnon to Calchas: you are always prophesying things unfavourable to me):
> "καὶ νῦν ἐν Δαναοῖσι θεοπροπέων ἀγορεύεις
> ὡς δὴ τοῦδ' ἕνεκά σφιν ἑκηβόλος ἄλγεα τεύχει,
> οὕνεκ' ἐγὼ κούρης Χρυσηΐδος ἀγλά' ἄποινα
> οὐκ ἔθελον δέξασθαι, ἐπεὶ πολὺ βούλομαι αὐτὴν
> οἴκοι ἔχειν"
> "this time again, prophesying among the Greeks, you maintain that because of this the far-shooter (Apollo) causes sorrows for them (the Greeks), because I was not willing to accept the splendid ransom for the daughter of Chryses, since I very much prefer to have her at home"[55]

Agamemnon recapitulates Calchas' speech A 93-100. The tone in which he does so is one of ironic disbelief as regards the correctness of Calchas' interpretation: the emphatic τοῦδ' ἕνεκα and ἐγώ, in combination with ὡς δή,[56] all indicate that Agamemnon finds it hard to believe that the misery of all Greeks is caused by his individual behaviour.[57] He insinuates that Calchas' interpretation results from a long-standing antipathy towards him, Agamemnon. A comparison of Calchas' actual words and Agamemnon's representation of them is revealing: Agamemnon does not refer to Chryses at all, i.e. he passes over in silence Calchas' point that in refusing the ransom for Chryseis he had, in fact, slighted (94: ἠτίμησ') a priest, and a priest of Apollo at that.[58] On the other hand, he adds something which was not mentioned by Calchas, viz. that he very much prefers to have Chryseis at home rather than accept the ransom. In other words, with the ἐπεί clause of 122-3 Agamemnon has moved away from Calchas' speech (in his eyes a malicious *accusation*) and turns to his *defense*: he had his motives for acting as he did.

From an example like this, where a speaking character represents words spoken by another character very much from his own point of view, it is only a small step to cases where a speaking character only *pretends* to quote somebody else's words, but, in fact, invents them. An example is found in

(23) Π 837-42 (Hector: dying Patroclus):
"ἆ δείλ', οὐδέ τοι ἐσθλὸς ἐὼν χραίσμησεν 'Αχιλλεύς,
ὅς πού τοι μάλα πολλὰ μένων ἐπετέλλετ' ἰόντι·
'μή μοι πρὶν ἰέναι, Πατρόκλεες ἱπποκέλευθε,
νῆας ἐπὶ γλαφυράς, πρὶν "Εκτορος ἀνδροφόνοιο
αἱματόεντα χιτῶνα περὶ στήθεσσι δαΐξαι.'
ὥς πού σε προσέφη, σοὶ δὲ φρένας ἄφρονι πεῖθε."
"poor you, Achilles was not, though excellent himself, of avail to you, who, I suppose, staying behind himself ordered you, who were going, many times: 'Do not come back to me, Patroclus driver of horses, to the hollow ships, before you have lacerated the bloody chiton of man-slaughtering Hector around his breast.' Thus he spoke, I suppose, to you and persuaded you in your foolish mind."[59]

Now we know that in fact Achilles had warned Patroclus in Π 80-100 not to take too many risks and to return as soon as he had brought relief to the battle near the ships. Hector, of course, has never heard these words of Achilles, but then his intention in Π 839-41 is not at all to reconstruct faithfully what Achilles might have said but only to gloat over his opponent's defeat. Just as in the first half of his triumph speech he reconstructs Patroclus' own hopes (830: που ἔφησθα) only to show their futility (833: νήπιε), because he himself (note the self-assured Ἕκτορος in 833) thwarted them;[60] so, in the second half, he invents this speech of Achilles (note που in 838 and 842) only to show how stupid (842: ἄφρονι) Patroclus was to give heed to it. In fact, Hector seems to try and drive a wedge between the two friends, placing Achilles in a definitely negative light: although himself an excellent warrior he did not protect Patroclus; staying behind himself he sent his friend into battle and, finally, he gave Patroclus a risky assignment, ordering him not to return until he had finished it.[61]

The most obvious examples of embedded speeches which formally are quotations, but in fact derive completely from the mind of the speaking character are embedded tis-speeches. These are speeches which a speaking character envisions to be spoken at some point in the future by an anonymous 'somebody' (τις). An example is

(24) Ζ 459-62 (Hector: Andromache):
"καί ποτέ τις εἴπησιν ἰδών κατὰ δάκρυ χέουσαν·
' Ἕκτορος ἥδε γυνή, ὃς ἀριστεύεσκε μάχεσθαι
Τρώων ἱπποδάμων, ὅτε Ἴλιον ἀμφιμάχοντο.'
ὥς ποτέ τις ἐρέει"
"And once somebody may say, seeing you weep: 'this is the wife of Hector, who was best in fighting of the horse-taming Trojans, when they fought around Troy.' Thus somebody will speak"[62]

Andromache had just suggested to Hector to stay in Troy and not to return to the battlefield (407-39). Hector answers that he must, and indeed wishes to, fight in the front line, even if he knows that Troy is doomed to fall (441-9). In this short moment of realism he projects a vision of the miserable life awaiting Andromache after the fall of Troy, when she will be forced to work as a slave for a Greek master (450-8). Her grief about this humiliating situation will receive fresh impulses (462: νέον ... ἄλγος) whenever a Greek bystander recognizes her and by his words (460-1) reminds her of her former status as wife of illustrious Hector. Then she will feel the loss of not just her husband, but of a man of such qualities as he, Hector, has (463: τοιοῦδε) to ward off the day of slavery. Although Hector tries to put himself mentally into the position of Andromache, the tis-speech reveals his own preoccupations (note that Andromache's name is not mentioned, but Hector's is): he devises a kind of oral epitaph for himself,[63] indicating how he hopes to be remembered, viz. as the best warrior before Troy. From Ζ 444-6 we already knew that this was the kind of κλέος Hector (as all heroes) is striving for. In De Jong (forth.) I have discussed all tis-speeches of the *Iliad* (both those embedded in the narrator-text, the "actual" ones, and those embedded in character-text, the "potential" ones) and my remarks here are based on that article. Since embedded tis-speeches are located in the future and are attributed to an anonymous person, they are no quotations, but imaginary ("potential") speeches. They are the (hopeful or fearful) evaluation by the speaking character of his own behaviour, which he - and this is characteristic for the Homeric shame culture - puts into the mouth of somebody else.[64]

Conclusion

Comparing the last examples of embedded speeches with those discussed at the beginning of this section, I conclude that embedded speeches display a range of varieties as regards their reliability: they can be truthful quotations or reports, they can be adapted to a greater or lesser degree or they can be wholly invented. In this respect embedded speeches differ from character-texts. The latter, being introduced by the NF_1, are, at least in the *Iliad*, to be regarded as reliable and correct quotations of a character's words,[65] the reliability being guaranteed by the Muses. Embedded speeches, being quoted by characters themselves, do not have this automatic stamp of authority. Only too often speaking characters are induced, either on account of their own emotional involvement or on account of the effects they wish their words to have on their addressee, to modify the words of others. In other words, with the number of embeddings the distance from the 'reality' of the primary fabula *increases* and therewith the reliability *decreases*. Thus, the difference between NF_1 and characters functioning as NF_2 is not only one of emotional involvement (cp. above pp. 159-60), but also of reliability as presentators of narrative information.

Another difference between NF_1 and speaking characters is that the former more frequently embeds direct than indirect speeches, whereas the latter more frequently embeds indirect than direct speeches. Characters seem to reserve the inclusion of *direct* speech for those cases where dramatic vividness is especially called for: when they wish

1. to draw attention to an important point in their story (Glaucus in Z 164-5)

2. to increase the apologetic (Agamemnon in T 101-5 + 107-11 + 121-4), persuasive (Odysseus in B 323-9 and I 254-8, Nestor in Λ 786-9) or taunting (Hector in Π 839-41) force of their speech

3. to externalize their own hopes/fears (tis-speeches). Embedded *indirect* speech is a less emphatic vehicle for representing the words of another. It is used when

4. what counts is content rather than impact. Thus, what is important in T 128-9 is the *content* of Zeus' oath (banishment of Ate from the Olympus). Vis-à-vis Patroclus Nestor quotes his father Menoetius directly, but merely reports (part of) Peleus' speech. Wishing to incite Aeneas, Apollo reminds him of the main point (that he will face Achilles) of what can be imagined as having been a long and bragging speech.

5. a speaker wishes to play down the importance of somebody else's words. By recapitulating Calchas' speech in an indirect form Agamemnon already shows that he does not wish it to be taken seriously. The indirect form further enables him to show his disapproval ('Calchas says this but I think it improbable') and to leave out unpleasant details (his own treatment of Chryses).

The analysis of embedded indirect and direct speech has, furthermore, confirmed that the tertiary level of focalization and narration-focalization is dominated by the hierarchically higher, secondary level of narration-focalization. This result is relevant to all interpretators of the Homeric text: passages in character-text which describe the perceptions, feelings, intentions, words of characters other than the speaker should not always be taken at face value, or worse, be forced to match other passages. The narrative information they contain is filtered by the F_3, NF_2 and NF_1 and in the course of this process many elements may be sifted out or slightly altered.

5.4. Repeated speech

Repeated speech is a phenomenon which can be regularly observed in the Homeric epics: parts of or even entire speeches are repeated verbatim in other speeches. Verbatim or almost verbatim repetition of verse-clusters is, of course, also found outside character-text in the narrator-text. Alexandrian scholars and, in modern times, the Analysts showed little appreciation for such repeated passages and marked them as spurious or tried to decide between original and copied versions. Pfudel (1891), Arend (1933) and Calhoun (1933) paved the way for a more favourable approach. Nowadays verbatim repetition of larger units is accepted as an exponent of the oral background of the epics, to be placed on a par with the formulas. It offers a singer time to relax and to consider how to continue his song. Thus, the presence of repetitions is explained genetically. Should we leave it at that or can repetitions also be given sense narratologically? Is verbatim repetition in itself significant? To answer these questions it is necessary to start by taking into account the narrative situation in which the repeated verse-clusters occur. I distinguish between

a. repetition of verse-clusters within simple narrator-text

b. repetition of verse-clusters within character-text

c. repetition of verse-clusters from simple narrator-text in character-text and vice versa.

These three categories of repetitions each call for their own approach. I will not go into **a**, which mainly concerns Arend's (1933) "typische Szenen" (see also Gruen 1977). For **c** I refer to section 6.2. Category **b** forms the subject of this section.

In Appendix V I have collected all cases of repeated verse-clusters in character-text (direct speech), defining as a verse-cluster the combination of at least two verses. The vital point in analyzing (examples from) this corpus will be to realize *on which level* the repetition is functional from a narratological point of view. Is the repetition intended by the speaker and does it have a function on the level of the communication between characters? Or are we dealing with a recurrence of phrases, which is neither intended nor understood by the characters as a repetition? In the last case, it is the $NeFe_1$, who, as recipient of *all* speeches, identifies the repetition as such and may accord a significance to it. I begin my discussion with the largest category of repeated speech: the messenger-speeches.

5.4.1. Messenger-speeches

In the *Iliad* we find 22 repeated messenger-speeches, collected in Appendix V A.[66] The repetition is to be analyzed as follows: character **a** instructs character **b** to transmit a message, often a command (*instruction* speech), which the latter delivers to character **c** (*delivery* speech). Character **b** is often a professional herald: Iris (see Hentze 1903), Idaeus, Thootes, Talthybius. Character **b** functions, therefore, first as addressee of character **a** and then as speaker to character **c**. Normally, *instruction* and *delivery* speech follow closely upon one another, the only exception being Nestor's instruction to Patroclus (Λ 658-662+794-803), which the latter delivers to Achilles in Π 23-27+ 36-45. Sometimes a messenger-speech is delivered twice: Hector presents Helenus' instruction (Z 87-97) first in a shortened, less detailed version to his men (Z 113-115) and then verbatim to his mother Hecabe (Z 269-78). Part of this same message recurs for a third time in the prayer to Athena by the priestess Theano: Z 306-310 ≅ 274-8 ≅ 93-7. Similarly, Agamemnon repeats in B 60-70 to his counsellors almost the complete speech of Oneirus/ 'Nestor' B 23-34, the main part of which is formed by Zeus' message B 11-5 = 28-32 = 65-70. The A-scholia, defending B 60-71 against Zenodotus, make an interesting remark:

τὰ δὲ ἀπαγγελτικὰ ἐξ ἀνάγκης δὶς καὶ τρὶς ἀναπολεῖται ταῖς αὐταῖς λέξεσι. καὶ οὐκ δυσωπητέον· ἀναγκαῖον γὰρ καὶ τοῖς συγκεκλημένοις βουλευταῖς διηγήσασθαι.

Messages are of necessity repeated two or three times with the same words. And one should not look with suspicion (at this technique), for it is necessary to tell the message also to the gathered councillors.

In other words, the fact that the NeFe$_1$ has already received certain information does not preclude that information from being repeated, when characters in the story need it. Thus, although the NeFe$_1$ has heard Zeus' message in B 11-5, it is nevertheless repeated, first to Agamemnon and then to the councillors. We see that in the case of messenger-speeches the NF$_1$, who decides after all whether or not to quote a character's words, makes the interest of the characters prevail over those of the NeFe$_1$, just as in other cases he intrudes upon the embedded focalization of his characters for the benefit of the NeFe$_1$.

Only seldom - but more than once: contra Richardson (1974: 261, ad *H. Dem.* 314-23) - does the NF$_1$ *not* give both instruction and delivery speech: Iris' message to the Trojans is summarily announced in B 786-7 (ἄγγελος ἦλθε ... ἀγγελίη ἀλεγεινῇ); Hector's *instruction* speech to Idaeus, which the latter delivers in Γ 250-258 to Priam, is only represented as ἔπεμπε ... Πρίαμόν τε καλέσσαι (Γ 116-7);[67] Idaeus' delivery of Agamemnon's message H 406-11 is summarized as speech-act mention in H 416 (ἀγγελίην ἀπέειπε) and Hera's instruction of Iris, delivered in Σ 170-80, is only briefly indicated in Σ 167 (ἄγγελος ἦλθε ... θωρήσσεσθαι ... πρὸ γὰρ ἧκε Ἥρη). Occasionally messengers even seem to speak entirely on their own initiative: not only is an instruction speech lacking, but even a small indication like those of B 786-7, Γ 116-7 and Σ 167. This applies to: Γ 130-8 (Iris: Helen),[68] Ξ 357-60 (Hypnus: Poseidon),[69] and Ψ 205-11 (Iris:

182

Winds).

The very nature of epic messenger-speeches - character **a** wishing to communicate something to character **c** with the help of character **b** as an intermediary[70] - requires the *delivery* speech to correspond as closely as possible to the *instruction* speech. In other words, the verbatim repetition is intended by the characters and functional on the level of their communication. A good example is Zeus' message to Hector (Λ 187-94), which is delivered by Iris (202-9) verbatim, except for the change of ὁρᾷ (187) into ὁρᾷς (202) and ἀναχωρείτω (189) into ὑπόεικε μάχης (204). Changes like these are the inevitable result of character **c** being referred to as 's/he' in the *instruction* speech and 'you' in the *delivery* speech, just as character **a** is 'I' in the *instruction* and 's/he' in the *delivery* speech, e.g.

(25) Γ 69-70 (Paris: Hector):
"αὐτὰρ ἔμ' ἐν μέσσῳ καὶ ἀρηΐφιλον Μενέλαον
συμβάλετ' ... μάχεσθαι"
"but bring me and Menelaus, dear to Ares, together in the middle to fight ..."

vs.

90-1 (Hector: Greeks and Trojans):
"(κέλεται) αὐτὸν δ' ἐν μέσσῳ καὶ ἀρηΐφιλον Μενέλαον
... μάχεσθαι."
"(Paris urges) that he himself and Menelaus, dear to Ares, fight in the middle"

A change in *local* deixis, as a result of character **b** moving from the position of character **a** to that of character **c**, is to be observed in the following example:

(26) Μ 345+348 (Menestheus: Thootes):
"ἐπεὶ τάχα τῇδε τετεύξεται αἰπὺς ὄλεθρος ...
εἰ δέ σφιν καὶ κεῖθι πόνος καὶ νεῖκος ὄρωρεν"
"because soon sheer destruction will take place here ...
but if there as well struggle and fury has arisen for them"

vs.

Μ 358+361 (Thootes: Ajaxes):
"ἐπεὶ τάχα κεῖθι τετεύξεται αἰπὺς ὄλεθρος ...
εἰ δὲ καὶ ἐνθάδε περ πόλεμος καὶ νεῖκος ὄρωρεν"
"because soon sheer destruction will take place there ...
but if here as well fighting and fury has arisen"

Apart from these small and inevitable changes, a messenger can also *deliberately* modify his instruction:[71] after all, a messenger is not only a (secondary) narrator, but also a (secondary) focalizer.

- s/he can change the mode of presentation of his/her message from direct into indirect speech.[72] Through the introduction of a verb of speaking s/he can then make explicit the tone of the message conveyed (example 27) or stress his/her role as an intermediary, i.e. as a mouthpiece of someone else's words (example 28):[73]

(27) Θ 402 (Zeus: Iris):
"γυιώσω μέν σφωῖν ὑφ' ἅρμασιν ὠκέας ἵππους"
"I will lame their swift horses under the chariot"

vs.

415-6 (Iris: Athena and Hera):
"ὧδε γὰρ <u>ἠπείλησε</u> Κρόνου πάϊς, ἢ τελέει περ,
γυιώσειν μὲν σφωῖν ὑφ' ἅρμασιν ὠκέας ἵππους"
"for thus did Cronus' son <u>threaten</u>, and he will make it a thing accomplished, to lame for both of you your swift horses under the chariot"[74]

(28) H 362 (Paris: Trojans):
"γυναῖκα μὲν οὐκ ἀποδώσω"
"the woman I will not give back"

vs.

392-3 (Idaeus: Greeks):
"κουριδίην δ' ἄλοχον Μενελάου κυδαλίμοιο
οὔ <u>φησιν</u> δώσειν· ἦ μὴν Τρῶές γε κέλονται."
"he (Paris) <u>says</u> that he will not give the lawful wife of glorious Menelaus: for sure the Trojans urge him to do so."

In (27) Iris through ἠπείλησε makes very clear that Zeus is angry and that Hera and Athena had better give heed to his message. In (28) the herald Idaeus, through the indirect form, dissociates himself from Paris' statement, which he, like the other Trojans, is not pleased with. For a last example I draw attention to Odysseus' diplomatic gift in I 677-88, where he has to report to Agamemnon Achilles' negative answer. Odysseus starts by answering (in chiastic order) Agamemnon's two questions of 674-5: 1) will Achilles help? and 2) has his anger come to an end? Ad 2: Achilles' anger has not stopped and 'he refuses you and your gifts' (678-9). By using as mode of presentation speech-act mention (ἀναί-νεται) Odysseus shrewdly avoids Achilles' far more agressive formulations in I 312 (ἐχθρὸς γάρ μοι κεῖνος ὁμῶς Ἀΐδαο πύλησιν) and 378 (ἐχθρὰ δέ μοι τοῦ δῶρα). Ad 1: Achilles will not help, but a) he leaves it to Agamemnon to save his men and b) he threatens to sail home (680-3). Here

Odysseus twice uses embedded indirect speech: in (a) to replace Achilles' third person imperative (346-7: φραζέσθω), in (b) to make explicit the illocutionary force of Achilles' threatening words in 356-63. It is to be noted that Odysseus does not mention Achilles' modifications of his own threats, which the latter makes in 618-9 and 650-5, as Ameis-H. rightly suggest "weil es für die Klärung der Lage zwecksmäßiger ist, wenn sich die Achäer jeder Hoffnung auf Achill völlig entschlagen." The last part of Odysseus' report (684-8) starts as embedded indirect speech (ἔφη παραμυθήσασθαι instead of Achilles' παραμυθησαίμην: 417), but from 685 ἐπεί onwards turns to embedded direct speech, capped by ὣς ἔφατ': 688. Once again Odysseus seems bent on driving home to his audience the seriousness of the Greeks' situation. Thus, his condensed report manages both to take the sting out of Achilles' words to Agamemnon, and yet to leave the main message, the perilous situation of the Greeks, intact.

- another way of modifying a message is by changing the order of presentation. E.g., whereas Paris in H 362-4 first had mentioned his refusal to give back Helen and then his offer to return the material goods, Idaeus (H 389-93) begins, by way of *captatio benevolentiae*, with the positive part of his message (Paris' offer) and only then adds the negative part (Paris' refusal).

- a messenger can also choose a different formulation: e.g. in example (28) above Paris refers to Helen as 'the woman', whereas Idaeus speaks of 'the lawful wife of glorious Menelaus'.[75] In choosing this formulation, Idaeus seems to take into account the fact that he is addressing the Greeks. At the same time it is indicative of his (and the other Trojans') sentiment that Paris should have given Helen back. An example of an apparently unintentional and therefore all the more revealing change in formulation is

(29) K 308 (Hector: the Trojans: I give a chariot and horses to him who would dare):
"νηῶν ὠκυπόρων σχεδὸν ἐλθέμεν"
"to go near the quick ships"

vs.

395 (Dolon: Odysseus and Diomedes):
"ἀνδρῶν δυσμενέων σχεδὸν ἐλθέμεν"
"(Hector urged me) to go near the enemy"

The different formulation in 395 is due to the fact that Dolon's situation has changed dramatically: before reaching the 'quick ships' of the Greeks he has been captured and now faces 'the enemy'.

- a messenger may also leave out parts of the message: the best example is
I 300-306 where Odysseus vis-à-vis Achilles tactfully suppresses the aggressive
final part of Agamemnon's *instruction* speech (I 158-61: δμηθήτω ... ὑποστήθω).[76]
- apart from these changes within the message, the messenger can also add
some words of his/her own,[77] either as a comment on (e.g. Idaeus in H 390) or
reinforcement of (e.g. Iris in Θ 423-4)[78] that message.

Conclusion

Messenger-speeches in the *Iliad* serve to convey a message from character a to
character c through the intermediary of character b. The messenger bridges a
distance in space between characters a and c (Olympus vs. earth; Trojan side
vs. Greek side; different parts of the Greek side) and often also a distance in
status (Zeus or other gods vs. humans). The verbatim repetition involved in
messenger-speeches is intended by the speakers themselves and is functional on
the level of the communication between characters. The NeFe$_1$, who hears both
instruction and *delivery* speech, has to put up with this redundancy. However,
his attention is kept alive by the many - indeed more than have been recognized
by scholars so far - smaller or greater alterations the messengers make in the
messages they transmit.[79] Like all speaking characters, messengers are (secondary)
focalizers and as such they often select, add to and interpret the information
they have to convey. Thus, from the very way in which Idaeus transmits the
μῦθον ᾿Αλεξάνδροιο (adding a curse in 390, changing the order of Paris' offer
and rejection, referring to Helen as 'the lawful wife of Menelaus', turning Paris'
direct speech into indirect speech) much can be learnt about his (presumably
the Trojan people's) ideas about Paris.

Another factor which influences the way in which a message is repeated is
the identity and status of the messenger's addressee, character c: Odysseus' tact
and versatility can be admired in the Embassy where he adapts Agamemnon's
message vis-à-vis Achilles and Achilles' message vis-à-vis Agamemnon. It is exactly
these alterations which make character b into more than an impersonal go-between.

5.4.2. Other cases of repeated speech

In the *Iliad* repeated speech is also found in other circumstances than the transmission of a message: these cases are collected in Appendix V B. The repetition

is here to be analyzed as the recurrence of identical (or almost identical) verse-clusters in two (or more) speeches, spoken by either the same or different speakers, addressing the same or different addressees. Occasionally speeches are repeated in their totality. They are marked in the Appendix with an asterisk. In this heterogeneous corpus of passages, a narratological significance cannot always be attributed to the repetition and in a number of cases we must be satisfied with a genetical explanation only, viz. that the similarity of situation allowed the poet to use (make his characters use) the same formulation. Thus, in (30) Sarpedon and Odysseus use the same threatening words, facing a weaker opponent:

(30) E 652-4 = Λ 443-5:
"σοὶ δ' ἐγὼ ἐνθάδε φημὶ φόνον καὶ κῆρα μέλαιναν
ἐξ ἐμέθεν τεύξεσθαι, ἐμῷ δ' ὑπὸ δουρὶ δαμέντα
εὖχος ἐμοὶ δώσειν, ψυχὴν δ' "Αϊδι κλυτοπώλῳ."
"And I proclaim here to you that slaughter and dark death
will be prepared by me and that, subdued by my spear, you
will give glory to me, but your soul to Hades, renowned for
his horses."[80]

In the following I shall, however, discuss examples where the repetition is functional, either on the level of the communication between characters, as in the case of messenger-speeches, or on the level of the reception by the NeFe$_1$, or on both levels. To decide whether a repetition is intended by a speaking character or whether it is only recognized as such by the NeFe$_1$, I have divided the material in four groups:

1. different speakers	- different addressees
2. different speakers	- the same addressee
3. the same speaker	- the same addressee
4. the same speaker	- different addressees

different speakers - different addressees

A speaker can deliberately repeat the words of another character, as is the case in Z 378-80 = Z 383-5 where the female servant, answering Hector's question, echoes his words in negated form; or in E 130-2 = E 819-21, where Diomedes reminds Athena of her own words.

It is to be noted that oaths, which in the Homeric epics are presented twice just like messages, are not, however, repeated verbatim:[81] Dolon's proposal for an oath to Hector (K 322-3) is actually sworn by Hector (K 329-31) in different words; the same holds true for Agamemnon's oath T 258-65, which follows upon the instruction by Achilles (T 176-7 = I 275-6 ≅ I 133-4, for the small difference see note 75). In these two cases the oath sworn is both longer and more force-ful.[82] Conversely, Hera's oath to Hypnus, which the latter had proposed in Ξ 275-6, is presented in summarized form by the NF$_1$ in Ξ 278-9.

A speaker can also repeat to a third person words spoken to him earlier by another, e.g.

(31) E 883-4 (Ares: Zeus):
"Κύπριδα μὲν πρῶτον σχεδὸν οὔτασε χεῖρ' ἐπὶ καρπῷ,
αὐτὰρ ἔπειτ' αὐτῷ μοι ἐπέσσυτο δαίμονι ἶσος"
"he (Diomedes) first hit Aphrodite in close fight on her hand near the wrist, but then he rushed like a daemon onto my-self"[83]

Ares here repeats the formulation Apollo had used to him in E 458-9. Note that the first verse of the repeated statement refers to the same event (Diomedes attacking Aphrodite), whereas the second verse refers to two different events (Diomedes attacking Apollo, Diomedes attacking Ares). Thus, the referent of μοι in E 459 is Apollo, in E 884 Ares. In all cases discussed so far the repetition can be logically accounted for, because an addressee has turned into a speaker.

More often, however, we find a different situation, viz. different speakers using the same words without being aware that other speakers had used them also. Only the NeFe$_1$, hearing both speeches, recognizes the repetition as such. In a case like

(32) K 402-4 (Odysseus: Dolon) = P 76-8 (Apollo: Hector):
"οἱ δ' ἀλεγεινοὶ
ἀνδράσι γε θνητοῖσι δαμήμεναι ἠδ' ὀχέεσθαι,
ἄλλῳ γ' ἢ Ἀχιλῆϊ, τὸν ἀθανάτη τέκε μήτηρ."
"they (Achilles' horses) are difficult to master or drive for another mortal than Achilles, whom an immortal mother bore."

the recurrence of words can be explained logically as due to knowledge shared by Odysseus and Apollo, but the repetition does not seem to have any special significance for the NeFe$_1$.[84]

This is different when repeated verse-clusters occur in speeches of characters who belong to two different camps (Greeks vs. Trojans or humans vs. gods). Then, the repetition, for the NeFe$_1$, can have the effect of a contrast.[85] A good example is:

(33) Δ 163-5 = Ζ 447-9:

"εὖ γὰρ ἐγὼ τόδε οἶδα κατὰ φρένα καὶ κατὰ θυμόν·
ἔσσεται ἦμαρ ὅτ' ἄν ποτ' ὀλώλῃ Ἴλιος ἱρὴ
καὶ Πρίαμος καὶ λαὸς ἐυμμελίω Πριάμοιο"

"For I know well this in my heart and spirit: there once will
be a day when holy Ilium and Priam and the people of Priam
with good spear will perish"[86]

With these words Agamemnon, the future victor, adhorts his troops (in Δ), whereas Hector, the future looser, expresses to his wife Andromache his determination to fight despite everything (in Ζ).[87] The same words in the mouth of Greek or Trojan get a different emotional colouring, a difference which can only be noticed and savoured by the NeFe$_1$.

different speakers - the same addressee

In Ε 529-32 = Ο 561-4 Agamemnon and Ajax adhort the Greeks with the same words. The fact that the addressee is the same in both cases is not relevant for the recurrence of the verse cluster. The same adhortation might also have been spoken by Hector addressing the Trojans. This is different in Λ 362-7 = Υ 449-54.[88] Here it is important that it is, in both cases, Hector who is addressed.[89] Both Diomedes and Achilles react with disappointment to the fact that Hector, the most important opponent for all Greeks, has escaped alive. They also show contempt (note κύον : 'dog') for their opponent, who has escaped only through the intervention of a god. Finally, they express their determination to kill Hector at a later occasion, a prophecy which only Achilles will fulfil. In the case of Υ 200-2 = Υ 431-3 again an important role is played by the fact that the addressee is the same (Achilles): Aeneas and Hector feel treated like 'a foolish child' (νηπύτιος) by Achilles. Now, Achilles had indeed advised Aeneas to retreat, in order not to be killed (Υ 196-8) and Hector to come near, in order to be killed all the sooner (Υ 429), both times marking himself as the superior fighter. Achilles' threatening words are used by other characters too (Υ 196-8 = Ρ 30-2: Menelaus is addressing Euphorbus and Υ 429 = Ζ 143: Diomedes is addressing Hippolochus), but when spoken by Achilles to Aeneas and Hector, heroes who are in principle (almost) his equal, they elicit from them an - as the NeFe$_1$ notices, the same - indignant reaction. My last example of this second group again shows the effect repetition can have, when the speakers belong to different camps (cp. above example 33). Priam has announced to Hecabe that he will go to Achilles and she reacts with a mixture of amazement, panic and rejection:

(34) Ω 203-5 (You must have lost your mind):
"πῶς ἐθέλεις ἐπὶ νῆας ᾿Αχαιῶν ἐλθέμεν οἶος,
ἀνδρὸς ἐς ὀφθαλμοὺς ὅς τοι πολέας τε καὶ ἐσθλοὺς
υἱέας ἐξενάριξε; σιδήρειόν νύ τοι ἦτορ."
"How can you wish to go alone to the Greek ships, to the
eyes of the man who has killed many noble sons of yours?
Your heart is of iron."

When Achilles asks Priam the same question in Ω 519-21,[90] it gives expression
to his amazement (cp. 483: θάμβησεν) and pity (516: οἰκτίρων). Viewing himself
for a moment through the eyes of Priam - and as the NeFe₁ knows, of Hecabe -
he understands the courage and at the same time the extreme sorrow (Ω 518)
of the old man, who is forced to come and face him. Priam, addressee of both
Hecabe and Achilles, might have noticed the repetition, but he does not comment
on it. The effect of the repetition seems to be intended for the NeFe₁: it stresses
the extraordinary nature of Priam's mission, which is acknowledged by friend
and foe.

the same speaker - the same addressee

It is in itself plausible that a speaker uses the same words on more than one
occasion. In Γ 285-7 = Γ 458-60 the repetition is intended by Agamemnon, who
claims, when the duel between Paris and Menelaus has come to an end, the fulfilment of the conditions of the fight agreed upon before. In A 37-8 = A 451-2
Chryses opens his prayers to Apollo with the same invocation. This repetition
corresponds to 'reality', where prayers can be expected to contain certain standard
elements. For the NeFe₁, however, the repetition also signals something else,
viz. that Chryses' first, aggressive prayer is now balanced by a propitious one
and that Apollo's anger will come to an end.[91]

Another effect of the recurrence of verse-clusters can be to characterize
the relation between speaker and addressee, e.g.

(36) Θ 39-40 = X 183-4:
"θάρσει, Τριτογένεια, φίλον τέκος· οὔ νύ τι θυμῷ
πρόφρονι μυθέομαι, ἐθέλω δέ τοι ἤπιος εἶναι."
"Keep faith, Tritogeneia (Athena), dear daughter: for I speak
not in earnest and I want to be kind to you."[92]

The repetition is indicative of Zeus' tender feelings towards his daughter Athena:
he can not easily say "no" to her. This 'characterizing' interpretation of Θ 39-40
and X 183-4 seems to be confirmed by the fact that both passages are a reaction

to words spoken by Athena, which on other occasions are used by Hera: Θ 32-7 = Θ 463-8 and Χ 179-81 = Π 441-3. Spoken by Hera, they elicit a very different reaction from Zeus: in Π he fulfils her demand, without answering her; in Θ he answers in a fairly aggressive way.

The most famous example of this third group is B 110-18 + 139-41 = I 17-28. Agamemnon declares that he has been misled by Zeus in believing that he could capture Troy and, disillusioned, suggests to his soldiers that they return home. In B he does not mean this suggestion to be taken seriously,[93] in I he does[94] and as Lohmann (1971: 212) notes: "Der identische Wortlaut macht die völlige Umkehrung des Sinnes noch wirkungsvoller". It is characteristic for Agamemnon's weak position as leader of the expedition that neither in B nor in I his words have the effect he intended them to have: in B the soldiers take his speech at face value and start making preparations for the return, in I Agamemnon's proposal is not discussed seriously at all. It is to be noted that, as in the case of example (34), the addressees do not (nor, as a matter of fact, Agamemnon himself) comment upon the repetitious character of I 17-28. It is left to the NeFe$_1$ to detect the significance of the repetition, "the complete reversal of meaning".

the same speaker- different addressees

An example of repetition intended by the speaker is

> (37) Σ 112-3 (Achilles: Thetis) = T 65-6 (Achilles: Agamemnon and Greeks):
> "ἀλλὰ τὰ μὲν προτετύχθαι ἐάσομεν ἀχνύμενόι περ,
> θυμὸν ἐνὶ στήθεσσι φίλον δαμάσαντες ἀνάγκῃ"
> "but let us subdue by force the impulse in our breast, and
> leave this here as passed and over, in spite of our grief"

Achilles must use these same words on two occasions in view of the difference in addressee. Just as he had announced his wrath first to Agamemnon and the Greeks (A 297-303) and then to his mother Thetis (A 408-12), he now renounces it first privately, in front of Thetis, and then officially, in front of Agamemnon and the Greeks.

In this group we also find examples of recurrent verse-clusters which characterize a speaker (cp. above example 36): e.g., B 371-3 + 374 = Δ 288 + 290-1 characterize Agamemnon as leader of the expedition, eager to reach his goal, the destruction of Troy, and Σ 56-62 = Σ 437-43 characterize Thetis as mother, proud of and at the same time concerned for her precious offspring.[95]

The last example of this fourth group is Ξ 200-7 = Ξ 301-6. Hera tells, first to Aphrodite and then to Zeus, the same false story, viz. that she intends to visit Oceanus and Tethys in order to settle a marriage problem for them. Hera invents this false story in the first place to persuade Aphrodite to give her 'love and seduction', which she needs to seduce Zeus. She motivates her helpfulness towards Oceanus and Tethys by referring to the service this couple rendered her in the past: they received and reared her after her mother Rhea and father Cronus were defeated. By helping them now in her turn, she will earn their eternal gratitude. The second time Hera tells this story, it is by way of answer to Zeus, who had asked her why she had come all the way to Mount Ida.[96] The invented story is now less relevant to the situation, and accordingly, Hera cuts it short: she leaves out the circumstances of the service rendered to her by Oceanus and Tethys and their gratitude. It is no coincidence that she leaves out exactly these details, since it was Zeus himself who defeated Hera's parents and, therefore, caused her to be adopted by Oceanus and Tethys. It would have been tactless to recall this incident in front of Zeus.

Conclusion

In this section I have discussed one category of repeated verse-clusters, viz. those occurring in character-text (category b of p. 180). It has turned out that for many cases the question I posed at the beginnning of this section could be answered positively, viz. that the repetition is not merely to be explained genetically, but also makes sense narratologically. The examples of repeated speech I discussed

    1. are functional on the level of the communication between characters and/or

    2. have a significance for the NeFe$_1$.

Ad 1. This is the case when

- character b repeats to character c what he had heard from character a (messages);

- character b echoes the words of character a, while addressing that same character a (question-answer, reminder);

Ad 2. This was found in the case of

- messenger-speeches, when the convention of verbatim reporting is broken and the messenger makes changes in his message (Idaeus distancing himself from Paris and adapting his message to his Greek audience; Odysseus leaving out the aggressive finale of Agamemnon's message to Achilles, subtly presenting Achilles' answer to Agamemnon);

- the (unintended) mirroring by one speaker of the words of another speaker. This then points to a dramatic contrast (fall of Troy as anticipated by victor and looser) or emphatic agreement (Priam's mission amazes friend and foe).

- the repeated use by one speaker of the same verse-clusters. This characterizes that speaker (Thetis as mother, Agamemnon as leader of the expedition) or the relation between speaker and addressee (Zeus' affection for Athena).

5.5. Summary

Almost half of the *Iliad* consists of character-text, the narrative situation of a character verbalizing his own focalization: $NF_1[NF_2C_x]$. This means that characters have a substantial share in the presentation of the story. In this chapter aspects of the presentation by characters have been investigated. What picture has emerged? What kind of presentators are Homeric characters and which factors play a role in their presentation? The position of characters as presentators, as compared to that other presentator of the *Iliad*, the NF_1, is summed up in the following three qualifications:

1. secondary. Characters are secondary narrator-focalizers, which means that the NF_1 decides when and for how long to let them speak and that the $NeFe_1$ also receives their speech.

2. internal. Whereas the NF_1 is external, the characters are *qualitate qua* internal narrator-focalizers: their speeches constitute an event on the level of the primary fabula and refer - except in the case of certain external analepses- to events in which the speakers are (or have been) themselves involved.

3. multiple. In comparison to the one NF_1 (and $NeFe_1$) there is a multitude of speaking characters (and addressees).

Ad 1. The double reception of speeches has proved to be of importance in the case of repeated speech (section 5.4): only the $NeFe_1$ can notice alterations in messenger-speeches, and interpret the recurrence of verse-clusters as significant.

Ad 2 and 3. Together these two qualifications account for the great variety and emotional or subjective colouring of the speeches. To illustrate this variety as concretely as possible I have (in section 5.1) compared the presentation by different characters of the same event. The comparison showed considerable differences in tone, evaluation, selection of details, vocabulary, etc. This led to the formulation of the following rule: the presentation by characters in character-text is conditioned by the identity of speaker and addressee and by the situation, i.e. the effect the speaker wants his words to have on the addressee.

The validity of this rule was further confirmed by the analysis of the embedded Bellerophontes-story (section 5.2) and of embedded speech (section 5.3). Section 5.3 also brought to light another difference between NF_1 and characters. The NF_1, on account of or rather through his association with the Muses, claims to be a reliable presentator. This reliability also pertains to his quotation of character-texts, which are supposed to contain the *ipsissima verba* of the characters. Characters, however, are not always dependable presentators of the words of others. The degree of reliability ranges from pure quotation, via indirect representation or summary, to pure invention (tis-speeches).

The results of sections 5.2 and 5.4 have shown that a (text-immanent, synchronic) narratological interpretation of the Homeric text offers a valuable, sometimes indispensable complement to genetical ones. The diachronic and comparatistic interpretations of the Bellerophontes-story had drawn attention to many interesting points, but had treated the Iliadic passage itself rather stepmotherly. This *external analepsis* is firmly integrated into the speech it forms part of. The speech in its turn serves a clear function in the confrontation between Diomedes and Glaucus. The many "omissions" scholars had noticed are in fact due to selection (focalization) by Glaucus, who wishes his story to be as rhetorically effective as possible. What 'remains' forms a coherent whole, with emphasis put on those details which are relevant to the story or to its rhetorical function (and that of the speech as a whole). In the case of repetition of verseclusters occurring in character-text, it has been demonstrated that interpretation should not stop at merely considering them "a natural feature of oral poetry". Repeated speech is functional on the level of the communication between characters and/or significant for the $NeFe_1$.

It will be understood that many other aspects concerning the presentation of the story in character-text have not been touched upon. I mention two suggestions for further research. In the first place there is the aspect of the influence of the NF_1 on character-text. As we have seen in chapter 1 (pp. 13-4) the scholiasts occasionally comment on a word/expression occurring in direct speech as deriving from the poet. On other occasions characters speak about things which they logically cannot know and their information derives from the poet: cp. bT-scholia ad Π 844-5, Bassett (1938: 131-40, who speaks of the λύσις ἐκ τοῦ ἀκροατοῦ), Kakridis (1982), and Macleod (ad Ω 203-5). A second route for further study concerns the analysis of conversations in the *Iliad*. This category of informal speech has not been covered by Fingerle and it seems rewarding to undertake an analysis of it according to insights gained by research in *discourse analysis*, for which see Levinson (1983: 284-370).

6. THE RELATION OF NARRATOR-TEXT (SIMPLE AND COMPLEX) AND CHARACTER-TEXT

In the previous chapters I have dealt with the three main narrative situations in the *Iliad* separately: simple narrator-text (ch.3), complex narrator-text (ch.4) and character-text (ch.5). In fact, these three narrative situations are, of course, integrated and together form a complex whole. It is only for the sake of a clear and systematic analysis that they have been treated separately. Occasionally I have drawn attention to the relation between the narrative situations, e.g. the fact that complex narrator-text often forms the transition from simple narrator-text to character-text. In this chapter I will look at (aspects of) this relation and integration more extensively.[1] A concrete point of contact between narrator-text and character-text is formed by the speech-formulas by which the NF_1 introduces and caps speeches of characters. In section 6.1 these speech-formulas will be analyzed in their function of attributive discourse. In 6.2 narrator-text and character-text are confronted with each other when they describe the same event.

6.1. Speech-formulas as attributive discourse

In the Homeric epics the transition from narrator-text to character-text and vice versa is almost without exception[2] marked explicitly by introductory and capping phrases. The reason for this explicitness must undoubtedly be sought in the oral background of the Homeric text: lacking visual signs like quotation-marks or indentation, the performing singer must mark the change from narrator-text to character-text and vice versa with words.[3] Since the *Iliad* has so many speeches, which all need to be accompanied by speech-markers, these speech-markers tend to be highly formulaic and I will henceforth refer to them as *speech-formulas*.

Scholarship on Homeric speech-formulas has mainly dealt with semantic or genetic questions. To the first, semantic category belong Jacobsohn (1935), Calhoun (1935), Couch (1937), Munoz Valle (1971) and Vivante (1975), who all concentrate on the interpretation of the fossilized (and therefore obscure) expressions ἔπος τ' ἔφατ' ἔκ τ' ὀνόμαζε and ἔπεα πτερόεντα. To the second, genetic category belong M. Parry (1937), Krarup (1941), Fournier (1946) and Edwards (1969, 1970), who analyze the system of the speech-formulas. A somewhat special position is occupied by Fingerle (1939: 306-72): he investigates the "Typik der Einführungs-und Abschlußformeln", taking into account also the type of speech introduced or the kind of action following. The high degree of stylization the Homeric speech-formulas display has led Fournier to deny them almost all meaning:

> La perception globale d'un changement de registre suffisait, les détails de l'annonce: épithètes, participes ou adverbes circonstanciels, restaient peu distincts et ne servaient qu'à remplir l'hexamètre. (1946: 68)

Fournier's extreme Parryism with its stress on "l'action tyrannique du mètre" has been modified by the investigations of Edwards, who draws attention to subtleties of expression which can be found even in this group of standard phrases. The approach to the Homeric speech-formulas that will be undertaken in this section can, I think, supplement the results obtained by Edwards and rehabilitate the speech-formulas by assigning to them their narratological function.

The Iliadic speech-formulas will be analyzed as forms of *attributive discourse*. This concept derives from the narratologist Prince, who defines it as

> les locutions et les phrases qui, dans un récit (...), accompagnent le discours direct et l'attribuent à tel personnage ou à tel autre- les "dit-il", "s'écriait-elle' ... qui régissent partiellement la circulation des voix et contribuent à situer la parole, son origine, son contexte et sa destination (1978: 305).[4]

Adducing numerous examples from modern novels, Prince demonstrates how form, extent, and distribution of attributive discourse can be revealing for the narrative itself or for the genre or period to which it belongs. To give one example, in Flaubert's *Madame Bovary* the heroine, when about to speak, is alternately referred to as 'Emma', 'Madame Bovary', 'she' or 'the young woman', depending on the situation in which she finds herself and the person to whom she speaks. Attributive discourse is also paid attention to by Bal (1977: 43 = 1983: 253-4): the NF_1, beforehand or afterwards qualifying a speech, directs, especially through his choice of a verb of speaking, the reception of that speech by the $NeFe_1$. Before yielding his power to speak to one of the characters, the NF_1, as it were, emphasizes his own authority.

In the *Iliad* the beginnings and the ends of speeches coincide (except for O 82 and Ψ 855) with the beginning and end of a verse. The speech-formulas are found in the verses preceding and following the speech, they are never intercalated in it.[5] The average length of an introductory formula is one verse, of a capping formula half a verse. The introductory formula normally contains the following elements: addressee-verb of speaking-speaker-additional information. The capping formula normally contains: an anaphoric (demonstrative) pronoun-verb of speaking. An example:

(1)   A 413+428:
      τὸν δ' ἠμεἰβετ' ἔπειτα Θέτις κατὰ δάκρυ χέουσα· ...
      Ὣς ἄρα φωνήσασ' ἀπεβήσετο
      And to him spoke in answer Thetis, shedding tears: ...
      Having thus spoken, she left

In the following I will have a closer look at these various elements of the introductory and capping formulas, to get an idea of how the NF_1 moulds the $NeFe_1$'s response to and interpretation of the speech enclosed by the speech-formulas.

The speaker
The *Iliad* does not show such subtle variations in denomination as Prince demonstrated for Flaubert's *Madame Bovary*. In the majority of cases the speaker is referred to by his name or patronymic, often accompanied by an epithet. Thus we find 5 times:

(2)   τὸν δ' ἀπαμειβόμενος προσέφη <u>πολύμητις Ὀδυσσεύς</u>
      and to him spoke in answer <u>Odysseus, of many devices</u>

This prevalence of proper names instead of indirect references or a simple 'he', 'she' is the consequence of the speech-formulas being formulaic: the combination proper name-epithet is one of the most formalized parts of the Homeric diction.

But the somewhat solemn announcement of the speaker should also, I think, be seen in the light of the encomiastic nature of the *Iliad* (see above section 3.4, p. 98): to be a 'speaker of words' and an 'accomplisher of deeds' (I 443: μύθων τε ῥητῆρ' ... πρηκτῆρά τε ἔργων) is the heroic ideal and accordingly the NF₁ celebrates the words of his characters as much as their martial feats.

There are, however, some instances of indirect reference instead of proper names. Upon examination, they turn out, almost without exception, to have a function: they stress the quality in which a speaker is speaking.

A 92: μάντις ἀμύμων ('excellent seer') instead of Calchas. In the ensuing speech (A 93-100) Calchas reveals the divine cause of the plague.

A 544 (and X 167, Ω 103): πατὴρ ἀνδρῶν τε θεῶν τε ('father of men and gods') instead of Zeus. This formula is found also outside attributive discourse, but its use in A 544 is "especially suitable" according to Kirk (ad loc.), "stressing as it does his (Zeus') august and autocratic side against Here's insinuation that he is just an ordinary husband".

Δ 403: υἱὸς Καπανῆος ('son of Kapaneus') instead of Sthenelus. Sthenelus will in the ensuing speech speak about his father's (unsuccessful) expedition against Thebes.

E 101: Λυκάονος ... υἱός ('son of Lycaon') instead of Pandarus. This seems to be a regular denomination of Pandarus, cp. e.g. Δ 89 and 93.

Z 144: Ἱππολόχοιο ... φαίδιμος υἱός ('splendid son of Hippolochus') instead of Glaucus. The ensuing speech contains a genealogy and at the end Hippolochus plays a role, cp. above ch. 5, n. 30.

Z 484: πόσις ('husband') instead of Hector. For the role of denomination in the Homilia see De Jong (1987).

H 384: ἠπύτα κῆρυξ ('the loud-voiced herald') instead of Idaeus. Idaeus is about to deliver an official message.

Λ 605 (and Λ 837, Π 626): Μενοιτίου ἄλκιμος υἱός ('valiant son of Menoetius') instead of Patroclus. This denomination is found regularly also outside attributive speech without a recognizable special effect.

T 286: γυνή ('the woman') instead of Briseis. Briseis will talk in her quality of former and future wife.

Φ 97: Πριάμοιο ... φαίδιμος υἱός ('splendid son of Priam') instead of Lycaon. Lycaon, in fact, pays for this status with his life, cp. Φ 105.

Φ 152: Πηλεγόνος ... φαίδιμος υἱός ('splendid son of Pelegon') instead of Asteropaeus. The ensuing speech contains a genealogy and in 159 the name Pelegon recurs.

X 79: μήτηρ ('his mother') instead of Hecabe. In the ensuing speech Hecabe, trying to persuade Hector to come into the city, will appeal to his reverence and love for her as his mother.

Ψ 304: πατήρ ('his father') instead of Nestor. Nestor is going to give advice to his son.

Ω 200: γυνή ('his wife') instead of Hecabe. Hecabe speaks as Priam's wife.[6]

Sometimes the NF₁ precedes the actual introductory formula by a description of the speaker: Calchas (A 69-72), Nestor (A 247-52), Thersites (Β 212-23), Thoas (O 281-4, and cp. N 216-8), Polydamas (Σ 249-52). In the cases of Calchas and Nestor this introduction accompanies their first, of Thersites and Thoas their only, and of Polydamas his last and most important performance as a speaker. Except for Thersites, these are no general or comprehensive descriptions, but they draw attention to the rhetorical abilities and good sense of the speaker. In other words, they serve to *recommend* the speaker to the NeFe₁. The tone of recommendation also recurs in the speech-formula itself:

(3) A 73 = 253 = O 285 = Σ 253:
δ σφιν <u>ἐὐφρονέων</u> ἀγορήσατο καὶ μετέειπεν
that man, <u>in kind intention to them</u>, took the floor and in their midst spoke[7]

Shorter versions of such speaker-recommendations are: Ἕλενος, οἰωνοπόλων ὄχ' ἄριστος (Ζ 76); κῆρυξ Ἰδαῖος, πεπνυμένα μήδεα εἰδώς (Η 278); Νέστωρ, οὗ καὶ πρόσθεν ἀρίστη φαίνετο βουλή (Η 325 = Ι 94); Πρίαμος, θεόφιν μήστωρ ἀτάλαντος (Η 366); following after the speech: ὁ γέρων ... πάλαι πολέμων ἐΰ εἰδώς (Δ 310).

The addressee

The addressee is referred to either by name or, more often, through the anaphoric demonstrative pronoun τόν, τήν, τοῖσι. In the majority of cases the addressee appears at the beginning of the speech itself in the form of a vocative, e.g.

(4) Ε 463-4:
υἱάσι δὲ Πριάμοιο διοτρεφέεσσι κέλευεν·
"ὦ υἱεῖς Πριάμοιο διοτρεφέος βασιλῆος"
And he spurred on the sons of Priam, nourished by Zeus:
"O sons of Priam, king nourished by Zeus"

Twice an introductory formula takes the addressee as its point of departure, containing a verb of *hearing* instead of speaking. The situation is that of warriors who, facing a stronger opponent, beg for their lives:

(5) Λ 137 ≅ Φ 98:
    ἀμείλικτον δ' ὄπ' ἄκουσαν
    (they begged) but they heard an unsoftened/relentless voice

In other words, ἀμείλικτον is focalized by the suppliants.[8] The effect is that the hearer/reader identifies with these suppliants and as it were hears the ensuing speech, spoken by the opponent, with their ears. A somewhat different effect is reached in

(6) Θ 4:
    αὐτὸς δέ σφ' ἀγόρευε, θεοὶ δ' ὑπὸ πάντες ἄκουον
    he himself (Zeus) spoke among them and all the gods listened
    thereat

Zeus is about to make an important statement and what is normally left implicit is now indicated explicitly, viz. that his addressees listen.[9] There is also a capping formula which, containing a verb of hearing, starts from the addressee rather than the speaker:

(7) Y 318 (≅ Φ 377 ≅ Ψ 161):
    Αὐτὰρ ἐπεὶ τό γ' ἄκουσε Ποσειδάων ἐνοσίχθων
    but after earth-shaker Poseidon had heard that

The effect is to illustrate the prompt reaction of the addressee: being asked to do something, he or she immediately (note αὐτίκα in Y 321, Φ 378, Ψ 162) hastens to execute that request.[10]

The verb of speaking[11]
The verb of speaking (both of introductory and of capping formula) appears as a finite verb and/or a participle. Often we find more than one verb: two predicates (e.g. in example 3) or predicate and participle (e.g. in example 2). Less often the verb of speaking appears as a participle only (e.g. Φ 529-30: βαῖνε χαμᾶζε, ὀτρύνων ...). A useful framework for discussing these verbs is offered by *speech act* theory.[12] When we speak, we perform three acts simultaneously:

"- a *locutionary* act: the utterance of a sentence with determinate sense and reference;
- an *illocutionary* act: the making of a statement, offer, promise etc. in uttering a sentence, by virtue of the conventional force associated with it; and
- a *perlocutionary* act: the bringing about of effects on the audience by means of uttering the sentence, such effects being special to the circumstance of utterance" (Levinson 1983: 236).

In the following pair of Iliadic introductory and capping formulas, the NF_1 merely indicates the locutionary act of the speaking character:

(8) A 58+68:
τοῖσι δ' ἀνιστάμενος <u>μετέφη</u> πόδας ὠκὺς ᾿Αχιλλεύς
"Ητοι ὅ γ' ὣς <u>εἰπὼν</u> κατ' ἄρ' ἕζετο
And standing up quick-footed Achilles <u>spoke</u> amidst them
- And <u>having thus spoken</u> he sat down again

In examples 9-12 the NF_1 also indicates the illocutionary force of the following speech:

(9) Ξ 478:
τῷ δ' ᾿Ακάμας ἔκπαγλον <u>ἐπεύξατο</u> μακρὸν ἀύσας
But over him Akamas very much <u>boasted</u>, shouting loudly

(10) Λ 130:
τὼ δ' αὖτ' ἐκ δίφρου <u>γουναζέσθην</u>
and the two of them <u>supplicated</u> from their chariot

(11) Κ 328:
ὃ δ' ἐν χερσὶ σκῆπτρον λάβε καί οἱ <u>ὄμοσσεν</u>
and he took the sceptre in his hands and <u>swore</u> to him

(12) Γ 38 = Ζ 325:
Τὸν δ' ῞Εκτωρ <u>νείκεσσεν</u> ἰδὼν αἰσχροῖς ἐπέεσσιν
And Hector seeing him (Paris) <u>rebuked</u> him with harsh words

The verb 'boast' in (9) indicates that the speech following is, in Searle's (1976) terms, *assertive*: the speaker tells how (he thinks) things are. Here, Acamas claims his victory over Promachus. The verb 'supplicate' in (10) indicates that a *directive* follows: the speaker tries to get another to do things. Here, the two brothers try to make Agamemnon spare their lives. The verb 'swear' in (11) indicates that a *commissive* follows: the speaker commits himself to do things. Here, Hector promises Dolon Achilles' horses. The verb 'criticize' in (12), finally, indicates that an *expressive* follows: the speaker expresses an emotion. Here, Hector expresses his discontent over Paris' behaviour.

Most capping formulas indicate the locutionary act only (ἦ, ἔφατο, εἰπών, φαμένη), but occasionally the illocutionary force of the speech is indicated (again), e.g.

(13) A 450+457:
τοῖσιν δε Χρύσης μεγάλ᾽ <u>εὔχετο</u> χεῖρας ἀνασχών
῞Ως ἔφατ᾽ <u>εὐχόμενος</u>
And among them Chryses <u>prayed</u> aloud, with his hands raised
Thus he spoke <u>praying</u>[13]

Sometimes the introductory formula only indicates the locutionary act, whereas the capping formula indicates the illocutionary act, e.g.

(14) H 123+161:
Νέστωρ δ᾽ ᾽Αργείοισιν ἀνίστατο καὶ <u>μετέειπεν</u>
῞Ως <u>νείκεσσ᾽</u> ὁ γέρων
Nestor stood up and <u>spoke</u> amongst the Greeks
Thus the old man <u>reproached them</u>[14]

In

(15) Ψ 178+184:
ᾤμωξέν τ᾽ ἄρ᾽ ἔπειτα, φίλον δ᾽ <u>ὀνόμηνεν</u> ἑταῖρον
῞Ως φάτ᾽ <u>ἀπειλήσας</u>
And then he (Achilles) started weeping and <u>called</u> his friend
<u>by name</u> ... Thus he spoke <u>with a (grim) pledge</u>

the difference between introductory and capping formula corresponds to a change of tone within the speech itself. Achilles starts by addressing his friend Patroclus, but mention of the twelve young Trojans' fate makes him think of Hector and the sad tone of farewell changes into a revengeful one.[15] Sometimes the speaker himself (also) indicates *expressis verbis* the illocutionary force of his words (example 16) or it is recognized by the addressee (example 17):

(16) O 660+665:
λίσσεθ᾽ ὑπὲρ τοκέων γουνούμενος ἄνδρα ἕκαστον
"τῶν ὕπερ ἐνθάδ᾽ ἐγὼ <u>γουνάζομαι</u> οὐ παρεόντων"
(Nestor) adjured them on behalf of their parents, supplicating each man
"on behalf of those who are not present I here <u>supplicate</u>"[16]

(17) Γ 59 = Z 333 (Paris: Hector):
" ῞Εκτορ, ἐπεί με κατ᾽ αἶσαν <u>ἐνείκεσας</u> οὐδ᾽ ὑπὲρ αἶσαν"
"Hector, since you <u>criticized</u> me justly and not unfairly"[17]

In (17) Paris refers back to Hector's speech Γ 39-57 (Z 326-31), which had been introduced with the verb νείκεσσεν (above example 12). Sometimes the illocutionary force of a speech as recognized by the addressee is contained in embedded focalization, e.g.

(18) Ω 265:
   ῞Ως ἔφαϑ', οἱ δ' ἄρα πατρὸς ὑποδείσαντες <u>ὁμοκλήν</u>...
   thus he (Priam) spoke, and they, scared by the <u>rebuke</u> of
   their father, ...

Priam's speech had in Ω 252 been introduced with ὁμοκλήσας ἐκέλευε.[18]

The perlocutionary act of a speech, its intended or unintended effect on the addressee, can also be indicated by the NF_1, e.g.

(19) N 788 (= H 120):
   ῞Ως εἰπὼν <u>παρέπεισεν</u> ἀδελφειοῦ φρένας ἥρως
   By such a speech the hero <u>made</u> his brother <u>change his
   mind</u>[19]

A passage which was disputed already in antiquity is

(20) Θ 97 (Diomedes has asked Odysseus to help him save Nestor)
   ῞Ως ἔφατ', <u>οὐδ' ἐσάκουσε</u> πολύτλας δῖος 'Οδυσσεύς
   Thus he spoke, but <u>he did not hear/give heed</u>, much-enduring
   illustrious Odysseus

Does οὐδ' ἐσάκουσε mean 1) Odysseus 'did not hear' (so bT-scholia) or 2) Odysseus 'did not give heed', i.e. 'turned a deaf ear to' (so Aristarchus, Ameis-H., Willcock, Andersen 1978: 113-4). I prefer the second interpretation in view of the way in which Diomedes' speech was introduced:

(21) Θ 92:
   σμερδαλέον δ' ἐβόησεν <u>ἐποτρύνων</u> 'Οδυσῆα
   he cried out loud <u>rallying</u> Odysseus

The unique formulation οὐδ' ἐσάκουσε - more frequent is οὔ τι προσέφη, e.g. in E 689 (on which see Beßlich 1966: 74) - seems a reaction to ἐποτρύνων: Diomedes urged Odysseus, but the latter did not respond.

Additional information

I distinguish between information which is available to the characters and information which reaches the NeFe₁ only. To the first category belong indications about gestures (e.g. χεῖρας ὀρεγνύς: 'stretching out his hands'), facial expressions (e.g. ὑπόδρα ἰδών: 'looking with a scowl'), emotions (e.g. χολωσαμένη: 'angry') or tone (e.g. ἀγανοῖς ἐπέεσσιν: 'with gentle words').[20] Often these indications, especially those of emotions and tone, further elaborate on what has already been indicated by the verb of speaking, e.g. Φ 480 νείκεσεν ... ὀνειδείοις ἐπέεσσι: 'she criticized ... with reproachful words'. But sometimes the illocutionary force of the speech is indicated by the additional information only. For example, an introduction like Φ 393 ὀνείδειον φάτο μῦθον ('he spoke a reproachful speech') indicates that an expressive speech will follow. In

(21) Θ 28-9 = Ι 693-4 ≅ 430-1:
"Ὡς ἔφαϑ', οἱ δ' ἄρα πάντες ἀκὴν ἐγένοντο σιωπῇ
μῦϑον ἀγασσάμενοι· μάλα γὰρ <u>κρατερῶς</u> ἀγόρευσεν.
thus he spoke, and they all fell silent in awe of his speech:
for he had spoken very <u>forcefully</u>.

I would consider the qualification κρατερῶς as due to the secondary focalization of the characters who have just heard the speech. The adverb occurs in a γάρ-clause following upon a verb of feeling (ἀγασσάμενοι), cp. above section 4.1.1, p. 112.

To the second category, information which reaches the NeFe₁ only, belong in the first place what I call truth-indications, i.e. indications given by the NF₁ for the benefit of the NeFe₁ as to how he is to understand the following speech. Thus, when it is told in Ξ 197.300.329 that Hera spoke δολοφρονέουσα ('planning trickery'), the NeFe₁ - not Zeus, the NeFe₂ - knows that he should not take the following speech at face value. The NF₁ can also give beforehand an indication as to the content of the speech, e.g.

(22) Ε 358-359:
πολλὰ λισσομένη χρυσάμπυκας <u>ᾔτεεν ἵππους·</u>
"φίλε κασίγνητε, κόμισαί τέ με <u>ὃς</u> δέ μοι <u>ἵππους</u>"
urgently pleading she (Aphrodite) <u>asked</u> him (Ares) <u>for his horses</u> with golden frontlet: "dear brother, provide for me and <u>give me your horses</u>"[21]

Apart from indicating the truth-value or content of a speech, the NF₁ can also evaluate a speech. Thus he can qualify it as a πυκινήν ... βουλήν ('a carefully constructed plan': B 55 = K 302),[22] or αἴσιμα ('proper things': Z 62 = H 121).[23] In the following cases I am inclined to ascribe the speech-evaluations not to the NF₁ but to characters: τοῖσι δὲ πᾶσιν ἑαδότα μῦθον ἔειπεν ('he spoke a speech pleasant to all': I 173) and ἅδε δ' Ἕκτορι μῦθος ἀπήμων ('the profitable speech pleased Hector': M 80 = N 748). The focalizing characters (all, Hector) are indicated in the dative, cp. above section 4.1.2, p. 119. Capping formulas only rarely contain additional information. A very effectful example is found in Ξ 475. Ajax has just killed a companion of Polydamas, who in his turn had killed the Greek Prothoènor. Ajax now shouts to Polydamas:

(23) Ξ 470-5:
"φράζεο, Πουλυδάμα, καί μοι νημερτὲς ἐνίσπες,
ἦ ῥ' οὐχ οὗτος ἀνὴρ Προθοήνορος ἀντὶ πεφάσθαι
ἄξιος; οὐ μέν μοι κακὸς εἴδεται οὐδὲ κακῶν ἔξ,
ἀλλὰ κασίγνητος ᾿Αντήνορος ἱπποδάμοιο
ἢ πάϊς· αὐτῷ γὰρ γενεὴν ἄγχιστα ἐῴκει."
Ἦ ῥ' εὖ γιγνώσκων, Τρῶας δ' ἄχος ἔλλαβε θυμόν.
"Look Polydamas and tell me the truth, is not that a worthy man to have been killed in exchange for Prothoenor? He seems to me indeed not to be a mean man nor (sprung) from mean parents, but to be the brother of horse-taming Antenor, or his son. For he looked most like him as to his race." He spoke, knowing perfectly well (who it was), and grief befell the Trojans.

Through the addition of εὖ γιγνώσκων the NF₁ indicates that Ajax only pretends not to know the exact identity of his opponent. His feigned ignorance drives home to the Trojans ever so strongly the loss of their companion.[24]

The anaphoric (demonstrative) pronoun
In almost all cases the capping formula contains ὥς ('thus'). Once a speech is referred back to (also) with ταῦτα:

(24) M 173:
"Ὣς ἔφατ', οὐδὲ Διὸς πεῖθε φρένα ταῦτ' ἀγορεύων
Thus he spoke, but he did not persuade Zeus' mind by saying those things.[25]

Finally, there is the following capping formula, containing as anaphoric pronoun τοιαῦτα:

(25) Ὣς οἱ μὲν <u>τοιαῦτα</u> πρὸς ἀλλήλους ἀγόρευον
Thus they were saying <u>such things</u> to each other[26]

The use of the somewhat unspecific τοιαῦτα ('such things') does not - as in Thucydides' *Histories*[27]- signal that the NF₁ has not quoted the *ipsissima verba*. This capping formula always follows after a cluster of speeches and τοιαῦτα indicates that the content of more than one speech is referred to. Taking the form of a μέν-clause it signals a change of scene. In the ensuing δέ- (once αὐτάρ-: Φ 514) clause, characters other than the speaker, often in another place, ask for our attention. The formula often marks a return from the divine entourage to the world of the heroes: E 431, H 464, Θ 212, Σ 368, Φ 514. The imperfect (ἀγόρευον) of the μέν-clause suggests that the action of the δέ clause takes place during this conversation. Thus, the δέ-clause reports simultaneous action (cp. Combellack 1939: 46), new stages in or even the completion of action which had begun already before the conversation. I discuss two examples. Poseidon/ 'Calchas' has given the Ajaxes new energy and they describe to each other this miraculous experience (N 68-75 and 77-80). Their conversation is concluded with

(26) N 81-3:
Ὣς οἱ μὲν τοιαῦτα πρὸς ἀλλήλους ἀγόρευον, ...
τόφρα δὲ τοὺς ὄπιθεν γαιήοχος ὦρσεν Ἀχαιούς
Thus they were saying things like that to each other, ..., but in the meantime the earth-mover (Poseidon) adhorted the (other) Achaeans behind them

Here the simultaneity of μέν- and δέ-clause is made explicit through τόφρα. My second example occurs in book Π. Patroclus has reported to Achilles the desperate situation of the Greeks and asked permission to enter the battle. With

(27) Π 101-2:
Ὣς οἱ μὲν τοιαῦτα πρὸς ἀλλήλους ἀγόρευον,
Αἴας δ' οὐκέτ' ἔμιμνε
Thus they were saying things like that to each other, but Ajax did not hold his stand any longer

the scene changes from Achilles' tent to the battlefield. The last thing we had heard about Ajax had been that he was defending the Greek ships with utmost vigour (O 745-6) and it is to be understood that during the very conversation between Achilles and Patroclus the situation has deteriorated further and that Patroclus' intervention has become all the more urgent.[28]

There is one capping formula without an anaphoric pronoun: Ἦ (ῥα) καὶ ... ('he or she spoke and ...'). The briefness of this formula corresponds to the situation in the story: the action co-ordinated by καί follows immediately upon the speech and except for Φ 233 the subject of this action is identical with the speaker.

Conclusion

In comparison to the transition from simple narrator-text to complex narrator-text the change from simple narrator-text to character-text and vice versa is marked in the *Iliad* systematically and extensively in the form of speech-formulas. Genetical factors (the oral background of the *Iliad*), but certainly also narratological ones account for this emphatic marking. In narratology the introduction and capping of direct speech is called attributive discourse. Attributive discourse signals a change not only in level of focalization, but also of narration. In the case of the *Iliad*, the NF_1, before temporarily handing over his prerogative of the verbal presentation of the story to one of his characters, acquits himself of his task as presentator with double vigour. In the introductory formula he indicates

- the speaker, mostly by his/her proper name + epithet, sometimes by an indirect reference, which then calls attention to the quality in which a speaker will speak;
- the addressee, mostly by a form of the anaphoric demonstrative pronoun ὁ, the proper name cropping up in the speech itself in the form of a vocative;
- the speech act (always the locutionary, often the illocutionary act);
- additional information, which either is also visible to the character, who functions as recipient of the speaker ($NeFe_2$): position, tone, emotions; or reaches the $NeFe_1$ only: truth-indications, summary of content.

The capping formulas are much shorter, containing

- most of the time an anaphoric (demonstrative) pronoun: ὥς, or (after clusters) τοιαῦτα;
- an indication of the speech act (always the locutionary, sometimes the illocutionary or perlocutionary act).

The NF_1 sometimes evaluates a speech or speaker either beforehand or afterwards. Through the attributive discourse (the combination of introductory and capping formula) the $NeFe_1$ is fully equipped to understand and interpret a speech properly.

The Iliadic speech-formulas, far from being produced automatically with a thoughtless formularity, bear witness once again to the importance of the NF_1's role as focalizer: he makes clear how he interprets the words spoken by the heroes and how he wishes the $NeFe_1$ to interpret them. This heightened activity of the NF_1 at the threshold of character-text is also indicative of the importance of the spoken word in the Homeric epics.

6.2. Narrator-text and character-text confronted

In previous chapters we have already come across several examples where the NF_1 and characters present the same event, or refer to the same person or draw on the same information:

- in section 3.3.3 I discussed the external analepses Λ 122-5 and Φ 34-46, inserted by the NF_1 to provide the $NeFe_1$ with background information necessary to understand following speeches.

- in section 4.2 I compared Π 3-4 and 7-10, where first the NF_1 and then Achilles illustrate the weeping of Patroclus by means of a simile.

- in section 5.1 an analysis was made of O 458-493, where one event, the breaking of Teucer's bowstring, is presented first by the NF_1 and then by three different characters.

Such cases of double presentation of the same event offer an excellent opportunity to confront the NF_1 and characters as presentators, to detect differences in their focalization and narration.[29] In this section I will discuss three more groups of passages which allow such a confrontation:

1. Orders and suggestions for action. These can be considered internal prolepses by characters of what later will be presented by the NF_1 as events.

2. Reports. These can be considered internal analepses by characters of events already presented by the NF_1.

3. Repeated motivation and information. These are passages where characters give a motivation or information which had already been given by the NF_1.

Central questions in the analyses carried out in this section will be 1) why is an event or information presented doubly and 2) what is the relation between the versions of NF_1 and characters: what are the differences and, conversely, what is the significance when NF_1 and characters use exactly the same words (category c of repeated verse-clusters, above section 5.4, p. 180)?

Orders and suggestions for action

When a character gives an order or makes a suggestion for action, these orders or suggestions often return in the narrator-text as events, when the NF$_1$ describes their execution, e.g.

(28) Θ 505-7 (Hector: Trojans):
ἐκ πόλιος δ' ἄξεσθε βόας καὶ ἴφια μῆλα
καρπαλίμως, οἶνον δὲ μελίφρονα οἰνίζεσθε
σῖτόν τ' ἐκ μεγάρων, ἐπὶ δὲ ξύλα πολλὰ λέγεσθε
bring from the city oxen and fat sheep, quickly, and get sweet wine and bread from the palace and collect much firewood besides

vs.

(29) Θ 545-7 (NF$_1$: NeFe$_1$):
ἐκ πόλιος δ' ἄξοντο βόας καὶ ἴφια μῆλα
καρπαλίμως, οἶνον δὲ μελίφρονα οἰνίζοντο
σῖτόν τ' ἐκ μεγάρων, ἐπὶ δὲ ξύλα πολλὰ λέγοντο
and they brought from the city oxen and fat sheep, quickly, and they got sweet wine and bread from the palace, and they collected much firewood besides[30]

The function of the repetition - here, as often, verbatim - in the narrator-text is clear: in this way the NF$_1$ signals that the order or suggestion is carried out exactly as the speaker had told.[31] From Bowra (1964: 256-8) it appears that this type of repetition, involving orders, is a general feature of all heroic poetry. Observe in this connection that the NF$_1$ often does not repeat in the narrator-text the intentions or fears which the speaking character expresses together with his/her order or suggestion. Thus, of the long chain of ὡς ... μή ... μή ... ὡς ... ἵνα-clauses following (Θ 508-16) after Hector's orders quoted in example (28), the NF$_1$ describes only the execution of the first final clause: ὡς κεν ... καίωμεν πυρὰ πολλά (508-9), becoming πυρὰ δέ σφισι καίετο πολλά (554). It is not without reason or narrative subtlety that Hector's other four projections (that the Greeks will not be able to escape in the dark of the night) are not repeated by the NF$_1$: the whole of book I will centre around this issue of the fate of the Greeks.[32]

However, the correspondence between character-text and narrator-text is not always as close as in example (28-29) and the other passages mentioned in n. 30. Thus, the NF$_1$'s description of the execution of an order or suggestion for action can be shorter than the character's utterance. An example is Σ 314,[33] where only one (δόρπον εἵλοντο) of Hector's four orders given in Σ 298-302

(δόρπον ἕλεσθε, φυλακῆς μνήσασθε, ἐγρήγορθε, δότω) is described as executed.
The non-repetition of Σ 299 might be ascribed to a certain eagerness of the
NF$_1$ to skip irrelevant details and turn (314: αὐτάρ) to the Greek camp. The
omission of 300-2 is, I think, significant. It confirms that the suggestion Hector
made there ('let those who are overanxious for their possessions distribute them
among the Trojans rather than lose them to the enemy') was not meant by him
to be taken seriously and executed. It served a purely rhetorical purpose, viz.
to discredit Polydamas (and his proposal) with the Trojans.[34]

More frequently, the version of the NF$_1$ is longer than that of the speaking
character, with new events, even new speeches cropping up. Thus, Menelaus'
order to the Trojans in Γ 103-7 to fetch two lambs and summon Priam to the
battlefield is first repeated by Hector to two heralds (indirect speech: Γ 116-7)
and is then described as executed in 245-58: not only do the heralds fetch two
lambs, but also wine and festive (φαεινόν: 247, χρύσεια: 248) utensils for the
libation. The NF$_1$ also specifies the name of one of the heralds, Idaeus, and
presents his summons of Priam in direct speech (250-8).[35]

In the third place, the versions of NF$_1$ and characters can differ not so
much in length as in tone and in choice of details. An example is Λ 828-32
(Eurypylus asks Patroclus to nurse his wound) vs. Λ 842-8 (the NF$_1$ tells the
NeFe$_1$ how Eurypylus nursed Patroclus' wound).[36] The central part of the two
passages, describing the removal of the arrow and washing out of the wound, is
more or less the same, the NF$_1$ being somewhat more detailed (829-30a = 844-46a).
Variations occur at the beginning and end: Eurypylus, who has to persuade
Patroclus to help him, uses the imperative σάωσον ἄγων (828) and stresses
Patroclus' ability to help him (831-2). In the corresponding lines, the NF$_1$ uses
an indicative ἄγε (842) and in detail describes the positive effects of Patroclus'
treatment (847-8). Where Eurypylus, suffering pain, had asked for 'soothing' and
'good' herbs (830-1: ἤπια φάρμακα ... ἐσθλά), the NF$_1$ tells that Patroclus applied
a 'bitter root, staying pain' (846-7: ῥίζαν ... πικρήν ... ὀδυνήφατον). Through
the specification of φάρμακα as ῥίζαν, the qualifications πικρήν, ὀδυνήφατον,
which suggest experience with that root,[37] and the stress put upon the effective-
ness of the treatment, the NF$_1$ in an implicit and subtle way confirms Eurypylus'
estimation of Patroclus' 'pharmacological' knowledge.

Reports

I consider as reports all those passages where one character tells to another what he/she (or they) has (have) just seen or experienced or where he/she recapitulates a series of events. Narrating implies focalizing and it will be seen how the reporting characters select, interpret and evaluate the events presented earlier by the NF$_1$. Although I take the NF$_1$-version as the standard to which the character-version is compared, it should not be forgotten that the NF$_1$-version is itself also a selection, interpretation and evaluation of the events of the (primary) fabula.

I start with a simple example:

(30) P 128-30 (NF$_1$: NeFe$_1$):
Αἴας δ' ἐγγύθεν ἦλθε φέρων σάκος ἠΰτε πύργον·
Ἕκτωρ δ' ἂψ ἐς ὅμιλον ἰὼν ἀνεχάζεθ' ἑταίρων,
ἐς δίφρον δ' ἀνόρουσε
Ajax came near bearing his shield like a tower: and Hector went and retreated into the throng of his companions again, and jumped on his chariot.

vs.

(31) P 166-8 (Glaucus: Hector):
ἀλλὰ σύ γ' Αἴαντος μεγαλήτορος οὐκ ἐτάλασσας
στήμεναι ἄντα, κατ' ὄσσε ἰδὼν δηΐων ἐν αὐτῇ,
οὐδ' ἰθὺς μαχέσασθαι
But you did not dare stand against great-hearted Ajax, having spotted his eyes in the battle of the enemies, nor fight with him directly.

The NF$_1$ in (30) leaves implicit that it was the sight of Ajax which made Hector retreat and also does not comment on this retreat. Glaucus in (31) interprets Hector's retreat as an act of cowardice, prompted by the sight of Ajax and heavily rebukes him (cp. the speech-introduction P 141: χαλεπῷ ἠνίπαπε μύθῳ).

A more complex case is B 56-71: Agamemnon reports to the councillors his visitation by 'Nestor'/the Dream sent by Zeus. What is remarkable about Agamemnon's report is that he immediately makes clear that he has seen through the human disguise of the Dream (56-8). How and when did he find out? The NF$_1$ tells that the Dream had assumed the appearance of Nestor, 'whom Agamemnon honoured most of his councillors' (20-1). The function of the relative clause is to explain to the NeFe$_1$ why the Dream chose this particular mask.[38] In the speech introduction of 22, however, the NF$_1$ refers to the speaker not as 'Nestor' but as θεῖος Ὄνειρος. This is a general rule to be observed in the Homeric epics, viz. that gods addressing humans in disguise are referred to in the speech-formulas by their *own* names.[39] The explanation is simple and related to the oral background of the epics: lacking visual helps like inverted comma's (cp. my own use of 'Nestor') the poet had to make his NF₁ use the real name in order to avoid misunderstanding. In his speech, 'Nestor'/the Dream itself provides Agamemnon with a clue as to his real identity, by saying (26): Διὸς δέ τοι ἄγγελός εἰμι: 'I am a messenger of Zeus to you'.[40] Then, when Agamemnon awakes, the NF₁ states that θείη δέ μιν ἀμφέχυτ' ὀμφή (41: 'the divine voice was poured around him'). Who is focalizing here? Is it the NF₁, who through θείη and ὀμφή (always of the voice of gods) wants to remind the NeFe₁ of the divine status of the Dream? Or is the choice of vocabulary due to Agamemnon's embedded focalization and does it signal that he realizes at this moment that it was not 'Nestor', but a *divine* Dream which has just appeared to him?[41] I prefer the second option, since 41 would then form a stepping-stone toward 56-8, which otherwise comes somewhat as a surprise. Another argument for taking 41 as focalized by Agamemnon is his description of the Dream's appearance in 58: the Dream resembled Nestor εἶδός τε μέγεθός τε φυήν τ' ('in appearance, stature and shape'). We know from other divine epiphanies that gods could also imitate a human voice (e.g. N 45: εἰσάμενος Κάλχαντι δέμας καὶ ἀτειρέα φωνήν).[42] The fact that Agamemnon does not mention resemblance of voice suggests that it was the Dream's divine voice which, together with his reference to himself as messenger of Zeus, revealed his true identity to Agamemnon. At the end of his report - the middle part is taken up by a repetition of Zeus' message, see above section 5.4, p. 181 - Agamemnon describes the Dream's departure as ᾤχετ' ἀποπτάμενος (71: 'he disappeared, flying away').[43] The NF₁ at that point had said ἀπεβήσετο (35: 'he went away'). The verb ἀποβαίνω is regularly used to describe a departure after a speech (cp. *LfgrE* II, s.v. βαίνω BII3b). Agamemnon's ἀποπτάμενος is more specific and suggests that the Dream left in a special dreamlike way.[44] Or was Agamemnon 'dreaming' that he saw the Dream fly away? After all, he woke up only *after* the Dream's departure (41, 71).

B 56-71 is only one of many places in the *Iliad* where a character reports or reflects upon a contact with a god. Such contacts between the divine and human worlds either take the form of a face-to-face meeting, with the god addressing the human person, or of an intervention, viz. when a god does not address a person, inciting him/her to do so and so, but intervenes directly in the course of events. In the latter case, characters reporting such an intervention have to base themselves on inference rather than direct perception. Hence, they usually express themselves in unspecified terms like δαίμων or τις θεῶν. But sometimes they do mention a specific name. Three examples:

INTERPRETATION OF THE NF₁	OF SPEAKING CHARACTER
Γ 380-2: <u>Aphrodite</u> transports Paris from the battlefield to his bedroom	Γ 439: (Paris: Helen) <u>Athena</u> has given victory to Menelaus
Λ 353: Hector is saved by the helmet which <u>Apollo</u> gave him	Λ 363: (Diomedes: Hector) you have escaped death, because <u>Apollo</u> saved you
Ψ 772: <u>Athena</u> makes Odysseus' limbs light; 774: <u>Athena</u> makes Ajax slip	Ψ 782-3: (Ajax: Greeks) the goddess who always helps Odysseus (= <u>Athena</u>) has tripped up my feet

In Γ the interpretations of NF₁ and Paris are in a way complementary to each other: addressing a critical and sarcastic Helen, Paris chooses to pass over in silence his own rescue by Aphrodite, and instead argues that Menelaus has been helped by Athena, i.e. has been lucky.[45] In archaic religious thinking it was customary to ascribe success to a god and here, where a Greek is involved, what was more natural than to think of Athena, constant supporter of the Greeks. Now the NF₁ had not mentioned any assistance of Athena and her non-intervention is referred to by Zeus in Δ 7-10. This confirms that Γ 439 is merely an inference or rhetorical argument of Paris.

In Λ both NF₁ and Diomedes connect Apollo with the event of Diomedes' spear ricocheting off Hector's helmet. However, the way by which both presentators reach that interpretation is not the same: the NF₁ speaks in terms of a divine gift; Diomedes is not, as the relative clause 364 makes clear (Apollo has saved you, 'to whom you surely pray before going into the din of spears'), referring to a special connection between Hector's helmet and Apollo (how should he know?), but speaks in general terms about Apollo protecting Hector.[46]

The situation in Ψ is complex (see also Köhnken 1981, Snell 1984). It should be realized that Athena's intervention is triggered by a prayer from Odysseus (770). Athena grants his prayer and not only makes his feet swift (as he had asked), but also (somewhat unexpectedly) makes Ajax slip. In his comment after the race, Ajax ascribes his own fall to Athena, not because he saw her act, nor because he could expect any action from her side (from 769: εὔχετ' ... ὃν κατὰ θυμόν it appears that Odysseus prayed in silence), but simply because Odysseus has won the race and Athena is known always to help Odysseus.[47] Much more could be said about these three passages from the point of view of Homeric religion or "Weltbild", but I do not intend to do so.[48] What I wanted to show is that when analyzing divine interventions in the *Iliad* one should distinguish systematically between the presentation and interpretation of the NF_1 and of the speaking characters. Differences between the two versions should not be ascribed, I think, to differences in religious beliefs or concepts between NF_1 and characters, but to a difference in narrative competence (the NF_1 is omniscient and knows more than the characters) or rhetorical situation (Paris wishing to excuse his own defeat vis-à-vis Helen).

My next example of a confrontation between narrator-text and character-text concerns the bird-omen of book M. The Trojans, led by Hector and Polydamas, are hesitating to cross the ditch around the Greek camp. They hesitate because of an eagle passing them 'along the left side' (i.e. the inauspicious side) holding in his claws a snake which he is forced to drop and which then falls amidst the Trojans (M 200-9). The Trojan soldiers intuitively interpret what they have seen as a negative omen, which is confirmed by Polydamas who sets himself up as seer and interprets the omen as a warning not to cross the ditch (211-29). His presentation of the omen (218-27) can be divided in three parts. He starts with a faithful report of its first phase: M 218-21 (ζωόν) ≅ 200-3 (ζωόν). Through the use of the deictic pronoun ὅδε (218) Polydamas indicates that he is here drawing on his (and the Trojans') own perception. From 221 onwards Polydamas' version starts diverging from that of the NF_1 or, as Bushnell (1982: 4) puts it, Polydamas starts "rewriting" the story. The NF_1 had described how the snake did not give up resistance, but, hitting the eagle with all his might, made him drop him. The eagle, with a cry, continues his flight (203-7). In his description of the struggle between snake and eagle the NF_1 betrays a certain admiration for the snake, who despite a seemingly lost position does not give up and, in the end, wins. The corresponding part of Polydamas' interpretation (221-2) strikes a different tone. Not a single word is said about the heroic fight of the snake, but instead Polydamas sides with the eagle: through ἄφαρ (221) he stresses the unexpected and sudden nature of the eagle having to let go his prey.[49] This, Polydamas imagines, means that the eagle loses his prey before reaching 'home' and thus fails to provide food to his 'children'. Commentators have been troubled by Polydamas' use of οἰκί' and τεκέεσσιν in connection with an eagle.[50] The introduction of these human terms is, I think, an indication that Polydamas is now making the transition to his exegesis proper: the application of the omen to the actual situation of the Trojans. This is the third part of his presentation: just as the eagle has failed to complete his mission with success, in like way the Trojans will not return safely 'home', once they have entered the Greek camp (223-5). With this exegesis Polydamas has provided the argument for his proposal of 216, viz. not to engage into a fight with the Greeks inside their camp. We see how Polydamas in his report gradually moves away from the presentation as given by the NF$_1$, starting with an eyewitness account, then supplementing projections of his own and, finally, reading a very specific meaning into the whole event. There is in the narrator-text no passage corresponding to the third, exegetic part of Polydamas' presentation and one could ask whether he is right in interpreting the whole scene as he does. For Hector the answer is clear: he severely rebukes Polydamas and proclaims to attach more importance to Zeus' promise (of victory) to him than to any bird-sign (231-50). The Trojans react with enthusiasm to Hector's words and follow his lead. The further course of events in the *Iliad* will show that Polydamas' warning was justified. This induces most commentators to find fault with Hector's words in 231-50.[51] Is their judgement appropriate? Only Erbse (1978: 6-7) defends Hector: "Aber was sollte Hektor tun? Den bisherigen Erfolg preisgeben? Das hieße auf dem Plan verzichten, in dem er eine (vielleicht die einzige) Rettungsmöglichkeit für Troia sieht. Hektors Größe besteht doch wohl gerade darin, dass er keine Zweifel an Erfolg aufkommen läßt und den Bedenken des Sehers seine begründete Zuversicht entgegensetzt." I would go one step further and ask whether the bird-scene as described by the NF$_1$ in M 200-9 really is an omen or whether it is only Polydamas' interpretation which makes us believe it is one.[52] The only concrete indication that M 200-9 is an omen is Διὸς τέρας αἰγιόχοιο (209: 'a sign from aegis-bearing Zeus'), which is an apposition to ὄφιν or maybe rather to αἰόλον ... μέσσοισι.[53] Is this the NF$_1$'s interpretation or is it part of the Trojans' embedded focalization (208: ἴδον)? In the latter case it would be *characters only* who interpret the bird-scene as an omen. I prefer this second option: it is nowhere stated that the eagle was sent by Zeus[54] nor does the NF$_1$ make clear *expressis verbis* (as in Σ 311-3) that Polydamas is right and Hector wrong. It is even illogical to assume that Zeus here sends a negative omen, since in 252-5 he openly supports the Trojans.[55] The NF$_1$'s presentation of the bird-scene in M 200-9 is, I think, deliberately ambiguous, making an interpretation as given by Polydamas possible, but not imperative.

My last example of a report is Thetis' recapitulation in Σ 444-456(+460-1) of the major events of the *Iliad* so far.[56] Aristarchus considered Σ 444-456 superfluous (οὐδὲν ἀναγκαῖον), against which verdict the bT-scholia (ad 444-56a) protest: when Thetis is allowed to speak about her marriage (432-5) why should she not talk about that 'for which she has come'? I think the passage allows a stronger defense. Let us take a closer look at the recapitulation, its content and relation to the NF₁'s version. Thetis mentions the following events:

> 1. 444-6 (ἔφθιεν): Agamemnon took away Achilles' girl, and grieving over her he (Achilles) ate his heart out;
> 2. 446 (αὐτάρ)-8 (ἐξιέναι): the Greeks were hemmed in their own camp by the Trojans;
> 3. 448 (τόν)-9: elders of the Greeks entreated Achilles, offering a rich compensation;
> 4. 450-2: Achilles refused to ward off disaster himself, but sent Patroclus (clad in his armour) and many troops;
> 5. 453-6: Patroclus almost captured Troy, but was killed by Apollo, who gave Hector the glory of victory;
> 6. 460 (ὃ γάρ)-1 (δαμείς): Patroclus, killed by the Trojans, lost Achilles' armour.

Ad 1. Starting her recapitulation at this point, Thetis leaves out the events leading up to Agamemnon's act. I shall argue below why Thetis starts at this point. Lines 444-5 are virtually identical with Π 56+58 (Achilles: Patroclus). The repetition (not intended by Thetis) signals to the NeFe₁ that Thetis here follows closely Achilles' interpretation of the origins of his wrath. Through ἄψ Thetis and Achilles underline the arrogance of Agamemnon's behaviour, who annulled a decision of all the Greeks.[57] Note also the contrast between active ἔξελον (the Greeks picked out for Achilles) vs. middle ἕλετο (Agamemnon took for himself). ὃ τῆς ἀχέων φρένας ἔφθιεν is Thetis' somewhat compressed description of what is in fact a complex emotion: Achilles is grieving over Briseis and angry at Agamemnon. As a result he abstains from the battle, but this inactivity also consumes his heart. Cp. A 491-2 (NF₁: φθινύθεσκε φίλον κῆρ αὖθι μένων, ποθέεσκε δ' ἀϋτήν τε πτόλεμόν τε), B 694 (NF₁: τῆς ὅ γε κεῖτ' ἀχέων) and Δ 513 (Apollo: Ἀχιλεύς ... ἐπὶ νηυσὶ χόλον θυμαλγέα πέσσει).

Ad 2. These verses, coming before the mention of the Embassy of I, must, strictly speaking, refer to Θ, the second fighting day. However, the combination ἐπὶ πρύμνῃσιν ἐείλεον recalls in general Zeus' Will, cp. A 409 (κατὰ πρύμνας ... ἐλσαι) and Σ 76 (ἐπὶ πρύμνῃσιν ἀλήμεναι). Thus, whereas Thetis nowhere mentions Zeus, the NeFe₁ is, all the same, reminded of Zeus' Will.

<u>Ad 3</u>. Thetis here, of course, refers to the Embassy of book I. She does not specify the names of the elders, just as in 440 she had not mentioned Briseis' name. Details like these do not serve the purpose of her story and she only gives the names of the main actors involved. Note that the name of Achilles does not occur anywhere in the entire speech. He is constantly referred to as 'he', which is suggestive for the way in which Achilles is uppermost in Thetis' mind. There simply is no other referent 'he' for her but Achilles.

<u>Ad 4</u>. Here Thetis establishes a connection[58] between two events (Embassy of I and Patroclus' performance as Achilles' 'stand-in' in Π), which in fact are not related. Thetis' presentation suggests that Achilles, as it were, compensated his own (αὐτὸς μέν: 450) refusal to re-enter the battle by sending Patroclus. She also pictures Achilles as the main instigator of the plan to send Patroclus into battle with his armour. In reality this was Nestor's idea (Λ 794-803), taken over by Patroclus (Π 36-45). Thetis, at this point, seems to be influenced by Achilles' own words, spoken to her in Σ 82, where he claims full and active responsibility for Patroclus' death: τὸν ἀπώλεσα.

<u>Ad 5</u>. Commentators have noted that περὶ Σκαιῇσι πύλῃσι (453) is not correct: "But this is not the place where we need expect the accuracy of a chronicler" (Leaf). Perhaps it is not simply a slip on Thetis' part. The Scaean gates form the main entrance to Troy and by situating Patroclus' fighting there, Thetis heightens the glory of the hero. In the same way, the *if not*-situation of 454-6- 454 mirrors Π 698-701+780, the εἰ μή-clause Π 786-867 - seems to exculpate Patroclus: in the end he loses Achilles' armour, but before that he fights very bravely (note also πολλὰ κακὰ ῥέξαντα) and almost captures Troy.

<u>Ad 6</u>. In 457-60 Thetis seemed to have come to the end of her recapitulation, making her request to Hephaestus. Yet, in 460-1 she once more turns to the past and adds the crucial point that Patroclus' death (the last event mentioned in her recapitulation (5)) had entailed the loss of Achilles' armour.

With the present tense verb form κεῖται (461) Thetis returns to the present once again and now for good, θυμὸν ἀχεύων recalling 443 ἄχνυται. This ring-composition enclosing the recapitulation gives a first indication that Σ 444-56+460-1 is firmly anchored in Thetis' whole speech. This brings me back to the question of the status of this passage. The main point of Thetis' speech is her request to Hephaestus to make new armour for Achilles (457-60). Everything else in her speech serves to lead up to this point and to persuade Hephaestus to comply with her request. What is Thetis' strategy? She does not, as might have been expected on account of Σ 395-405, fall back on the *do ut des*-principle, but instead appeals to Hephaestus' compassion for herself (endowed with a mortal man and a mortal son) and for her son, who during the short span of his life is miserable. The recapitulation starts as an explanation of ἄχνυται. Why is Achilles grieving? Because (asyndeton explicativum) Agamemnon took away his girl (Σ 443-5). We now understand why Thetis starts at this point, leaving out the Chryseis-episode. From this point onwards an inevitable chain of events leads up to Patroclus' entering the battle with Achilles' armour, losing it and causing by his death new grief to Achilles. The function of the recapitulation is, therefore, both to motivate Thetis' request (Achilles' armour is lost and must be replaced so that he can avenge his 'faithful companion') and to argue why Hephaestus should make it (to alleviate Achilles' unhappiness during his short life). From Hephaestus' answer (463-7) it appears that Thetis' words have struck home: he regrets not being able to change Achilles' mortality and brevity of life, but promises to make splendid new armour.

Repeated motivation and information

In examples (32-3) we see how a motivation given by the NF_1 is 'repeated' on the level of the character-text:

(32) A 195-6 (NF_1: $NeFe_1$: Athena came down):
προ γὰρ ἧκε θεὰ λευκώλενος Ἥρη,
ἄμφω ὁμῶς θυμῷ φιλέουσά τε κηδομένη τε.
for white-armed Hera sent her forward, loving and caring for both (Achilles and Agamemnon) equally in her heart.

vs.

(33) A 208-9 (Athena: Achilles: I have come to stop your anger):
προ δέ μ' ἧκε θεὰ λευκώλενος Ἥρη,
ἄμφω ὁμῶς θυμῷ φιλέουσά τε κηδομένη τε.
and white-armed Hera sent me forward, loving and caring for both of you equally in her heart.

Why this double presentation? The answer is simple when we realize that Athena in (33) is answering a question of Achilles (A 202: τίπτ' αὖτ', αἰγιόχοιο Διὸς τέκος, εἰλήλουθας; 'why have you come, child of aegis-bearing Zeus?'). In other words, the information provided earlier by the NF_1 to the $NeFe_1$ is relevant also on the level of the communication between characters and therefore repeated, here even verbatim. In the same way Z 386-9, which repeats the information of Z 372-3, is triggered by a question from Hector (Z 377); N 256-8, which repeats

247-8, which in its turn repeats N 156-68, is triggered by Idomeneus' question in 250; N 780-3, which repeats N 761-4, is triggered by Hector's question 770-2; Σ 184, which repeats Σ 168, is triggered by Achilles' question 182.[59] Once again (cp. above section 5.4.1, p. 181) we see that in the *Iliad* the fact that certain information or a motivation has already reached the $NeFe_1$ does not prevent it from being repeated on the level of communication between characters, if these characters need (or, as is the case here, ask for) this information. Conversely, the fact that a motivation or information will be given in character-text does not lead to the suppression of that information in the narrator-text. Only seldom does a speech surprise the $NeFe_1$ with new information (at least with regard to the primary fabula).

6.3. Summary

I sum up the main results of this section according to the two central questions posed at its beginning. The double presentation of an event or information, i.e. once in narrator-text and once in character-text, is functional, in the case of
- orders or suggestions, because the NF_1, who repeats character-text, in this way confirms (to the $NeFe_1$) that the order or suggestion is executed exactly as it had been formulated;
- reports, because the speaking character, who 'repeats' narrator-text, informs another character (Agamemnon in B, Thetis in Σ) or brings forward his specific interpretation (Polydamas in M). Certain reports (Paris in Δ, Diomedes in Λ, Glaucus in P, Ajax in Ψ) are not so much informative, but rather give expression to the emotions of the speaking character. Paris tries to defend himself, Diomedes is disappointed because he did not kill Hector and also wants to insult his opponent, Glaucus is angry with Hector, Ajax is stunned, but also disappointed about his own bad luck.
- repeated motivation or information, because the NF_1 never leaves his $NeFe_1$ groping in the dark, yet also allows characters to give this information to other characters, if they ask for it.

Confrontation of narrator-text and character-text in these cases of double presentation brings to light verbatim repetitions, quantitative and qualitative differences and even downright discrepancies. Verbatim repetition signals (to the $NeFe_1$) that an order or suggestion is carried out exactly as prescibed or that a reporting character is giving a faithful eyewitness report (Polydamas in M 218-21 ζωόν).

Quantitative differences are either the result of the NF_1 describing the execution of an order or suggestion with more detail (e.g. in Γ 245-59) or conversely in abridged form, which then, e.g. in Σ 314, provides a valuable clue as to how seriously we are to take a character's words (here Hector's suggestion to divide up Troy's riches). In her recapitulation, Thetis of course confines herself to the main events in so far as they are relevant for her rhetorical aim, which is to stress Achilles' grief (over Briseis and Patroclus) and to describe how his armour was lost by Patroclus.

Qualitative differences are often due to the difference in engagement or rhetorical situation between the NF_1, who recounts events of the past, and characters, who are immediately involved in those events and react emotionally to them (Glaucus in P) or try to influence their course (Eurypylus in Λ).

Discrepancies are mainly found in reports and are due to the fact that these reports serve a rhetorical purpose: advocating a less risky strategy than Hector, Polydamas in M invents the detail of the eagle being unable to feed his young at home and interprets the whole bird-scene as a negative omen; wishing to bring home to Hephaestus the sorrows of Achilles' brief heroic life, Thetis in Σ depicts her son as the inventor of the armour-exchange plan and in this way emphasizes his share in the death of his friend.

With this direct confrontation of the NF_1 and characters I have come to the end of my analysis of the presentation of the story in the *Iliad* and it is time to strike a balance. This will be the object of the next and final chapter.

7. CONCLUSION. NARRATORS AND FOCALIZERS

> A mon avis, l'importance de la contri-
> bution de la narratologie à l'étude de
> la littérature se situe dans l'usage
> heuristique. (M. Bal, *Femmes Imaginaires*)

As Aristotle said (*Poetics* 7), well-constructed plots must have a beginning, a middle, and an end. If one regards the Introduction and chapters 1-2 as the beginning, the analyses carried out in chapters 3-6 as the middle, it is now time to tell the end of my story, 'that which is inevitable, or as a rule, the natural result of something else', although I certainly do not hope that after this end 'nothing else follows'.

In the following I will make concluding remarks about the model used, the narratological approach, the presentation of the story, and narrators and focalizers.

The model

If the results in the field of Homeric scholarship laid down in the preceding chapters are accepted, Bal's narratological model has proved in practice to be a powerful means of interpretation. Although it was originally developed in connection with modern written novels, it could be shown to be fully applicable also to an epic text with an oral background dating from the beginnings of Western civilization.

Specifically, Bal's model enables us to see in a very clear way the serious shortcomings of the time-honoured dogma of Homeric objectivity. As a matter of fact, it is precisely as an "instrument with which (readers) can describe narrative texts" that Bal introduces her model (1985: 3, 4, 6, 10). It also helps us to solve old problems of interpretation, while at the same time it raises interesting new ones. And fortunately so. A model that claimed to provide a panacea to all questions connected with a work of art of the complexity and depth of the *Iliad* would be pretentious and, what is worse, boring.

Since the questions of interpretation are all of 'local' interest and do not pertain to the interpretation of the *Iliad* as a whole, they are not easily summarized. Yet, since focalization is the most novel and most controversial part of Bal's narratological model, I wish to recall here some interpretations in which focalization plays a decisive role. If we analyze Γ 128 as (implicit) embedded focalization, we acquire another testimony for Helen's feelings of guilt about her role in the outbreak of the war; if we assume that the simile Δ 141-7 is directed not to the characters, but to the NeFe₁, there is no reason to call it the 'most curious simile of *Iliad* and *Odyssey*'; if we grant that νίκη in H 312 is focalized by Ajax, who rejoices about what he considers a victory, there is no contradiction with the fact that that duel had been stopped before a decision had been reached; if we realize that the only indication for M 200-9 to be 'an omen sent by aegis-bearing Zeus' (209) allows an analysis as embedded focalization, Polydamas' interpretation becomes less sacrosanct, Hector's confidence in Zeus less overbearing; if we accept the rule that secondary narration-focalization dominates tertiary narration-focalization, Hector's 'quotation' of Achilles' words to Patroclus in Π 837-42 need not be taken as a serious reconstruction, but can, rather, be seen as a self-invented construction meant to hurt Patroclus; if we consider the fact that the priamel X 158-61 is presented in primary focalization, and that the simile X 162-6 is assimilated to the (secondary) focalization of the gods, there is no "puzzling inconsistency" between the two passages; if we realize that Ω 583-6 is focalized by Achilles, it appears that Achilles is himself very much aware of his own irascible temper.

I conclude that Bal's narratological model has proved its worth and promises good results also when applied to other classical texts. There are two points on which I have thought it necessary to

    1. correct the model and

    2. improve on its application.

Ad 1. In section 4.1.1 I have argued that indirect speech should be analyzed under the heading of focalization, not of narration as is done by Bal (1985: 37-

42). Indirect speech is a form of embedded focalization: the NF_1 represents words of a character, while that character does not become NF_2.

<u>Ad 2.</u> I have paid more attention to the layer of the *text* than narratologists are wont to do. They analyze the text almost exclusively in connection with the question of "who speaks" and further seem to consider it the entrance, to be hurried through, in search for the more intriguing layers of *story* and *fabula*. The reason for this relative neglect of the text-layer by narratologists might be a historical one: text-interpretation has traditionally been the occupation of philologists and the new approach offered by narratology promised precisely to look at the *content* of those words, the story they tell. In my opinion, however, the text-layer deserves the close interest of narratologists too. As a general principle I would say that a narratological analysis should indicate as precisely as possible how aspects of the story manifest themselves in the text and, conversely, how textual phenomena lead one to trace aspects of the story. Thus, we have seen in the *Iliad* how certain particles, evaluative and emotional words/ expressions, the presence of a dative can signal/confirm that we are dealing with embedded focalization; how the demonstrative pronouns in the expressions ἤματι κείνῳ, ἤματι τῷδ' are indicative of the temporal relation between speaker and events, how in the narrator-text an iterative verb form indicates a summary, the pluperfect a pause or the situation found by a character upon arriving somewhere. In stressing this correlation between text and story - which has not been done sufficiently by Bal (1985) - I do not intend to blur or weaken the distinction narration : focalization, as some critics of Bal's model have proposed: Bronzwaer (1981), Genette (1983), and Briosi (1986). This distinction remains vital if only for the simple reason that one cannot narrate without focalizing, while one can focalize without narrating: in Γ 28 it is Menelaus (as F_2) who considers Paris a 'sinner' (ἀλείτην), yet it is the NF_1 who narrates this.

But the analyses carried out in this book have also in another way demonstrated the interest of the text-layer. This is best illustrated schematically. We have come across the following five situations:

224

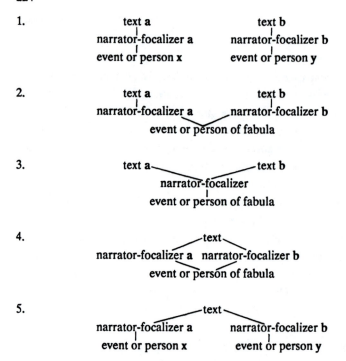

1.

text **a**   text **b**

narrator-focalizer **a**   narrator-focalizer **b**

event or person **x**   event or person **y**

2.

text **a**   text **b**

narrator-focalizer **a**   narrator-focalizer **b**

event or person of fabula

3.

text **a**   text **b**

narrator-focalizer

event or person of fabula

4.

text

narrator-focalizer **a**   narrator-focalizer **b**

event or person of fabula

5.

text

narrator-focalizer **a**   narrator-focalizer **b**

event or person **x**   event or person **y**

<u>Ad 1.</u> This is what is found most often, viz. two different narrator-focalizers focalizing different events or persons and talking about them in different words.

<u>Ad 2.</u> Two different narrator-focalizers can also talk about the same event or person in different words. I recall here one example, O 458-93, where the four focalizers, NF_1, Teucer, Ajax and Hector, refer to the intervening god as Ζεύς, δαίμων, θεός and Ζεύς, respectively.

<u>Ad 3.</u> This situation is found less often, but we have seen how Glaucus in Π 521-2 and Π 541-2 chooses to bring forward different aspects of Sarpedon, in accordance with the person he is addressing.

<u>Ad 4 and 5.</u> These two situations are particular for a text with an oral background and formulaic composition like the *Iliad*: different narrator-focalizers can express their focalization of different (5) or of the same (4) events or persons in exactly the same words. In sections 5.4 and 6.2 I have demonstrated that such verbatim repetitions, by two characters or by the NF_1 and one or more characters, almost always turn out to be either functional on the level of the communication between characters or significant for the $NeFe_1$, recipient of all texts, or both.

We see how *identical* text-passages can derive from different narrator-focalizers and refer to the same or different events or persons of the fabula; how *different* text-passages can derive from the same or different narrator-focalizer(s) and refer to the same or different events or persons of the fabula. In short, the text-layer is not just a transparent, uncomplicated passage to the layers of story and fabula, but has its own complications and intriguing aspects.

The narratological approach

Speaking about verbatim repetition, I have, in fact, already touched upon one of the aims of this study, mentioned in the Introduction: to push interpretation further than genetical explanation only. Narratology is not interested in how a narrative text comes about, but, taking the finished product (whether recited or written) as its point of departure, it analyzes the way in which its words evoke a (fictional) world inhabited by (fictional) people and the way in which the hearer/reader forms an opinion of this world and its inhabitants. This narratological approach brings with it its own questions: not why did Homer leave out the horse Pegasus in Z 155-202, but what kind of picture does Glaucus present to Diomedes of his forefather Bellerophontes and, indirectly, of himself. Not how formulaic are the speech-formulas, but how does the NF_1 program through them the $NeFe_1$'s interpretation of and reponse to a character's speech? Not how could Homer make his task easy through the automatical repetition of messenger-speeches, but how and when do messengers succeed in making clear their own feelings through small changes in the messages they have to convey? Not why did Homer add the "unnecessary" recapitulation of Σ 444-56 (+460-1), but why does Thetis tell Hephaestus this particular combination of events?

I conclude that a narratological approach can indeed broaden the scope of Homeric scholarship, just as Latacz had prophesied (Introduction xii).

The presentation of the story

The primary aim of this study has been to analyze and describe systematically the presentation of the story in the *Iliad*. From chapter 1, where I gave a survey of ancient and modern opinions on this matter, it appeared that most scholars repeat each other in qualifying the Homeric narrative style as objective and impersonal. My first move to question this dogma has been to apply to the *Iliad* a basic narratological principle, viz. the distinction author : narrator. To speak of the poet vs. the characters, as most Homerists do, is to compare apples with pears: the poet does not stand on a par with the characters, does not form part of the poem like them, but stands above them, in fact has *created* them. Apart from the characters, the poet has also called to life a 'person', which I have throughout referred to by the *functions* he fulfils: the primary narrator-focalizer (NF$_1$). Together, NF$_1$ and characters are the presentators of the story in the *Iliad*.

This principle opened the way to pursue the question further: if one agrees that the poet does not intrude personally in his work, how about the NF$_1$ and the characters? Are they also objective, neutral and impersonal in their presentation? As for the characters, scholars have always affirmed that their speeches (character-text), which take up 45% of the whole text, are subjective. In chapter 5 I analyzed this subjectivity more precisely in terms of focalization: speaking characters function as NF$_2$, which means that they verbalize their views on and interpretation of events of the present, past and future. Their presentation is conditioned by their own identity, status, personality and emotions, by those of the characters they are addressing, by the situation in which they find themselves, and by the effect they wish their words to have. However, characters also take part in the presentation of the story *outside* their own speeches, viz. in the cases of embedded focalization, which make up about 5% of the whole text. Whenever the NF$_1$ describes in the narrator-text what a character sees, feels, strives for, fears or says (indirect speech), we again see events through characters' eyes. The presence in secondarily focalized passages of evaluative and affective words/expressions, which are elsewhere found only in character-text, confirmed this assumption concerning the characters' share in the presentation. In section 4.2 we have seen that the emotions of characters even permeate certain comparisons and similes in the narrator-text.

Thus, the presentation in about 50% of the *Iliad* is subjective, emotional and committed. But how about the other half, how about the presentation by the NF$_1$? Here I first had to track down the activity of the NF$_1$ as presentator, since, apart from the Muse-invocations, his presentation remains implicit. My point of departure was the theoretical premise that the NF$_1$ too, like the characters, addresses someone, tells his story to someone: the primary narratee-focalizee (NeFe$_1$). By analyzing passages where this NeFe$_1$ is appealed to in one way or another by the NF$_1$ (passages with a second person verb form, negated statements, *if not*-situations, analepses and prolepses, motivation and presupposition, attributive discourse) I could

1. demonstrate that there is indeed a deliberate presentation of events also in the narrator-text and, thus, that "the story does not tell itself" and

2. recover perhaps not what the NF_1 himself thinks about the events and persons he tells about, but at least how he seems to want his addressee, the $NeFe_1$ (and in the end us, the historical reader) to interpret and react to them.

It appeared that the rhetoric of the NF_1, which for the ancient scholiasts had been manifest everywhere, but which in modern times, except for Bassett, Booth and Griffin, had disappeared into the background, is aimed mainly at eliciting admiration and (sometimes) pity for the heroes, their deeds and words. There is one group of passages where the NF_1 in a very oblique way tells us something about himself: the Muse-invocations. Applying Lesky's principle of "doppelte Motivation" I have argued that through addressing the Muses the human NF_1 augments rather than diminishes his self-esteem as presentator: it is he who *de facto* presents the story, but the cooperation of the Muses authorizes his story and underscores his art and professionality as a (singing) storyteller.

The basis of my entire investigation of the presentation of the story was the distinction between the five narrative situations: simple narrator-text, complex narrator-text, character-text, tertiary focalization, and embedded speech. Thus, Plato's important couple *diegesis haple* and *mimesis* was firmly re-established (narrator-text vs. character-text) and at the same time refined (simple vs. complex narrator-text, tertiary focalization and embedded speech as subcategories of character-text). The introduction of the category of embedded focalization in particular has, by giving a more accurate account of the share the NF_1 and the characters have in the presentation, proved of great heuristic value.

Narrators and focalizers
My thesis that the presentation of the story in the *Iliad* is not objective, neutral, or impersonal does not mean that I suggest to describe it now simply by the opposites of these qualifications, viz. as subjective, engaged and emotional. In fact, I think that it is best characterized as *multiple*. Despite the uniformity bestowed upon the Iliadic text by the unity of metre (both narrator-text and character-text are composed in dactylic hexameters), the formulas and the typical scenes, this narrative has more variety of presentation than many a modern novel. There are the NF_1, the 'you' of second person verb-forms, the anonymous 'they' of φασί-utterances, anonymous secondary focalizers ('a man', or collective of female servants, soldiers), named secondary focalizers, anonymous speakers

(actual tis-speeches), some 80 named speaking characters, tertiary focalizers, hypothetical speakers (potential tis-speeches) and tertiary speakers (characters quoted by other characters).

All these narrator-focalizers and focalizers together, operating on different levels of narration and focalization, shape our interpretation of the *Iliad*, each adding his piece of (factual, coloured, contradictory, exaggerated, untrue) information. All this information is relevant to the hearer/reader, who receives it through $NeFe_1$, Fe_2, $NeFe_2$, Fe_3, $NeFe_3$, as long as he or she realizes who is speaking and who is focalizing. Even untrue information (e.g. Helen's statement that her brothers are ashamed to join the Greek enterprise) is relevant in that it tells us something about the character who brings forward that information. It might be regarded as typical for the "early Greek capacity for viewing things separately" (Perry 1937) that so many different characters or groups of characters have their share in the presentation of the story: Andromache as well as Hector, young Antilochus as well as old Nestor, soldiers as well as leaders, mortal heroes as well as immortal gods, Trojans as well as Greeks.

My conclusion that one of these presentators, the NF1, who alone is responsible for half of the total text, viz. the simple narrator-text, is *human*, i.e. is not the Muse(s), has wider implications. I submit that the *Iliad* mainly presents a human vision of the events around Troy: of course, there are the gods who almost continually watch the events on earth. Yet, I do not think that we, the historical reader, are in the end supposed ourselves to see the events from this divine perspective: only in about 12% of the total text are the gods focalizing- not counting secondary focalization, they speak only 166 of the 677 speeches -, the remaining 88% being focalized by the human NF_1 or human characters. The gods watch human affairs as a kind of match, each god supporting his favourite team (Greeks or Trojans) or player. They watch as long as they care to watch and at times turn away their eyes. For the human characters, who are directly involved in the events, these events are real, frightening, pleasing, overwhelming, and, above all, inescapable. They see what their human nature allows them to see and at times their blindness with regard to their own fate is signalled by the NF_1 through νήπιος ('fool'). The NF_1 sees (and thereby makes us see) both: the heroes fighting bravely, often unaware of what fate has in store for them and the gods watching (sometimes not watching) them. This double focus is again an instrument of the NF_1's rhetoric: the sustained interest of the gods confirms the heroic stature of the characters and strengthens the $NeFe_1$'s *ad-*

miration; the gods' pity for certain heroes, but also their occasional playing down of the importance of human struggle, incites the NeFe₁'s *pity*. The NF₁ never turns away his eyes, never minimalizes the exertions of his heroes (and for that matter his own activity as presentator) and the NeFe₁, far from being allowed to close his eyes to certain events is, drawn into them forcefully. Only this powerful, yet masterfully concealed, rhetoric explains the fascination, in Homeric terminology 'the spell' (κηληθμός), in which the *Iliad* has held its readers through the ages.

APPENDIX I
adjectives of war/fighting

In this appendix I have collected the attributive adjectives found together with the four main words for war/fighting in the *Iliad*.[1] They have been grouped according to the narrative situation in which they occur: simple narrator-text (first column), complex narrator-text (second column) and character-text (third column). The second column is only included in order to offer a complete inventory of the material, but does not play a role in my argument in section 3.1.1, p. 43 and will not further be gone into.

	simple narrator-text	complex narrator-text	character-text
μάχη			
ἀλεγεινός[2]	Τ 46, Υ 43	Σ 248	
ἀλίαστος			Ξ 57
δακρυόεις		Ν 765	Π 436
δριμύς	Ο 696		
κάρτιστος			Ζ 185
καύστειρα			Δ 342, Μ 316
κυδιάνειρα[3]	Δ 225	Ξ 155	Ζ 124, Η 113, Θ 448, Μ 325, Ν 270, Ω 391
πολύδακρυς	Ρ 192		
φθισίμβροτος	Ν 339		
π(τ)όλεμος[4]			
αἱματόεις		Τ 313	Ι 650
ἀλίαστος	Υ 31		Β 797
ἀργαλέος			Ξ 87
δακρυόεις	Ε 737, Θ 388		Ρ 512
δήϊος	Δ 281, Ρ 189		Ε 117, Η 119.174, Τ 73, Φ 422

	simple narrator-text	complex narrator-text	character-text
π(τ)όλεμος			
δυσηλεγής		Υ 154	
δυσηχής	Ν 535	Β 686	Η 376.395, Λ 524.590, Σ 307
θρασύς		Κ 28	Ζ 254
κακός			Α 284, Δ 15.82 Ν 225, Π 494
λευγαλέος			Ν 97
ὀΐζυρός		Γ 112	
ὀλοός			Γ 133
ὁμοίΐος	Ν 358, Ο 670, Σ 242		Ι 440, Ν 635 Φ 294
πευκεδανός	Κ 8		
πολύαιξ	Υ 328		Α 165
πολύδακρυς			Γ 165, Χ 487
στυγερός		Δ 240	Ζ 330, Τ 230
φθισήνωρ	Κ 78	Β 833, Λ 331	Ι 604, Ξ 43
ὑσμίνη			
κρατερός	Β 40, Δ 462, Ε 84.627, Η 14, Ν 838.522, Ξ 448, Π 567.645.764.788, Ρ 289.543, Σ 343, Τ 52	Ε 712, Η 18 Π 648, Φ 207	Β 345, Ε 200.530, Λ 190.205.468, Μ 347.360, Π 447.451, Ρ 15
φύλοπις			
αἰνός	Ε 496, Ζ 1.105, Λ 213, Π 677	Π 256	Δ 15.65.82, Ε 379, Λ 278, Σ 171
ἀργαλέος			Λ 278
κρατερός	Σ 242		

Notes

1. For a full survey of the epithets of war see Paraskevaides (1984: 39-43).

2. The same οὕνεκα-clause recurs in Σ 248, Τ 46, Υ 43. In Σ 248 I analyze it as embedded focalization, describing the Trojan fear; in Τ 46 it is focalized doubly: the motivation of the NF₁ now coincides with that of the characters then; in Υ 43, finally, the clause follows after ἐκύδανον ('were triumphant') and is focalized solely by the NF₁.

3. It is interesting to note that this adjective, one of the few downright positive qualifications of war, is used almost exclusively by characters.

4. I have left out of account πολέμου ... ἐπιδημίου ὀκρυόεντος in Ι 64, because we are here dealing with a very special kind of war, viz. civil war.

APPENDIX II
on the/this/that day

The use by the NF₁ of the expression ἤματι κείνῳ ('on that day') indicates that he is temporally removed from the events he presents. To argue this point is the objective of this appendix.

The Homeric language has one anaphoric demonstrative pronoun: ὁ, ἡ, τό (refers to something, -body just mentioned; it can also be cataphoric, referring to something, -body to be mentioned) and three demonstrative pronouns: ὅδε, ἥδε, τόδε (refers to what is near the speaker); οὗτος, αὕτη, τοῦτο (refers to what is near the addressee); (ἐ)κεῖνος, -νη, -νο (refers to what is neither near the speaker nor near the addressee, i.e. often to something, -body which/who is not present or belongs to past/future).

With ἦμαρ ('day') we find the following combinations:

	simple narrator-text	complex narrator-text	character-text
ἤματι τῷ ('on the/that day')	4	-	17
ἤματι τῷδ' ('on this day')	-	-	5
ἤματι κείνῳ ('on that remote day')	2	2	1

ἤματι τῷ

This expression is used both by the NF₁ and by characters in their speeches. Except for P 401, it is always followed by a ὅτε-clause,[1] making clear the temporal orientation. When used by a character ἤματι τῷ, ὅτε refers most of the times (15 out of 17) to an event of the past, e.g.

> (1) Γ 189 (Priam is speaking: I was elected an ally of the Phrygians):
> ἤματι τῷ ὅτε τ' ἦλθον 'Αμαζόνες ἀντιάνειραι
> on that day when the Amazones, a match for men, came[2]

In two cases (Θ 475, X 359) the expression refers to the future. The NF₁ uses the expression in B· 743 and X 471 to refer to an event which has taken place before the time covered by the *Iliad*, in N 335 in a (timeless) simile. In

(2) P 400-1:
τοῖον Ζεὺς ἐπὶ Πατρόκλῳ ἀνδρῶν τε καὶ ἵππων
ἤματι τῷ ἐτάνυσσε κακὸν πόνον.
Such a devastating struggle of men and horses over Patroclus'
body did Zeus stretch on that day.

no ὅτε-clause follows and we must ourselves determine the temporal orientation. At this point, it is useful to turn to the combination

ἤματι κείνῳ

The expression is used once by a character (Σ 324) and then refers to an event which for that character (Achilles) too belongs to the past.[3] It is used twice by the NF₁ (B 482, Δ 543) in contexts very much like P 401:

(3) B 482-3 (Agamemnon was like a bull amidst cows):
τοῖον ἄρ᾽ Ἀτρεΐδην θῆκε Ζεὺς ἤματι κείνῳ
ἐκπρεπέ᾽ ἐν πολλοῖσι καὶ ἔξοχον ἡρώεσσιν.
such did Zeus make Agamemnon on that day, conspicuous
among many and pre-eminent among heroes.

On account of the deictic force of (ἐ)κεῖνος it seems warranted to suppose that ἤματι κείνῳ in B 482 and Δ 543 (and by analogy in P 401) signals that for the speaker (the NF₁) the events belong to the past. A somewhat exaggerated translation would be: 'on that remote day in the past'. This temporal orientation of the NF₁ seems to persevere in the two instances of this expression occurring in secondarily focalized passages:

(4) B 37:
φῆ γὰρ ὅ γ᾽ αἱρήσειν Πριάμου πόλιν ἤματι κείνῳ
for he (Agamemnon) thought that he would capture Priam's
city on that day.

and

(5) Φ 516-7:
μέμβλετο γάρ οἱ τεῖχος ἐϋδμήτοιο πόληος
μὴ Δαναοὶ πέρσειαν ὑπὲρ μόρον ἤματι κείνῳ.
for he (Apollo) cared for the wall of the well-built city,
lest the Greeks would destroy it against fate on that day

The words underlined contain the secondary focalization of Agamemnon and

Apollo, respectively. They hope/fear that something will happen on that very day, that is to say, for them 'today'. Nevertheless, we find ἤματι κείνῳ, which corresponds to the temporal orientation of the NF₁ (looking back on the past), rather than of the characters (engaged in the present). The explanation for B 37 might be that it forms part of an internal prolepsis by the NF₁ (for this terminology see section 3.3.3): B 36-40, in which the NF₁ contrasts his own knowledge of future events to the ignorance of Agamemnon, who cherishes false hopes. In Φ 517, again knowledge of the future (fate), this time residing with Apollo, is involved.

ἤματι τῷδ'

The temporal distance of the NF₁ from the events he presents also appears from the fact that this expression (where τῷδ' refers to what is near to the speaker) is never found outside direct speech. Only characters, who are themselves involved in the events they refer to, use 'this day'. Note that σήμερον ('today') is also found in direct speech only: H 30.291, Θ 141, Λ 431, Τ 103, Υ 127.211.

ἤματι τούτῳ

This expression is used neither by the NF₁ nor by characters. The only thing we can learn from the fact that the NF₁ does not use it, is that his addressee, the NeFe₁, is also temporally removed from the events presented.

In sum, the fact that the NF₁ uses ἤματι κείνῳ and never ἤματι τῷδ' or ἤματι τούτῳ indicates that for him, as for his addressee, the events presented belong to the (remote) past.

Notes

1. According to Ruijgh (1971: 494) ἤματι τῷ, ὅτε is a more elaborate doublet of ὅτε. The combination is always found at the beginning of a verse - where ὅτε does not fit in metrically - and is probably an old formula.

2. According to Fränkel (1955: 24, n. 3), the expression does not refer to a particular day, but to a certain situation.

3. More in particular, Achilles seems to emphasize, through the use of ἤματι κείνῳ, the irrevocability of the past.

APPENDIX III

φασί-utterances in Iliad and Odyssey

Total number of occurrences in *Iliad* and *Odyssey*: 42
A. with definite subject: 8

narrator-text	character-text
-	I 234 (sc.Τρῶες), P 637 (sc.φίλοι ἑταῖροι), Φ 569 (ἄνθρωποι), α 33 (sc. βροτοί), β 238 (sc. μνηστῆρες), η 322 (οἵ μιν ἴδοντο λαῶν ἡμετέρων), λ 176 (sc.πατὴρ καὶ υἱός), τ 383 (ὅσοι ἴδον ὀφθαλμοῖσιν ἡμέας ἀμφοτέρους)

B. with indefinite subject ('they say', 'on dit'): 34
B1. φασί-utterance concerns information which the speaker cannot confirm as having seen with his own eyes:

narrator-text	character-text
B 783	Δ 375 (cp. φάσαν in 374), Π 14, Ω 615, α 189, γ 84.188.212, δ 201, ν 249, π 143

B2. φασί-utterance refers to somebody's descent:

narrator-text	character-text
-	E 635, Z 100, Y 105.206, Φ 159, α 220, δ 387, σ 128

B3. φασί-utterance contains a reputation or universally admitted fact, which the speaker mentions either to confirm or to falsify:

narrator-text	character-text
P 674, ζ 42	E 638, I 401, Λ 831, N 631, T 96.416, Ψ 791, Ω 546, γ 245, π 418, σ 261, τ 267, ψ 125

Remarks

Ad category B1: the circumstance that a speaker can not draw on his or her own perception is often expressed explicitly in the context: Δ 374-5 (οὐ γὰρ ἔγωγε ἥντησ' οὐδὲ ἴδον), Ω 614 (που), γ 184-7 (οὐδέ τι οἶδα ... πεύθομαι), δ 200-1 (= Δ 374-5).

In α 189 and ν 249 'Athena' effectively uses φασί-utterances to mask her own omniscience as a god and strengthen the credibility of her human disguise.

In Π 14, α 189 and π 143 the φασί-utterance stresses the idea of distance (between Achilles and his home) or isolation (of Laertes, who lives withdrawn from the others out of grief over his absent son).

Ad category B2: these φασί-utterances seem a more modest variant of birth-claims through εἰμί, φημί, εὔχομαι, εὔχεται: see Muellner (1976: 69-78, esp. p. 78).

α 220 might also be put in category B1: Telemachus is not sure whether Odysseus really is his father, since he has never seen him himself: αὐτὰρ ἐγώ γε οὐκ οἶδ' (215-6).

Ad category B3: for ζ 42, cp. Bassett (1938: 90): "this is a more idealized conception than we find in the *Iliad*. There Olympus belongs to the story, as the scene of many interesting episodes. Here the poet presents the popular conception of his own day, "as men say"."; and Spieker (1969: 139): "das φασί hat einen versichernden Charakter ... φασί ἔμμεναι der Olymposbeschreibung muß man auffassen als pointiertes εἰσί."

In π 418 Penelope falsifies a reputation: cp. also E 635 in category B2.

In Ψ 791 φασί seems to make ὠμογέροντα a kind of quotation, a nickname of Odysseus (the adjective is a *hapax* and means something like 'a ripe old man').

The φασί-utterances of this category often contain a superlative or superlative-like expression and in this respect they again are related to εὔχεσθαι-statements (see Muellner 1976: 79-83): N 631 (περὶ φρένας ἔμμεναι ἄλλων), P 675 (ὀξύτατον δέρκεσθαι), T 95 (ἄριστον).416 (ἐλαφροτάτην), Ω 546 (κεκάσθαι), π 419 (ἄριστον), ψ 124 (ἀρίστην).

APPENDIX IV
δαίμων in the Homeric epics

The following figures form the point of departure for the interpretation of Homeric δαίμων as proposed in N. van der Ben & I.J.F. de Jong, 'Daimon in Ilias en Odyssee', *Lampas* 17 (1984), 301-16, and which is summarized in section 5.1, p. 158. All figures (except those under f) concern *Iliad* and *Odyssey*.

(a) Occurrences of θεός and δαίμων:

θεός		δαίμων	
772		60	
Iliad	*Odyssey*	*Iliad*	*Odyssey*
402	37	28	32

(b) Distribution of δαίμων over narrator-text and character-text:

narrator-text		character-text	
12		48	
Iliad	*Odyssey*	*Iliad*	*Odyssey*
11	1	17	31

(c) Cases in which δαίμων occurs:

nominative		other cases	
narrator-text	character-text	narrator-text	character-text
4	36	8	12

(d) Of the 36 nominative occurrences in character-text, the activity of the δαίμων is directed to:

speaker	addressee	a third person
23	6	7

(e) Of the 40 nominative occurrences, the tense of the predicate of which δαίμων is subject is:

present	aorist	future
7	31	2

(f) Of the 40 times the nominative singular θεός occurs in the *Iliad* in character-text, it is 10 times as subject of a distributive-iterative subjunctive (E 129, Z 228, I 703, N 743, P99, T 159, Y 130, Φ 103) or potential optative (K 556-7, Y 100-1).

APPENDIX V

repeated speech in the *Iliad*

A. Messenger-speeches

In the following, those parts of *instruction* (I) and *delivery* (D) speeches are cited which correspond either verbatim or almost verbatim. Between brackets are passages which are added (by instructor or messenger) or changed substantially (by the messenger).

			speaker	addressee
-	(I)	B 11-15	Zeus	Oneirus
	(D)	B 28-32 [+33-4]	Oneirus	Agamemnon
-	(I)	B 158-165	Hera	Athena
	(D)	B 174-181	Athena	Odysseus
-	(I)	Γ 68-73 [+74-5]	Paris	Hector
	(D)	Γ 88-94	Hector	Greeks/Trojans
-	(I)	Δ 65-67	Hera	Zeus
	(D)	Δ 70-72	Zeus	Athena
-	(I)	Δ 193-197	Agamemnon	Talthybius
	(D)	Δ 204-207	Talthybius	Machaon
-	(I)	Z 87-97 [+98-101]	Helenus	Hector
	(D)	Z 269-278	Hector	Hecabe
-	(I)	H 38-40 [+41-2]	Apollo	Athena
	(D)	H 49-51 [+52-3]	Helenus	Hector
-	(I)	H 362-364	Paris	Trojans
	(I)	H 374-378	Priam	Trojans
	(D)	H 388-397	Idaeus	Greeks
-	(I)	Θ 402-408	Zeus	Iris
	(D)	Θ 416-422 [+423-4]	Iris	Athena/Hera
-	(I)	I 122-157 [+158-161]	Agamemnon	Nestor/Greek leaders
	(D)	I 264-299 [+300-306]	Odysseus	Achilles
-	(I)	I 417-420+427-429	Achilles	Odysseus
	(D)	I 684-687+690-692	Odysseus	Agamemnon/Greek leaders

			speaker	addressee
-	(I)	K 208-210	Nestor	Greek leaders
	(D)	K [406-8+]409-411	Odysseus	Dolon
-	(I)	K 308-312	Hector	Trojans
	(D)	K 395-399	Dolon	Diomedes
-	(I)	Λ 187-194	Zeus	Iris
	(D)	Λ 202-209	Iris	Hector
-	(I)	Λ 658-662+794-803	Nestor	Patroclus
	(D)	Π 23-27+36-45	Patroclus	Achilles
-	(I)	M 343-350	Menestheus	Thootes
	(D)	M 356-363	Thootes	Ajaxes
-	(I)	O 160-167	Zeus	Iris
	(D)	O 176-183	Iris	Poseidon
-	(I)	Π 454-457	Hera	Zeus
	(D)	Π 671-675	Zeus	Apollo
-	(I)	P 654-655	Ajax	Menelaus
	(I)	P 689-693	Menelaus	Antilochus
	(D)	Σ [19+]20-21	Antilochus	Achilles
-	(I)	Ω 113-116	Zeus	Thetis
	(D)	Ω 134-137	Thetis	Achilles
-	(I)	Ω 146-158	Zeus	Iris
	(D)	Ω 175-187	Iris	Priam
-	(I)	Ω [290-1+]292-295	Hecuba	Priam
	(D)	Ω [308-9+]310-313	Priam	Zeus

Remarks

In the cases of B 158-165 = B 174-181 and Π 454-457 = Π 671-675, we see that what in fact is an order to character **b** is transmitted by that same character to character **c**, who then executes the order.

For Γ 68-73 [+74-5] = Γ 88-94, cp. Plutarch *Moralia* 741D-743C.

In the case of Δ 65-67 = Δ 70-72 character **c** is present at the moment the instruction speech is spoken. The role of the intermediary (Zeus) is, therefore, not so much to carry a message from one place to another as to *authorize* what character **a** (Hera) wishes to impose on character **c** (Athena).

H 38-40[+41-2] = H 49-51[+52-3] is a special case, since here Apollo does not directly instruct Helenus. The latter 'gathered in his mind', as a seer, the deliberation of Apollo and Athena and transferred it in somewhat altered form to Hector.

Note that in the case of K 208-210 = K [406-8+]409-411 and K 308-312 = K 395-399 the *instruction* speech is not really meant to be delivered as a message. Especially Dolon had not intended to repeat Hector's instruction to anybody else, but is forced to do so when captured by Odysseus and Diomedes.

In Π 23 Patroclus replaces Nestor's οἱ γὰρ ἄριστοι (Λ 658) by the formulation of Eurypylus, which he has heard in Λ 825.

B. Other cases of repeated speech

Speeches which are repeated in their totality are marked with an asterisk. In the fourth column is indicated to which of the four groups mentioned on p. 186 the repeated verse-cluster belongs.

		speaker	addressee	group
-	A 37 -38	Chryses	Apollo	3
	A 451-452	Chryses	Apollo	
-	A 411-412	Achilles	Thetis	1
	Π 273-4	Patroclus	Myrmidonians	
-	A 453-5	Chryses	Apollo	1
	Π 236-238	Achilles	Zeus	
-	B 110-118+139-141	Agamemnon	Greeks	3
	I 17 -25 +26 -28	Agamemnon	Greeks	
-	B 371+373-4	Agamemnon	Nestor	4
	Δ 288+290-1	Agamemnon	Ajaxes	
-	Γ 285-287	Agamemnon	Trojans/Greeks	3
	Γ 458-460	Agamemnon	Trojans/Greeks	
-	Δ 15 -16	Zeus	other gods	1
	Δ 82-84	somebody	his neighbour	
-	Δ 60 -61	Hera	Zeus	3
	Σ 365-366	Hera	Zeus	

		speaker	addressee	group
-	Δ 163-165	Agamemnon	Menelaus	1
	Z 447-449	Hector	Andromache	
-	E 130-132	Athena	Diomedes	1
	E 819-821	Diomedes	Athena	
-	E 175-176	Aeneas	Pandarus	1
	Π 424-425	Sarpedon	Lycians	
-	E 221-223	Aeneas	Pandarus	1
	Θ 105-107	Diomedes	Nestor	
-	E 373-374*	Dione	Aphrodite	1
	Φ 509-510	Zeus	Leto	
-	E 458-459	Apollo	Ares	1
	E 883-884	Ares	Zeus	
-	E 529-532*	Agamemnon	Greeks	2
	O 561-564	Ajax	Greeks	
-	E 652-654	Sarpedon	Tlepolemus	1
	Λ 443-445	Odysseus	Socus	
-	Z 46 -50*	Adrestus	Menelaus	1
	Λ 131-135	Peisander/	Agamemnon	
		Hippolochus		
cp.	K 378-381	Dolon	Odysseus/Diomedes	
-	Z 378-380	Hector	female servant	1
	Z 383-385	female servant	Hector	
-	H 79 -80	Hector	Greeks/Trojans	4
	X 342-343	Hector	Achilles	
-	Θ [31+]32 -37*	Athena	Zeus	2
	Θ [462+]463-468	Hera	Zeus	
-	Θ 39 -40	Zeus	Athena	3
	X 183-184	Zeus	Athena	
-	Θ 173-174	Hector	Trojans	3
	Λ 286-287	Hector	Trojans	
	O 486-487 [+488a]	Hector	Trojans	
	P 184-185	Hector	Trojans	
-	K 402-404	Odysseus	Dolon	1
	P 76 -78	Apollo	Hector	

		speaker	addressee	group
-	Λ 362-367*	Diomedes	Hector	2
	Υ 449-454	Achilles	Hector	
-	Λ 792-3	Nestor	Patroclus	1
	Ο 403-4	Patroclus	Eurypylus	
-	Λ 800-801	Nestor	Patroclus	1
	Π 42 -43	Patroclus	Achilles	
	Σ 200-201	Iris	Achilles	
-	Ξ 195-196	Aphrodite	Hera	1
	Σ 426-427	Hephaestus	Thetis	
-	Ξ 200-207	Hera	Aphrodite	4
	Ξ 301-306	Hera	Zeus	
-	Π 441-443	Hera	Zeus	2
	Χ 179-181	Athena	Zeus	
-	Ρ 30 -32	Menelaus	Euphorbus	1
	Υ 196-198	Achilles	Aeneas	
-	Σ 56 -62	Thetis	Nereids	4
	Σ 437-443	Thetis	Hephaestus	
-	Σ 112-113	Achilles	Thetis	4
	Τ 65 -66	Achilles	Agamemnon	
-	Σ 385-386	Charis	Thetis	2
	Σ 424-425	Hephaestus	Thetis	
-	Υ 200-202	Aeneas	Achilles	2
	Υ 431-433	Hector	Achilles	
-	Υ 315-317a	Hera	Poseidon	1
	Φ 374-376	Xanthus	Hera	
-	Ω 203-205	Hecabe	Priam	2
	Ω 519-521	Achilles	Priam	

Remarks

In the case of Ε 652-4 = Λ 443-445 there is a small difference, viz. Odysseus saying ἤματι τῷδ' ἔσσεσθαι (Λ 444), Sarpedon ἐξ ἐμέθεν τεύξεσθαι (Ε 653). Odysseus' formulation seems a reaction to Socus' σήμερον in Λ 431.

The differences between Athena's (Θ 31) and Hera's addressing of Zeus (Θ 462) is due to difference in identity of speaker (Athena is addressing her father, Hera her husband) and mood (Hera is angry: 461).

1. For Homer as "educator of the Greeks" see Verdenius (1970: 3-20).

2. From 393c and 397b it appears that λέξις includes φωνή ('voice') and σχῆμα ('gesture'): Plato is clearly thinking of poetry being performed (drama) or recited (epic). In antiquity even reading always meant reading aloud, i.e. the reader 'performing' the text. See Herington (1985).

3. Plato does not say anything about the quantitative relation between (1) and (2) in the *Iliad*. Incorrectly Koster (1970: 40): "Wie das bei Homer aussieht, hat Platon 396E beschrieben ... Der diegetische Teil überwiegt also nach Platon bei Homer". In 396e Plato is speaking about hypothetical narratives to be performed by the Guardians (note the future tense χρήσεται) and his reference to the Homeric epics here only concerns their mixed manner of narration.

4. Cp. Cornford (1941: 80): "dramatic representation"; Vicaire (1960: 221): "représentation active"; Koster and Fuhrmann: "Darstellung"; Else (1972: 23): "impersonation".

5. Adam & Rees (1963: 143); White (1979: 96): "pure third-person narrative"; Cornford (1941:8 1); Genette (1972: 184 = 1980: 162 n. 2, and cp. 1977: 392): as an argument he refers to ἄκρατον in 397b (should be d), but the interpretation of this passage is difficult (for a good exposition of the problem here see Annas 1981:94).

6. I have already brought forward these arguments in De Jong (1985a: 18 n. 11).

7. Cp. Friedman (1955: 1161-2): "showing what a thing is" vs. "telling how he feels about it"; Stanzel (1964: 11), Genette (1972: 75 = 1980: 163) and Chatman (1978: 146). The distinction "showing-telling" was first introduced by the literary critic Lubbock (see note 45), who nowhere refers to Plato.

8. Both historically, Homer as the first tragedian: 1448b 34-49a 2 (cp. Plato *Republic* X 607a, 595c and *Theaetetus* 152e) and structurally: 1449b 16-20, 1451a 22-30, 1459a 30-b 37.

9. If in the following I compare Aristotle with Plato this is done from a systematical rather than a historical point of view. Aristotle was a pupil of Plato from 367-347 and it is only logical to suppose that the choice of some of his subjects was influenced by the topics raised by his teacher. However, since he nowhere explicitly refers to Plato nor to his ideas we can only guess the exact degree of polemics in the *Poetics*. On this problem see Lucas (1968: xxii) and Fuhrmann (1979: 86-90).

10. For discussion see Lucas (1968: 66-7). Koster (1970: 46) and Genette (1977: 393) choose the bipartite, Fuhrmann (1973: 87) and Van der Ben & Bremer (1986) the tripartite interpretation. I feel a slight preference for the latter.

11. Bywater (1909: 316): "His aim apparently is to show that although narrative is an element in every epic, it is reduced to a minimum in the best epic, that of Homer"; Lucas (1968: passim), Koster (1970: 68), Lanser (1981: 20).

12. Bywater (1909: 100-101): "a grave inconsistency"; Lucas (1968: 226 ad 60a 8)

"this is a restricted use of μίμησις as in Pl. *Rep.* 392 D ff. According to A's normal usage the epic poet is a μιμητής regardless of whether he uses direct speech."

13. This leads to misleading conclusions like the following: Lanser (1981: 20, n. 13): "in this passage ... he (Aristotle) implies that diegetic discourse because it is not mimesis in the narrower, technical sense of imitated speech, *is not art*" (my italics).

14. Lucas (1968: 226 ad 60a 6): "it is surprising if all the poets of the cycle, to say nothing of later epic poets, denied themselves the pleasure of putting speeches into their characters' mouths ... In fact passages of direct speech occur in the scanty fragments."; (ad 60a 8): "one may wonder how Antimachos expanded twenty-four Books ... if he did not give his heroes a generous allowance of speeches."

15. Lucas (1968: 227 ad 60a 9): "Anyway the distinction is between *narration* and impersonation" (my italics); Koster (1970: 68): "Andere Ependichter mühen sich im ganzen Werk ab, selbst zu reden und führen selten andere ein."

16. A curious (and to me incomprehensible) defense of this ὀλίγα is given by Gudeman (1934: 105-6): "aber auch die rein erzählenden Stellen, besonders in der Odyssee, stehen in gar keinem quantitativen Verhältnis, weder an Zahl noch an Umfang, zu den übrigen Partien, in denen Homer, die Forderung des ἕτερόν τι γιγνόμενον, glänzend erfüllt. Jene narrationes konnten daher als eine quantité négligeable hier ausgeschaltet werden."

17. E.g. the translator of the Loeb edition, Hamilton Fyfe (1927: 96 note a): "When Aristotle says 'the poet speaks himself' ... he refers not to the narrative, of which there is a great deal in Homer, but to the preludes ... in which the poet, invoking the Muse, speaks in his own person."

18. Of course, this refinement remains unobserved by the adherents to the other interpretation, e.g. Lucas (1968: 67): "Apparently A. does not distinguish between passages in which poets narrate and those in which they speak personally as in invoking the Muse or commenting on their story, e.g. Il. 23.176."

19. Cp. Heirman (1972: 16): "Plutarch was not a professional theorist, but a first rate pedagogical lecturer"; and Schenkeveld (1982: 62): "We should not forget that Plutarch has not written a theoretical dissertation on the nature of poetry, but a very practical guide".

20. For a more detailed discussion of the structure of *De audiendis poetis* see Heirman (1972: 22-5) and Schenkeveld (1982).

21. I base this opposition "explicitly-implicitly" on the opposition between λόγων and πραγμάτων in 19d 13-e 15: αὗται μὲν οὖν αἱ τῶν λόγων ἀποφάσεις καὶ δόξαι παντός εἰσι κατιδεῖν τοῦ προσέχοντος· ἑτέρας δ' ἐκ τῶν πραγμάτων αὐτῶν παρέχουσι μαθήσεις ('Now those *verbal* assertions and opinions may be observed by any attentive reader, but they (sc. poets) supply other lessons *by the course of events itself*'). The notion 'implicitly' is indicated once again in σιωπώμενον (19e 18: 'silently').

22. The remainder of chapter IV is devoted to the method of balancing passages,

i.e. neutralizing bad opinions by looking for their good counterparts. Here it is no longer the poet who judges, but the reading young man. The transition to this second part is not sharply marked by Plutarch: Heirman (1972: 25) puts it at 20d 13, Schenkeveld (1982: 69) somewhere between 19e and 20c and I at 20c 25.

23. Heirman (1972: 32) states the fact, but gives no reason: "Apparently, Plutarch found Homer the most suitable for his moralistic approach to education and specifically the heroism of the Iliad."

24. Plutarch's actual order is slightly different: A: 19a 15 (τῶν λεγομένων); A1: 19b 16-c 2; B: 19c 2 (τῶν πράξεων); B1: 19c 3-4; B2: 19d 6-8;, A2: 19d 9-10; B2: 19d 11-12, C: 19d 14-20c (ἐκ τῶν πραγμάτων αὐτῶν).

25. Key words are τέρπειν and θέλγειν. For this whole question of didacticism see Verdenius (1970: 20-7 and 1983: 31-4), Hainsworth (1970: 93). Let me give one example, taken from Verdenius (1970: 21), who is a moderate defendant of Homer's didacticism: A 237 is supposed to be "superfluous from a dramatic point of view" and inserted by Homer "to enlighten his audience on natural causes", in other words Homer is here a "lecturer in botany". I contend, together with Kirk (ad 234-9), that the many details supplied in A 235-7 do have a clear dramatic function, viz. to add "emphasis and emotional force" to Achilles' oath, make it more "impressive" and therefore "effective".

26. I do not agree with the particular examples here given by Plutarch - Hera's and Zeus' anger are clearly conditioned by the story - but agree with him that the interpretation of the hearer/reader can be shaped by the reactions of characters in the text: see section 3.2 and n. 41 of that chapter.

27. See Schmidt (1969: 39-65) and Richardson (1980). Schenkeveld (1970) argues that Aristarchus, whose views are represented in the A-scholia, also used a theory of poetics in establishing the text, its main points being consistency and functionality.

28. In collecting these scholia I have consulted Bachman (1902: 15-6) and von Franz (1943: 35-7) and the index of Erbse (1969-1983). In my text I shall not always indicate whether I am dealing with A- or bT-scholia. The numbers in brackets refer to Erbse's line-numbers.

29. Plato's tripartite division is also cited in other scholia (on Hesiod, Theocritus, Dionysius Thrax). See Severyns (1938: 79-81) and Koster (1970: 105-7).

30. The verb διηγέομαι is used as a general term for the narrating activity of the poet, both in the narrator-text and the speeches (for the latter case, see e.g. scholion on A 366a); διήγησις can refer to the story in general (e.g. A 8-9 (72).304a, K 558-63 (59), Ξ 153b (46).226-7 (70), P 301-3 (86), Υ 410 (75), Φ 34b (95)) or to a certain type of stories (ἦν δέ τις: 'there was a man called': E 9a, K 314; or embedded narratives: A 366b, I 232a.524a¹+a², Λ 677-761 (71), or to the activity of narration (A1a (11).7b.11b (5), B 494-877 (96), M 175-81b (71).Ξ 347-51 (85), P 648a1. διήγημα means 'story', 'anecdote', both as told by the poet (e.g. N 665a) or by a character (e.g. Λ 671-761.785-9, T 101).

31. A direct influence is advocated by Adam (1889); Richardson (1980: 265) speaks

of "a considerable influence"; Schmidt (1969: 43) seems less convinced and see also Lucas (1968: xxii-iii).

32. See further scholia on H 62a, K 488-90, Λ 262-3, Π 101-11, P 58a, Φ 299-300b. In German narratological studies we often find 'berichten/Bericht' on a par with 'erzählen/Erzählung': Friedemann (1910: 143 et passim), Stanzel (1964: 11).

33. At I 685 and Π 202c, 203a the scholia comment on similar abrupt transitions to indirect and direct speech, respectively, found in speeches.

34. According to the scholion on Δ 127a (59-61) and the author of *On the sublime* 27.1 these abrupt transitions are a form of *apostrophe*. For this whole group of scholia see De Martino (1977).

35. Note that the passage from the *Iliad* is here quoted with a different inter-punction from that given in the Monro-Allen text. With this interpunction, making O 347 indirect speech, O 348 is closely comparable to Δ 303 and Ψ 855; with the Monro-Allen interpunction, making O 347 part of the direct speech, the transition is less abrupt: ἐκέκλετο μακρὸν ἀΰσας is a perfectly normal speech-introduction, cp. Z 66.110, Θ 172, Λ 285, O 424.485, Π 268.

36. For more examples see Schmidt (1969: 57-8).

37. See further Schmidt (1969: 56-7) and Richardson (1980: 273-4).

38. The debate on Homer's nationalism is still continuing: (pro) Ameis-H. (e.g. ad Θ 130 and passim), Bassett (1938: 218), Howald (1946: 32-3), Van der Valk (1953, 1985); (contra) Kramer (1946: 12-3 and 112-4), Kakridis (1956); (moderate position) Gomme (1954: 42-3), Reinhardt (1961: 120-3: Homer anti-Trojan, but less vehemently than the tradition), Richardson (1980: 274), Griffin (1980: 4-5, 23: the difference in characterization of Greeks and Trojans is "vital to the Iliad, no mere chauvinism"), Müller (1984: 90: "the pro-Achaean bias of the poem generates its own counterpart: the greater the successes of the Achaeans on the battlefield, the more the Trojan victims evoke the poet's sympathy").

39. I do not agree with the scholiasts here: 225-8 also contains pathetic undertones (ἥβης: 'prime of youth' and ἐκ θαλάμοιο: 'straight from the bedroom').

40. (bT) Δ 127a.146a, H 104-8, O 365b, Π 692-3.787, Y 2a; (T) N 603. In N 603 and O 365b the term ἀναφώνησις is used instead of ἀποστροφή. The A-scholia are also interested in apostrophes (O 582b, Π 20.584, P 702), probably because often textual problems are involved (see discussion on ἔλεν/ἔλες at Π 697a[1]). They also note (at Π 586.697a[1], P 705) the switch from addressing a character to speaking about him.

41. See Richardson (1980: 272-3). This same principle also forms the basis for the scholiastic technique of the λύσις ἐκ τοῦ προσώπου: discrepancies in the text can be explained - λύσις means the solution to a problem (ζήτημα) such as formulated e.g. by Porphyrius - by taking into account who is speaking. Thus, when Menelaus is called a μαλθακὸς αἰχμητής ('faint-hearted warrior') in P 588, this is not in contradiction with the rest of the *Iliad*, since it is (an angry) Poseidon who is speaking here. See Dachs (1913).

42. See Schmidt (1969: 82 n. 36) and scholion ad Π 844-5.

43. Cp. also Milman Parry (1928: 148-54), who discusses this group of scholia together with two other ones where epithets (in speeches) are commented upon by scholiasts: οὐ κόσμου χάριν, ἀλλὰ πρός τι ('not for the sake of ornament, but with a special meaning') and οὐ τότε, ἀλλὰ φύσει ('not in this case, but in general, (by nature)').

44. Hamburg-edition (1957: 523). As an example of "trockene Wahrheit" Schiller mentions Z 119-236, where Homer describes the meeting of Glaucus and Diomedes "als ob er etwas Alltägliches berichtet hätte." Other scholars, however, treat Z 234-6 as a subjective element: category 4, pp. 18-9.

45. For the idea that the story "seems to tell itself" cp. Lubbock (1921: 113):

> The scene he (Guy de Maupassant) evokes is contemporaneous, and there it is, we can see it as well as he can. Certainly he is "telling" us things, but they are things so immediate, so perceptible, that the machinery of his telling, by which they reach us, is unnoticed; the story appears to tell itself. Critically, of course, we know how far that is from being the case, we know with what judicious thought the showman is selecting the points of the scene upon which he touches. But the *effect* is that he is not there at all.

and Benveniste (1966: 241):

> A vrai dire, il n'y a même plus de narrateur. Les événements sont posés comme ils se sont produits à mesure qu'ils apparaissent à l'horizon de l'histoire. Personne ne parle ici: les événements *semblent se raconter eux-mêmes*. (my italics)

46. I do not take into account J. Schmidt, *Das subjektive Element bei Homer*, 20. Jb. des K.K. Staatsgymn. im III Bezirk (Wien) 1889, because he only presents an endless series of quotations, without systematizing them or arguing why he considers these passages subjective.

47. For the second type of subjectivity see Cesareo (1898) and Drerup (1921: 446-66).

48. Cp. Gaunt (1976: 65):

> It will no doubt be said that these comments are essentially subjective. It is high time for classical literature to be criticised, as all other literatures are, with a limited degree of subjective comment.

and Griffin (1980: 104)

> Here again, ..., it will prove possible to meet the criticism that we are reading into the poem things that really are not there at all, and misrepresenting a smooth and objective surface by the arbitrary intrusion of subjective emotion.

49. Interpretators of Virgil show a marked tendency to stress the (unsubtle) Homeric objectivity as against Virgil's (subtle) subjectivity, cp. e.g. Otis (1963: 41-96) and Williams (1983: 164-214). A more sympathetic approach to the Homeric narrative style is found in Gransden (1984: 9-30).

50. Cp. also Effe (1975: 140-1).

51. Cp. Bassett (1938: 100):

> What might have been, or what could not have happened, is purely subjective
> ... (the objective narrator) would have described what actually happened.

52. Not all scholars are convinced that apostrophes are a mark of subjectivity:

> Bei diesem Stilmittel handelt es sich offensichtlich um eine weithin formelhaft
> verwendete, technische Konvention aus dem Bereich mündlicher Improvisation,
> um ein automatisiertes Element der epischen Kunstsprache dem man - im Unter-
> schied zum späteren Epos - keine oder allenfalls eine nur sehr geringe emotionale
> Aussagekraft zusprechen darf. (Effe 1983: 177)

For this question see further note 12 of chapter 3.

53. As a parallel to this type of passages I draw attention to the *Chanson de Roland* (1401-3 = 1420-2)

> Que de bons Français y perdent leur. jeune vie!
> Ils ne reverront plus leurs mères ni leurs femmes
> ni ceux de France qui les attendent aux ports.

54. A similar contrast between narrator-text and speeches is indicated by Létoublon (1983: 25)

> récit objectif, fait par un narrateur omniscient effacé derrière les événements
> qu'il rapporte, et qui parle de tous les personnages à la troisième personne" vs.
> "les récits chez Alkinoos, qui ne sont présentés que par le biais d'une narration
> subjective et rétrospective.

55. E.g. in 'Die epische Poesie und Goethe', *Goethejahrbuch* 1895 (I quote from Friedemann 1910: 1):

> Was verlange ich von einem dichterischen Roman? Dies: daß er zuerst ... wie
> das homerische Epos, nur handelnde Personen kennt, hinter denen der Dichter
> völlig und ausnahmslos verschwindet, so, daß er auch nicht die geringste Meinung
> für sich selbst äußern darf ... am wenigsten über seine Personen, die ihren
> Charakter, ihr Wollen, Wähnen, Wünschen ohne seine Nach- und Beihilfe durch
> ihr Tun und Lassen, ihr Sagen und Schweigen exponieren müssen.

56. (1972: 90 and 101 = 1980: 49 and 62):

> l'analepse est ici en quelque sorte ponctuelle, elle raconte un moment du passé
> qui reste isolé dans son éloignement, et qu'elle ne cherche pas à raccorder au
> moment présent en couvrant un entre-deux non pertinent pour l'épopée, puisque
> le sujet de l'Odyssée, comme le remarquait déjà Aristote, n'est pas la vie
> d'Ulysse, mais seulement son retour de Troie. (101 = 62)

57. As an additional argument to those mentioned in my article I draw attention to ψ 74-5 (ψ 74 = τ 393), where Eurycleia recounts to Penelope how she had recognized the scar. I have also noticed that my interpretation is practically in accordance with that of Austin (1966: 310-1)

> The whole story is virtually Eurykleia's remembrance of Odysseus. The details
> go beyond Eurykleia's actual memory to mingle with what only Odysseus could
> have known, but it is her character as nurse which dictates the nature of the
> digression. She, the nurse, who now sees the grown man, projects him back
> into his childhood and tries to integrate her perception of the stranger with
> her knowledge of the youth.

I have argued that Eurycleia can indeed know every detail of Odysseus' adventure because the latter told everything on his return home (τ 464-6).

58. 1961: 70-77:

> As he (an author) writes, he creates ... an implied version of "himself" that is different from the implied authors we meet in other men's work ... in this distinction between author and implied author we find a middle position between the technical irrelevance of talk about the artist's objectivity and the harmful error of pretending that an author can allow direct intrusions of his own immediate problems and desires...
>
> we cannot easily tell from the plays whether the man Shakespeare preferred blondes to brunettes or whether he disliked bastards, Jews, or Moors ... (but) the implied Shakespeare is thoroughly engaged with life, and he does not conceal his judgment on the selfish, the foolish, and the cruel.

1. Important parts of Genette (1972) and Bal (1977) have been translated into English: see my bibliography. I will give page-references to both the original French publications and the English translations.

2. With 'narrative texts' or 'narratives' I refer to an epic or novel *in its entirety*, i.e. the combination of narrator-text and character-text from cover to cover. Since I am primarily interested in the aspect of presentation, i.e. in the question of who is presenting, I will not further distinguish between narrative and non-narrative parts (descriptions, argumentations, etc.) in the narrator-text: see Bal 1985: 126-34).

3. Cp. also the following warning by Christopher Isherwood in his introductory note to *Goodbye to Berlin*

> Because I have given my own name to the 'I' of this narrative, readers are certainly not entitled to assume that its pages are purely autobiographical ... 'Christopher Isherwood' is a convenient ventriloquist's dummy, nothing more.

4. For an analysis of this opening-scene see Bühler (1976) and cp. also Effe (1975) for Heliodorus as "personaler Erzähler".

5. The term is introduced by Genette (1972: 206 = 1980: 189) as follows: "Pour éviter ce que les termes de vision, de champ et de point de vue ont de trop spécifiquement visuel, je reprendrai ici le terme un peu plus abstrait de focalisation, qui répond d'ailleurs à l'expression de Brooks et Warren: "focus of narration"."

6. This becomes clear in particular in Genette (1983: 48), in the course of his reply to, in fact, rejection of Bal (1977): "focalisateur, s'il s'appliquait à quelqu'un, ce ne pourrait être qu'à celui qui focalise le récit, c'est-à-dire le narrateur."

7. I refer to the narrator and focalizer, which are neutral function-indications, with 'he', although strictly speaking 'it' would me more accurate. Whenever I speak of characters I use he/she, since characters are representations of persons.

8. Of course, fictional persons and the fictional world can very much resemble historical persons and places; yet, when forming part of a narrative, they are not the same as these persons and places. Cp. for this question Forster (1976: 55-6) and Dolezel (1980).

9. Narratives where this suggestion is not upheld, i.e. where the narrator says that he is inventing the events and characters are eighteenth century anti-novels like Diderot's *Jacques le Fataliste* or Sterne's *Tristam Shandy* and contemporary postmodernist novels.

10. Bal thus rejects Genette's first type of focalization, "le récit non-focalisé, ou à focalisation zéro", which would be represented by the classical narrative, i.e. the narrative with an omniscient narrator (1972: 206 = 1980: 189). Let me give one example. The otherwise 'invisible' NF_1 of Somerset Maugham's short story *Lord Mountdrago* gives the following description of this character:

> He had a fine presence: he was a tall handsome man, rather bald and somewhat
> too stout, but this gave him solidity...

The presence of a focalizer, of an interpreting medium, is betrayed in a small detail like "somewhat <u>too</u> stout": "too" implies a norm or personal taste against which the character is evaluated.

11. What is the role of the F_1 in cases of embedded focalization? In principle, the F_1 suppresses his own focalization in favour of that of the F_2, but the vision of this F_2 is given within the all-encompassing vision of the F_1. The focalization can also be *double* or *ambiguous* (Bal 1985: 113-4). Finally, the F_1 can *intrude upon* the focalization of the F_2, as e.g. in Forster's *A Passage to India*

> While thinking of Mrs. Moore she <u>heard</u> sounds, which gradually grew more
> distinct. The *epoch-making* trial had started, and the superintendent of Police
> was opening the case for the prosecution.

The verb "heard" signals that what follows is focalized by the F_2, "she", but the qualification "epoch-making" can only derive from the omniscient NF_1, who knows the sensational turn the trial is going to take.

12. The content of this speech by a secondary narrator-focalizer need not necessarily be a narrative - just as the narrator-text can contain non-narrative passages: see above note 2 -, indeed most of the time it is (part of) a conversation, a description, an adhortatory speech etc. However, to make clear the structural relationship between narrator-text and character-text, the term secondary *narrator* has been chosen.

13. To give one more example: the six different descriptions of Emma Bovary's eyes as listed by Julian Barnes in *Flaubert's Parrot*, London 1984, p. 80 are the result of a difference in focalizer: the NF_1, her adoring husband, her lovers Leon and Rodolphe, as well as Emma herself.

14. This situation forms the exception to the rule of symmetry. Only when the secondary focalization consists of indirect speech, an internal secondary focalizee corresponds to an internal secondary focalizer: 'character x said to character y to prepare the horses' Here C_y functions as internal secondary focalizee. However, when the embedded focalization consists of perceptions or thoughts, there is no internal secondary focalizee, since human characters cannot 'receive' other characters' perceptions and thoughts, except through words. In these cases an external secondary focalizee corresponds to an internal secondary focalizer. The external $NeFe_1$ does get to know the thoughts, perceptions of the F_2 and this situation of asymmetry can in itself create a certain effect, cp. Bal (1985: 137): "When a character does not hear what another character thinks, and readers do receive information concerning these thoughts, readers may easily come to expect too much of such a character."

15. Examples of categories I and II are discussed in Bal (1977: 41-2 = 1983: 252-3 and 1981: 46-7). Category III (indirect speech) has not been analyzed by her in terms of focalization, but (in my opinion) incorrectly under the heading 'narration': Bal (1985: 134-9). Indirect speech is a form of embedded focalization, because the responsibility for the wording lies with the NF_1, who can choose more or less exactly to represent the words of a character, but the content of these words represents the thoughts/emotions etc. of the character, not of the NF_1.

16. This example neatly shows the role of the NF_1 in the case of an embedding: here we are told to suppose that the content of the character's thoughts was in Dutch. It is the NF_1 who has translated them into English. Uspenskij (1975: 56-61) draws attention to a very similar phenomenon in Tolstoj's *War and peace*: characters which are supposed to speak in French are partly quoted in that language and partly in Russian, a translation by the NF (or 'author' as Uspenskij says).

17. I disagree with Bronzwaer's (1981: 197) analysis of the sentence "Oedipus said that *Momma* was beautiful" as "N narrates: Oedipus (F) said that Momma (N) was beautiful." Just as in the case of "what the devil" in my example (11), I would ascribe "Momma" to the F_2 Oedipus, not to the NF_1.

1. The total percentage of narrator-text (both simple and complex) is 55%. Since the percentage of complex narrator-text (embedded focalization) cannot be given exactly - I have estimated it at about 5% -, the percentage of simple narrator-text of necessity cannot be be given exactly either.

2. See Genette (1972: 122-44 = 1980: 86-112), who calls this aspect "durée"/ "duration" and Bal (1985: 68-77). In section 3.3.3 another aspect of the handling of 'time' (order) will be discussed and there more scholarship will be mentioned.

3. Bal (see previous note) discusses rhythm only on the level of the story, not (as I do) also on that of the text. This is in general a disadvantage of her book, viz. that the relations between the three layers are not worked out systematically. The different aspects of the story-layer also have their correlates in the text-layer. The rigorous separation of the layers is understandable from a didactic point of view, but unsatisfactory from a scholarly one.

4. I use "presented time" and "time of presentation" instead of Müllers "erzählte Zeit" vs. "Erzählzeit" or Bal's "fabula-time" vs. "story-time", since I consider rhythm to be a matter of both focalization and narration.

5. For descriptions filling a pause see Bal (1985: 76-7; 129-33).

6. For more elaborate discussions of 'war' in the *Iliad* see Marg (1942), Wulfert (1955), Harrison (1960), and cp. also Taplin (1980: 15-6) and Schein (1984: 82-4).

7. Cp. e.g. Suerbaum (1968: 153): "*Der Dichter* der Odyssee gehört in Hinsicht auf die Technik des Erzählens zum Typ des *allwissenden Dichters*" (my italics). In this formulation his remark is void: every poet is *qualitate qua* omniscient, since he (re)creates the events. It only makes sense to distinguish between omniscient and restricted narrator-focalizers. One of the few Homerists who explicitly and consistently uses the term 'narrator' is Effe (1983, and see his note 1 on p. 171).

8. See Genette (1972: 228-34 = 1980: 215-23), who distinguishes between posterior, anterior, simultaneous and intercalated narration.

9. The same idea of degeneration is voiced by one of the characters, Nestor (A 271-2), who, himself spanning three generations (A 250-2), is endowed with a surpassing strength (Λ 636-7).

10. The NF$_1$ nowhere refers to himself in such a way as to make clear his sex: the θεὸν ὥς of M 176 provides no clue, since θεός in Homer can refer to both gods and goddesses (cp. e.g. A 516, where Thetis is speaking: ὅσσον ἐγὼ μετὰ πᾶσιν ἀτιμοτάτη θεός εἰμι).

11. Cp. Stanzel (1979: 258): "(im Vergleich zum) körperlosen (aber nicht unper-sönlichen) auktorialen Ich ..."

12. See Zyroff (1971), Parry (1972), Matthews (1980), and Block (1982). For a literary-theoretical approach see Culler (1981: 345-54).

13. For a general discussion of the "potentielle Autoreflexivität des narrativen Diskurses" see Hempfer (1982), who defines it as: "die prinzipielle Möglichkeit

des Erzählens, das Erzählen selbst und nicht nur die Geschichte zum Gegenstand des Diskurses zu machen."

14. Lenz (1980: 31-4) suggests:
> Der Widerspruch zwischen Musenanruf zu Beginn und Äußerung der Eigeninitiative am Ende erklärt sich somit daraus, daß für den Schiffskatalog das den epischen Vortrag einleitende hymnische Proöm und der sowohl hymnische als auch epische Themen einleitende Musenanruf zusammenfallen.

I give a different explanation on p. 48.

15. Cp. Klotz (1965: 14):
> Die Muse verliert nach und nach an Macht und Gewicht. Sie ist es nicht mehr, die, geglaubt oder behauptet, das Lied verkündet: der Erzähler selbst erhebt unumwunden seine Stimme, freilich nicht, ohne sich bei der Gottheit zu versichern und die Muse um Beistand zu bitten.

16. The whole passage M 175-81 was rejected by ancient commentators, followed by Ameis-H. and Leaf, but cp. Zielinski (1905: 430-1):
> eine interessante Klage des Dichters über die Schwierigkeiten, in die ihn die Beobachtung des Incompatibilitätsgesetzes stürzt

and Latacz (1977: 97-8)
> Das Ideal der göttlichen Allwissenheit, die nichts auslassende, vollkommene Abspiegelung also, kann der Dichter nicht erreichen. Aber der Charakter des Stoßseufzers, den diese Aussage trägt, macht deutlich, dass er die Illusion des Vollständigen und Universellen jedenfalls angestrebt hat.

17. Both aspects of this passage have also been commented upon by the scholiasts: (rhetorical question) οὐδὲν δὲ ἔχουσιν εἰς ἐπαιτίασιν, ἀλλ' αὔξουσι τὸ μέγεθος τῆς ὑπὲρ Π. μάχης (A-scholia); (breaking-off) ἡ ἀποσιώπησις τὸ πλῆθος ηὔξησεν (bT-scholia). A comparable rhetorical question is found in γ 113-4 (Nestor is speaking).

18. Cp. also Ameis-H. ad l.: ᾗσι φρεσί: "kraft eigenen Geistes, eigener Erinnerung, ohne Beistand der Muse".

19. For subj.+ ἄν, κεν in a principal clause as emphatic future, see Monro (253) and Chantraine (210-1). Almost the same phrase recurs in δ 240-1 (Helen speaking), λ 328-9.517-8 (Odysseus speaking), again in situations where a speaker, faced with a huge quantity of facts, declines to tell all. Most commentators take 488 as having a potential nuance under the influence of the ἄν + optative clause which follows (490-2): "I could not tell by name - not even if ... - unless the Muses reminded me of how many ..." This would then, according to Krischer (1965), followed by Lenz and Kirk, mean that the poet is not going to give the names of the mass (in contrast to those of the leaders), but their number. Against this interpretation plead: 1) that in the ensuing catalogue only twice numbers of men are given instead of the ships; 2) that apodosis (names) and protasis (number) do not refer to the same; 3) that the logical implication of the passage would be: if the Muses give me the number, I can give the names.

20. Ameis-H., followed by Kirk, mention as a parallel μ 78, but a better one is γ 115-7.

21. As a consequence of the interpretation sketched in note 19, Kirk (ad l.) states that 493 is "the final, summarizing verse" and he translates αὖ with "so". This is incorrect: see *LfgrE* I s.v. 1αⲟⲁα ('andererseits', 'dagegen').

22. Note that in Σ 377 the NF₁ intrudes (with his own admiration) upon the secondary focalization of Thetis (372: εὖρε). In the Odyssean instances of this expression (ζ 306, η 45, θ 366, ν 108) the object of admiration is not always of a divine nature. Cp. Treu (1969: 84): "In den älteren Belegstellen ist tatsächlich noch etwas von einem göttlichen Wunder enthalten."

23. Cp. also Ameis-H. ad E 703: "Zur Andeutung der Menge, indem diese Formel durch Hervorhebung des ersten und letzten das Ganze zusammenfaßt". It is interesting to see that the answer to the Λ 299-300 question consists first of a list of names of the leaders (301-3) and then a simile for the πληθύς (305-9). As in B 488-92, the NF₁ shows his reluctance to give the names of the mass. One of the few places where the mass is endowed with names is E 676-8.

24. Some scholars (e.g. Minton 1960: 304 and Beye 1966: 352) have reasoned the other way around and interpret E 703-4 etc. also as questions directed to the Muses.

25. Differently Bassett (1938: 31): "the poet *casually* invokes the Muses to emphasize the reality of a particular action or episode" (my italics).

26. Δ 457.459, E 38, Z 5.9, Θ 256, Λ 92.420, M 191.378.438, N 170.809, Ξ 402.442, O 454, Π 284.307.399.593, P 597, Φ 392. Cp. also in character-text Λ 738 and Π 558, where the implication is that to be first in doing something is laudatory.

27. Cp. also Kirk (ad B 485-6): "The contrast between divine omniscience and human ignorance is of course a common one."

28. Cp. Lenz (1980: 40): "Unterschiedlich ist lediglich der Grad der Genauigkeit und Zuverläßigkeit". I do not agree with the interpretations Krischer and Lenz give for κλέος: Krischer (1965: 9) contrasts κλέος = the story to 'knowledge of the Muses' = the catalogues; Lenz (1980: 40-1) considers the general indication of the theme in the proem the result of κλέος whereas the remainder of the poem originates in the Muses' knowledge.

29. This idea of the autopsy of the Muses is based in the first place on πάρεστε ('you are present', sc. at the moment and place of the events of the fabula). Others (e.g. Lesher 1981: 12-3) also point to the original meaning of οἶδα: 'I have seen' (from the Indo-European root *weid-*, also present in Latin *video* and German *wissen*).

30. For the great value attributed to an eyewitness report cp. θ 487-91 and Murray (1981: 92-4), Walsh (1984: 8-19).

31. Cp. Thornton (1984: 36, n. 20): "What is described is ... a privilege rather than a weakness".

32. In contrast to an amateur like Achilles in I 186-9. Cp. also Redfield's (1979: 98-9) remark on θεά:

he addresses her, relatively informally as 9εά. This vocative is proper, not to
a prayer such as this invocation but to a face-to-face conversation with a
goddess ... To pray to a goddess simply as 9εά ... assumes that the correct
goddess will know she is being addressed and this in turn assumes a preexisting
relation between speaker and goddess.

33. Lesky's analysis is accepted by Murray (1979: 96-8), but rejected by Walsh
(1984: 11-3) as "naive psychology".

34. Cp. J. Wackernagel, *Vorlesungen über Syntax* I (Basel) 1920: 109-11: "Es wird
eine ideale Person angeredet, etwa "wenn du, Hörer des Dichters, dabei gewesen
wärest, hättest du ihn nicht schlaff gesehen"."

35. I owe this parallel to Gerry Wakker.

36. Cp. Block (1982: 13): "the narrator suggests to the audience its own active
observing presence, by attributing to it the fear and confusion with which *he
intends the scene to be understood*" (my italics). Grammarians (K.G. 1: 232,
Chantraine: 220-1, Goodwin: 162) tend to analyze this type of optative as potential,
but in view of the persuasion inherent in them ('you would surely', not 'you
would probably') it seems better to analyze them as counterfactual.

37. Cp. R.G. Austin, *Virgil Aeneid IV* (Oxford) 1973: ad l.: "the vivid present
subjunctive puts the distant scene actually before the reader's eyes as it happens."

38. K.G. (1: 212-3) analyze Δ 421 and Π 638 as "Potential der Vergangenheit":
"da konnte ergreifen, oder hätte ergreifen können, da ergriff wohl".

39. A good example of such an anonymous focalizer can be found in the first
pages of Part Two of Flaubert's *Madame Bovary*, where the city of Yonville is
described as seen by a traveller, who is referred to with "on" or "vous". See
also Bal (1981-2).

40. Or as the anonymous author of *On the sublime* says (26.3): the use of the
second person verb form makes the hearer ἐμπαθέστερον ('more moved'), προσεκ-
τίκωτερον ('more attentive') and ἀγῶνος ἔμπλεων ('full of anxiety'). Cp. also
the bT-scholion ad Δ 223a:+προσευκτικὸν+ δὲ λίαν εἰς Ἀγαμέμνονα τὸν
ἀκροατὴν ποιεῖ.

41. For this terminology see Leech (1974: 106-8). I am grateful to Miek Hoffmann,
who has helped me find my way in the vast literature on negations.

42. See Weinrich (1975: 55): "die Verneinung setzt immer eine positive Erwartung
voraus, die dann verworfen wird. Ebensogut kann man sagen, die Verneinung
setze immer eine positive Vorinformation voraus, aus der sich überhaupt erst die
Erwartung bilden kann."

43. On the passage Π 140-4 see Armstrong (1958: esp. 346-7), Shannon (1975: 27,
30, 70) and Bannert (1984). Note that the passage was rejected by Zenodotus,
followed by Ameis-H.

44. Of the 252 γάρ-clauses in the Iliadic narrator-text, 70 occur after a negated
statement. Other examples from the first five books: B 37.39.687.688.755.834,

Γ 453.454, Δ 480.532.543, E 87.517.622.667.

45. I leave out of account altogether: 1) regular (litotic) combinations like οὐδ' ἀπίθησε ('and he/she did not disobey'), for which see Donnelly (1929-30); 2) cases where the negative statement follows after a positive statement and only repeats the information of that first statement, e.g. Λ 350 καὶ βάλεν, οὐδ' ἀφάμαρτε ('and he hit and did not miss').

46. Other examples: A 318-9 (refers back to A 181-5).495-6 (A 393-412), O 240 οὐδ' ἔτι κεῖτο (O 9: κείμενον).

47. Cp. A 511, Δ 401, E 689, Z 342 etc., where a character does not answer when addressed. In general see Beßlich (1966).

48. Other examples: N 30, Ξ 228, P 463.

49. A 330, B 419.642, Γ 302, Δ 198, E 89.90.94.333.621.674, H 433, Θ 126, K 336, Λ 376, M 3.53.113.184.304.351.460, N 302.510.513.521.712, Ξ 18, O 236.274.674.708, Π 601.676, P 9.401.497.702, Y 8.398.421, Φ 495.608, X 136.200.328.371, Ψ 388.690.

50. Cp. E 621-2 = N 510-1. Other examples: A 490-1 (and cp. B 686); with forms of τλῆ, ἔτλη: E 21 (cp. Ameis-H.: "was man unter solchen Verhältnisse hätte erwarten sollen"), Θ 78-9, P 733-4, Φ 608-10, X 136-7; with forms of μένειν: Ξ 488-9, Π 659.

51. Other examples: E 94.571, N 142, Ξ 33, O 407.450.585.617.651, Π 815, P 276.292. A comparable effect is reached in M 393 with ὅμως (and cp. καὶ ὥς in the positive statement Π 363).

52. Other examples: Γ 348 = H 259 = P 44, Λ 96.236.352, M 184.404-5, N 371-2 = 397-8.607, Π 813, Y 398, X 328.

53. For an example of a wounding-scene where the NeFe₁ knows more than the characters involved, see Δ 127-87, to be discussed below section 4.2, p. 125.

54. Other examples: Λ 80 (reacts to 78-9), M 262 (261-2), N 808 (806-7), Ξ 423-4 (422-3), T 312-3 (312: τέρποντες), X 295 (294-5), Ψ 100 (99).184 (182-3).

55. Other examples: B 419.873, Γ 302, E 674-5, M 3 (and cp. 9).113-5, P 497-8, Y 466. The last 4 examples contain μέλλω, to which I return below p. 87 and cp. Basset (1979: 60-1) on the use of μέλλω to announce a tragic destiny: "Cette valeur est la plus fréquente, soit qu'il s'agisse d'un malheur à venir, soit qu'on indique que les espoirs qui animent les personnages ne seront pas réalisés (l'expression a souvent alors la forme négative)."

56. Comparable passages are Λ 497-501, N 521-5.674-6, P 377-80. 401-11. All these passages with 'character x has not heard ...', except the one in X, have been suspected by ancient and modern commentators of being interpolations (see Leaf ad ll.), most probably because they present non-events and as such could be 'missed'. Especially Aristarchus was always keen on making the story to be told as economically as possible: see Schenkeveld (1970).

57. See Griffin (1980: 109-10) and Segal (1971b).

58. I disagree on this point with Griffin (1980: 97): "the pattern of her weaving is unimportant". Better: Segal (1971b: 40) "Her embroidery ... contains the symbols of life and hope."

59. Fenik (1968: 175) calls them "extreme situations". Schadewaldt's use of "beinahe" and "fast" (1938: 15, 55, 70, 150, 153) refers to something else, viz. the phenomenon that in the *Iliad* a programmatic announcement (e.g. Zeus' announcement of Hector's victory in Λ 191-4) is not executed straightaway, but with many chances of fulfilment first being "bypassed".

60. Kühner-Gerth (1: 214) discuss E 22; (2: 469) Λ 750, E 897, Θ 90.132; Cp. also Chantraine (226-7) and Tabachovitz (1951: 47-9). For the three optative cases see K.G. (1: 232), Chantraine (220-1).

61. Leaf (ad Y 289) finds this "whole sentence, with its long chain of unrealised possibilities, by no means in the Homeric manner."

62. For a detailed discussion of the relation Diomedes-Nestor in the *Iliad* see Andersen (1978: 111-24).

63. The function of this passage seems to be to heighten the suspense: Diomedes now has to save Nestor 'on his own' (99: αὐτός περ ἐών).

64. On the denomination ὁ γέρων see also below chapter 6, note 6.

65. Leaf (ad N 725) has completely overlooked this connection between *if not*-situation and speech, in particular the telling contrast between λευγαλέως-ἀπήμονες: "(Polydamas') ultimate advice to hold a council on the advisibility of retreat is at least surprising, and shews him in the light of a *mere coward, instead of a sage adviser*" (my italics).

66. A different interpretation is given by Fränkel (1976: 83), viz. that the poet enhances Patroclus' heroism, by letting him almost take Troy, and by the fated course of events being maintained only through the intervention of a god.

67. According to the *LfgrE* I s.v. ἀναλκείη (col. 778) the expression ἀναλκείῃσι δαμέντας (P 320.337 and cp. Z 74) is in itself not pejorative.

68. The epithet ὑψίπυλον is found only in these two near captures and in Z 416, where the real capture of Thebes is mentioned.

69. In view of the echoing of ὑμεῖς ... ἐρητύειν ἐπέεσσιν (B 75) in σοῖς δ' ἀγανοῖς ἐπέεσσιν ἐρήτυε (164 and 180) and ἀγανοῖς ἐπέεσσιν ἐρητύσασκε (189) I do not agree with Bergold's (1977: 13) interpretation of 75: "sie sollen den ungestümen Kampfeswillen mässigen und in die geordneten Bahnen einer disziplinierten Schlachtvorbereitung lenken."

70. I follow Ebeling (255) in taking οὐ ... πω as temporal ('not ... yet'), not as modal (so Willcock "and still ... they would not").

71. For other instances of divine jealousy, see *LfgrE* I s.v. ἄγαμαι B 2bβ (col. 33-4).

72. Notice also the Trojans' joy at seeing Hector return 'unharmed' (307-10) and, conversely, Ajax' joy at his 'victory' (312: see also below, ch. 4, pp. 101-2).

73. Cp. Andersen (1981: 326) in reply to Levy (1979), who had maintained that gods were at some stage thought to be mortal: "Ares dying in the brazen jug is not only hypothetical and past possibility, it is an ad hoc possibility in Book 5. The scene must be understood first, in the light of the general tenor of that book, in which some gods appear rather too human ... and ... second ... in the light of the fact that the Ares-paradeigma is coloured by its context (388a = 311a)."

74. For a discussion of the relation between tradition and history see Häußler (1976: 21-38), who also gives the relevant scholarship.

75. Cp. Stallmach's (1968: 36) analysis of another, normal counterfactual (Π 686-7): "eine Denk-, keine Realmöglichkeit".

76. For the idea that fate coincides with the traditional ("historical") course of events, see Heden (1912: 177), Fränkel (1976: 63-4) and Redfield (1975: 133). Fate can also coincide with the specific plot of the Διὸς βουλή, which presumably has been invented by the poet of the *Iliad*, rather than taken over from tradition. Such a 'literary' exploitation of fate does not mean that it was not seen as a religious concept anymore, just as the 'divine machinery' does not rob the gods of their religious status.

77. Genette (1972: 90 = 1980: 48) speaks of "récit premier" as "le niveau temporel de récit par rapport auquel une anachronie se définit comme telle". He is inclined to take the boundaries of the "récit premier" as flexible, including e.g. in the case of the *Odyssey* Odysseus' travel stories. I disagree and consider these travel stories a flash-back (external analepsis). Cp. also my strict definition of mirror-stories vs. the looser one of Létoublon: de Jong (1985a: 18, n. 3).

78. See also Müller (1970) and Rutherford (1982: 153-8) on prolepses concerning Sarpedon, Hector, Patroclus and Achilles.

79. But not always interpreted rightly by them, cp. O 270-80, where Zeus thunders in support of the Greeks, an omen which is interpreted as favourable by the Trojans, who attack the Greeks with even more gusto.

80. For a survey of scholarship and an analysis of dramatic irony in the *Odyssey* see Dekker (1965). The study by J. Piechowski entitled *De ironia Iliadis* (1856) is not very useful, since here a great number of passages are simply collected without commentary or systematics.

81. Other examples: B 38, M 113-5, Π 685-7, P 497-8, Σ 311-3, Y 466. νήπιος is also found outside prolepses: B 873-5, M 127-30, Y 264-6, X 445-6.

82. After an optimistic speech (Σ 298-309), optimistic embedded focalization (B 37, M 110-2.125-6, P 495-6, Y 464-5) or a description of activities which imply optimism (B 872, Π 684-5, X 440-4). Observe that the prolepses following after νήπιος are often in a negative form (cp. Kirk ad B 38).

83. Cp. Otis (1963: 70): "*infelix* is a key-word - a finger-pointing word - that foreshadows future tragedy and at the same time expresses sympathy: it is the

word for those who oppose fate or whom fate opposes but are yet worthy of true pity".

84. For a full discussion of μέλλω in the Homeric poems see Basset (1979: 35-107). My examples of μέλλω forming part of a prolepsis coincide with Basset's série II ("destinée dans le passé") except for Λ 54, Π 460, which Basset analyzes (p. 51) as examples of his série I ("imminence dans le passé"). Note that in those cases where a character itself will bring about the fulfilment of the event announced in the prolepsis (Zeus in B 39, Λ 54, O 601) μέλλω acquires a sense of intentionality, which Basset, in my opinion incorrectly, recognizes for his série I only, e.g. ad Λ 21-2 (p. 51), Λ 700-3 (p. 53) or ζ 135-6 (p. 55).

85. In F. Truffaut, *Hitchcock*. London 1969, 128. I owe this reference to Albert Rijksbaron.

86. Cp. Austin (1966: 311): "digressions are not a release from tension, but a concentration of tension"; Müller (1984: 109): "(the) seeming digressions and endless descriptions are, like still shots or slow-motion sequences, moments of heightened suspense".

87. Two other effective internal analepses are Φ 4-5: the reference to the panic of the Greeks and Hector's triumph on the previous day underscores the contrast with the present situation, where Achilles is routing the Trojans; Ψ 63-4 (at the moment Patroclus' ghost comes to Achilles, the NF$_1$ tells that Achilles was fast asleep, 'for he had tired his body pursuing Hector').

88. Cp. Kullmann (1964: 20): "Dabei ist sehr auffallend, daß Vergangenes und Künftiges in den direkten Reden der epischen Personen stärker zum Ausdruck kommt als durch Bericht"; the same observation already in Balensiefen (1955: 21).

89. Griffin (1980: 130) in my opinion takes one step too many when he says (on account of O 361-6): "(it) conveys the poet's sense of vain human effort, and also the divine scale, on which nothing achieved or endured by men *can be really serious*" (my italics). This last addition robs the whole *Iliad* of its *raîson d' être*.

90. Cp. Moulton (1977: 72): "the simile does convey an impression of overwhelming force, somehow random or uncommitted in the very ease of its exercise".

91. Cp. Reinhardt (1961: 267-9: the passage deals with "Ruhm und Vergänglichkeit") and Schein (1984: 30): "the effect is to set the brilliant deeds of Achilles and the Trojan War as a whole in an ironic perspective that makes them no less beautiful or heroic but much more affecting".

92. On the description of objects in the *Iliad* in general see Willenbrock (1944).

93. Other examples: Z 395-7 (cp. in Andromache's speech 413-28), K 314-7 (378-81), N 427-33 (464-6, but note that the information of 466 is new), Ξ 463 (473-4), O 430-2 (437-9), P 575-7 (589-90), Y 382-5 (389-92, and see Jordan 1905: 117-8 and Reinhardt 1961: 430), Φ 141-3 (157-9 and 184-7).

94. For presupposition in linguistics see Levinson (1983: 167-225); in literary theory Culler (1981: 111-31). My use of presupposition comes closest to Culler's

"pragmatic presupposition".

95. Less often we find ἐπεί, e.g. K 79.500-1, Λ 498, Π 639, Υ 270, Φ 163, Ψ 743. Once οὕνεκα: B 580. For examples of γάρ see below notes 98 and 99. For a linguistic analysis of γάρ and ἐπεί see Rijksbaron (1976: 67-106).

96. Cp. also Lang (1984: 154, n. 27): "the ubiquity of gar in the Histories ... is evidence of the historian's readiness to explain. To what extent this readiness is a result or in anticipation of audience reactions is, of course, impossible to say, but it seems likely to be considerable."

97. Cp. also Gährken (1950: 28): "Der Zuhörer möchte sich verwundert fragen, wieso Achill dazu kam".

98. Other examples: B 221, Δ 437, Θ 311, Λ 180.600, Ψ 530-1.865. Often the γάρ-clause does not so much give a causal explanation as an elaboration: A 12, Δ 467.518, Λ 74, P 727, Σ 373-4, Φ 180.

99. Other examples: E 51, Λ 111-2, Σ 168.311, T 49, Φ 24, Ψ 137. Note that in all these cases, except B 409, the word to be explained is in runover position.

100. For "digressif-permanent" τε see Ruijgh (1971), for the use of gnomic aorist, present/perfect indicative in similes esp. 255-66, distributive-iterative subjunctive 291-2.

101. This idea was advocated for the first time by Platt in *AJP* 24 (1896: 28-38) and is supported by e.g. Severyns (1948: 153-64), Fränkel (1976: 44), Lesky, RE suppl. XI s.v. Homeros (748: "Die Gleichnisse, die ja wie Fenster einen Blick auf die Umwelt Homers freigeben").

102. I base myself on Ruijgh (1971: 359-60, 374, 877-84), who provides numerous examples. These other categories of "permanent facts" can, but need not be, characterized by τε or gnomic aorist.

103. Remarkable in this respect is the use of the article with demonstrative force in A 11 τὸν Χρύσην ('that man Chryses'): (Ameis-H.) "den aus der Sage oder aus andern Liedern bekannten", (Willcock) "either Chryses was a well-known figure in the saga or else the poet wishes to give the impression that he was"); and in Υ 147 τὸ κῆτος ('that monster').

104. The same topographical vagueness in Virgil's *Aeneid*, see Heinze (1915: 350-4).

105. "Weder konnte ja der Sänger gemeinsame 'Erinnerung' reaktivieren (niemand, weder er noch seine Hörer, war dabeigewesen) noch konnte er direkte 'Aktualisierung' evozieren (denn Dimensionen wie die geschilderten waren ihm wie sein Publikum empirisch unbekannt ...) Die raumzeitliche Koordinatensystem seiner Erzählung mußte also vom Sänger 'fingiert' und von seinen Hörern dementsprechend 'rekonstruiert' werden."

1. I have come across only one discussion of perspective in the *Iliad*: Balensiefen (1955: 61-4), whose conclusion, however, I do not share: "Alles Geschehen der Ilias wird grundsätzlich aus des Dichters eigener Perspektive gesehen. Er bedient sich keines Mediums, das für ihn sieht und erzählt."

2. This list does not give all Homeric verbs of perceiving (e.g. παπταίνω: 'look around' is lacking), but only those which are found construed with an object, containing the embedded focalization. The same criterion is used in the case of the verbs of thinking/feeling and speaking.

3. Notice that μέγα ἔργον only occurs in embedded focalization (M 416: σφισι φαίνετο), or character-text (Λ 734, Π 208, T 150).

4. Other examples: K 524 (μέρμερα: 'baneful'), Ξ 13 (ἀεικές: 'grievous'), Φ 527 (πελώριον: 'monstrously big') and X 370 (ἀγητός: 'admirable'). See also below section 4.3.

5. Other examples: N 207 (υἰωνοῖο), Ξ 156 (αὐτοκασίγνητον καὶ δαέρα), Φ 469 (πατροκασιγνήτοιο). As a matter of fact, substitution of a proper name by an indirect reference is also found outside secondarily focalized passages, e.g. A 441: (τὴν) ... πατρὶ φίλῳ ἐν χερσὶ τίθει: 'and her he put back in her dear fathers hands'. This whole subject of denomination deserves a more detailed investigation.

6. Cp. A 23 (ἱερῆα).331 (βασιλῆα), Δ 402 (βασιλῆος), Φ 207 (τὸν ἄριστον) and ἀρχόν (B 703 = 726, B 778).

7. Cp. Macleod (ad Ω 702): "the lack of the name is expressive: 'him' can mean only one person to Cassandra and the Trojans".

8. Differently Ameis-H., who maintain that the Trojans see Patroclus. This problem, whether the trick works or not, is not discussed in Van Scheliha (1943). For the "Waffentausch" in general see Reinhardt (1961: 308-40).

9. Note that in a modern text the same effect might have been reached by printing 'Achilles', meaning 'Patroclus pretending to be Achilles'. Such typographical indications, however, could not be used in a text like the *Iliad*, which was originally meant to be heard. Cp. also below section 6.1, p. 196 on the necessity of speech-introductions.

10. A comparable case is Ω 355 (ἄνδρ' ὁρόω) vs. 352-3 (τὸν ... ἐφράσσατο ... Ἑρμείαν). Cp. also (no embedded focalization): K 82-5 (after 81) and Φ 150 (139-41).

11. Other examples: A 56 (refers back to 51-2), Δ 467 (463-6), E 95-6 (87, 93-4).166 (144-65).572 (570).711-2 (703-10), etc.

12. Cp. Denniston (1954: 416): "In Homer, οὖν almost invariably follows ἐπεί or ὡς, in a subordinate temporal clause, which refers to something previously described or implied". Of the 34 cases of οὖν in the Iliadic narrator-text 18 are found in the context of a perception-passage: Γ 21.30.154.396, E 95.711, H 17, Θ 251, Λ 248.575.581, Ξ 440, Π 419, P 198, Σ 222.530, Φ 49.418.

13. Another example is M 336. Γ 396-7 is somewhat problematical since the NF₁ had told that Aphrodite had assumed the shape of an old woman (386-8). I favour the interpretation of Bergold (1977: 118): (in 396-7) "wird die Maske der alten Frau langsam gehoben".

14. Other examples: A 600 (ποιπνύοντα repeats in a different formulation 597-8), Γ 30-1 (29), H 308-9 (307; cp. E 515 which repeats 514).

15. Cp. Smith (1981: 141, n. 127) with reference to the *Hymn to Aphrodite*: "It appears that an emphasis on sight is made when an emotional reaction is to be immediate, as when Aphrodite first sees Anchises (56 f.), when Anchises first sees Aphrodite (84), when he first sees her in her true form (181 f.), or now when he will first see Aineias (278 f.)."

16. Other examples: A 599-600, H 214-6, Θ 278-9, M 208-9, N 86-7.494-5, O 279-80.

17. Other examples: E 95-9.571-2, H 17-20, Λ 459-60, Ξ 440-1. It is interesting to note that many perception-passages form part of *circumstantial* ὡς or ἐπεί-clauses (for examples see note 12): "when there not only exists a temporal relationship between a ὡς/ἐπεί-clause and its main clause, but the main clause also expresses *a reaction to* what is expressed in the ὡς/ἐπεί-clause - a reaction which is based upon *an observation by* the subject of the main clause of the event(s) referred to in the subordinate clause -, such a ὡς-clause may be said to express the circumstances that occasion the event of the main clause." (Rijksbaron 1976: 115, my italics)

18. Other examples of perception-passages followed by a speech: Γ 154 (followed by direct speech 156-60: this indirect presentation of Helen's beauty was much admired by Lessing in his *Laokoon* xx1), Δ 79-80 (82-4).148-9 (155-62).151 (184-7).232 (234-9).240 (242-9).255 (257-64).283 (285-91).311 (313-6), E 166 (171-8).596 (601-6) etc. Only very seldom is a perception described in direct speech which has not been prepared by embedded focalization: e.g. Λ 526-7, Π 127.

19. Other examples: Γ 157 (τοιῆδ'), Δ 243 (οὕτως), E 174-5 (τῷδ' ... ἀνδρὶ, ... ὅδε).604 (κεῖνος).717 (οὕτω).761 (τοῦτον), Θ 282 (οὕτως), etc.

20. Cp. Jordan (1904: 6): "... durch welches Mittel der Dichter seine Helden in Bewegung bringt, er läßt den einen von anderen erblickt werden ... dieses Mittel ... wird sehr oft in der Ilias verwendet, so oft daß es sich als beliebtestes erweist." Cp. also Hellwig (1964: 90-3).

21. Other examples: Δ 467, E 166.565, N 560, Ω 699.

22. This procedure in drama is, of course, conditioned by the rule of *unity of place*. For novels cp. Hatcher (1944: 358, n. 3): "To the device A voit disparaître B may be compared the far more frequent A voit paraître B, which serves to usher a new character on stage." She gives as an example from Flaubert, *Madame Bovary*: "Alors on vit descendre du carosse un monsieur vêtu d'un habit court ..."

23. The correspondence with perception-passages becomes very clear e.g. in B 188 (κιχείη) next to 198 (ἴδοι ... ἐφεύροι) or Δ 89-91 (εὗρε) next to 200-2 (ἐνό-ησεν). An interesting passage in this respect is *Odyssey* ε 58 (τέτμεν) to which corresponds 73-5 (θηήσαιτο ἰδὼν ... θηεῖτο): here it is made explicit that the

whole description ε 59-73 has been focalized by Hermes. See also Müller (1968: 123-37) and Elliger (1975: 128-32).

24. On Achilles breaking his fast here, see Edwards (1987: 89).

25. Cp. K.G. (1: 152): "das griechische Plusquamperfekt ... eignet ... sich wie das Imperfekt zu Beschreibungen und Schilderungen."
Imperfect: B 171, Γ 125-8.384, Δ 331-2, Z 324, I 189-90, K 152.154.155 (εὖδ').182, Λ 474, N 460, O 240-2, T 6, Ω 84-5.162.164.166.473-6.
Pluperfect: B 19 (κέχυϑ'), Δ 329.331 (ἔστασαν).334.367, E 356, Z 373, K 153.155 (ἔστρωτο).156.

26. Other examples: B 171, Γ 128, Δ 334-5, E 795, Λ 474-81, M 122-3, Σ 3-4.373-80.

27. Examples: B 23 εὖδεις (refers back to 18-9), Δ 340 (333-5), K 37 (34), O 245 (240), T 8 τοῦτον (4: Πατρόκλῳ). For the relation in Z 326 of χόλον τόνδ' ('this anger') and the embedded focalization of 321-4, see Hijmans (1975).

28. For this kind of deliberation-passages see Arend (1933: 106-115) and Voigt (1972). Deliberations can also be presented as monologues, see Fenik (1978a) and for a comparison between "stumme Überlegung" and "Gesprächsstellen" see Barck (1976: 33-6).

29. Other examples: A 430 (βίη ἀέκοντος), B 473 (διαρραῖσαι).690 (πολλὰ μόγησας), Γ 28 (ἀλείτην).112 (ὀϊζυροῦ), Δ 402 (αἰδοίοιο), M 103 (διακριδόν), P 365 (αἰπύν). See further below section 4.3.

30. For a general discussion of final clauses in Homer see Wakker (1987).

31. Other examples of this type of indirect question (not preceded by a question verb): B 794, Δ 334-5, H 415-6, I 191, K 189, Ξ 507, Σ 508, X 321, Ψ 749.

32. Other examples of correspondence between final clauses and direct speech: H 439 (340), Σ 147 (143-4), T 354 (348), Ψ 435-7 (428), Ω 285 (287). Additional indications that final clauses are secondarily focalized are: the so called sympathetic datives in E 24 and M 334; the correspondence in Φ 249-50 with the deliberation-passage Φ 137-8 and in Υ 464-5 the contrast between the intention of the character and the omniscience of the NF$_1$ (466).

33. Sometimes ὡς is used with a causal nuance, e.g. Z 109, Π 600. See Monro (238-9) and Ruijgh (1971: 538-40).

34. Other examples: γάρ: E 22 (after οὐδ' ἔτλη περιβῆναι, cp. Ameis-H. "Diese objektiv vom Dichter gegebene Begründung für seine Flucht ist zugleich die Erwägung die Idaios bestimmt"), Φ 24 (δειδιότες); οὕνεκα: A 11 (χολωϑείς), Σ 248 (ἔχε τρόμος), Ψ 386-7 (χωομένοιο); ὅτ(τ)ι: A 56 (κήδετο), E 326 (τίεν), Ξ 407 + X 292 (χώσατο), O 156 (ἐχολώσατο), Π 531+ P 568 (γήϑησεν), Ψ 556 (χαίρων).

35. Other examples: γάρ: A 56, E 566, K 355, M 125, N 214, O 596, Π 609.713.866, Σ 34, Φ 468; ἐπεί: M 407, Φ 146. It is to be noted that not all causal clauses

following upon a deliberate and conscious action are focalized doubly, e.g. Z 300: Theano opened the door of Athena's temple 'for her the Trojans had made priestess of Athena'. Here the γάρ-clause does not give Theano's reason for opening the door.

36. Cp. also above ch. 3, example 59. Other examples: γάρ: M 52, O 612, P 625, Φ 51; οὕνεκα: Λ 54, T 54-6, Y 409; ἐπεί: B 171, E 536, P 577.

37. Other examples: Z 108-9.501-2, M 106-7.125-6.261-2, N 41-2.89, Π 281-2, P 286-7.395-7, Ω 167-8.

38. Other examples: A 536-8 (in her ensuing speech Hera dissimulates her knowledge), B 3-4 (at this stage Zeus keeps his plan secret), O 728 (Ajax thinks he is going to die and retreats, but when he adhorts his men in 733-41, he nowhere expresses his pessimism), Φ 468-9 (αἰδώς had not figured in Apollo's speech). See also De Jong (1985c: 518), where I suggested that the flash-back about Odysseus' scar is effectively presented as embedded focalization (with Eurycleia as F_2), because Penelope is not (yet) to recognize Odysseus.

39. The same question could be asked in Σ 343-5, X 442-4, and Ψ 40-1.

40. There does not exist a systematic treatment of Homeric indirect speech (but cp. Létoublon 1983: 38-40), presumably because it is not found very frequently.

41. In fact, there are more possibilities, here irrelevant, of speech representation: for a synopsis of recent scholarship see Rimmon-Kenan (1983: 106-16).

42. Hentze (1904: 14), and cp. Von Scheliha (1943: 378), suggests that the predominance of direct speech is the result of "der noch mangelhaften Ausbildung der Syntax, da die Formen der erzählten Rede noch nicht so allseitig entwickelt oder doch noch nicht so geläufig waren, daß größere Gedankenreihen sich darin ohne Schwierigkeiten wiedergeben ließen". This seems unlikely in view of the fact that declarative verbs + infinitive are already found in Mycenaean tablets, e.g. PY ED 704, 5-6. I am not convinced either by Friedemann (1910: 158-9), who ascribes the rarity of indirect speech to a primitive narrative style: "die Abstraktionsfähigkeit reicht nicht so weit, Einzelheiten unter bestimmten Gesichtspunkte zusammenzufassen und das Wichtige vom Unwichtigen zu scheiden."

43. Other examples: Z 240-1, I 179-81, Λ 47-8 = M 84-5, Y 5-6, Ψ 196-8.

44. Cp. Führer (1967: 148, n. 22), who rightly notes that "dem Volk wenigstens eine indirekte Rede bisweilen zugestanden wird."

45. Orders to soldiers: A 313, B 280, M 49-50.467-8, O 687-8, etc.; to servants: Γ 259-60, I 10-12.658-9, O 119-20, Σ 343-4.469, X 442-3, Ψ 39-40; to individuals: Γ 119-20, Δ 229-30, Λ 273-4 = 399-400, Π 145.727-8, Y 4-5, Ψ 563-4.

46. Other examples: Γ 120.260, Θ 319, I 660-1, etc. Cp. also LfgrE I s.v. ἄνωγα B (col. 692): "In der Erz. wird es meistens da gebraucht, wo zu erwarten ist, daß die Aufforderung usw. ohne weiteres befolgt werden wird". Sometimes it is only the backward referring particle οὖν which indicates that an order is obeyed, e.g. A 54 ἀγορήνδε καλέσσατο λαὸν 'Αχιλλεύς which is followed in 57 by οἱ δ' ἐπεὶ οὖν ἤγερθεν.

47. Other examples: Σ 167 (followed by direct speech 170-80), Ψ 204 ἕζεσθαι ... ἀνήνατο (205: οὐχ ἕδος). In Δ 301-2 and Ψ 854 the indirect speech even merges into direct speech.

48. Other examples: B 597-8, N 666-8.

49. For literature on the shield see Friedrich (1975: 50-1) and cp. also Taplin (1980).

50. For this type of dative see Chantraine (74, par. 96): "dans certains tours, le datif d'intérêt exprime le point de vue, la situation ou le sentiment d'une personne"; and K.G. (1: 421).

51. Other examples: δηΐων ἀνδρῶν ἀλεωρήν in M 57 and O 533.

52. Other examples: N 2, P 131.548-9.

53. Other examples: Δ 115, H 481 (πρίν λεῖξαι), O 588, Π 322, Φ 578. Note that πρίν + infinitive need not always have a final nuance: N 172, Ξ 19, X 156. Cp. Chantraine (315): "Il y a une différence entre l'exemple de Π 332, (cf. Θ 453, N 172, etc.) et celui de Z 464 (cf. O 588, etc.): le premier constate un fait, le second exprime une intention."

54. Contrast E 63-4, where the relative clause explaining ἀρχεκάκους clearly derives from the NF₁.

55. Cp. Kakridis (1971: 110) and Griffin (1980: 97): "it shows her aware of her own role in causing all distress". I disagree with Bergold (1977: 55): "hier zeigt er (sc. the poet, IdJ) sie beinahe kindlich unbekümmert. Nur aus ganz weiter Distanz scheint sie an dem Geschehen, dessen Mittelpunkt sie eigentlich ist, teilzuhaben, ja nicht einmal teilzuhaben, sondern es nunmehr zur Kenntnis zu nehmen" and with Macleod (1983: 11): "she is detached enough to be the artist of her own fateful deeds".

56. Cp. K.G. (1: 561-2): "Das Reflexivpronomen kann im Griechischen ... auch ... in Nebensätzen gebraucht werden, wenn dieselben *aus der Seele des Subjektes im Hauptsatze*, also als Gedanken desselben, ausgesagt werden."

57. For πελώριος see also below, section 4.2, p. 130.

58. This section is a revised version of my article 'Fokalization und die homerische Gleichnisse': de Jong (1985b). Cp. also Bremer (1986). For an interesting discussion of subjectivity in Virgilian similes see Williams (1983: 165-83: "the problem of aspect in similes"). As a matter of fact, Williams (as many Virgil-scholars, see note 49 of chapter 1) stresses the objectivity of the Homeric similes too much (see also below note 69).

59. I follow Coffey (1957: 113) in distinguishing between comparisons, which have no finite verb of their own, and similes, which do have one or more.

60. For syntax see Ruijgh (1971: 846-84); classifications according to subject-matter Wilkins (1919-20) and Scott (1974: 56-95).

61. See also Scott (1974: 42-50). I have not been able to consult: H. Storch, *Die Erzählfunktion der homerischen Gleichnisse* (diss. Tübingen) 1937 and W. Elliger, *Gleichnis und Vergleich bei Homer und den griechischen Tragikern* (diss. Tübingen) 1956.

62. Figures based on the appendix in Scott (1974: 191-200).

63. Cp. the following passage from D. Lodge's *Small World*:
> The spin-drier cycle of Hilary Swallow's washing machine makes a sound *not unlike a jetplane*, especially when she punches the button to stop the motor, and the piercing whine of the rotating drum dies away, falling in pitch, *just like* the engines of a jumbo jet ... *The similarity does not strike Hilary* ... for the sound made by a jet engine is less *familiar* to her than it is to her husband ... (my italics).

64. This same simile occurs in I 14-5, there in connection with Agamemnon. For this repetition see Moulton (1977: 103-4).

65. Is the repeated emphasis on the darkness of the water (3: μελάνυδρος, 4: δνοφερόν) meant to illustrate the mental state of Agamemnon and Patroclus (so Fränkel 1921: 21 and n.1 and cp. Scott 1979: 194, who qualifies the simile as "psychological")? According to the *LfgrE* II s.v. δνοφερός, this word does not have the association 'gloomy'. The other occurrences of μελάνυδρος (Π 160, Φ 257, υ 158) do not point to an association with a dark mood.

66. Other examples of comparisons or similes referring to the same event: M 132-6:167-72 (speech Asius), Π 742-3: 745-50 (Patroclus' speech can be considered one long and ironic simile, see Moulton 1979: 287). One could also compare Ξ 295-6, where the NF₁'s statement concerning Zeus' passion is as it were surpassed by the long priamel in Zeus' speech (315-28), see Race (1982: 36).

67. For the symbolic function of the imagery of the "Glanz der Waffen" see Krischer (1971: 36-8).

68. An extra argument for this interpretation might be the accusative ὥς τ' ἀστέρ(α) after τὸν ... παμφαίνοντ'. Cp. also Fränkel (1921: 48): "Warum mit einem Mal diese ganz andere Stimmung? Weil wir hier den Achaierhelden mit den Augen des Priamos sehen" and Coffey (1957: 118, n. 21): "X 26, where the primary function of the simile is to illustrate a warrior's appearance. But by implication the psychological reaction of Priamos to the appearance of Achilles is illustrated."

69. And an antidote to Williams (1983: 166):
> such objectivity toward the context is certainly one aspect of similes that can be traced back to the Homeric models. It is the poet who claims to see and establish the similarities between the context and the simile; there is no suggestion that the characters in the narrative would have viewed the situation in the terms of the simile. In this sense, the simile is authorial, impartial, objective.

70. Not all comparisons and similes occurring in a secondarily focalized context are assimilated: Δ 141-7 (see above, p. 125), Λ 474-81 (secondary focalizers in the context are Ajax and Menelaus, who 'found' Odysseus encircled by Trojans. The simile from 480 on is anticipatory. As we have seen earlier (pp. 108-9 and

n. 26) find-passages often contain interventions of the NF$_1$).

71. Again, not all comparisons and similes containing emotional elements can be related to one of the characters of the story, e.g Y 403-5, where Poseidon's joy in the simile does not correspond to joy of any of the characters.

72. Cp. Bergold (1977: 24): "Denn was ihn erwartet, verdeutlicht Homer dadurch, daß er *gewissermaßen im Parallelverlauf mit Menelaos' Blick auf Paris* eine gleichnishafte Szene erstehen läßt" (my italics).

73. At first sight Agamemnon's *joy* seems incongruous with the *fear* of the goatherd in the simile. In De Jong (1985b: 270) I gave the following explanation: "um so besser verstehen wir jetzt dessen (Agamemnon's) Freude, weil wir uns realisieren, wie furchterregend diese Wolke von Griechen ihren Gegnern vorkommen wird". To this I would now add as a parallel H 214-6, where Ajax' martial appearance makes the Greeks rejoice, the Trojans and Hector shudder. The Greeks rejoice, because they realize that Ajax looks fearsome to his opponent.

74. Cp. Ameis-H. ad H 61: "die folgende Schilderung der gelagerten Heere erscheint als das den Augen der zuschauenden Götter sich darbietende Bild".

75. Cp. Fränkel (1921: 22-3) and Camps (1980: 58): "Hector *as seen by the people on the other side* is compared to an ominous dogstar" (my italics).

76. To the similes of my 1985 discussion I have now added similes where the context contains the verb μένω ('await'), because here clearly a perception is implied of the approaching enemy (whose place in the simile is taken by a menacing animal or multitude of hunters, dogs).

77. Cp. Michel (1971: 95, n. 127): "Bemerkenswert ist auch die Zweiteiligkeit des Gleichnisses: aus der Sicht der Gefährten ist Aineias wie der anführende Widder; er dagegen sieht die Gefährten sich folgen, wie ein Hirt die Herde dem Leittier folgen sieht."

78. This simile is analyzed in De Jong (1987a: 116).

79. Note how the three assimilated similes O 586-9.618-22.624-9 describe a gradual process: at first the Greeks await the arrival of the Trojans, then their hearts are troubled and finally they turn to flight. Cp. also Moulton (1977: 68-71).

80. Is the trumpet sounded by the attackers or the besieged? Leaf mentions both possibilities, showing a slight preference for the second alternative, which is adopted by Willcock. I follow Moulton (1977: 107, n. 51) in preferring the first alternative.

81. Other examples of assimilated similes preparing for following speeches: M 299-308 (prepares 310-28), N 471-7 (481-6), O 271-8 (286-99), Σ 318-23 (324-42), Y 164-75 (178-98), X 93-7 (99-130).162-6 (168-76).410-11 (416-28). In the case of Θ 555-61 and Φ 573-82 the speeches (Θ 497-541 and Φ 553-70) *precede* the assimilated similes.

82. Cp. Ameis-H.: "Die vorher nicht erzählte Ankunft der Helden bei den Troern wird im Vergleich vorausgesetzt."

83. Cp. Achilles in X 394, Hecabe in X 434-5, Priam in Ω 258-9, Poseidon in N 54 and Hector himself in Θ 539-40 and N 825-7.

84. Note the subtle way in which Achilles' approach is described: in 92, when Hector (implicitly) focalizes him for the first time, he is ἆσσον ἰόντα ('coming nearer'), during the time of Hector's monologue he has come close enough (131: σχεδόν) for him to discern details: Achilles' helmet and especially his fearful Pelian spear.

85. In the simile Γ 33-7 a traveller is frightened by a snake; in Λ 26-8 and 38-40 snakes form the (apoptropaeic) ornaments on Agamemnon's corslet and shield; in M 201-9 a snake offers fierce resistance to an eagle.

86. The three exceptions are: E 842.847, P 360. Note that M. Parry (1928: 198-9) discusses πελώριος as an example of an "épithète particularisée".

87. A somewhat comparable case is N 470-86, where the NF₁ first says that Idomeneus did not 'like a stripling' panic at the arrival of Aeneas (outward appearance), then compares him to a boar opposing a multitude of hunters, but preparing to defend his life dearly (first indication as to how Idomeus views the situation). To his companions Idomeneus declares that he fears Aeneas because he is so much younger than himself. Idomeneus' advanced age, which was seen by the NF₁ in N 470 as an advantage, is evaluated by Idomeneus himself as a disadvantage (484-6).

88. Note the middle ὀρῶντο, which indicates that the gods watched *with interest*. Fränkel (1921: 78) saw the connection ("Zuschauer sind nicht die Troer und Achaier, sondern die Götter"), but did nothing with it: "Das Gleichnis X 162 sagt nicht viel mehr als was die vorangehende Verse schon geschildert hatten ... Nun galt es das Bild breiter auszumalen."

89. Cp. above section 3.3.2, p. 70 for the "divine audience" in the *Iliad*.

90. For the function of such human observers in similes cp. Webster (1958: 232): "the herdsman who perceives the storm or fails to prevent the lion's ravage is not simply a picturesque addition to the simile, but adds a further point of correspondence: the event has relevance for some responsible person."

91. The same suggestion was made by Latacz (1966: 148): "so daß dann in der rhetorischen Frage ... die unausgesprochenen Antwort impliziert wäre 'darüber können ja doch nur die Feinde froh werden!'".

92. Note especially the similarity between Z 4 μεσσηγὺς Σιμόεντος ἰδὲ Ξάνθοιο ῥοάων and Θ 560 μεσηγὺ νεῶν ἠδὲ Ξάνθοιο ῥοάων.

93. See Ruijgh (1971: 619-20) for the ὡς εἰ + optative construction.

94. For this question and several possible answers, see Leaf (ad Δ 75), Fränkel (1921: 30), Bergold (1977: 150-1), Moulton (1979: 292, n. 40) and Erbse (1980: 262-3).

95. Cp. *LfgrE* I s.v. Ἄρης B 2bββ (1255-6): "Falls prädikativ, würde es den Eindruck, den Leonteus auf die Tr. macht, wiedergeben". Cp. also X 132, where

ἴσος Ἐνυαλίῳ is assimilated to Hector's focalization.

96. In B 627, E 576, Θ 215, Λ 295.604, N 295.328.500.528.802, O 302, Π 784, P 72.536.

97. Griffin does not refer to Opelt at all. Another striking absence in his article is the *LfgrE*: indeed his "paper would have been a lot easier to prepare" (45) if he had consulted this work, where it is very often indicated (either sub B(edeutung) or G(ebrauch)) whether a word occurs exclusively or mainly in direct speech: cp. e.g. s.v. αἰδώς, βάζω, δύσμορος.

98. I discuss these exceptions in 'Homeric Words and Speakers. An Addendum', which will appear in *JHS* 108 (1988), 188-91.

99. E.g. those of R. Quirk a.o., *A Grammar of Contemporary English* (London) 1974, 267 and R. Hetzron, 'On the Relative Order of Adjectives', in H. Seiler (ed.), *Language Universals* (Tübingen) 1978, 165-84. Evaluative: words/expressions which are "susceptible to subjective measure" (Quirk 267), i.e. which are "the expressions of the speaker's personal opinion" (Hetzron 181), e.g. 'beautiful', dangerous', 'good'; affective: words/expressions which give expression to the emotions of the speaker, e.g. 'horrible', 'marvellous' (Hetzron 181). By descriptive I mean adjectives "susceptible to objective measure, including those denoting size or shape, adjectives denoting age, color, material, provenance" (Quirk 267).

100. Other examples: (with μήδομαι) Δ 21, H 478, Φ 19; (φρονέω) Δ 219, K 486, Π 73.701.783, X 320; (μητιάω) Σ 312.

101. One should also take into consideration that to dishonour an opponent's dead body (either by leaving it uncared for or by actual mutilation) is in itself not an unusual custom in the *Iliad*, hence is not considered a negative action as such: P 39-40.125-7.255, Σ 179, Ψ 21, etc. Cp. also Aristotle's remark quoted in Erbse's apparatus ad Ω 15-16 (Achilles is pulling Hector around Patroclus' grave): ἔστι δὲ λύειν καὶ εἰς τὰ ὑπάρχοντα ἀγαγόντ' ἔφη ὅτι τοιαῦτα ἦν: 'the solution is also to take into account the existing customs, that they were like that.'

102. In Δ 21, Π 373.701.783, X 320.395, Ψ 176. Cp. Leaf (ad Ψ 176): "the word means only that what he did was ill work *for his victims*", Bassett (1933: 44) and Adkins (1960: 31): "to say of an action 'it is agathon (kakon) to do X' is simply to say that it is beneficial (harmful) to do X, without passing any moral judgement on the rightness or wrongness of X."

103. As Bassett notes (1933: 45), ἀεικής acquires a moral overtone in the *Odyssey* (in the mouth of characters): γ 265, λ 429, ψ 222. According to Segal (1971: 15 n. 2) "the word also has a strong moral note in Il. 9.70, 15.496, 19.124." I do not agree with Segal that moral issues are at stake here, but rather events/circumstances which are appropriate (note the litotes: 'not unseemly') to someone's status: as king (l 70), as warrior (O 496), as offspring of Zeus (T 124).

104. There are other passages where the contrast between charm, beauty on the one hand and defilement on the other results in such pathos: Π 796-9, P 51-60, Σ 23-4, X 401-4. See Griffin (1980: 134-8) on the "beauty brought low" motif.

105. Cp. *LfgrE* II s.v.: 'maßlos', "wohl nicht (wie ὑπὲρ αἶσαν, ὑπέρμορον) 'gegen das Schicksal' (sc. die vorgegebene Eroberung Troias)".

106. Cp. υ 121 where the ἀλεῖται are the suitors as focalized by Odysseus.

107. Unless stated otherwise, the numbers given in this and the following figures take into account Iliadic occurrences only.

108. Ω 217.299.372.386.405.552.634.659.

109. It is interesting to note that ἀγητός in Χ 370 is combined with εἶδος, which according to Clay (1974: 130) is (in comparison to the other words for 'shape': φυή, δέμας) "subjective, requiring the presence of an onlooker".

110. The distinction between literal and figurative instances of αἰπύς is based on the *LfgrE* s.v. Other examples in embedded focalization: Ξ 507 = Π 283, Π 651. Examples in direct speech: Ζ 57, Κ 371, Λ 441, Μ 345 = 358, Ν 773, Ξ 99, Π 859, Ρ 155.244, Σ 129.

111. Cp. also Griffin (1986: 46), who notes that λίην occurs 41 times in the Homeric epics, of which only once in narrator-text: ξ 461. This one exception again concerns embedded focalization, since the passage "describes Odysseus' unspoken thoughts".

112. *Iliad*: Ε 876, Ξ 84, Τ 92; *Odyssey*: δ 92, κ 394, λ 410.555, ο 344, ρ 287.474.484, σ 273, ω 97.

113. Leaf, Ameis-H., Willcock, Kirk. The bT-scholia (ad 2a) say: ὡς ἐπὶ ἰδίοις ἀλγῶν δυσφημεῖ αὐτήν: 'as if feeling sorrow for his own affairs, the poet speaks ill of her (sc. the wrath)'. Redfield (1979: 100) also notes that οὐλόμενος, except for Α 2, only occurs in direct speech, but I disagree with his conclusion: "it has a tone of subjectivity and expresses a personal rejection of another person or personified thing. The bard thus brings before us his personal reaction, *almost his distaste for*, his theme" (my italics).

114. Cp. Griffin (1986: 45), who calls attention to two exceptional cases of ἦ in narrator-text in the *Odyssey*: φ 99 (again an internal prolepsis) and χ 31 (embedded focalization).

115. See also *LfgrE* s.v. δήϊος B2a and b. The cases of δήϊος in embedded focalization are: (explicit) Β 544, Κ 358, Ν 395, Ρ 272.667; (implicit) Μ 57 ≅ Ο 533, Μ 264 (with Greeks as implicit F₂), Ν 556 (Antilochus), Ο 548 (Melanippus), Π 591 (the man), Σ 208 (the inhabitants of the beleaguered city).220 (the inhabitants of the city).

116. αἰδοῖος in Β 514, Ζ 250, Φ 479 and πελώριος in Ε 842.847, Ρ 360 seem to be purely descriptive.

117. Cp. the interesting analysis by Eide (1986) of the five epithets of χείρ. His conclusion: "παχύς and στιβαρός are used of the hand acting, while βαρύς, θρασύς, and ἄαπτος are *emotionally laden and denote the hand primarily as a harmful instrument*" (my italics).

1. The following scholars incorrectly mention the figure of 67%: Latacz (1974: 395), Fenik (1978a: 68), Taplin in *CR* 31 (1981: 103).

2. Cp. Lämmert (1955: 196): "Der Erzähler erzählt den Gesprächsakt wie ein anderes Geschehen des äußeren Vorgangs. Die Aussage der Personen aber vermag sich vom Fortschritt der Handlung zu lösen."

3. Cp. also Lohmann (1970: passim), who suggests that in certain speeches the poet counts upon his audience to remember another speech, in order that they experience the effective contrast between the two speeches.

4. For more detailed surveys of scholarship on the Homeric speeches, see Latacz (1970) and Lohmann (1970: 1-7).

5. Cp. Barck (1971) on Menelaus as "Zwischenszenencharakter".

6. Until this speech, Menelaus' opinions on the Trojans and Paris had only been presented in embedded focalization (B 589-90, Γ 28) or briefly in direct speech (Γ 100 and 351-4).

7. A good discussion of N 620-39 in Michel (1971: 110-13).

8. Exceptions are of course monologues, which are not heard by other characters, but by the NeFe₁ only. Sometimes a character can prefer not to express his/her feelings. An example is Δ 401-2, where Diomedes does not answer Agamemnon's taunting speech (370-400). Only later (Ι 34-5) does it appear that on that occasion he had felt hurt in his pride as a warrior.

9. Cp. also Lohmann (1970: 96-130) on "Perspektivenwechsel".

10. Cp. bT-scholia ad Π 558a: τῶν πεπραγμένων αὐτῷ ὑπομιμνήσκει πρὸς ἀμύνης ὑπόμνησιν: 'he reminds (them) of the things done by him (Sarpedon) with a view to reviving their defensive spirit'.

11. This resemblance (note also a detail like ἠερίη: 'in the morning': 497, 557) implies that Hera has actually seen Thetis and Zeus together, just as Zeus feared in 522-3. She has not overheard what they discussed, but when she sees him at his return on the Olympus, she guesses that they have secretly contrived something (536-8).

12. A good discussion of all references to this wall (both in narrator- and in character-text) is found in Thornton (1984: 257-60).

13. Note that Achilles ascribes the whole enterprise of the wall to Agamemnon alone, thus making him the chief butt of his sarcasm: πονήσατο (Ι 348), ἔδειμε, ἤλασε (349), κατέπηξεν (350), δύναται (351).

14. Cp. the pertinent remark of the bT-scholia (ad Ξ 139-41): 'we always find some invective against Agamemnon as regards his behaviour towards Achilles. But now the opposite is found. And it is *in accordance with the situation* to offer an excuse to Agamemnon, viz. that the Greek army is in distress not because of his fault, but because of Achilles' intemperate behaviour' (my italics).

15. Other external analepses which are told more than once: about Hera and Heracles (Ξ 250-61 and O 18-30), Laomedon (E 638-42.648-51, H 452-3 and Φ 441-57), earlier confrontations between Achilles and Aeneas (Υ 90-6 and 188-94) and between Achilles and Lycaon (Φ 57-9 and 76-82), marriage of Thetis and Peleus (Σ 84-5.432-4, Ω 59-61).

16. In my analysis I shall not go into the genetical question of which details of the story are invented *ad hoc*: for this question see Willcock (1964, esp. 144-5 on Δ 372-99). These three passages are also discussed by Hebel (1970: 32-3, 81-3, 85-7) and Andersen (1978: 34-8, 79-80, 130-1).

17. Austin (1966: 300). Note that in his reaction Sthenelus (Δ 404-10) tries to play down the force of the paradigm.

18. Two other explanations have been offered: 1) (Ameis-H. and Willcock) the poet wishes to explain why the leading city of Mycenae had nothing to do with the Expedition against Thebes; 2) (Hebel 1970: 82) Ag. wishes to stress the contrast between Diomedes and Tydeus: whereas Tydeus was less successful in words (Mycenae-episode) than in deeds, Diomedes is 'less in fighting, but better in words' (399-400). The first explanation is based on extratextual arguments, the second cannot be valid, because it is nowhere stated that Tydeus was not a man of words. In fact, he did at first convince the Mycenaeans (380), who only changed their mind because of an external factor (divine intervention).

19. I see no reason to reject line 808, as Aristarchus proposed. See Leaf ad loc.

20. To remind a god(dess) of earlier assistance is in general a recurrent item in prayers, cp. A 453-5 = Π 236-8.

21. This is also the conclusion of Hebel (1970: 12): "Der Stoff tritt hinter dem Zweck zurück" and (26): "jeder Erzähler erzählt so ... wie es seinem Wesen in der gegebenen Situation entspricht".

22. I adopt Aristophanes' reading μάχην instead of μάχης.

23. Cp. Vivante (1982: 18-26) for the principle that through epithets "points of arrest are brightened into focus".

24. See Van der Ben & de Jong (1984). To the bibliography given there (on p. 313) should be added: Chantraine (1954), Dietrich (1976: 307-21), Tsagarakis (1977: 98-116) and Erbse (1986: 259-73).

25. Older scholarship maintained that these external analepses or digressions (this word has in itself already a depreciatory ring) are often *not* connected to their context: e.g. Lillge (1911: 83-4), Heinze (1903: 407): "Wo und wann immer es dem Dichter beliebt, läßt er die Rede zur Erzählung werden, mag das auch der realistisch betrachteten Situation *so unangemessen wie möglich sein*." (my italics). For this question see also Austin (1966: 295-7).

26. Note especially at the beginning of Antenor's story (207: 'I have received both as guests and entertained them in my palace') and end (224: 'we marvelled beholding Odysseus' appearance').

27. Cp. Y 188-94 and Φ 441-57.

28. Another example is Ξ 125 (Diomedes claims that his father Tydeus surpassed all in wealth and military prowess): τὰ δὲ μέλλετ᾽ ἀκουέμεν ('but those things you must know from hearing'), cp. Basset (1979: 78): "Ces origines lui semblent assez illustres pour être vraisemblablement connues des Grecs". The converse situation is found in I 527-8, where Phoenix seems to be the only one who knows this story (presumably because he is old and the events told took place long ago).

29. I do not agree with Kirk (ad loc.) that "the stress on Agamemnon's reliance on hearsay seems unnecessary" nor with Hebel (1970: 81-2): "Der Sprecher (Agamemnon) ist in der Situation zu sehr mit seinem Gefühl beteiligt. Sein Zeugnis allein wäre nicht objektiv genug, um wirklich zu wirken. Die Augenzeugen aber, die er erwähnt, sind unbeteiligte, objektive Autorität." Why would Agamemnon, telling something of the past, be "beteiligt" and the actual witnesses be "unbeteiligt"? I submit that 374-5 is inserted by Agamemnon to compensate for the fact that he has not himself witnessed what he is going to narrate. This device is sometimes called authentication (Dolezel 1980).

30. This exception is Aelion (1984), who gives an analysis à la Propp of the B.-story, as found in Homer and in Pindar, *Olympian* 13.

31. For a concise inventory of the omissions see Willcock (ad Z 155).

32. The NF$_1$ introduces Glaucus and Diomedes as 'son of Hippolochus' (repeated in 144 and cp. in Glaucus' speech: 206) and 'son of Tydeus' (cp. in Diomedes' speech: 222-3), respectively, thus anticipating the theme of ancestry to follow.

33. Such verbal exchanges are a regular preliminary to fighting: see Fingerle (1939: 130-149), Fenik (1968: 32, 101, 161) and Létoublon (1983b).

34. Note in the simile the repeated ἀνδρῶν (146, 149) and cp. Φ 464-6, where human beings are again compared to leaves, this time by Apollo, who indicates the tininess and relative insignificance of the human race.

35. For a survey of opinions on the remarkable lines Z 232-6 see Calder (1984).

36. In Z 159 I take as object of ἐδάμασσε B. (cp. Ameis-H.), not the Argives (scholia, Willcock). The γάρ-clause, together with the ἐπεί-clause in 158, provide an explanation why Proetus can give orders to B. This information is necessary to understand the story, whereas a possible domination of the Argives by Proetus is not.

37. For a discussion of B.'s epithets (especially ἀμύμων and δαΐφρων) see Amory Parry (1973: 23-8).

38. Only the bT-scholia have paid attention to this verse : εὖ τὸ μὴ εἰπεῖν 'ἔφασαν ἄλλοι', ἀλλ᾽ αὐτὸς ὁ πεπειραμένος ('it is good that the poet does not say "said others", but he himself (B.) being the one who experienced it').

39. For a discussion of the three possible interpretations of καί in 200, see

Leaf (ad 200-2). I follow the interpretation of Monro ("even he, whom they had formerly loved"), because throughout Glaucus had emphasized B.'s divine protection: 156, 171, 183.

40. Cp. Reinhardt (1961: 218): "alles das vom nachblickenden Zuschauer vom Ufer aus gesehen, ...". Ameis-H. draw attention to another effect of ὄψεαι: "um die unzweifelhafte Ausführung seines Entschlusses hervorzuheben."

41. Comparable to Ι 359-61 are Δ 353-5 and Θ 470-2. There too the tone is sarcastic ("a sneering remark": Willcock (ad Δ 353); "even more sarcastic": Kirk (ad Δ 353), who incorrectly mentions Agamemnon as subject of ὄψεαι in Ι 359; "höhnend": Ameis-H. (ad Θ 471).

42. Cp. the A-scholia (ad Σ 154-6, 30-33 and ad 174, 79-80) and Segal (1971: 23-4): (there are) "grounds for questioning whether Iris' statement is to be taken at face value".

43. According to the bT-scholia (ad Π 12-3a), followed by Leaf and Willcock, all four questions are ironical, Achilles knowing perfectly well why Patroclus is weeping. I disagree on account of 1) ᾤκτιρε ('he felt pity') in 5; and 2) the simile (7-10), the tone of which is teasing (cp. above 4.2, pp. 125-6), but not ironical or even scornful (see Moulton 1977: 103 n. 41).

44. The bT-scholia also connect ὑπερβασίης with Achilles, but in a different way: λεληθότως ὑπεραπολογεῖται ἑαυτοῦ, ὡς ἀδικηθεὶς ὠργίσθη ('implicitly he excuses himself: he only became angry after first having been wronged himself').

45. Embedded direct speech: Β 60-70.323-9, Δ 178-81, Ζ 164-5. 460-1.479 (πατρός ... ἀμείνων), Η 89-90.301-2, Θ 149, Ι 254-8, Λ 786-9, Μ 318-21, Π 203-6.839-41, Τ 101-5.107-11.121-4, Χ 107.498, Ψ 576-8.
Embedded indirect speech: I have not made an exhaustive list, but offer an approximate figure of 70-90 cases.

46. I leave out of account here embedded speeches concerning messages. In the *Iliad* messages are almost always presented twice (once at the moment of instruction, once at the moment of delivery) and, accordingly, they will be discussed in 5.4 (repeated speech).

47. Cp. Austin (1966: 30). I do not share, however, his idea that Agamemnon tells the story "to explain how delusion entered the world" nor Willcock's (ad 132-3): "The whole of the foregoing paradeigma is evidently an attempt to explain why such a hero as Herakles had been subservient to so poor a figure as Eurystheus", because this robs the external analepsis of its relevance in the context.

48. A recent, good discussion of this very complex and difficult concept is Wyatt (1982), who also gives earlier scholarship: p. 248, n. 1 (one should add Bremer 1969: 99-112 and Saïd 1978: 76-83).

49. According to Erbse (1986: 11-7), Ate is a "Neuschöpfung Homers".

50. Cp. the bT-scholia (ad Τ 95a): καὶ ἐν οἷς ἐλεεινολογεῖται ὑψοῖ ἑαυτόν,

εἰκάζων τῷ μεγίστῳ θεῷ ('even when he is engaged in arousing pity he elevates himself, comparing (himself) to the greatest god') and Van Erp Taalman Kip (1971: 59-60): "Zeus' verblinding ... bewerkte dat hij niet doorzag dat hem onrecht werd aangedaan; Agamemnon daarentegen doorzag niet dat hij onrecht deed. Het aspect *van het alleen maar slachtoffer zijn*, krijgt door deze bedrieglijke parallel nog grotere nadruk" (my italics).

51. Another example is Z 207-10 (Hippolochus to Glaucus, see above p. 166) and cp. Hebel (1970: 60), who gives examples from later literature. One could further compare E 197-200 (Lycaon advising his son Pandarus), I 442-3 (Peleus instructing Phoenix when he leaves together with Achilles for Troy), Σ 326-7 (Achilles promising Menoetius the safe return of his son) and Ψ 144-9 (Peleus praying to the river Spercheius for the safe return of Achilles. Note in Ψ 145 κεῖσε instead of δεῦρο, which betrays the geographical orientation of the speaker (NF₂), Achilles, not of the quoted speaker (F₃), Peleus).

52. Cp. the bT-scholia ad Λ 786-9: (Nestor and Odysseus quote Menoetius and Peleus) ἵνα μὴ δόξωσιν οἱ ἀκούοντες μήτε ᾿Οδυσσέα μήτε Νέστορα τοὺς λέγοντας, ἀλλὰ τὸν πατέρα ('in order that those who are listening (Achilles, Patroclus) do not think they hear Odysseus or Nestor speak, but their fathers.') A very similar remark is found ad B 323a.

53. Λ 784 = Z 208 (Glaucus embeds words of his father) and cp. Z 444-5 (Hector is speaking).

54. Other examples: (embedded indirect speech:) Γ 430-1, Θ 229.233-4; (embedded direct speech:) Π 203-6.

55. Other examples of recent embedded speeches: Θ 372 = Ο 77 (refers to A 503-10), I 35 (Δ 370-400), Κ 392-9 (Κ 303-12+319-27+329-31), Μ 235-6 (Μ 216-29), Ξ 96-7 (Ξ 74-81), P 174 (P 166-8), Σ 191 (Σ 136-7).

56. For δή see Denniston (1978: 233): "After verbs of saying, thinking, hoping and fearing: implying, at most, that what follows is false; at least, that it is not unquestionably true."

57. This disbelief also appears from καὶ ὧς ('even so') in 116: although he does not believe Calchas' interpretation to be correct, he is prepared to do what is best for the army.

58. Cp. Van Erp Taalman Kip (1971: 12): "Met deze woorden (111-3) negeert hij volkomen het pijnlijke karakter van zijn optreden tegen Chryses."

59. Other examples: (embedded indirect speech:) H 131, I 234-5.240.241-3.305-6, N 54, Ξ 45-7. In the case of P 26-7 it is difficult to decide whether Hyperenor indeed has said this (the NF₁'s version in Ξ 516-9 does not mention a speech) or whether it is invented *ad hoc* by Menelaus. Note that in the case of embedded speeches referring to words spoken in the time period *before* that covered by the *Iliad*, we are never able to compare the represented version with the 'original' one: cp. above pp. 174-5 on the speeches of Menoetius and Peleus in Phthia. In the case of I 410-6 and Φ 277-8, which seem to contradict each other (cp. Λ 794-5 ≅ Π 36-7 ≅ 50-1), one might either consider one of the two versions an "autoschediasma" or "Augenblickserfindung" (so Willcock 1977: 48-9) or consider

the two speeches to be spoken by Thetis at different occasions, Φ 277-8 presumably following after the moment Achilles has chosen for the first alternative Ι 412-3.

60. Cp. in a very similar situation Achilles' words to the dying Hector X 331-5 (note που ἔφης: 331 and νήπιε: 333). See Lohmann (1970: 159-60).

61. Both Lohmann and Willcock (1977: 47: the words "characterize him (Hector) as lacking in real judgement and true understanding") take Π 838-41 as a serious reconstruction by Hector, which I think it is not.

62. Other embedded tis-speeches: (in speeches of Hector:) Z 479, H 89-90.301-2, X 107; (Agamemnon:) Δ 178-81; (Sarpedon:) M 318-21; (Menelaus:) Ψ 576-8. One could further compare Θ 149, where Diomedes imagines what Hector will say, when he, Diomedes, flees for him. Hector's actual words are found in Θ 161-6.

63. The embedded tis-speech of H 89-90 is another such 'epitaph' composed by Hector himself: see De Jong (forth.).

64. Cp. Dodds (1951: 18): "The strongest moral force which Homeric man knows is not the fear of god, but respect for public opinion."

65. Cp. Létoublon (1983b: 41): "Quand il (sc. l'auteur du récit épique) rapporte des paroles au style direct, il fait semblant de croire et de vouloir faire croire qu'elles ont été réellement prononcées telles quelles."

66. Homeric messenger-speeches are discussed by Pfudel (1891: 9-16), Fingerle (1939: 266-70), Hebel (1970: 137-41) and Létoublon (1987).

67. Bergold (1977: 93 n. 3) wonders how Idaeus knows the formulation Γ 256-8, which Paris had used to Hector (Γ 73-5), but which the latter had not repeated to the Trojans and Greeks. He considers it a (pardonable) inconsistency on the part of Homer, who only cares for "die Assoziation des Publikums bei der Wieder-holung des Wortlautes". Also problematic is Γ 253-5, where Idaeus uses almost the same words as Iris vs. Helen in Γ 136-8.

68. For a discussion of Iris' initiative here, see Hentze (1903), Bergold (1977: 54-5) and Kirk (ad Γ 121).

69. Explanations for Hypnus' behaviour are given by the bT-scholia ad Ξ 354-5 and 357-8 and by Ameis-H. ad O 41.

70. Note that messenger-speeches in drama are of a very different nature: they are reports of events not presented on stage, not the transmission of another character's words (see Bremer 1976). Iliadic messenger-speeches which come closest to such reporting speeches are Π 23-7 and Σ 20-1.

71. This has been insufficiently recognized by Létoublon (1987), who very much stresses the "fidelity" of the Homeric messenger.

72. In the case of Δ 65-7 vs. Δ 70-2 we find the reverse, viz. an indirect *instruction* speech being turned into a direct *delivery* speech.

73. Note that in general character b identifies him-/herself as a messenger by mentioning character a as the source of his/her words (e.g. B 26: Διὸς δέ τοι ἄγγελός εἰμι: 'I am a messenger from Zeus to you'). Exceptions are Hector in Z 269-78, who does not mention Helenus, presumably because he is his superior in command (cp. H 67-91 where again Hector does not mention Helenus, but instead says: ὄφρ' εἴπω τά με θυμὸς ἐνὶ στήθεσσι κελεύει: (listen to me) 'in order that I say what my spirit in my breast commands me'); Patroclus in Π 23-7+36-45, who does not mention Nestor, presumably in order not to irritate Achilles.

74. Other examples: Γ 88 (κέλεται), Μ 355 (ἠνώγει), Ο 176 (κέλευσε).179 (ἠπεί-λει).180 (ἄνωγε).

75. Cp. Hebel (1970: 139-40). Other examples: B 175 (ἐν νήεσσι πολυκλήϊσι πεσόντες) instead of B 159 (ἐπ' εὐρέα νῶτα θαλάσσης); Γ 89 (κέλεται Τρῶας ... Ἀχαιοὺς τεύχεα ... ἀποθέσθαι) instead of Γ 68 (κάθισον Τρῶας ... Ἀχαιούς): this change might be due to Hector's recent experience of being attacked by the Greeks (Γ 79-80); Δ 205 (Μενέλαον ἀρήϊον ἀρχὸν Ἀχαιῶν) instead of Δ 195 (Μ. ἀ. Ἀτρέος υἱόν): note that the MSS. are hesitating; Z 269 (Ἀθηναίης ἀγελείης) instead of Z 88 (Ἀ. γλαυκώπιδος); Ι 276 (ἥ θέμις ἐστίν, ἄναξ, ἤ τ' ἀνδρῶν ἤ τε γυναικῶν) instead of Ι 134 (ἥ θέμις ἀνθρώπων πέλει, ἀνδρῶν ἠδὲ γυναικῶν): note that the formulation of Ι 276 recurs in Τ 177. In both cases it is Achilles who is addressed, which might account for the (urgent) vocative.

76. Other examples of omissions: Hector in Γ 88-94 leaves out Γ 74-5, which formed the conclusion of Paris' speech. Note that Γ 73-5 recur in Idaeus' speech to Priam Γ 256-7 (see above n. 67); in Z 269-70 Hector leaves out the details of the location of Athena's temple and the opening of the door (cp. Z 88-9).

77. Note that character a in his/her *instruction* speech can also give personal comment, not repeated by the messenger: Z 98-101 (Helenus describes his fear for Diomedes, whom he considers a greater danger than Achilles); in P 692-3 we find a final αἴ κε + subj. clause (cp. Wakker 1987) in which character a indicates the result he hopes to achieve with his message. Cp. also Ω 116 αἴ κέν ... λύσῃ, which is transmitted by Iris in 137 as λῦσον.

78. Aristarchus rejected these verses as being not in tune with Iris' ethopoiia. However, as Hentze (1903: 325-6) - and before him Pfudel (1891: 13) - remarks, Iris has received from Zeus a rather free instruction, viz. to turn back Athena and Hera (Θ 399-400: πάλιν τρέπε). Cp. Ο 201-4, where Iris even adds an entire speech of her own, to convince Poseidon. Other examples of additions made by messengers: B 33-4, Η 52.393 (ἦ μὴν ... κέλονται), Κ 406-8, Σ 19.

79. Cp. e.g. Calhoun (1933: 19, ad B 11-15 = 28-32 = 65-70): "He (the listener) waits expectantly for the dream to begin the actual words with which he has just heard him charged, and he knows that verbatim repetition may begin at any moment. When it does begin, he listens with the pleasure of satisfied expectancy, which is sharply interrupted when the speech does not stop at the moment expected but goes on"; and Segal (1971: 5): "The very sameness of recurrent patterns makes the listener all the more sensitive to variation when it occurs".

80. Other examples: A 453-5 = Π 236-8 (prayer); E 175-6 = Π 424-5 (enemy wreaking havoc); E 373-4 = Φ 509-10 (wounding); Θ 173-4 = Λ 286-7 = O 486-7 (+488a) = P 184-5 (adhortation); Z 46-50 = Λ 131-5, cp. K 378-81 (supplication); P 30-2 = Y 196-8 (threat); Ξ 195-6 = Σ 426-7 (polite phrase).

81. Cp. Arend (1933: 122-3): "Nur selten wird der Inhalt des Schwures nach der Aufforderung bei der Ausführung wiederholt". In the case of Y 315-317: Φ 374-6, where we are dealing with two oaths which have completely independent origins, but happen to have the same formulation, I am inclined to explain the repetition genetically only.

82. Cp. Arend (1933: 123, ad K 329-31 vs. 322-3): "Um Dolon zu den Spähergange zu verlocken, malt er aus, wie jener schon von den Pferden dahingetragen wird."

83. Another example might be A 411-2 = Π 273-4. Patroclus in Π uses words which Achilles had used in A in his conversation with Thetis, but which he most probably had also repeated on other occasions to Patroclus. Ameis-H. consider the words more appropriate in A than in Π. According to the bT-scholia (ad Π 273-4), however, they give Patroclus' appeal to the Myrmidonians more weight.

84. In the case of Λ 800-801 = Π 42-3 = Σ 200-201 the repetition is partly due to similarity of situation (the Greeks are endangered by the Trojans) and partly to common knowledge. The expression ὀλίγη δέ τ' ἀνάπνευσις πολέμοιο (Λ 801 = Π 43 = Σ 201: 'only brief is respite in battle') to my opinion is sententious (note τε: Ruijgh 1971: 653+661 and Willcock: "proverbial remark"), rather than specific, as Leaf takes it: "there is so little respite from war that even a short breathing space will be precious, as no actual victory can be won without Achilles himself".

85. Cp. Bowra (1958: 96): "With his recurring passages, he (the poet) can give one emotional colour here and another there, and by reminiscence of an earlier scene he can implicitly point a contrast."

86. Other examples: Δ 15-6 = Δ 82-4. The almost exact recurrence of Zeus' words in the anonymous tis-speech creates a tragic contrast, because the NeFe₁ by now knows that Zeus has decided to continue the war, whereas the Greek and Trojan soldiers still reckon with the possibility of peace; E 221-3 = Θ 105-7. Here the same words are first spoken by the proud Trojan owner of the horses, then by the proud Greek captor of these same horses.

87. Cp. Schadewaldt (1959: 227): "Hinter diesem Wissen um den einmal kommenden Untergang steht unausgesprochen ein 'und doch'. Hektor bedarf um zu kämpfen nicht einmal die Hoffnung." I prefer this interpretation to that of Ameis-H. (ad Δ 163-5): "schmerzliche Resignation".

88. Other examples: Σ 385-6 = Σ 424-5, where both Charis and Hephaestus address Thetis with the same polite phrase (cp. Ξ 195-6 = Σ 426-7 above n. 80); Π 441-3 = X 179-81, where first Hera and then Athena react to Zeus' hesitation to let a doomed man die.

89. Λ 362-6 is often considered a weak variant of Y 449-54. The passage is defended by Andersen (1978: 136-7).

90. In comparison to Hecabe's version Achilles' version shows two minor differences: instead of ἐθέλεις ('you want') we find ἔτλης ('you dared': with the semantic element of both courage and suffering): when Hecabe speaks Priam still has to go, when Achilles speaks he has already dared to go; instead of the third person ἐξενάριξε (the man who killed), Achilles uses the first person ἐξενάριξα (I who killed). For the combination relative pronoun + verb in first person, see K.G. (1: 88 Anm. 5) and cp. e.g. β 166-7.

91. Müller (1984: 56-7) notes a similar function for A 362-3a = Σ 73-4a. At the moment the Διὸς βουλή has reached its dramatic climax (Achilles' sorrow over Patroclus), the NeFe₁ is reminded of its starting point (Achilles' sorrow over Briseis): "formal identity points to substantive difference".

92. Another example is Δ 60-1 = Σ 365-6, which is symptomatic of Hera's feelings of frustration towards Zeus: although she occupies, by birth and marriage, a position of high rank among the Olympians, she feels overruled by Zeus.

93. This double intention of the speech in B explains the presence of 119-138 (where Agamemnon discusses the pros, but especially the cons of the return) which are lacking in the I version. In fact, the B speech has *three* different layers of meaning: (1) for the speaker, Agamemnon, who purposefully says something else than he thinks; (2) for the NeFe₂, the Greek soldiers, who take Agamemnon's words at face value; and (3) for the NeFe₁, who knows that it is Agamemnon who is being deceived by Zeus.

94. Curiously enough the bT-scholia (ad I 17) think that I 17-28 is also a test, i.e. is not meant to be taken seriously. Ameis-H. consider the repetition in I "befremdend" and Willcock stops his interpretation at the (to my mind insufficient) level of a genetical explanation: "Such repetition of situations and of the lines that go with it is a natural feature of oral poetry."

95. The repetition H 79-80 = X 342-3 characterizes Hector as being very concerned for his own body, that it should receive the proper burial rites. Against this background Achilles' dishonouring of Hector's body is all the more dramatic.

96. Létoublon (1985: 68) offers an interesting interpretation of the difference between εἶμι in 200 (+205:304) vs. ἔρχομαι in 301. εἶμι emphasizes the *determination* of the speaker to go (Hera must convince Aphrodite that it is necessary that she go), whereas ἔρχομαι is more neutral (Hera answers Zeus' question as casually as possible).

1. Cp. also Barck (1976: 37-6) on "Wort und Tat als Bauelemente des frühen Epos". Analyzing book A Barck shows how intimately words (= character-text) and deeds (main part of the narrator-text) are connected with each other.

2. For such cases of "omitted speech-formulas" see Combellack (1939).

3. Cp. Combellack (1939: 43): "the quotation-marks of recited poetry".

4. Prince cites authors like G. Flaubert and N. Sarraute who avow to be bothered by the monotony of "he said", "he answered", etc. Cp. already for this problem Cicero, *Laelius, de amicitia* 1.3: quasi enim ipsos induxi loquentis, ne "inquam" et "inquit" saepius interponeretur ('for I have, so .to speak, brought them on stage speaking themselves in order to avoid too frequent insertion of "said I" and "said he"').

5. For intercalated speech-introductions in an epic text, cp. e.g. Virgil, *Aeneid* 1.321: ac prior "heus" <u>inquit</u> "monstrate" ...

6. I hesitate to attach too much significance to the denomination ὁ γέρων/ γεραιός of Nestor (Δ 310, H 161, K 190), Priam (Γ 181.191, X 37.77, Ω 252. 424.715) or Chryses (A 35). Nestor and Priam are the old men *par excellence* on both sides and are referred to often as 'the old man' also outside attributive discourse. Yet the qualification is not without poignancy in Δ 310 (cp. πάλαι), H 161 (Nestor has in the preceding speech stressed his old age) and X 36.77 (Priam tries to persuade Hector to come inside by pointing at his own old age. Cp. ἐπὶ γήραος οὐδῷ: 60 and γέροντος: 75). In the case of Chryses the use of ὁ γεραιός (A 35) is in tune with Agamemnon's γέρον in 26 and the NF₁'s γέρων in 33.

7. The meaning of ἐϋφρονέων is somewhat ambiguous: 'with good sense' or 'with good intent'. See Leaf (ad A 73). I do not see Kirk's point (ad A 74-83) that the "cautious, not to say devious, tone" of Calchas' speech contrasts "piquantly with ἐϋφρονέων in 73". In my opinion ἐϋφρονέων , which should be taken closely with σφιν, indicates that the speaker will suggest something which is to the benefit of his addressees. Calchas in A 73 is about to reveal the cause of the plague, thereby opening a way to end it.

8. Cp. the bT-scholia ad Λ 137a: ἀμείλικτον ἑαυτοῖς, δικαίαν δέ ('relentless for themselves, the suppliants, but in fact, righteous'); and *LfgrE* I s.v.: "ungerührt, von der Stimme jemandes, der bei einer Rede, die sich an sein Gefühl wendet ungerührt bleibt. Der Unterredner erkennt dies am Ton der Stimme, ehe er den Sinn der Worte versteht, daher Adj. zu ὄπα".

9. Comparable are Θ 492 and Π 232 (cp. 249).

10. In B 16, Δ 198, M 351.442, P 256.694 we find both a verb of speaking and a verb of hearing. All the speeches capped, except for P 694, contain a request and ἀκούω means not just 'hear', but 'give heed to' (cp. οὐδ' ἀπίθησεν in Δ 198). In P 694 ἀκούω stresses the fact that Menelaus' speech (in which he reports Patroclus' death) makes a great impression on Antilochus.

11. Only twice is the verb of the introductory formula not strictly speaking a

verb of speaking: Κ 476 δεῖξεν ('he pointed out', note in Odysseus' speech οὗτος ... οὗτοι) and Μ 342 προΐει ('he sent forth').

12. I base myself here on the synopsis given by Levinson (1983: 226-83).

13. Other examples: εὔχομαι: Α 43, Ε 121, Ζ 311, Κ 295; νεικείω Β 243; ὀτρύνω: Δ 310; κελευτιάω: Ν 125; λίσσομαι Φ 98.

14. Other examples: εὐχόμενος: Ε 106 (cp. introduction in 101: μακρὸν ἄϋσε); ἐποτρύνων: Μ 442 (439: ἤϋσεν ... γεγωνώς); ἀπειλήσας: Φ 161 (152: προσεφώνεε); λισσόμενος: Π 46 (20: προσέφης).

15. Another example is Θ 184 (ἐκέκλετο: 'he spurred on') vs. 198 (ἔφατ' εὐχόμενος: 'he spoke boasting'). In the course of his speech Hector becomes more and more confident about his power to destroy the Greeks. These examples remind us of the fact that a speech consists of a number of utterances and can, therefore, give expression to different speech acts. The verb of speaking of the introductory or capping formula will normally indicate the global or dominant speech act of a speech.

16. Other examples: Δ 184 θάρσει (cp. introduction 183: ἐπιθαρσύνων).359 οὔτε ... νεικείω (336: νείκεσσεν: Agamemnon takes back his words: 357), Ε 492 ἐνιπήν (471: νείκεσεν), Φ 74 γουνοῦμαι (71: ἐλλίσσετο). Speeches marked as directive (verbum dicendi: ἐκέκλετο, ἐκέλευσε, ὄτρυνεν) always contain one or more imperatives and/or an adhortative subjunctive.

17. Other examples: Β 277 ὀνειδείοις ἐπέεσσιν (cp. 222: λέγ' ὀνείδεα), Γ 438 μή ... ἔνιπτε (427: ἠνίπαπε). Interestingly enough three of the four cases concern Paris, who shows himself very sensitive about criticism from others.

18. Cp. also Μ 413, Ψ 417.446 and ἄχος γένετ' εὐξαμένοιο in Ν 417= Ξ 458.486, capping speeches introduced by ἐπεύξατο (Ν 413, Ξ 453.478).

19. Other examples: ὄτρυνε: Δ 73, Ε 470.792, Ζ 72, etc.; φρένας/θυμὸν πεῖθε/ἔπειθε: Δ 104, Ζ 51; θυμὸν ... ὄρινε: Β 142, Γ 395, Δ 208, Λ 804, Ξ 459, Ρ 123; ἵμερον ὦρσε γόοιο: Ω 507; ἔτρεψεν ... φρένας: Ζ 61.

20. Other examples: position: ἀγχοῦ ἱστάμενος (passim); facial expressions: κάκ' ὀσσόμενος (Α 105), ἐπιμειδήσας (Δ 356); emotions: βαρὺ στενάχων (Α 364, Δ 153), (κατὰ) δάκρυ χέων/-ουσα (Α 357.413), ὀλοφυρόμενος (Ε 871), μέγ' ὀχθήσας (Α 517 etc.: for this expression see Scully 1984), χολωτοῖσιν ἐπέεσσιν (Δ 241); tone: ἀταρτηροῖς ἐπέεσσιν (Α 223), κερτομίοις(ι) (ἐπέεσσι) (Α 539, Δ 6, Ε 419), χαλεπῷ ... μύθῳ (Β 245, Ρ 141), αἰσχροῖς ἐπέεσσι (Γ 38, Ζ 325, Ν 768), (μύθοισι) μειλιχίοισι(ν) ἐπέεσσι (Δ 256, Ζ 214.343), ὀνειδείοις ἐπέεσσι (Φ 480), κρατερὸν ... μῦθον (Α 25.326, Π 199). Cp. also the adverbs κακῶς (Α 25), αἰσχρῶς (Ψ 473) and ἐλεεινά (Χ 37).

21. Other examples: in the form of indirect speech: see above ch. 4.1.1, p. 117 and n. 47); varia: Δ 357 πάλιν δ' ὅ γε λάζετο μῦθον, Ο 660 ὑπὲρ τοκέων γουνούμενος ('begging on behalf of their parents'), Υ 15 Διὸς δ' ἐξείρετο βουλήν ('he asked about Zeus' plan'). In the case of Ψ 350 one can hesitate whether the ἐπεί-clause summarizes the content of Nestor's speech 306-48 or whether it refers to words of Nestor not further quoted. To this group can also

be reckoned Γ 191 and 225 where the NeFe₁ is informed beforehand that the descriptions given by Priam in the ensuing speeches concern Odysseus and Ajax, respectively (above section 4.1.1, p. 104).

22. Curiously enough the proposals contained in both speeches which are qualified as πυκινὴν ... βουλήν will turn out to be failures. Agamemnon's test of the troops almost ends in an untimely return home and Hector's plan ends with the death of its executor, Dolon. Cp. Van Erp Taalman Kip (1971: 26-7): "er van uitgaande dat de peira geen verstandig plan was, moet men tot de conclusie komen dat het woord πυκινὴν hier enigzins mechanisch gebruikt is. Toevalligerwijs lijkt dit de tweede keer dat het vers voorkomt ook zo te zijn."

23. Not strictly belonging to the attributive discourse are those passages where the NF₁, as it were, reacts to words of characters: B 419 = Γ 302, Γ 243-4, K 332, Π 46-7.249-52, Σ 312-3.

24. Cp. the bT-scholion ad Ξ 475a: διὰ τῆς ἐπιφωνήσεως τὸ ἦθος τῶν λόγων παρέστησεν ὁ ποιητής, ὅτι τὸ ὅλον ἐν εἰρωνείᾳ ἐξέφερεν ὡς ἀμφιβάλλων ('through the added remark the poet makes clear the nature of the speech, viz. that he (Ajax) has uttered the whole of it in irony, as if being in doubt').

25. Cp. in character-text: ταῦτ(α) ἀγορεύεις (H 357, K 250, M 231, Π 627, Σ 285), τοῦτον (sc. μῦθον) ἀγορεύεις (H 359, M 233), ταῦτ' ... βάζεις (Δ 355). Except for K 250, the speaker refers back to things said which *displease* him.

26. E 274.431, H 464, Θ 212, N 81, Π 101, Σ 368, Φ 514. Closely related are Z 312-3 and Ω 141-2.

27. Thucydides announces in his famous "Methodenkapitel" (*Histories* I.22) that it is impossible for him to quote the *ipsissima verba* of the historical figures and that instead he will compose their speeches himself adhering 'as closely as possible to the general sense of what was actually said'. As a consequence Thucydides most of the times introduces speeches with τοιάδε and caps them with τοιαῦτα.

28. The other instances (see above n. 26) can be analyzed as follows: simultaneous action: E 275 (cp. 239-40).432-3 (cp. 344-6), Θ 213-5 (cp. 170-1); completion: Z 313 (cp. 280), H 465 (cp. 442), Σ 369 (cp. 146-8). In Φ 514 (note αὐτάρ instead of δέ) there is no connection with earlier action. For Ω 143 see Krischer (1971: 95).

29. Arend (1933: 10) has wholly overlooked such differences: "Auch die Wiederkehr des Gleichen bei Erzählung und Wiedererzählung ist durch die Objektivität der archaischen Dichtung gerechtfertigt. Es gibt nur einen Ausdruck für einen Vorgang, mag nun eine Person mehrmals nacheinander oder mögen verschiedene Personen denselben Vorgang erzählen."

30. Other examples: A 141-6: A 308-11; A 565a: A 569a; Δ 101-3: Δ 119-21; E 261 (σὺ δέ)-4: E 321-4 (note E 319-20, where Diomedes' orders are explicitly recalled); H 331-43: H 430-2+435-41; Λ 512-3: Λ 517-20 (note 516: οὐδ' ἀπίθησε); Ξ 219: Ξ 223b; Π 495-6: 532-3; Π 724: Π 732; P 479-80: P 482-3a; T 347-8: T 352 (ἣ δ')-4.

31. I recall that orders presented in *indirect speech* are also regularly followed by a statement of their realization: cp. above section 4.1.1 p. 117.

32. Other examples A 147.566-7, H 343, Π 725, P 480 (ὄφρα μάχωμαι). A case where an intention (final-clause) is repeated is T 348 (ἵνα ... ἵκηται) ≅ 354 (ἵνα ... ἵκοιτο).

33. Another example is Π 678-83: Π 667-75 and cp. 454-7 (what is left out by the NF₁ is the embalming by the relatives, in other words the NF₁ only describes what is done by Apollo, the addressee of Zeus in 667-75).

34. Cp. Ameis-H. and Willcock (ad Σ 300-2): "These words are aimed at Polydamas and those who think like him."

35. Other examples: E 605-6: E 699-702; H 194: H 200 + speech 202-5; M 76-8: M 84-7; P 717-21: P 722-53.

36. Another example is Ψ 237-48: Ψ 250-7. Whereas Achilles in his order-speech had paid much attention to the identification of Patroclus' bones after the cremation and further twice referred to his own (impending) death (244, 247-8), the NF₁ stresses the grief (252: κλαίοντες) of Patroclus' companions collecting the bones of their 'beloved' friend.

37 Cp. the bT-scholia (ad Λ 830c): ὡς ἀλγῶν πραέα φάρμακα βούλεται. ὁ δὲ εἰδὼς ῥίζαν πικρὰν βάλλει ('as one suffering pain he (= Eurypylus) wants soothing herbs. And he (= Patroclus), as one knowing, applies a bitter root').

38. In other words, the Dream chooses his mask in accordance to his addressee, cp. also Iris, who assumes, when about to address Helen, the shape of a Spartan woman, 'whom Helen loved most' (Γ 388). I disagree with Kirk (ad B 56-9), who says that the description in B 20-1 serves "to introduce him (= Nestor) to the audience". Nestor had already been introduced to the audience in A 247-52.

39. Cp. B 795 (Iris = 'Polites'), Γ 129 (Iris = 'Laodice').389 (Aphrodite = 'Spartan woman'), N 231 (Poseidon = 'Thoas'), Υ 82+103 (Apollo = 'Lycaon'), X 238 (Athena = 'Deiphobus'), Ω 378+389+410+432 (Hermes = 'young man').

40. In other words, I take this "breaking of the Dream's verisimilitude" as intended and not as the result of abbreviation by the poet of a longer description (so Kirk ad B 20-1).

41. Line B 41 would then be a more subtle variant of B 807, Γ 396-7, N 66, P 333-4, where it is stated explicitly that a character sees through the human disguise of a god.

42. Other examples: P 555, Y 81, X 227. Cp. for this question of human and divine voice Clay (1974).

43. As Kessels (1978: 43-4) notes, ἀποπτάμενος need not imply that the Dream really *flew* away. It can also mean 'disappeared very quickly'.

44. That Dreams depart in a special way becomes clear from δ 838-9 (simple narrator-text).

45. Cp. the bT-scholia (ad Γ 439-40a): οἶαι τῶν ἠσχημονηκότων αἱ ἀπολογίαι διὰ τὴν Ἀθηνᾶν φησι νενικῆσθαι, ὥσπερ οὐκ ἐκ τῶν ἐναντίων διὰ τὴν Ἀφροδίτην αὐτὸς σωθείς. ('such as are the defenses of people who have disgraced themselves, he (Paris) says that he has been defeated by Athena, as if he himself has not, conversely, been saved by Aphrodite.')

46. Cp. Y 450-1 (Achilles: Hector), corresponding to 443-4 in simple narrator-text. Here the NF₁ interprets what happens in terms of a divine intervention, not a divine gift.

47. Notice that both Odysseus (770) and Ajax (782) refer to Athena simply by θεά. For this see Redfield (1979: 99).

48. For a detailed discussion of the complicated theme of divine gifts/divine interventions see Van der Mije (1987).

49. See *LfgrE* I s.v. ἄφαρ B 1a: "(erstaunlich) schnell, z.T. auch plötzlich". I prefer this interpretation to that of Ameis-H.: "sofort, nach seinem Erscheinen".

50. Ameis-H. (ad 221): "aus der Menschenwelt entnommene Züge"; Willcock (ad 222): "a quaint sort of humanising of the eagle".

51. Stockinger (1959: 34): "Daß Hektor ein Tor war, das sagt uns der Dichter durch den Gang der Ereignisse in Buch XIV und XVI, die dem Polydamas und seiner Zeichendeutung recht geben. Es lohnt sich nicht, wie Hektor zu handeln!"; Schadewaldt (1970: 32): "In Wahrheit und auf weitere Sicht ist Hektor auch hier bereits im Unrecht und auch hier der Vermessene"; Redfield (1975: 145): "this is the beginning of Hector's error. He is unable to hear Polydamas' advice".

52. All commentators take M 200-9 as describing an omen: Schadewaldt (1970: 32): "ein bedenkliches Vogelzeichen"; Redfield (1975: 145): "the omen (which is also from Zeus) warns of failure"; Erbse (1978: 6): "das böse Zeichen kann nicht hinweggedeutet werden".

53. ὄρνις in M 200 is no sure indication, since it can mean both 'bird' and 'bird-omen'. It is perfectly possible to take it as 'bird', followed by the specification αἰετός: cp. H 59 (ὄρνισιν ... αἰγυπιοῖσι), ε 51 (λάρῳ ὄρνιθι), τ 548 (αἰετὸς ὄρνις).

54. Cp. Θ 247, Ω 315, β 146-7, where it is explicitly told by the NF₁ that Zeus sent an eagle. In ο 160-4 we find another bird-scene where an eagle is involved, without Zeus being mentioned (but cp. Telemachus' prayer in 180). The situation in β 146-76 is somewhat comparable to M 200-50. Cp. Sternberg (1978: 64): "His (Halitherses') optimistic reading ultimately proves, of course, to be right; but this must not blind us to its wrong-headedness. At this point in the narrative, when we examine it in the light of the expositional information communicated so far and of the plain meaning of the symbol itself, we are, alas, compelled to question its validity, or even dismiss it as wishful thinking".

55. This contradiction, naturally, troubled the commentators, cp. Reinhardt (1961: 272): "Wir mögen den Widerspruch als Willen auf das Ferne und das Nächste hin erklären, zunächst stehen wir nicht anders als die Troer vor einem Rätsel".

56. The *Iliad* contains one more recapitulation: A 366-92, for which see Kirk (ad 366-92) and De Jong (1985a).

57. Cp. *LfgrE* I s.v. ἄψ B1c (col. 1782), ad ἄψ in Π 54.58, Σ 445: "wo ἄψ die Brutalität des Beraubens, Wegnehmens, Entreißens, unterstreicht, vgl. dagegen αὖτις (Ι 368) von der Reziprozität des Gebens und Wieder(weg)nehmens die hier ausdrücklich geleugnet wird."

58. For ἔνθα as a connective particle see *LfgrE* II, s.v. B2b.

59. A somewhat different case is Π 517-9, where Glaucus prays to Apollo to heal his wound, which (as the NF$_1$ already told in 510-1) was bothering him.

BIBLIOGRAPHY

Journals are abbreviated according to Marouzeau.
The following works are referred to by name of author only:

Ameis-H.:
    K.F.Ameis & C.Hentze, *Homers Ilias*, Leipzig
    1.1 (^{5}1894), 1.2 (^{5}1900), 1.3 (^{4}1894), 1.4 (^{4}1896), 2.1 (^{3}1896), 2.2 (^{3}1894),
    2.3 (^{3}1896), 2.4 (^{3}1896).
Chantraine:
    P. Chantraine, *Grammaire Homérique* II, Syntaxe, Paris 1963.
Ebeling:
    H. Ebeling (ed.), *Lexicon Homericum* I,II, Leipzig 1880.
Kirk:
    G.S. Kirk, *The Iliad: a Commentary*. I. Books 1-4, Cambridge 1986.
K.G.
    R. Kühner & B. Gerth, *Ausführliche Grammatik der Griechischen Sprache*,
    II.1,2, Hannover/Leipzig 1898/1904.
Leaf:
    W. Leaf, *The Iliad* I,II, London ^{2}1900-2.
LfgrE
    Lexikon des frühgriechischen Epos, fasc. 1-11, Göttingen 1955-1984.
Macleod
    C.W. Macleod, *Homer Iliad Book XXIV*, Cambridge 1982.
Monro
    D.B. Monro, *A Grammar of the Homeric Dialect*, Oxford ^{2}1891.
Willcock
    M.M. Willcock, *The Iliad of Homer* (I,II), London 1978, 1984.

- -

M.H. Abrams
    1953. *The Mirror and the Lamp. Romantic Theory and the critical Tradition*,
    Oxford.
J. Adam & D.A.Rees
    ^{2}1963. *The Republic of Plato*, Oxford.
L. Adam
    1889. *Die aristotelische Theorie vom Epos und ihre Entwicklung bei Griechen
    und Römern*, Wiesbaden.
A.W.H. Adkins
    1960. *Merit and Responsibility*, Oxford.
R. Aelion
    1984. 'Les mythes de Bellérophon et de Persée. Essai d'analyse selon un
    schéma inspiré de V. Propp', *Lalies* 4, 195-214.
A.R. Amory Parry
    1971. 'Homer as Artist', *CQ* 21, 1-15.
    1973. *Blameless Aegisthus. A Study of* ἀμύμων *and other Homeric Epithets*,
    Mnemosyne Supplementa, Leiden.

Ø. Andersen
1978. *Die Diomedesgestalt in der Ilias*, Symbolae Osloenses Vol. Suppl. 25, Oslo/Bergen.
1981. 'A Note on the Mortality of Gods in Homer', *GRBS* 22, 323-8.
1987. 'Myth, Paradigm and 'spatial Form' in the Iliad', in Bremer & de Jong (1987).
T.M. Andersson
1976. *Early Epic Scenery (Homer, Vergil, and the Medieval Legacy)*, Ithaca, New York.
J. Annas
1981. *An Introduction to Plato's Republic*, Oxford.
W. Arend
1933. *Die typischen Szenen bei Homer*, Problemata 7, Berlin.
J.I. Armstrong
1958. 'The Arming Motif in the Iliad', *AJPh* 79, 337-354.
E. Auerbach
1953. *Mimesis. The Representation of Reality in Western Literature*, Princeton.
J.N.H. Austin
1966. 'The Function of Digressions in the Iliad', *GRBS* 7, 295-312.
1975. *Archery at the Dark of the Moon. Poetic Problems in Homer's Odyssey*, Berkeley/Los Angeles/London.
W. Bachmann
1902. *Die aesthetischen Anschauungen Aristarchs in der Exegese und Kritik der homerischen Gedichte*, Teil I, Beilage z.Jahrbericht d. Kön.Alt Gymnasium in Nürnberg, Nürnberg.
M. Bal
1977. *Narratologie. Essais sur la signification narrative dans quatre romans modernes*, Paris (²1984, Utrecht). An English translation of the first chapter 'Narration et focalisation' appeared in *Style* 17 (1983), 234-69.
1981. 'Notes on narrative Embedding', *Poetics Today* 2, 41-59.
1981-2. 'On Meanings and Descriptions', *Studies in 20th Century Literature* 6, 100-48.
1985. *Narratology. Introduction to the Theory of Narrative*, Toronto.
E. Balensiefen
1956. *Die Zeitgestaltung in Homers Ilias*, Diss. Tübingen.
H. Bannert
1984. 'Die Lanze des Patroklos', *WS* 18, 27-35.
C. Barck
1971. 'Menelaos bei Homer', *WS* 84, 5-28.
1976. *Wort und Tat bei Homer*, Spudasmata 34, Hildesheim.
E. Barmeyer
1968. *Die Musen. Ein Beitrag zur Inspirationstheorie*, München.
L. Basset
1979. *Les emplois périphrastiques du verbe grec μέλλειν*, Collection de la maison de l'Orient méditerranéen ancien, no. 7, série philol. 1, Lyon.
S.E. Bassett
1921. 'The Function of the Homeric Simile', *TAPhA* 52, 132-147.
1933. 'Achilles' Treatment of Hector's Body', *TAPhA* 64, 41-65.
1938. *The Poetry of Homer*, Sather Classical Lectures 15, Berkeley.
J.T. Beckmann
1932. *Das Gebet bei Homer*, Diss. Würzburg.
N. van der Ben
1980. 'De Homerische Aphrodite-hymne 1', *Lampas* 13, 40-77.

N. van der Ben & I.J.F. de Jong
 1984. 'Daimon in Ilias en Odyssee', *Lampas* 17, 301-16.
N. van der Ben & J.M. Bremer
 1986. *Aristoteles Poetica*, Amsterdam.
E. Benveniste
 1966. *Problèmes de linguistique générale*, Paris.
W. Bergold
 1977. *Der Zweikampf des Paris und Menelaos*, Bonn.
S. Beßlich
 1966. *Schweigen - Verschweigen - Übergehen. Die Darstellung des Unaus-gesprochenen in der Odyssee*, Bibl. der klass. Altertumswiss. W.F. 2, Heidelberg.
C.R. Beye
 1966. *The Iliad, the Odyssey, and the Epic Tradition*, New York.
E. Block
 1982. 'The Narrator speaks: Apostrophe in Homer and Vergil', *TAPhA* 112, 7-22.
W.C. Booth
 1961. *The Rhetoric of Fiction*, Chicago.
C.M. Bowra
 ²1958. *Tradition and Design in the Iliad*, Oxford (first ed. 1930).
 ²1964. *Heroic Poetry*, London (first ed. 1952).
B.K. Braswell
 1971. 'Mythological Innovation in the Iliad', *CQ* 31, 16-26.
J.M. Bremer
 1969. *Hamartia. Tragic Error in the Poetics of Aristotle and in Greek Tragedy*, Amsterdam.
 1976. 'Why Messenger-speeches?', in: J.M.Bremer, S.Radt, C.J.Ruijgh (eds.) *Miscellanea Tragica in honorem J.C. Kamerbeek*, Amsterdam, 29-48.
 1986. 'Four Similes in Iliad 22', in: F. Cairns (ed.), *Papers of the Liverpool Latin Seminar 5*, Liverpool, 367-73.
J.M. Bremer & I.J.F. de Jong (eds.)
 1987. *Homer: beyond Oral Poetry. Recent Trends in Homeric Interpretation*, Amsterdam.
S. Briosi
 1986. 'La narratologie et la question de l'auteur', *Poétique* 68, 507-19.
W.J.M. Bronzwaer
 1981. 'Mieke Bal's Concept of Focalization: a Critical Note', *Poetics Today* 2, 193-201.
W. Bühler
 1967. 'Das Element des Visuellen in der Eingangsszene von Heliodors Aithiopika', *WS* 10, 177-85.
I. Bywater
 1909. *Aristotle on the Art of Poetry*, Oxford.
W.M. Calder III
 1984. 'Gold for Bronze: Iliad 6, 232-6', in: K.J. Rigsby (ed.), *Studies Presented to Sterling Dow*, Greek, Roman and Byzantine monographs 10, Duke University, 31-5.
G.M. Calhoun
 1933. 'Homeric Repetitions', *UCPCPh* 12, 1-26.
 1935. 'The Art of Formula in Homer: ἔπεα πτερόεντα', *CPh* 30, 215-27.
W.A. Camps
 1980. *An Introduction to Homer*, Oxford.

294

P. Cesareo
　　1898. *Il subbiettivismo nei Poemi d'Omero*, Palermo.
P. Chantraine
　　1954. 'Le divin et les dieux chez Homère', *Entretiens Fondation Hardt* 1,
　　47-94
S. Chatman
　　1978. *Story and Discourse: Narrative Structure in Fiction and Film*, Ithaca,
　　New York.
H. Clarke
　　1981. *Homer's Readers. A Historical Introduction to the Iliad and the Odyssey*,
　　Newark.
D.B. Claus
　　1975. 'Aidôs in the Language of Achilles', *TAPhA* 105, 13-28.
J. Clay
　　1974. 'Demas and aude. The Nature of Divine Transformation in Homer',
　　Hermes 102, 129-36.
M. Coffey
　　1957. 'The Function of the Homeric Simile', *AJPh* 78, 113-132.
D. Cohn
　　1978. *Transparent Minds: Narrative Modes for Presenting Consciousness in
　　Fiction*, Princeton.
F.M. Combellack
　　1939. 'Omitted Speech Formulas in Homer', *UCPCPh* 12, 43-56.
F.M. Cornford
　　1941. *The Republic of Plato*, Oxford.
H.N. Couch
　　1937. 'A Prelude to Speech in Homer', *TAPhA* 68, 129-40.
J.D. Craig
　　1967. 'χρύσεα χαλκείων', *CR* 17, 243-5.
J. Culler
　　1981. *The Pursuit of Signs: Semiotics, Literature, Deconstruction*, London.
H. Dachs
　　1913. *Die λύσις ἐκ τοῦ προσώπου. Ein exegetischer und kritischer
　　Grundsatz Aristarchs und seine Neuanwendung auf Ilias und Odyssee*, Diss.
　　Erlangen.
A.F. Dekker
　　1965. *Ironie in de Odyssee*, Leiden.
R. Delasanta
　　1967. *The Epic Voice*, Den Haag/Paris.
J.D. Denniston
　　²1978. *The Greek Particles*, Oxford.
B.C. Dietrich
　　1967. *Death, Fate and the Gods. The Development of a Religious Idea in
　　Greek Popular Belief and in Homer*, London.
E.R. Dodds
　　1951. *The Greeks and the Irrational*, Sather Classical Lectures 25, Berkeley.
L. Dolezel
　　1980. 'Truth and Authenticity in Narrative', *Poetics Today* 1.3, 7-25.
F.P. Donnelly
　　1929-30. 'Homeric Litotes', *CW* 23, 137-40 and 145-6.
E. Drerup
　　1921. *Homerische Poetik I. Das Homerproblem in der Gegenwart*, Würzburg.

G.E. Duckworth
1931. 'Proanaphonesis in the Scholia to Homer', *AJPh* 52, 320-38.
1933. *Foreshadowing and Suspense in the Epics of Homer, Apollonius and Vergil*, Princeton.
M.W. Edwards
1969. 'On some 'Answering' Expressions in Homer', *CPh* 64, 81-7
1970. 'Homeric Speech Introductions', *HSPh* 74, 1-36.
1980. 'Convention and Individuality in Iliad 1', *HSPh* 84, 1-29.
1987. 'The Conventions of a Homeric Funeral', in: J.M. Betts, J.T. Hooker, J.R. Green (eds.), *Studies in Honour of T.B.L. Webster I*, Bristol, 84-92.
B. Effe
1975. 'Personale Erzählweisen der Erzählliteratur der Antike', *Poetica* 7, 135-57.
1983. 'Epische Objektivität und auktoriales Erzählen', *Gymnasium* 90, 171-86.
T. Eide
1986. 'Poetical and Metrical Value of Homeric Epithets', *SO* 111, 5-18.
W. Elliger
1975. *Die Darstellung der Landschaft in der Griechischen Dichtung*, Untersuchungen zur antiken Literatur und Geschichte 15, Berlin.
G.F. Else
1972. *The Structure and Date of Book 10 of Plato's Republic*, Heidelberg.
H. Erbse
1969-83. *Scholia Graeca in Homeri Iliadem (scholia vetera) I-VI*, Berlin.
1978. 'Hektor in der Ilias', in: H.G. Beck & A. Kambylis & P. Moraux (eds.), *Kyklos*, Festschrift R. Keydell, Berlin/New York, 1-19.
1980. 'Homerische Götter in Vogelgestalt', *Hermes* 108, 259-74.
1986. *Untersuchungen zur Funktion der Götter im homerischen Epos*, Berlin.
A.M. van Erp Taalman Kip
1971. *Agamemnon in Epos en Tragedie*, Assen.
O. Falter
1934. *Der Dichter und sein Gott bei den Griechen und Römern*, Würzburg.
B.C. Fenik
1968. *Typical Battle Scenes in the Iliad. Studies in the Narrative Techniques of Homeric Battle Description*, Hermes Einzelschriften 21, Wiesbaden.
1978a 'Stylization and Variety: Four Monologues in the Iliad', in Fenik 1978b, 68-90.
B.C. Fenik (ed.)
1978b. *Homer. Tradition and Invention*, Leiden.
A. Fingerle
1939. *Typik der homerischen Reden*, Diss. München (typescript)
R. Finnegan
1977. *Oral Poetry*, Cambridge.
G. Finsler
1914. *Homer I*, Leipzig.
E.M. Forster
1976. *Aspects of the Novel*, Harmondsworth, (first edition 1927).
H. Fournier
1946. 'Formules homériques de référence avec le verbe "dire"', *RPh* 20, 29-68.

296

H. Fränkel
　1921. *Die homerischen Gleichnisse*, Göttingen.
　1955. 'Die Zeitauffassung in der frühgriechischen Literatur', in: *Wege und Formen frühgriechischen Denkens*, München, 1-22.
✓　³1976. *Dichtung und Philosophie des frühen Griechentums*, München, (first ed. 1951).
M.L. von Franz
　1943. *Die aesthetischen Anschauungen der Ilias-Scholien* II, diss. Zürich, 35-7.
K. Friedemann
　1910. *Die Rolle des Erzählers in der Epik*, Leipzig.
N. Friedman
　1955. 'Point of View in Fiction. The Development of a Critical Concept', *Publ. of the Modern Language Ass. of America* 70, 1160-84.
P. Friedrich & J. Redfield
　1978. 'Speech as a Personality Symbol: the Case of Achilles', *Language* 54, 263-88.
　1981. 'Contra Messing', *Language* 57, 901-3.
R. Friedrich
　1975. *Stilwandel im homerischen Epos. Studien zur Poetik und Theorie der epischen Gattung*, Heidelberg.
W.H. Friedrich
　1982. 'Von den homerischen Gleichnissen und ihren Schicksalen', *A&A* 28, 103-30.
W. Füger
　1978. 'Das Nichtwissen des Erzählers in Fieldings Joseph Andrews. Baustein zu einer Theorie negierten Wissens in der Fiktion', *Poetica* 10, 188-216.
R. Führer
　1976. *Formproblem-Untersuchungen zu den Reden in der frühgriechischen Lyrik*, Zetemata 44, München.
M. Fuhrmann
　1973. *Einführung in die antike Dichtungstheorie*, Darmstadt.
B. Gährken
　1950. *Die Partikel* γάρ, Diss. Münster (dact.).
J.H. Gaisser
　1969a. 'A Structural Analysis of the Digressions of the Iliad and the Odyssey', *HSPh* 73, 1-43.
　1969b. 'Adaptation of Traditional Material in the Glaucus-Diomedes Episode', *TAPhA* 100, 165-76.
D.M. Gaunt
　1976. 'Judgement and Atmosphere in Epic', *Ramus* 5, 59-75.
G. Genette
　1969. 'Vraisemblance et motivation', in: *Figures II*, Paris, 71-99.
　1972. 'Discours du récit', in: *Figures III*, Paris, 67-267. Engl. Translation *Narrative Discourse*, Ithaca, New York 1980.
　1977. 'Genres, 'types', modes', *Poétique* 32, 389-421.
　1983. *Nouveau Discours du récit*, Paris.
A.W. Gomme
　1954. *The Greek Attitude to Poetry and History*, Berkeley.
J.H. Greenberg (ed.)
　1966. *Universals of Language*, Cambridge, Mass.
K.W. Gransden
　1984. *Virgil's Iliad. An Essay on Epic Narrative*, Cambridge.

J. Griffin
   1976. 'Homeric Pathos and Objectivity', *CQ* 26, 161-85.
   1978. 'The Divine Audience and the Religion of the Iliad', *CQ* 28, 1-22.
   1980. *Homer on Life and Death*, Oxford.
   1986. 'Homeric Words and Speakers', *JHS* 106, 36-57.
K. Gross
   1970. 'Götterhand und Menschenhand im homerischen Epos', *Gymnasium* 77, 365-75.
P.J. Gruen
   1977. *Battle Revenge in Homer's "Iliad". A Contribution to the Understanding of Narrative Patterns in the Early Greek Epic.* Diss. Columbia 1976, Ann Arbor.
A. Gudeman
   1934. *Aristoteles Poetik*, Berlin/Leipzig.
R. Häußler
   1973. 'Der Tod der Musen', *A&A* 19, 117-45.
   1976. *Das historische Epos der Griechen und Römer bis Vergil, Studien zum historischen Epos der Antike, I. Teil: Von Homer zu Vergil*, Heidelberg.
R. Harriott
   1969. *Poetry and Criticism before Plato*, London.
J.B. Hainsworth
   1970. 'The Criticism of an Oral Homer', *JHS* 90, 90-8.
F.E. Harrison
   1960. 'Homer and the Poetry of War', *G&R* 7 (1960), 9-19
A.G. Hatcher
   1944. 'Voir as a Modern Novelistic Device', *Philological Quarterly* 23, 354-74.
V. Hebel
   1970. *Untersuchungen zur Form und Funktion der Wiedererzählungen in Ilias und Odyssee*, Diss. Heidelberg.
E. Hedèn
   1912. *Homerische Götterstudien*, Uppsala.
R. Heinze
   1903. *Virgils epische Technik*, Leipzig.
L.J.R. Heirman
   1972. *Plutarchus 'De audiendis poetis'*, diss. Leiden.
B. Hellwig
   1964. *Raum und Zeit im homerischen Epos*, Spudasmata 2, Hildesheim.
K.W. Hempfer
   1982. 'Die potentielle Autoreflexivität des narrativen Diskurses und Ariosts Orlando Furioso', in: E. Lämmert (ed.) *Erzählforschung. Ein Symposion*, Stuttgart, 130-56.
C. Hentze
   1903. 'Das Auftreten der Iris im zweiten, dritten u. fünften Buch in der Ilias', *Philologus* 62, 321.
   1904. 'Die Monologe in den homerischen Epen', *Philologus* 63,12-30.
J. Herington
   1985. *Poetry into Drama. Early Greek Tragedy and the Greek Poetic Tradition.* Sather Classical Lectures 49, Berkeley.
A. Heubeck
   1978. 'Homeric Studies Today: Results and Prospects', in: Fenik 1978b, 1-17.
B.L.Hijmans
   1975. 'Alexandros and his Grief', *GB* 3, 177-89.
J.C. Hogan
   1973. 'Aristotle's Criticism of Homer in the Poetics', *CQ* 68, 95-108.

E. Howald
    1946. *Der Dichter der Ilias*, Zürich.
G. Jachmann
    1958. *Der homerische Schiffskatalog und die Ilias*, Köln/Opladen.
H. Jacobsohn
    1935. 'Zum homerischen ἔπος τ' ἔφατ' ἔκ τ' ὀνόμαζεν', *Zeitschrift für vergleichende Sprachforschung* 62, 132-40.
I.J.F. de Jong
    1985a. 'Iliad 1.366-392: a Mirror Story', *Arethusa* 18, 1-22.
    1985b. 'Fokalisation und die homerischen Gleichnisse', *Mnemosyne* 38, 257-70.
    1985c. 'Eurykleia and Odysseus' Scar: Odyssey 19.393-466', *CQ* 35, 517-8.
    1987a. 'Silent Characters in the Iliad' in Bremer & de Jong (1987), 105-21.
    1987b. 'The Voice of Anonymity: tis-speeches in the Iliad', *Eranos* 85 (1987), 69-84.
H. Jordan
    1905. *Der Erzählungsstil in den Kampfszenen der Ilias*, Breslau.
J.Th. Kakridis
    1949 *Homeric Researches*, Lund.
    1956 'Homer, ein Philhellene?' *WS*, 26-32.
    1982 'Μετακένωσις', *WS* 16, 5-12.
J.C. Kamerbeek
    1962. 'Problematiek van de vergelijkingen in Homerus' Ilias', *Forum der Letteren* 3, 33-47.
A.H.M. Kessels
    1978 *Studies on the Dream in Greek Literature*, Utrecht.
G.S. Kirk
    1962. *The Songs of Homer*, Cambridge.
    1976. *Homer and the Oral Tradition*, Cambridge.
A. Kleinlogel
    1981. 'Götterblut und Unsterblichkeit. Homerische Sprachreflexion und die Probleme epischer Forschungsparadigmata', *Poetica* 13, 252-79.
V. Klotz
    1965. *Muse und Helios. Über epische Anfangsnöte und -weisen in Romananfänge. Versuch zu einer Poetik des Romans*, Berlin.
A. Köhnken
    1976. 'Die Narbe des Odysseus. Ein Beitrag zur homerisch-epischen Erzähltechnik', *A&A* 22, 101-14.
    1981. 'Der Endspurt des Odysseus. Wettkampfdarstellung bei Homer und Vergil', *Hermes* 109, 129-48.
S. Koster
    1970. *Antike Epostheorien*, Palingenesia V, Wiesbaden.
J.M. Kramer
    1946. *De Ilias als vredesgedicht*, Amsterdam.
P. Krarup
    1941. 'Beobachtungen zur Typik und Technik einiger homerischer Gesprächsformeln', *C&M* 4, 230-47.
T. Krischer
    1965. 'Die Entschuldigung des Sängers (Ilias B 484-493)', *RhM* 108, 1-11.
    1971. *Formale Konventionen der homerischen Epik*, Zetemata 56, München.
C. Kraut
    1863. *Die epische Prolepsis, nachgewiesen in der Ilias*, Programm des Königlichen Gymnasiums in Tübingen, Tübingen.

W. Kullmann
1952. *Das Wirken der Götter in der Ilias. Untersuchungen zur Frage der Entstehung des homerischen "Götterapparats"*, Berlin (Diss. Berlin 1952).
1968. 'Vergangenheit und Zukunft in der Ilias', *Poetica* 2, 15-37.

M.L. Lang
1983. 'Reverberation and Mythology in the Iliad', in: C.A. Rubino & C.W. Shelmerdine (eds.) *Approaches to Homer*, Austin, Texas, 140-64.
1984. *Herodotean Narrative and Discourse*, Cambridge, Mass.

E. Lämmert
1955. *Bauformen des Erzählens*, Stuttgart.

S.S. Lanser
1981. *The Narrative Act. Point of View in Prose Fiction*, Princeton.

J. Latacz
1966. *Zum Wortfeld "Freude" in der Sprache Homers*, Heidelberg.
1974. 'Zur Forschungsarbeit an den direkten Reden bei Homer (1850-1970)', *GB* 2, 395-422.
1977. *Kampfparänese, Kampfdarstellung und Kampfwirklichkeit in der Ilias, bei Kallinos und Tyrtaios*, Zetemata 66, München.
1981. 'Zeus' Reise zu den Aithiopen (zu Il. 1, 304-495)', in: G. Kurz & D. Müller & W. Nicolai (eds.), *Gnomosyne*, Festschrift f. Walter Marg, München, 53-80.
1982. 'Realität und Imagination. Eine neue Lyrik-Theorie und Sapphos φαίνεταί μοι κῆνος-Lied', *MH* 42, 67-94.

D.J.N. Lee
1964. *The Similes of the Iliad and the Odyssey compared*, Melbourne.

G. Leech
1974. *Semantics*, Harmondsworth.

A. Lenz
1980. *Das Proöm des frühgriechischen Epos*, Bonn.

J.H. Lesher
1981. 'Perceiving and Knowing in the Iliad and Odyssey', *Phronesis* 26, 2-24.

A. Lesky
1961. *Göttliche und menschliche Motivation in homerischen Epos*, Sitz. Berichte Heidelberg 4.

F. Létoublon
1983a. 'Le miroir et la boucle', *Poétique* 40, 19-35.
1983b. 'Défi et combat dans l'Iliade', *REG* 96, 27-48.
1985. *Il allait pareil à la nuit, les verbes de mouvement en grec: supplétisme et aspect verbal*, Paris.
1987. 'Le messager fidèle', in: Bremer & de Jong (1987).

S.C. Levinson
1983. *Pragmatics*, Cambridge.

H.L. Levy
1974. 'Homer's Gods: a Comment on their Immortality', *GRBS* 20, 215-8

F. Lillge
1911. *Komposition und poetische Technik der Διομήδους ἀριστεία. Ein Beitrag zum Verständnis des homerischen Stiles*, Gotha.

J. Lintvelt
1981 *Essai de typologie narrative. Le "point de vue"*, Paris.

D. Lohmann
1970. *Die Komposition der Reden in der Ilias*, Berlin.

P. Lubbock
1921. *The Craft of Fiction*, New York.

300

D.W. Lucas
1968. *Aristotle Poetics*, Oxford.
J. Lyons
Semantics I, II, 1977.
C.W. Macleod
1983. 'Homer on Poetry and the Poetry of Homer', in: *Collected Essays*, Oxford, 1-15.
W. Marg
1942. 'Kampf und Tod in der Ilias', *Antike* 18, 167-79.
F. de Martino
1977. 'Omero fra narrazione e mimesi (Dal poeta ai personaggi)', *Belfagor* 32, 1-6.
B. McHale
1978. 'Free Indirect Discourse: a Survey of Recent Accounts', *Poetics and Theory of Literature* 3, 249-87.
G.M. Messing
1981. 'On Weighing Achilles' Winged Words', *Language* 57, 888-900.
C. Michel
1971. *Erläuterungen zum N der Ilias*, Heidelberg.
W.W. Minton
1960. 'Homer's Invocations of the Muses. Traditional Patterns', *TAPhA* 91, 292-309
C.W. Moulton
1974. 'Similes in the Iliad', *Hermes* 102, 381-97.
1977. *Similes in the Homeric Poems*, Hypomnemata 49, Göttingen.
D. Mülder
1910. *Die Ilias und ihre Quellen*, Berlin.
F. Müller
1968. *Darstellung und poetische Funktion der Gegenstände in der Odyssee*, Diss. Marburg.
G. Müller
1947. *Die Bedeutung der Zeit in der Erzählkunst*, Bonn
M. Müller
1970. 'Knowledge and Delusion in the Iliad', *Mosaic* 3.2 (1970), 86-103 = J.Wright (ed.) *Essays on the Iliad*, Indiana 1978, 105-23.
1984. *The Iliad*, London.
L.C. Muellner
1976. *The Meaning of Homeric* εὔχομαι *through its Formulas*, Innsbruck.
I. Munoz Valle
1971. 'Interpretacíon de la fórmula homérica ἔπος τ' ἔφατ' ἔκ τ' ὀνόμαζεν', *Emerita* 39, 305-14.
P. Murray
1981. 'Poetic Inspiration in Early Greece', *JHS* 101, 87-100.
S.R. van der Mije
1987. 'Achilles' God-Given Strength', *Mnemosyne* 40, 241-67.
J.L. Myres
1954. 'The Structure of the Iliad, Illustrated by the Speeches', *JHS* 74, 122-41.
W. Nicolai
1983. 'Rezeptionssteuerung in der Ilias', *Philologus* 127, 1-12.
J.A. Notopoulos
1938. 'Mnemosyne in Oral Literature', *TAPhA* 69, 465-93.
R. Oehler
1925. *Mythologische Exempla in der älteren griechischen Dichtung*, Diss. Basel.

I. Opelt
        1978. 'Gefühlswörter bei Homer und in den Argonautika des Apollonius
        Rhodius', *Glotta* 56, 170-90.
B. Otis
        1963. *Virgil. A Study in Civilized Poetry*, Oxford.
N. Page
        1973. Speech in the English Novel, London.
H.A. Paraskevaides
        1984. *The Use of Synonyms in Homeric Formulaic Diction*, Amsterdam.
A. Parry
        1956. 'The Language of Achilles', *TAPhA* 87, 1-7.
M. Parry
        1928. *L'épithète traditionnelle dans Homère. Essai sur un problème de style
        homérique*, Paris.
        1937. 'About Winged Words', *CPh* 32, 59-63.
R. Peppermüller
        1962. 'Die Glaukos-Diomedes-Szene der Ilias. Spuren vorhomerischer Dich-
        tung', *WS* 75, 5-21.
B.E. Perry
        1937. 'The Early Greek Capacity for Viewing Things separately', *TAPhA* 68,
        403-27.
G. Petersmann
        1973. 'Die monologische Totenklage der Ilias', *RhM* 116, 3-16.
        1974. 'Die Entscheidungsmonologe in den homerischen Epen', *GB* 2, 147-69.
E. Pfudel
        1891. *Die Wiederholungen bei Homer. I: Beabsichtigte Wiederholungen*, Beilage
        zum Jahresb. der königlichen Ritter-Akademie, Liegnitz.
M.A. Piwowarczyk
        1976. 'The Narratee and the Situation of Enunciation: a Reconsideration of
        Prince's Theory', *Genre* 9, 161-77.
D.M. Porter
        1973. 'Violent Juxtaposition in the Similes of the Iliad', *CJ* 68, 11-21.
G. Prince
        1973. 'Introduction à l'étude du narrataire', *Poétique* 14, 178-96.
        1978. 'Le discours attributif et le récit', *Poétique* 35, 305-13.
        1982. *Narratology: The Form and Functioning of Narrative*, The Hague.
P. Pucci
        1978. 'The Language of the Muses', *Proc. Comp. Lit. Symp.* 11, 163-86.
W.H. Race
        1982. *The Classical Priamel from Homer to Boethius*, Mnemosyne Suppl. 74,
        Leiden.
L. Radermacher
        ²1938. *Mythos und Sage bei den Griechen*, Brünn.
L.P. Rank
        1951. *Etymologiseering en verwante verschijnselen bij Homerus*, Assen.
J.M. Redfield
        1975. *Nature and Culture in the Iliad. The Tragedy of Hector*, Chicago.
        1979. 'The Proem of the Iliad. Homer's Art', *CPh* 74, 95-110.
M.D. Reeve
        1973. 'The Language of Achilles', *CQ* 23, 193-5.
K. Reinhardt
        1961. *Die Ilias und ihr Dichter*, Göttingen.

302

N.J. Richardson
    1974. *The Homeric Hymn to Demeter*. Ed. and Comm., Oxford.
    1980. 'Literary Criticism in the exegetical Scholia to the Iliad: a Sketch', *CQ* 30, 265-87.
A. Rijksbaron
    1976. *Temporal and Causal Conjunctions in Ancient Greek. With Special Reference to the Use of ἐπεί and ὡς in Herodotus*, Amsterdam.
S. Rimmon
    1976. 'A Comprehensive Theory of Narrative: Genette's Figures III and the Structuralist study of Fiction', *Poetics and Theory of Literature* 1, 33-62.
S. Rimmon-Kenan
    1983. *Narrative Fiction: Contemporary Poetics*, London/New York.
B. Romberg
    1962. *Studies in the Narrative Technique of the First-Person Novel*, Lund.
F. van Rossum-Guyon
    1970. 'Point de vue ou perspective narrative', *Poétique* 4, 476-97.
C. Rothe
    1914. *Die Odyssee als Dichtung und ihr Verhältnis zur Ilias*, Paderborn.
R.B. Rutherford
    1982. 'Tragic Form and Feeling in the Iliad', *JHS* 102, 145-60.
C.J. Ruijgh
    1971. *Autour de "TE épique"*, Amsterdam.
    1981. 'L'emploi de ἤτοι chez Homère et Hésiode', *Mnemosyne* 34, 272-87.
S. Said
    1978. *La faute tragique*, Paris.
W. Schadewaldt
    1938. *Iliasstudien*, Leipzig.
    ³1959. *Von Homers Welt und Werk*, Stuttgart.
    ²1970. 'Hektor in der Ilias', in: *Hellas und Hesperien I*, Zürich/Stuttgart, 21-38.
S.L. Schein
    1980. 'On Achilles' Speech to Odysseus, Iliad 9.308-429', *Eranos* 78, 125-31.
    1984. *The Mortal Hero. An Introduction to Homer's Iliad*, California.
R. von Scheliha
    1943. *Patroklos. Gedanken über Homers Dichtung und Gestalten*, Basel.
D.M. Schenkeveld
    1970. 'Aristarchus and "Ὅμηρος φιλότεχνος', *Mnemosyne* 23, 162-78.
    1982. 'The Structure of Plutarch's 'De audiendis poetis'', *Mnemosyne* 35, 60-71.
G. Schmeling
    1981, 'The Authority of the Author; from Muse to Aesthetics', *Materiali e Contributi per la Storia della Narrativa Greco-latina* 3, Perugia, 369-377.
M. Schmidt
    1969. *Die Erklärungen zum Weltbild Homers und zur Kultur der Heroenzeit in den bT-Scholien zur Ilias*, Zetemata 62, München.
M. Schneidewin
    1878. *Die homerische Naïvetät*, Hameln.
R. Scholes & R. Kellogg
    1966. *The Nature of Narrative*, Oxford.
R. Scodel
    1982. 'The Achaean Wall and the Myth of Destruction', *HSPh* 86, 33-53.
W.C. Scott
    1974. *The Oral Nature of the Homeric Simile*, Mnemosyne Suppl. 28, Leiden.

S. Scully
1984. 'The Language of Achilles. The ὀχθήσας formulas', *TAPhA* 114, 11-27.
J.R. Searle
1976. 'A Classification of Illocutionary Acts', *Language in society* 5, 1-23.
G.G. Sedgewick
1935. *Of Irony, especially in Drama*, Toronto.
C.P. Segal
1971a. *The Theme of the Mutilation of the Corpse in the Iliad*, Mnemosyne Suppl. 17, Leiden.
1971b. 'Andromache's anagnorisis: Formulaic Artistry in Iliad 22.437-476', *HSCP* 75, 33-58.
A. Severyns
1938. *Recherches sur la Chrestomathie de Proclos* II, Liège.
1948. *Homère III, l'artiste*, Bruxelles.
R.S. Shannon
1975. *The Arms of Achilles and Homeric Compositional Technique*, Mnemosyne Suppl. 36, Leiden.
P. Shorey
1922. 'The Logic of Homeric Similes', *CPh* 17, 240-59.
P.M. Smith
1981. *Nursling of Mortality. A Study of the Homeric Hymn to Aphrodite*, Frankfurt a/M.
B. Snell
³1955. *Die Entdeckung des Geistes*, Hamburg.
1984. '"Endspurt des Odysseus"', *Hermes* 112, 129-36.
W. Söffing
1981. *Deskriptive und normative Bestimmungen in der Poetik des Aristoteles*, Amsterdam.
R. Spieker
1969. 'Die Beschreibung des Olympos (Hom. Od. ζ 41-7)', *Hermes* 97, 136-61.
J. Stallmach
1968. *Ate. Zur Frage des Selbst- und Weltverständnisses des frühgriechischen Menschen*, Beiträge zur klassischen Philologie 18, Meisenheim am Glan.
F. Stanzel
1964. *Typische Formen des Romans*, Göttingen.
1979. *Theorie des Erzählens*, Göttingen.
G. Steinkopf
1937. *Untersuchungen zur Geschichte des Ruhms bei den Griechen*, Diss. Halle.
M. Sternberg
1978. *Expositional Modes and Temporal Ordering in Fiction*, Baltimore/London.
K. Stierle
1975. 'Der Gebrauch der Negation in fiktionale Texten', in: H. Weinrich (ed.), *Positionen der Negativität*, Poetik und Hermeneutik 6, München, 235-62.
H. Stockinger
1959. *Die Vorzeichen im Homerischen Epos. Ihre Typik und ihre Bedeutung*. Diss. München, St. Ottilien.
G. Strasburger
1954. *Die kleinen Kämpfer der Ilias*, Diss. Frankfurt.
R. Strömberg
1961. 'Die Bellerophontes-Erzählung in der Ilias', *C&M* 22, 1-15.
W. Suerbaum
1968. 'Die Ich-Erzählungen des Odysseus. Überlegungen zur epischen Technik der Odyssee', *Poetica* 2, 150-77.

304

J. Svenbro
1976. *La parole et le marbre. Aux origines de la poétique grecque*, Lund.
D. Tabachovitz
1951. *Homerische εἰ-Sätze*. Eine sprachpsychologische Studie, Lund.
O. Taplin
1977. *The Stagecraft of Aeschylus*, Oxford.
1980. 'The Shield of Achilles within the Iliad', *G&R* 27 (1980), 1-21.
A. Thornton
1984. *Homer's Iliad: its Composition and the Motif of Supplication*, Hypomnemata 81, Göttingen.
O. Tsagarakis
1977. *Nature and Background of Major Concepts of Divine Power in Homer*, Amsterdam.
B.A. Uspenskij
1975. *Poetik der Komposition. Struktur des künstlerischen Textes und Typologie der Kompositionsform*, Frankfurt a/M.
M. van der Valk
1953. 'Homer's Nationalistic Attitude', *AC* 22, 5-26.
1985. 'Homer's Nationalism, again', *Mnemosyne* 38, 373-6.
W.J. Verdenius
1970. 'Homer, the Educator of the Greeks', *Mededelingen Koninklijke Akademie van Wetenschappen* nr. 33.5, Amsterdam.
1983. 'The Principles of Greek Literary Criticism', *Mnemosyne* 36, 14-59.
P. Vicaire
1960. *Platon. Critique littéraire*, Paris.
P. Vivante
1970. *The Homeric Imagination*, Indiana.
1975. 'On Homer's Winged Words', *CQ* 25, 1-12.
1982. *The Epithets in Homer, a Study in Poetic Values*, Yale.
C. Voigt
1972. *Überlegung und Entscheidung. Studien zur Selbstauffassung des Menschen bei Homer*, Beiträge zum klassischen Philologie, Meisenheim am Glan (reprint of Berlin 1934 edition).
G.J. de Vries
1963. 'Het tertium comparationis in de homerische vergelijking', *Forum der Letteren* 4, 41-53.
G.C. Wakker
1988. 'Purpose Expressions in Homeric Greek', in: A. Rijksbaron & H. Mulder & G.C. Wakker (eds.), *In the Footsteps of Raphael Kühner*, Amsterdam.
G.B. Walsh
1984. *The Varieties of Enchantment. Early Greek Views of the Nature and Function of Poetry*, Chapel Hill/London.
T.B.L. Webster
1958. *From Mycenae to Homer. A Study in Early Greek Literature and Art*, London.
J.A. White
1982. 'Bellerophon in the Land of Nod. Some Notes on Iliad 6.53-211', *AJPh* 103, 119-27.
N.P. White
1979. *A Companion to Plato's Republic*, Oxford.
J. Wieniewski
1924. 'La technique d'annoncer les événements futurs chez Homère', *Eos* 27, 113-33

E.G. Wilkins
   1919-20. 'A Classification of the Similes of Homer', *CW* 13, 147-50 and
   154-59.
M.M. Willcock
   1964. 'Mythological Paradeigma in the Iliad', *CQ* 14, 141-54.
   1977. 'Ad hoc Invention in the Iliad', *HSPh* 81, 41-53.
H. Willenbrock
   1944. *Die poetische Bedeutung der Gegenstände in Homers Ilias*, Marburg/Lahn
   (reprinted 1969).
G. Williams
   1983. *Technique and Ideas in the Aeneid*, New Haven/ London.
P. Wulfert
   1955,. *Handeln und Ethik des Kriegers in der Ilias*, Diss. Münster.
W.F. Wyatt
   1982. 'Homeric ἄτη', *AJPh* 103, 247-76.
Th. Zielinski
   1899-1901. 'Die Behandlung gleichzeitiger Ereignisse im antiken Epos', *Philologus Suppl.* 8, 405-49.

INDEX OF SUBJECTS

Greek words are listed separately below.

INDEX OF PASSAGES

CPSIA information can be obtained
at www.ICGtesting.com
Printed in the USA
LVOW09s0425291117
557893LV00010B/251/P

9 781853 996580